The Prussian Welfare State

before 1740

1. Bronze Statue of the Great Elector by Andreas Schlüter

The Prussian Welfare State
before 1740

Reinhold August Dorwart

Harvard University Press
Cambridge, Massachusetts
1971

To

Juanita

Preface

The use of the term "welfare state" in title and text presumably requires both explanation and defense. There are those who would reserve this term exclusively for the social service state of the twentieth century. I obviously do not accept the arrogation of the broad concept of "welfare state" to an exclusive period of history. In the Introduction I argue that three stages of "welfare state" have accompanied the development of the Western political tradition in the last five hundred years. This study is concerned with the first of these stages as witnessed by the legislative and regulative acts of the Hohenzollern princes of Brandenburg-Prussia. Because, in this period before 1740, we are concerned with dynastic states, the ruling prince is predominant in determining the concept of state, the function of princely office, and the definition of welfare.

The historical problem involves the varying and differing definitions of "welfare" itself. Fundamental is the basic difference between the welfare of the individual and the general welfare, with the attendant problem of reconciling the two with each other. Each of the six parts of this study concerns itself with a distinct area of public life within which the Hohenzollern rulers sought to promote individual welfare, the common good, or both simultaneously.

Perhaps the most intriguing experience for me in describing the areas of state intervention, in the era before 1740, was the realization of the almost complete identity of these areas with practically every area of regulation by the state in contemporary society. Anti-poverty, consumer protection, minority rights, concern for the moral implications of clothing styles, extension and availability of education to all citizens at all levels, certification of teachers and health practitioners, urban development, anti-pollution measures to protect water and air, draft evasion by university matriculation, concern for the old, the sick, the unemployed, the discharged veteran, sanitation and fire security measures, and, of course, the primary issue of public security, law and order, all equally concern dynastic prince and modern democratic republics.

A welfare state is based upon compulsion, on exercise of the police power to regulate the actions of the individual. Compulsory school attendance, removal of fire hazards, quarantine of the sick, price and fee control, building and zoning codes, public support for the needy and sick are but a few illustrations. Compulsion and intervention by public authority by some indefinable law of nature seems traditionally to produce a counter resistance by the individual.

The history of the past five centuries seems to underscore the problem and difficulty of determining the nature of "welfare" by the individual "in general" and the state "in particular."

I am grateful to the Research Foundation of The University of Connecticut for a grant which made it easier for me to complete this study. I owe a special debt to Mrs. Selma I. Wollman of the Foundation staff for her personal interest and conscientious efforts in preparing a final, faultless copy for the publisher.

R.A.D.

Mansfield Center, Connecticut
8 June 1970

Contents

1 Introduction: The Theory of the Welfare State   1

Part I
Sumptuary Legislation

2 Moral Behavior   27
3 The Life Cycle   30
4 Clothing and Personal Decoration   45

Part II
Urban Affairs

5 The Marketplace   54
6 Public Works and Urban Development   77
7 City Sanitation—Streets and Wells   85

Part III
The Unprivileged and Underprivileged Society

8 Wayfaring Life in Electoral Brandenburg   94
9 The Jews in Brandenburg   112

Part IV
Education, Schools, and Culture

10 The Reformation and Education in Germany   143
11 Education in Brandenburg-Prussia, 1540-1650   151
12 Ideas and Writers Influencing Education in the Seventeenth Century   160
13 Development of a School System, 1650-1740   167
14 Gymnasium and University, 1650-1740   194
15 The Advancement of Learning   214

Part V
Public Health and Medical Sciences

16 The State Board of Medicine and Public Health   240
17 Medical Education   255
18 The Apothecary and Public Health   268
19 Epidemics and Practical Medicine   284

Part VI
Public Security

20   Fire Protection   293
21   Police Protection   305

22   Conclusion   310

Bibliography   315

Index   325

Illustrations

1   Bronze Statue of the Great Elector by Andreas Schlüter   frontispiece
2   Kindelbier: Celebration after Christening   32
3   A Bridal Couple   32
4   Wedding Dancers and Costumes of the Sixteenth Century by Hans Schäuffelein   38
5   Wedding Dancers and Costumes of the Sixteenth Century by Heinrich Aldegrever   38
6   Peasant Dancers of the Sixteenth Century by Albrecht Dürer   38
7   Funeral Procession of the Sixteenth Century by Hans Burgkmair   42
8   Costumes of the Sixteenth and Seventeenth Centuries   47
9   Buying Jewelry   61
10   Market Scene in the Sixteenth Century   61
11   A Vagrant Family   61
12   The Quacksalver Makes His Pitch   61
13   Landsknechte: Soldiers of the Sixteenth Century   108
14   A Natural History Collection   108
15   City Plan of Berlin by J. B. Schultz of 1688   233
16   Royal Palace and Great Elector Statue   236
17   Throne Room in the Berlin Palace   236
18   The Apothecary Arrives with His Clyster   272
19   Tobacco Smoking in 1630   272
20   Toothextracting at the Fair   283
21   An Apothecary Shop   283
22   Fire-fighting in the Seventeenth Century   299
23   Night Watch   299

Except where otherwise indicated, the illustrations are old prints of uncertain origin, found in the following publications:

Frontispiece. Photograph from Georg Dehio, *Geschichte der Deutschen Kunst.* vol. III (Berlin: Walter de Gruyter, 1926), p. 253.
2. Engraving by Abraham de Bosse, from Max von Boehn, *Die Mode im siebzehnten Jahrhundert* (Munich: F. Bruckmann, 1913), p. 90.
3. From Eduard Duller, *Deutschland und das deutsche Volk,* vol. IV (Leipzig: G. Wigand, 1845), plate 45.
4. Woodcut by Hans Schäuffelein, from Alwin Schultz, *Das Häuslichen Leben der Europäischen Kulturvölker vom Mittelalter bis zur Zweiten Hälfte des XVIII Jahrhunderts,* (Munich & Berlin: R. Oldenbourg Verlag, 1903), p. 361.
5. Woodcut by Heinrich Aldegrever, from Schultz, p. 361.
6. Copper engraving by Albrecht Dürer, from Schultz, p. 400.
7. Woodcut by Hans Burgkmair, from Schultz, p. 415.
8, 19. From Schultz, pp. 249, 329.
9, 10, 11, 12, 14, 20, 21, 22, 23. From Wolfgang Bruhn, *Deutsche Kulturbilder Deutsches Leben in 5 Jahrhunderten 1400-1900* (Hamburg: Cigaretten Bilderdienst, 1934), illustrations 112, 62, 6, 74, 82, 27, 51, 75, 85.
13. From E. Thiel, *Geschichte des Köstums* (Berlin: Henschelverlag, 1960), p. 157.
15. From Max Arendt, E. Faden, O. F. Gandert, *Geschichte der Stadt Berlin* (Berlin: E. S. Mittler & Sohn, 1937), endpaper map.
16, 17. Photographs from E. Redslob, *Barock und Rokoko in den Schlössern von Berlin und Potsdam* (Berlin: Rembrandt-Verlag, 1954), pp. 7 and 19.
18. Engraving from von Boehn, *Die Mode,* p. 100.

The Prussian Welfare State
before 1740

Abbreviations

C. C. Magdeb.	Christian Otto Mylius, ed., *Corpus Constitutionum Magdeburgicarum*
C. C. March.	Christian Otto Mylius, ed., *Corpus Constitutionum Marchicarum*
Cod. Dipl. Brand.	Adolf Riedel, ed., *Codex Diplomaticus Brandenburgensis*
Cod. dipl. brand. cont.	Georg W. von Raumer, *Codex diplomaticus brandenburgensis continuatus*
Kurm. Ständ. Joach.	Walter Friedensburg, ed., *Kurmärkische Ständeakten aus der Regierungszeit Kurfürst Joachims II*
Quellen brand-preuss.	Hans Bahr, ed., *Quellen zur brandenburgischen-preussischen Geschichte*
UA	*Urkunden und Actenstücke zur Geschichte des Kurfürsten Friedrich Wilhelm von Brandenburg*

1

Introduction:

The Theory of the Welfare State

Every state, then, is a welfare state.

Leonard Krieger

For the past twenty-five years there has been a "confused dialogue" about the nature and concept of the welfare state.[1] It is not surprising that much of the confusion revolves around the definition of "welfare" itself. Further confusion derives from certain misconceptions about the origin and historical evolution of the Western welfare state and the legal sanction upon which the welfare state is predicated.

All of the recent writing about the welfare state asserts that the phrase is of recent origin and generally credits William Temple, Archbishop of York, with first using the term in 1941 to describe Labour Britain.[2] The phrase was next applied to the Rooseveltian New Deal. Some writers see the origin of the welfare state itself in the Bismarckian social insurance legislation of the 1880's.[3] Asa Briggs traces some aspects of the Bismarckian welfare state to the "cameralism" of the eighteenth century.[4]

In my view, it is not historically correct to trace the origin of the welfare state, as a theory and concept of state, to the social policy of Bismarck or to the use of the term by Archbishop Temple. The idea of a welfare state is much older than the twentieth century. A particular phase or form of the welfare state originated in the late nineteenth century in response, most recent writers agree, to certain "social and economic contingencies." But the welfare state in general, throughout the last five hundred years, has been a response to changing historical contingencies. The idea of the welfare state has been part of the Western tradition since the secularization of political life in the later Middle Ages.

Writers who, like Jacob Viner and Charles Frankel, describe it as of recent origin, are in agreement that the welfare state "is a rejection of the

---

1. See Charles I. Schottland, ed., *The Welfare State: Selected Essays,* for a collection of essays on the contemporary welfare state written since 1950. This is a broad and inclusive selection, also providing a useful bibliography.

2. William Temple, Archbishop of York, *Citizen and Churchman* (London, 1941), pp. 20-39; quoted in Schottland, *Welfare State,* pp. 20-24.

3. Sidney B. Fay, "Bismarck's Welfare State," *Current History* 18 (1950): 1-8, 65-70, 129-133.

4. Asa Briggs, "The Welfare State in Historical Perspective," *Archives Européennes de Sociologie [European Journal of Sociology]* 2 (1961): 221-258; quoted in Schottland, *Welfare State,* pp. 25-45, see p. 34.

laissez-faire or 'liberal' system which substantially prevailed in the Western world in the nineteenth century."[5] But the welfare state did not emerge in history as theory, concept, or actuality at the point of rejection of nineteenth-century liberalism and laissez-faire. It is, perhaps, more accurate historically to say that the contemporary form and concept of the welfare state developed as a response to new historical contingencies which appeared when "Western society cast its fate irreversibly with machinery, cities, productivity, and economic growth."[6]

The Three Stages of Welfare State

If one can reject the misconceptions about the origin of the modern welfare state held by most recent writers, as well as about the historical singularity of the twentieth-century form, then it can be asserted that the modern welfare state has passed through three stages of growth during the last five hundred years.

The first stage began in the later Middle Ages and continued into the eighteenth century. It extended from the pole of medieval paternalism to that of dynastic mercantilism. The second stage, influenced by the doctrines of the Enlightenment (natural law, laissez-faire, and the natural rights of the individual), rejected paternalistic intervention by the state. It was to be identified with the political democracy, liberalism, and laissez-faire of the nineteenth century. The third and present stage may well have begun with the social insurance of Bismarck but certainly acquired its distinctive character in the twentieth century. It is this third stage to which recent historiography attempts to apply exclusively the term "welfare state." In this third stage the laissez-faire doctrines of the second stage have been rejected, and the concept of state intervention of the first stage has been restored.

The common denominator of all three stages is the police power legally inherent in the state and the exercise of that power to promote "welfare." The distinguishing marks of each stage involve differing attitudes toward the extent of state intervention, the areas of intervention, and the definition of "welfare," both individual and general, to be promoted by the state. The evolution of the welfare state is a dynamic process adjusting in theory and actuality to historical changes in political and social institutions and in human values. The underlying philosophy, the ultimate goals to be achieved, the degree of intervention in public and private life, the element of coercion or restriction of the rights of the individual,

5. Jacob Viner, "The United States as a Welfare State," in *The Nation's Economic Objectives,* ed. Edgar O. Edwards (Chicago: University of Chicago Press, 1964), pp. 151-167; quoted in Schottland, *Welfare State,* pp. 247-252, see p. 247.
6. Charles Frankel, *The Democratic Prospect* (New York: Harper & Row, 1962), pp. 125-144; quoted in Schottland, *Welfare State,* pp. 207-213, see p. 209.

all are a composite mirror which reflects a particular definition of "welfare state." Those who would reserve the term "welfare state" exclusively for the present stage might look for the warning signals of an impending fourth stage, to be seen in the factors of mass or gutter democracy, in the psychology of confrontation and demonstration as "the people" attempt to define concepts of "welfare." The fourth stage may well be characterized by moral laissez-faire with individual conscience replacing the police sanction of the state as the determinant for individual and community behavior.

This study is concerned with the development of the first stage of the modern Western welfare state, and more particularly with the welfare state of the Hohenzollern princes of Brandenburg-Prussia. The first stage appeared in the European cities of the later Middle Ages. New problems of internal administration were created by the secularized, materialistic activities associated with urban growth, commercial expansion, and a new affluence. With the new burgher wealth, luxury and extravagance became a moral issue; the new wealth challenged the traditional morality and class structure. Sumptuary legislation was the first attempt by city governments to protect individual welfare and morality. Urban problems connected with the market place (e.g., consumer protection, occupational monopolies); social problems of poverty, idle vagabonds, and minority groups required legislative regulation. The new middle class and the state required men educated in a new direction.

The cities, however, were only the microcosm of the future welfare state. They revealed the need and they showed the way. Territorial and "national" states soon took over the legislative and regulative functions performed by the cities. The secular state, with growing awareness of its "public" responsibility, expanded the perimeters of welfare to include public education, public health, public security in all forms, and social welfare.

Polizeistaat

During the late fifteenth and early sixteenth centuries, the term *Polizei* came into use to designate broad areas of individual and community activity which required legislative regulation in order to preserve good order in society and to promote the general welfare and common good. Later German historians adopted the term *Polizeistaat* to describe the type of state which developed after 1500. Offering both legal and substantive definition, *Polizeistaat* does not lend itself to a simple, unambiguous translation. A literal translation of "police state" denies completely the goal of the general welfare. The only proper translation of *Polizeistaat* is "welfare state."

Those who are disturbed by equating *Polizeistaat* with *Wohlfahrtsstaat* are captives of twentieth-century definitions of police state and of welfare state. Although there seems to be no "coherent philosophy" underlying the third stage of the welfare state, all definitions of it emphasize social welfare and services in the form of material protection against the hazards and evils of the modern industrial economy. Schottland defines the contemporary welfare state as "a modern democratic Western state in which the power of the state is deliberately used . . . to effect a redistribution of income."[7] Dean Roscoe Pound defines the twentieth-century welfare state as "a service state."[8] Harry Girvetz modifies this by defining the welfare state as "a social service state."[9]

In a technical or legal sense, the *Polizeistaat* might best be defined as "a regulative state." The welfare state that emerged during the Renaissance was no more and no less than a product of the police power legally inherent in the state, the power to regulate the activities of the individual either for his own welfare or for the common good. The instrument was the police power to regulate. The goal or purpose was the promotion of welfare, individual and general. What constitutes welfare in any period of history determines the stage or kind of welfare state arrived at at that point. But the basic definition of welfare state must concern itself with the nature and theory of the state itself. Regulation, intervention, compulsion, and restriction of individual action, under the legal authority of the police power of the state, to achieve an ultimate end of the common or individual good are the hallmarks of a welfare state.

The idea or theory of the welfare state would be less immune to definition and less subject to controversy if the meaning or nature of "welfare" itself were reducible to a uniform or static definition. But this has not been the historical pattern. The prevention of crime, maintenance of internal peace and order, the protection of life and property have traditionally, consistently, and continuously been basic functions of the coercive power of the state. Promotion of the general welfare in terms of security against civil disorder is so fundamental that the word "police" in the last two centuries has become identified almost exclusively with this function.

During the three hundred years between 1500 and 1800, public authority intervened in the private and civil sector by means of a great variety of regulative acts (police ordinances) designed to promote the public and individual welfare. During this first stage the areas subject to inter-

---

7. Schottland, *Welfare State,* p. 11.
8. Roscoe Pound, "The Rise of the Service State and Its Consequences," in *The Welfare State and the National Welfare,* ed. Sheldon Glueck (Cambridge, Mass.: Addison-Wesley Press, 1952), pp. 211-234; quoted in Schottland, *Welfare State,* pp. 201-206, see p. 201.
9. *International Encyclopedia of the Social Sciences,* s.v. "Welfare State."

vention and regulation and the welfare purposes of state experienced a changing emphasis. At the start, there was a greater concern for the individual, with religious and moral overtones. By the end of the seventeenth century, however, the emphasis had shifted to the common good, the general welfare, with economic overtones. Mercantilist and cameralist doctrines accented economic improvement and development of the political community for the enhancement of state power. Despite the shift of emphasis, the general welfare was not neglected in the sixteenth century, and the welfare of the individual was safeguarded and advanced by mercantilist princes. Some contemporary writers like Bossuet, at the end of the seventeenth century, believed that the purpose of royal power was "to ensure the public welfare." In Germany, Veit von Seckendorff as early as 1656 declared that a chief function of government was the establishment of good order and laws "for the welfare [*Wohlfahrt*] and general good [*gemeinen Nutz*] of the fatherland."[10] In contrast, in 1688, the elector of Brandenburg asserted that the primary goal of all Christian regents was "the happiness and welfare of their lands and subjects" and that he had in all his territories earnestly sought "to further the well-being of our loyal subjects . . . and to preserve to each one his rights."[11] Until 1740 the welfare of the individual was still a major concern to the Hohenzollern rulers. After that the welfare of the individual was a by-product of the power and economic prosperity of the state. Individual rights were forced to yield to the requirements of the common welfare and security. As Fritz Hartung points out, the achievement of the common welfare led to the fullest development of state power.[12] As power and national security became equated with public welfare, the rights and welfare of the individual receded in emphasis. It was not until the twentieth century that the primary goal of the welfare state again became the welfare of the individual, this time in the form of social services.

The evolution of the Western welfare state cannot be fully understood without determining the philosophical foundation on which the idea of the welfare state was based. There were two major determining influences affecting this philosophical foundation. At the beginning there was a Christian-feudal heritage that was displaced in the age of the Enlightenment by the twin forces of rationalism and natural law. To determine the philosophical basis of the welfare state in the general European context as well as in Germany one needs to consider the origin of the *idea* of a welfare state. Leonard Krieger raises an

---

10. Veit Ludwig von Seckendorff, *Teutscher Furstenstaat*, p. 203.
11. Christian Otto Mylius, ed., *Corpus Constitutionum Magdeburgicarum*, pt. 3, no. 1, p. 3 (cited hereafter as *C. C. Magdeb.*).
12. Fritz Hartung, "Der Aufgeklärte Absolutismus," in *Staatsbildende Kräfte der Neuzeit, Gessammelte Aufsätze*, p. 158.

interesting point in this regard: "The question arises . . . whether the idea of the welfare state has had any independent status vis-a-vis the actuality of it."[13] There is no doubt about the actuality of the welfare state in the practical legislation or regulation exercised by the governing authorities, and one has to agree with Krieger that the idea of a welfare state did exist in the Western tradition during and following the Middle Ages.

Krieger's definition of "welfare" as service of the governor to the governed needs, however, to be viewed with caution. In defining the aim of state as *salus populi,* the common interest, the general welfare, he relies perhaps too heavily on the ancient tradition of state as a *res publica* concerned with the *salus populi.* During the later Middle Ages and the two centuries following the Protestant Reformation, it was less the common interest and general welfare than the private conduct of the governed that was the concern of the governor. This explains why so large a segment of the welfare regulation was sumptuary in nature. Although police regulation by the state of private conduct is older than the Middle Ages, I agree with John M. Vincent, who believed that the idea that the moral and spiritual welfare of his subjects was the proper concern and duty of a prince originated in the religious and paternalistic nature of the medieval conception of government.[14]

The medieval conception of government in time became influenced by Roman traditions, once Roman law was reintroduced into Western Europe after the twelfth century. But medieval government, administrative institutions, and the functions of the prince were based on the dual foundations of Germanic tribal traditions and feudalism. The Frankish conception of kingship regarded the kingdom as the personal property of the king to be administered by the personal servants of the king's household. The Roman concept of the state as a public thing administered by public officials to achieve public aims was replaced by the idea of the personal authority of Germanic kings derived from tribal origins.

By the time of the Carolingians (ca. A.D. 800), the idea of state experienced a change vital to the nature of the welfare state in later centuries. While the Roman idea of a *res publica* was still unfamiliar, the powers, collective duties, and responsibilities basic to the notion of state reappeared in the Frankish empire of the Carolingian dynasty. Continuing to regard the kingdom as his personal property, the Frankish king now recognized that he had duties to those in his territories. A public interest appeared if not a state in the public sense. The authority of the Carolingian king was held of God. In the Carolingian state the community of peoples (who would be citizens of a *res publica*) were

---

13. "The Idea of the Welfare State in Europe and the United States," *Journal of the History of Ideas* 24 (1963): 553-568.
14. *Costume and Conduct in the Laws of Basel, Bern, and Zurich, 1370-1800,* pp. 1-2.

held together by a communal faith. The welfare (spiritual as well as material) of this community was accepted as a responsibility and duty by Charlemagne and his successors in their theocratic concept of state. The function of the king was to protect the church, foster education, maintain peace, provide justice, and supervise the moral life of his subjects. In fulfilling these functions for the community, Charlemagne asserted that he should have the aid of his subjects *pro nostra omnium communi salute* ("for the common welfare of us all"). There were duties for king and subjects; they were duties derived from the law of God. "Le bien de tous exige donc le dévouement à la même oeuvre de salut voulue par Dieu [The good of all requires therefore dedication to the same goal of welfare desired by God]."[15]

Until the secularization of the modern state beginning in the sixteenth century, the concept of duties and obligations of king and subject was based on divine principles. And, until the full impact of the Age of Reason changed political theory in the seventeenth and eighteenth centuries, divine-right principles guided the monarchs of the Age of Absolutism. This explains to a large extent the concern for the moral and spiritual life of subjects expressed in the edification function or ethical mission, which Krieger sees as central to the idea of the welfare state.[16]

The patriarchal or paternalistic nature of the medieval conception of government had its origins, aside from religious influence, chiefly in the feudal-manorial framework of medieval society. The basic character of the feudal state was the antithesis of the public nature of the ancient or modern state. The feudal state was based on personal rather than public or civic relationships, either of lord and vassal in the feudal hierarchy or of manorial lord and serfs at the economic level. Obligations, duties, and rights were not those of citizen and state but were part of a personal relationship. The public and private functions of the patriarchal feudal prince were undifferentiated. The prince's concern for the utilitarian and moral welfare of his dependents was part of his patrimonial jurisdiction. To concern himself with the welfare and personal conduct of his subjects was not a fulfillment of a public responsibility but a personal and paternalistic undertaking with overtones of obligations based on divine principles (sanction).

These comments on the origin of the idea of the welfare state in the early modern era in the religious and paternalistic nature of the medieval conception of government can, however, be misleading. In the first place, there *was* no state which provided for the welfare of its citizens. The

---

15. For most of these thoughts about the Carolingian concept of state, I am indebted to an excellent article by Louis Halphen, "L'idée d'état sous les carolingiens," *Revue Historique* 185 (1939): 59-70.

16. Krieger also stresses the utilitarian function. Ernst Troeltsch also argues that the Thomistic and Catholic theory of the state was that the purpose of the state is confined to utilitarian welfare and legal justice (*The Social Teaching of the Christian Churches,* 1:314).

"state" was a property holder fulfilling his personal obligations. But those obligations, satisfied by secular princes prior to the modern era, were the fundamental ones of protection and justice. What one would define as welfare in terms of human needs was furnished primarily by the medieval Christian Church. Problems of moral conduct, of poverty, misery, and ignorance were to be solved by Christian charity as administered by the Church. Not until responsibility for the secular needs of humanity and concern for the regulation of private conduct pass completely into the hands of secular governments can one speak of the actuality of a welfare state. The theory and the function of the welfare state had medieval origins, but it came into existence at the point where modern states and secular forms of government came into being.

Wilbur K. Jordan sees "one of the few great cultural revolutions in western history" in "the momentous shift from men's primarily religious preoccupations to the secular concerns that have moulded the thought and institutions of the past three centuries."[17] With regard to this religious preoccupation, Ernst Troeltsch maintains that in the early Christian Church, the Church's response to suffering caused by the existing social system was simply the work of charity. There was no program of social reform, no effort to remove poverty or the causes of social distress. The aim of almsgiving, ostensibly to alleviate suffering and want, was as much to benefit the giver as the receiver, because it awakened the spirit of love. During the Middle Ages the Church completely relieved the state of the burden of charity, even if ineffectively.[18] As early as the fourteenth century, however, changes in the social-economic system created an urban environment in which the secular needs of mankind increasingly became the concern of men and governments. Jordan states that in England, poverty was first systematically attacked in the sixteenth century with private gifts and then with state legislation to eradicate its causes. But the studies of Kent R. Greenfield and John M. Vincent more appropriately associate the birth of the modern welfare state with the sumptuary legislation of the late medieval cities.[19] Regulation of local economic activities and of the private conduct of its citizens by the city government provided a historical model for later territorial and national mercantilist and welfare states. Manners and morals, producer and consumer, public health, education, poverty, idleness were all regulated by the secular acts of municipal, territorial, and national governments.

In writing about "the welfare state" in the United States since the New Deal, Sidney Hook states that "The social philosophy behind the

---

17. *Philanthropy in England, 1480-1660*, p. 16.
18. Troeltsch, *Social Teaching*, pp. 133-138.
19. Kent R. Greenfield, *Sumptuary Law in Nürnberg;* Vincent, *Costume and Conduct.*

welfare state is vague and inchoate."[20] Legislation, he says, "did not flow from any doctrinaire theory." Troeltsch says much the same thing about the medieval scene: "The Christian social doctrine of the Middle Ages was as far removed from being a programme of social reform as was the social teaching of the Early Church."[21] The question arises whether the centuries between these eras produced any conscious social philosophy beyond the paternalistic heritage from the Middle Ages. The answer may be found by defining the welfare state specifically in terms of its objectives and purposes. However vague the social philosophy behind the twentieth-century welfare state may be, its legislative acts seek to provide for the economic security of its citizens against the evils, hazards, and distress produced by a modern industrial economy and society, which must cope with the radical changes and rapid developments of modern science and technology. Whether it be full employment, security against illness or old age, insurance against accident and disease, assurance of a decent standard of living in regulating wages and hours, or placing education at all levels within the reach of all, it is clear that the contemporary welfare state intervenes in the natural order of things to protect and insure the material needs of the individual citizen. Without doctrinaire motivation, the twentieth-century welfare state appears to have developed a social conscience, perhaps to atone historically for the evils introduced by the theories of *raison d'état* of the mercantilist state and to compensate for the imbalances, human abuses, and neglect of human needs and opportunities under laissez-faire doctrines.

Five hundred years earlier, in the Renaissance atmosphere of secularism, urbanization, and a changing society, municipal legislation in fifteenth-century Nuremberg concerned itself with price regulation, wage control, and consumer protection. Accepted concepts of the regulative power of the state made the city council of Nuremberg responsible for policing the streets and marketplaces, and for keeping good order in the city. It issued building regulations, concerned itself with public sanitation and the prevention and extinction of fires, looked after the poor, regulated crafts, and supervised the religious life of the pre-Reformation city.[22]

Unlike the contemporary welfare state, the first stage of the Western European welfare state equated welfare with peace and justice, with good order in public life. While the objectives differ, in both cases we see expressions of what Sidney Hook has called "compulsory cooperation"

20. "Welfare State—A Debate That Isn't," *New York Times Magazine,* November 27, 1960, p. 27; see also Schottland, *Welfare State,* p. 165.

21. *Social Teaching,* p. 303.

22. Greenfield, *Sumptuary Law,* p. 9.

regulated by the state for the good of the general welfare. The common ground of all welfare states consists not in a particular definition of welfare so much as in the regulative function of the state necessary to achieve the common good or the individual welfare. If the most recent manifestation is a "social service state," the term *utilitas* was used as early as the sixth to ninth centuries as synonymous with general welfare. *Utilitas publica* and *utilitas generalis* were defined as *salus, stabilitas, ordǫ,* and *securitas.* Emphasis throughout the Middle Ages was on stability, peace, justice, and the protection of the Church. In the fifteenth century the concept of "good order" was extended to sumptuary legislation and the regulation of the marketplace.[23] As a result of the Protestant Reformation, the spiritual welfare of subjects became a proper state responsibility. The responsibility of the state to promote welfare was continuously extended or modified, and the nature and definition of welfare reflected changing historical contingencies. What remained constant was the responsibility of the state to regulate, to intervene, to promote welfare, to attempt to find the balance-point between *Gemeinnutz* and *Eigennutz,* the general as opposed to the personal welfare.

Wilbur K. Jordan concludes that by the end of the Elizabethan period in Tudor England "it was generally agreed that all men must somehow be sustained at the level of subsistence, that the hopelessly derelict were proper charges on the society, and that the state must intervene to secure these ends if private charity should fail."[24] To these goals he adds the social rehabilitation of the poor and their children and combatting the ignorance which produces poverty by making available opportunities for education. But Jordan stresses the role of private philanthropy in solving in England those problems that on the Continent were the concern of the state. He believes that the cause of this singular development in England can be discovered in the peculiar nature of the English Reformation. "Calvinism was in England sublimated into a sensitive social conscience."[25] Private charity in England after the Elizabethan period, on the basis of "voluntary cooperation," did for humanity what the state's social conscience is attempting to achieve in the twentieth century.

To distinguish between the welfare state as originally defined and as it is defined today, in both its specific acts of regulation and its underlying philosophy, one needs to recognize the primary emphasis placed

23. See Walther Merk, "Der Gedanke des gemeinen Besten in der deutschen Staats- und Rechtsentwicklung," in *Festschrift Alfred Schultze zum 70. Geburtstage,* ed. Walther Merk, pp. 451-494 passim.

24. "The English Background of Modern Philanthropy," *American Historical Review,* vol. 66, no. 2, p. 401.

25. *Philanthropy in England,* p. 18.

upon sumptuary legislation in the early welfare state. Sumptuary regulation of the daily life of citizens prevailed throughout Europe from the Middle Ages to at least the end of the eighteenth century. Sumptuary legislation in deed and philosophy was the very epitome of the paternalistic *Polizeistaat*. Medieval paternalism, with its religious sanction, manifested itself as the personal concern of prince or city council for the right and proper private conduct of the individual. The sumptuary legislation of the welfare state from the fifteenth to the eighteenth century was as much concerned with the moral conduct and activity of the citizen as with his material and secular needs. The purpose of sumptuary legislation was to restrict luxury and extravagance in personal habits; these were the products of sinful vanity and pomp and, in turn, produced financial hardship and poverty. Because of this underlying concern for the moral welfare of the governed, sumptuary legislation is customarily associated with the development of the Protestant ethic after the Reformation of the sixteenth century.[26]

Both Greenfield and Vincent, on the basis of their studies of sumptuary legislation in German and Swiss cities before and after the Reformation, believe this to be a misconception.[27] Sumptuary legislation antedated the Protestant Reformation by two centuries, and the specific details and regulations of this legislation were not altered by the Reformation. This type of legislation arose to curb and restrain abuses that threatened the moral and economic welfare of the citizen. Because of the gradual development, refinement, expansion, and eventual stereotyping of this type of regulation over a period of several centuries, it is difficult to find an underlying theory of a welfare state on which the legislation was predicated. The philosophy of the welfare state prior to the eighteenth-century Enlightenment was simply based upon the paternalistic conceptions of government inherited from the Middle Ages. There were fundamentally two areas of paternalistic regulation. One had to do with the Christian-moral aspects of private conduct. The secular arm of government was used to preserve the Christian virtues and to curb the sinful instincts of profanity, indecency, and extravagance. The other area concerned the general police power of the state to maintain civil order and to serve the public interest. The two areas were by no means isolated from each other. Restriction of luxury, extravagance, and social uppishness reflected economic as well as moral motivation. Efforts to relieve poverty and disease reflected a basic charitable concern for individual suffering; but the economic welfare of a state was also promoted by an

26. E.g., ibid., pp. 146-151.
27. See Vincent, *Costume and Conduct,* and Greenfield, *Sumptuary Law.* See also J. M. Vincent, "European Blue Laws," in *Annual Report of the American Historical Association,* 1897, pp. 355-373.

employed and productive citizenry enjoying at least a minimum level of subsistence.

During the Middle Ages and in the early modern state prior to the Enlightenment, the sanction or justification upon which the regulative intervention of the state or prince was based was divine law. As that royal apologist for divine right monarchy, James I of England, so cogently argued, God made princes responsible for the welfare of those who were entrusted to their rule. Since the era of the Enlightenment, perhaps even in the seventeenth century, divine sanction was replaced under the influence of the political philosophers by natural and rational sanction. The concept of the prince as the first servant of the state was not hallowed by divine right. It was based on a contract theory and the preachings of the inalienable natural rights of the governed. Only in the eighteenth century can one find a suggestion of a doctrinaire social philosophy based on the half-baked formulae of the philosophes and expressed in the form of a supposedly enlightened despotism.

An analysis of the idea of the welfare state in terms of its origins, definitions, and philosophical foundations over a period of some five hundred years makes several things clear. The purpose and goals of the welfare state remain fairly constant, consistent with the basic definition of the welfare state as a regulative agency promoting "welfare." The variant elements are the definition of "welfare" and the sanction or justification upon which the regulative intervention was based. The concept of "welfare" and the basic sanction have varied over the centuries, reflecting the changing social-economic framework within which contemporary historical forces operated. The welfare state as a functioning actuality has been a fluid reality, an ad hoc affair, intervening in the moral and material daily life of its subjects to compel them to do what they naturally would not do or to restrain them from doing what they naturally would, to the end of promoting the welfare of the individual and of preserving the public interest.

The Prussian Form of Polizeistaat

When Sidney Hook, in 1960, analyzed the twentieth-century version of the welfare state, he wrote that "those who criticize the welfare state seek to prove, in an attempt to discredit it, that it has an unsavory genealogy which can be traced to the traditions and practices of Prussian absolutism tempered by a paternalistic concern for the well-being of its subjects."[28] It is perhaps true that by the eighteenth century the regulation of private life and activity under the police power of the state had achieved such

28. "Welfare State," p. 27.

intensification under the Hohenzollern rulers that the Prussian state epitomized the European *Polizeistaat.* If this was true, it was only because of the development in Prussia of a relatively more efficient administrative and bureaucratic machinery to enforce police regulations. But the Prussian welfare state was part of the universal evolution of ideas and practices in Western Europe after the Middle Ages. There was a universal climate of ideas pervading the European state system, although the ideas did not express themselves uniformly in all the member states. A heritage of Germanic, feudal, and Christian ideals created the paternalistic forms of regulation of private and public life. A universal divine sanction imposed upon paternalistic princes a responsibility to God for the welfare of subjects.

Fundamental to any welfare state is police power, the element of force or compulsion, the authority inherent in the office of government. According to Wilhelm Dilthey, "It is the relationship of the rights and duties of government as the power to rule the members of a state through force, and of the welfare principle as the purpose, from which all power manifestations are justified."[29] Dilthey further believes that there is a moral order fundamental to the rights and duties of office and basic to the law of the state. There are three factors intertwined here: the moral duties of the ruler, the rights or power of the ruler derived from the authority of his office to fulfill these duties, and the welfare of the individual, which it is the purpose of the state and therefore the duty of the ruler to provide. The origin of the duties and rights of the ruler as well as the ruled derived from Germanic and Christian traditions. The Protestant Reformation intensified a moral-religious bond between the ruler and the citizens among the northern Protestant states. By the seventeenth century, however, the theoretical foundations of the state and function of the prince had been divorced from theological principles. The derivation of state authority from God had been replaced by the contract theory. Natural law and reason had become the foundation of the authority of the state. But one factor remained constant—the purpose of authority, whatever the foundation on which that authority was based. The purpose of state and of authority was to provide for the welfare of the individual and to compel all individuals to work for the general welfare. Prior to the Enlightenment, the only limitation on the power of the prince was responsibility to God. After the Enlightenment, heralded by Pufendorf, Thomasius, and Wolff, the power of the state was limited by reason and natural law as expressed in the social contract.

If, by the eighteenth century, the Prussian *Polizeistaat* had acquired a status, a character of such distinct historical significance that it may possibly be described as the prototype of the later European welfare state,

---

29. Wilhelm Dilthey, *Zur preussischen Geschichte,* ed. Erich Weniger, p. 155.

this certainly was not true in the two preceding centuries. Until the end of the seventeenth century there was little, if any, uniqueness or independence in the theories and practices underlying the government of the Hohenzollern princes. The ideas that moved the latter were adopted from the greater German scene. Not until the very end of the seventeenth century did Brandenburg contribute leadership for Germany in the realm of ideas.

In the very best and most charitable analysis, Brandenburg operated in phase with, if not in imitation of, the ideas, theories, and philosophy of state dominant at the national level or prevailing in the leading territories and imperial cities, such as Saxony and Nuremberg. This was clearly evident in the development of the concept of the *Polizeistaat* after 1500. Although the Christian-feudal prince had concerned himself with the security and moral welfare of his subjects, and city councils had legislatively regulated the internal life of German cities, it was not until after 1500 that the word *Polizei* came into use to designate legislative and administrative regulation of the internal civil life to promote general welfare. The definition of the early welfare state as a *Polizeistaat* may best be observed in the identification of the borrowed French term *Polizei* with the German phrases, *Gemeine Nutz* and *Gemeine Beste* ("general welfare" and "general good"). From the French *polir* ("to establish good order") the word *Polizei* was adopted into the German legal language in the early sixteenth century. As there was no German equivalent, it could not be translated precisely; it connoted order, welfare, security. The towns of Germany probably used the term first. Not until the great efforts to reform the constitution of the Holy Roman Empire between 1495 and 1521 did the word and concept of "police" regulation become part of the legislative and legal vocabulary of imperial, territorial, and municipal administration.[30]

In 1495 at the Diet of Worms, Bertold, Archbishop of Mainz and leader of the reform party in the Holy Roman Empire, wanted to reorganize the administration of the Empire. He proposed to place under an imperial regency (to govern in the absence of the Emperor) the internal matters of civil administration that establish good order, welfare, peace, and security. To describe these aspects of government Bertold adopted the Burgundian *pollicie* as *Pollucy* [police]. Under *Pollucy* he included such items as blasphemy, the cost of clothing, itinerant musicians and entertainers, beggars, gypsies, excessive drinking, usury, and the adulteration of wine.

The word *Polizei* was not used again until 1521, when it was introduced

---

30. *Handwörterbuch der Staatswissenschaften,* 4th ed., s.v. "Polizei"; see also Joseph Segall, *Geschichte und Strafrecht der Reichspolizeiordnungen von 1530, 1548, 1577,* pp. 12-13.

by Emperor Charles V. Charles had to communicate with the German Estates in French and had to use the French-Burgundian term *Polizei* for lack of a German equivalent. The Diet of Worms of 1521 was the model diet as far as the origin and prototype of a *Reichspolizeiordnung* ("imperial police ordinance") is concerned. Charles requested the Estates to counsel him on "how to establish justice, peace, good order, and police in the Empire [*guet ordnung und policeien*]." A draft of a police ordinance in the following years proposed including under police regulation such things as fraud in the wool trade, musicians, entertainers, beggars, gypsies, usurious contracts, monopolies, excessive drinking, luxury in clothes, and other extravagances in personal and social behavior, blasphemy, profanity, immorality, Jewish usury, uniform weights and measures, and security on the highways.

The word *Polizei* was probably first used in an official, legislative document in 1530, the "Römischer Keyserlicher Majestät Ordnung und Reformation guter Pollicei im Heiligen Römischen Reich," issued by Emperor Charles V. It recurred in the police ordinance of 1548, whose title descriptively spoke of "guter Pollicey zu befürderung des gemeynen nutz [good police order for the benefit of the general good]." By 1577 the imperial ordinance was actually called *Policey Ordnung* ("police ordinance"). At first an imperial police ordinance was a loose collection of separate statutes dealing with particular problems: blasphemy, immorality, luxury and extravagance, usury, security. Collectively the imperial ordinance sought to establish order in the Empire. By 1577 the police ordinance consisted of a single statute with various articles dealing with problems identified as "police" matters.

The proclamation of imperial police ordinances gained general use for the word *Polizei* throughout Germany after 1530. The imperial ordinances became models for the territorial police ordinances issued in the sixteenth and seventeenth centuries. In the tumultuous days of the Reformation era, imperial edicts were ineffective in establishing good order or in furthering the public good. Nevertheless, the concept of a *Polizeistaat* as a state regulating the activities of individuals for the promotion of the general welfare was adopted by the territorial princes, including the Hohenzollern of Brandenburg. By the eighteenth century the word *Polizei* had become synonymous with *Wohlfahrt* or *Gemeine Nutz*. It implied legislative and administrative regulation in the private and public life of the civil community in order to establish good order and security and to advance the common good.

The language, the terminology, and the concept can be traced to the influence of imperial legislation. But effective legislative regulation by means of police ordinances occurred at municipal and territorial levels. For two hundred years the rulers of Brandenburg-Prussia justified their police ordinances on the grounds of their "paternalistic concern for the advancement of the common good [*Landes-Väterlicher Vorsorge zu Beförderung des allgemeinen Bestens*]."

In the sixteenth century there was no universal principle or theory to guide governing authorities in their legislative regulation. Provisions of police ordinances were an ad hoc response to conditions which threatened the security, good order, morality, or happiness of the prince's subjects. In the seventeenth century, Germany produced a number of political philosophers who began to develop a philosophy of government and a theory of state. Foremost among these was Veit von Seckendorff. In 1656, in his *Teutscher Fürstenstaat*,[31] Seckendorff gave perhaps the best formal, legalistic definition of the *Polizeistaat* and offered a blueprint for action for German princes. He regarded the chief function of government as the establishment of laws "for the welfare and common good of the fatherland." The purpose of law, he argued, was not to advance the personal interests of the prince or to please special persons; laws and ordinances were to be established on a just basis for the good of all uniformly, because laws of a police nature apply to citizens and subjects. He then proceeded to catalog areas requiring such laws of a police nature.

Princes were to:
1. establish peace, order, and justice in their lands
2. provide adequate food supplies, encourage increase of population, and assure economic livelihood for all
3. encourage a moral and decent behavior of subjects and a good Christian upbringing for youth at home and at school
4. require church attendance, forbid blasphemy, profanity, and drunkenness
5. preserve proper distinction between social classes in respect to conduct, clothing, and general consumption
6. establish building codes to assure proper construction and protection of public health and issue fire ordinances to protect property and life
7. promote public health by proper measures against pestilence and contagious disease; by assurance of pure water, clean air, sanitary streets, uncontaminated food and drink; by appointment of learned physicians, surgeons, and midwives; by adequate care of the poor, the needy, and orphans in hospitals, in poorhouses, or through poor relief; and by protection against the evils of brandy and tobacco
8. promote economic prosperity by encouraging the virtues of industriousness, thrift, and obedience and by discouraging idleness,

31. Pp. 203-232.

extravagance, roguery, begging, vagabondage, and parasitic charlatans of all kinds
9. prevent usury by keeping Jews out of the territory or by carefully regulating them
10. protect the consumer against monopoly and high prices
11. establish a uniform system of weights and measures
12. regulate the consumption of food at festive celebrations and extravagance in clothing by means of sumptuary legislation.

The theory of the welfare state defended by Seckendorff was to a large extent both a codification of the ad hoc legislation of the previous two centuries and a program of action to be followed by many German princes until the eighteenth century. But already at the end of the seventeenth and in the early eighteenth century a new theory and philosophy of state was emerging in Brandenburg-Prussia. Thomasius and Pufendorf developed a theory of the state based on a social contract; the authority of the ruler was based on natural law rather than divine law. This theory was significantly expanded by Christian Wolff into a philosophy of the Prussian welfare state of the eighteenth century.[32] Although Dilthey has stated that Wolff "was the philosopher of the welfare state under the first three Prussian kings," Wolff's philosophy and influence were really felt only in the reign of Frederick the Great and had little, if any, impact on Frederick William I. In 1721 Christian Wolff's *Vernünfftigen Gedanken vom gesellschaftlichen Leben der Menschen* first introduced ideas of the Enlightenment into German administrative theory.[33] There is a major distinction between the idea of the welfare state found in Seckendorff's writings and the "cameralistic welfare state" of which Wolff was the founder. Seckendorff saw the chief function of government as the furthering of "welfare and common good." Wolff defined the purpose of the state as "the furtherance of the common welfare and security." Otto Hintze recognized the distinction in his introduction to Volume VI of the *Acta Borussica: Die Behördenorganisation* when he stated that "The cultural pupose and the welfare purpose receded before the power purpose . . . *Raison d'état* dominated in all areas. [Der Kulturzweck und der Wohlfahrtszweck tritt vor dem Machtszweck zurück . . . Die 'Staatsraison' dominirt auf allen Gebieten]."[34]

32. Perhaps the best exposition and analysis of the welfare state in the eighteenth century and the influence of Wolff on its theoretical development is that of Dilthey, *Preussischen Geschichte*, pp. 152-183. See also Hartung, "Der Aufgeklärte Absolutismus"; A. M. Donner, "Over de Term 'Welvaartsstaat'," in *Mededelingen der Koninklijke Nederlandse Akademie van Wetenschappen,* new series, vol. 20, no. 15, pp. 551-565.
33. Hartung, "Der Aufgeklärte Absolutismus," p. 157.
34. *Acta Borussica: Die Behördenorganisation,* vol. 6, pt. 1, p. 6.

A new definition of the welfare state emerged in the idea of state [*Staatsidee*] of Wolff. The emergence of the state on the basis of a social contract, in the argument of the philosopher of the Enlightenment, meant that the dominant drive of the state was the struggle for power, for independence from outer and inner restraints. It was a Hobbesian state. The general welfare was ostensibly the goal, but it was dependent upon the state's power to establish external security, internal peace, and prosperity for all. General welfare and security were theoretically equated, but welfare was secondary to security. The *Machtszweck* [power], as Hintze put it, came first. In the competitive state system of the eighteenth century, the sovereignty of the absolute monarch determined what the general welfare was.

With the emergence of the eighteenth-century state based on natural law and reason, there followed also a subtle change in the function of the welfare state. This change expressed itself in the conflict between individual rights and the common welfare. From natural law was derived the prinple of the limitation of individual rights, or the principle of the general welfare. Individual welfare was subordinated to the common good. According to Dilthey, the first person to make this derivation was Christian Wolff. In the absolute (or "enlightened") monarchy of the eighteenth century, the individual was not able to compel the observance of his rights by the state. "On the contrary," as Hartung paraphrased Wolff, "the state has the obligation to devise useful means 'for the promotion of the general welfare and security' and to make those arrangements necessary for fulfillment, but at the same time has the right to compel its subjects to obey its orders, whereby it is expressly emphasized that the subjects are obliged to do willingly all that which the government decrees."[35]

Wolff's principles had their greatest influence upon the theory and actuality of the welfare state under Frederick the Great; they formed the philosophical basis on which the civil laws of the Prussian state (*Allgemeines Preussisches Landrecht*) were codified in 1794. This was the welfare state of the Age of Enlightenment, the welfare state of "unsavory genealogy" to which Sidney Hook referred.

The year 1740 thus takes on significance as a watershed year in the evolution of the welfare state in Prussia. Wolff's rational philosophy was developed while he was Professor of Mathematics and Philosophy (1706-1723) at the University of Halle. But Halle was also the center of German Pietism, which had a dominant influence in forming the conception of the welfare state held by Frederick William I. Theological principles and divine sanction may have yielded in theory before the teachings of Pufendorf, Thomasius, and Wolff, but not in actuality until after Frederick William I.

---

35. "Der Aufgeklärte Absolutismus," p. 157. See Christian Wolff, *Vernünfftigen Gedanken von dem Gessellschaftlichen Leben der Menschen*, pp. 459-460.

The distinction between individual welfare and general welfare, based on the principle of limitation of individual rights for the common good, represented in the eighteenth century a change in the purpose of the state. Between 1500 and 1740 there had been a shift of emphasis from the moral, spiritual, and material welfare of the individual to the general welfare. Security, justice, and internal peace had concerned the medieval and Renaissance ruler, and to this extent there had existed a concept of the general welfare of a community. In fact, the very introduction of the word *Polizei* in the imperial ordinances of the sixteenth century to signify concern for "good order" in internal civil administration emphasized the Germanic concern for promotion of the *general good*. It is more than a semantic argument to say that prior to the eighteenth century the German princes and city councils, moved by a Christian conscience, were primarily concerned with the individual's welfare. The promotion of the common good advanced individual welfare and happiness. But in the eighteenth century, power became the primary goal of the absolute monarch, and *raison d'état* the justification of that power. *Raison d'état* became the equivalent of the common and general welfare. The strength, the wealth, the security of the state could be achieved only if the principle were accepted that the common good took precedence over individual rights. The common good could be achieved only by force or compulsion, the exercise of the police power that is fundamental to any welfare state. Nineteenth-century liberalism rejected this concept, but neither completely nor uniformly.

Generically and historically, in concept and actuality, the term "welfare state" has therefore a much longer history than that attributed to it by writers of the last twenty-five years. Fritz Kern used the term *Wohlfahrtsstaat* as early as 1928.[36] German writers have used the term *Polizeistaat* to describe a welfare state for an even longer period.

Since the fifteenth century, the welfare state has passed through three stages. Promotion of the general welfare, however defined, was a constant factor common to all three stages. What distinguished each stage from the other was the underlying philosophy, the purpose and definition of welfare, and the role of government.

The elemental function of any state, whatever its form of government, is the preservation of law and order. Without this there can be no basis for individual welfare and security. In this fundamental sense, Leonard Krieger correctly maintains that "every state, then, is a welfare state." When government responsibility goes beyond this elemental function and assumes responsibility for the welfare of the citizens of the state within

36. "Vom Herrenstaat zum Wohlfahrtsstaat," *Schmoller's Jahrbuch für Gestezgebung, Verwaltung, und Volkswirtschaft* 52 (1928): 393-415.

the political framework of law and order, then the welfare state begins to emerge.

The modern welfare state emerged when historical contingencies could no longer be satisfied by the functions of "protection and justice" of the feudal state and by the humane services of the Christian Church. Urbanism, commercial economy, and new social classes were the historical contingencies whose challenge could be met only by a secularization of public authority or government. The heritage of the Middle Ages, however, was preserved in the paternalistic concern and legislative acts of the new secular princes. Divine sanction was the foundation for welfare legislation. Responsibility to God for the welfare of subjects and citizens enhanced the concept of a paternalistic prince.

During the first stage of the Western welfare state, from the sixteenth to the eighteenth centuries, there was a steady shift of emphasis in the scope and purpose of welfare. A primary moral-religious concern for the spiritual welfare of the individual was gradually replaced by a concern for the general welfare, the common good. The state assumed responsibility for the poor, the unfortunate, and the misfits of society. Market regulation, expansion of educational facilities, promotion of public health, and urban development profited from the direct intervention of government. This state intervention was tangibly expressed through the regulative, police legislation of the rising, bureaucratic, mercantilist-cameralist state. The climax of this first stage was reached when divine sanction was replaced by natural law and reason as the moral and juridical basis of state intervention. The rights of the individual and the general welfare were subordinated to the security and power purposes of the absolute state of the Enlightenment.

The nineteenth century, in theory at least, and in England perhaps more than on the Continent, under doctrines of laissez-faire and political liberalism, witnessed a rejection of governmental intervention.[37] In practice, governmental responsibility to protect the individual, to maintain order, to promote the public health, safety, morals, education, and the general welfare never really wavered. In Germany, it is probably correct to say that there was a direct, lineal projection of the cameralist welfare state in the social insurance program of Bismarck.

As the urban, commercial, secular development of the sixteenth and seventeenth centuries could be dealt with only by the regulative, police measures of the earlier *Polizeistaat,* so it was discovered in the twentieth century that the social and economic contingencies of a highly industrialized society required a rejection of laissez-faire and an extension of governmental intervention.

---

37. See John B. Brebner, "Laissez-Faire and State Intervention in Nineteenth Century Britain," in *The Making of English History,* ed. Robert L. Schuyler and Herman Ausubel (New York: Dryden Press, 1952), pp. 501-510.

The modern welfare state, throughout its history, has been an ad hoc response by government to ever-changing historical conditions. This response has taken the form of regulating the actions of individuals to promote the general welfare and protect the individual. The definition of the welfare to be achieved has had constant elements, but it has also varied from the preservation of corporate class privilege to the concept of equality of opportunity. Whatever the definition and scope of welfare, and whatever the form of government which seeks to promote it, the legal foundation for the welfare state is the police power of the state to regulate. This entails the necessary and adjunct element of compulsion, of limitation on the liberty of the individual. With the rejection of divine sanction and responsibility of the prince to God, a critical problem was posed. The problem was one of socio-political calculus. When is the maximum limit of the state's power of compulsion of the individual reached? The counterpart to this question is, at what point does the individual's right to resist government compulsion assert itself?

From natural law the eighteenth century derived a principle of natural rights, proclaimed in 1794 in the Prussian Law Code, which declared that "the universal rights of man are founded on the natural freedom to seek and to further his own welfare without injury of the rights of any other."[38] The general welfare in effect is the totality of "the rights of the others." Individual man as a moral man, however, is not capable of limiting his own rights. Therefore, the state, moved by moral duty and the social contract, must use its power to define and promote the general welfare. But the state, too, is incapable of limiting its power. This may well explain the nineteenth-century reaction of laissez-faire and liberalism against the concept of government intervention and regulation of the individual.

The inherent danger to individual freedom in the growth of the power of the state in the name of the general welfare is what alarms critics of the contemporary welfare state. Roscoe Pound argues that "the service state . . . must be a bureau state," which may easily lead to a totalitarian or absolute state.[39] Donald R. Richberg, perhaps disillusioned by New Deal experience, feels that "a comprehensive welfare state must be a police state."[40] He feared the growth of the bureaucratic power of state, arguing that political power wielded by public officials who administer the welfare state can become a tyranny.

Thus the interpretations of welfare state are like a point-counterpoint dialogue, with government intervention and compulsion on one side and laissez-faire liberalism on the other. Fulfillment of the individual and the

---

38. *Allegemeines Landrecht für die preussischen Staaten,* ed. Schering, 4 vols., 2d ed., rev. (Berlin: A. Nauck, 1869), Introduction, p. 10, par. 83.

39. "Rise of the Service State," p. 202.

40. "Liberalism, Paternalism, Security, and the Welfare State," in Glueck, *Welfare State and National Welfare,* pp. 235-261; quoted in Schottland, *Welfare State,* pp. 184-194, see p. 185.

good life for all are recognized as the ultimate goal by the protagonists of both sides of the dialogue. The need for law and order and social services provides the justification for the exercise of police regulation and limitations on the rights of the individual. The right to dissent and to resist government compulsion is defended on the grounds of the individual's natural rights and freedom. Individual and state cloak themselves with an appeal to morality. Unfortunately and tragically, the ideal, moral man and the ideal, moral state have been, since Plato, no more than a philosophical construction.

Part I
Sumptuary Legislation

I

Sumptuary Legislation

The concept of intervention by the state in private life for the furtherance of the public good perhaps never manifested itself so intimately as
under the category of sumptuary legislation. Here the regulation of individual conduct for the benefit of the individual and the community can
be most closely observed. Sumptuary regulation of the manners and
morals of "everyman" was the very essence of paternalism. This paternal
concern *(väterliche Sorge)* was more than a legalistic stereotype. Until at
least the eighteenth century, the prince acted as the father of his people,
concerned with their moral, spiritual, and material welfare.

There is nothing unique or innovative about the idea of sumptuary
regulation by the Hohenzollern rulers in Brandenburg-Prussia. There was
ample precedent among the German territories and imperial cities as early
as the fourteenth century, as the work of Greenfield and Vincent has
shown.[1] The oldest police regulation in Brandenburg history, pre-Hohen-
zollern in origin, was issued in 1334 for the cities of Berlin and Cölln
and was completely sumptuary in content.[2]

One of the early police ordinances effective in the Hohenzollern lands
was issued by Margrave John of the Neumark at Cüstrin in 1540.[3] The
ordinance defined the police power as being concerned with the prosperity,
well-being, increase, and livelihood of the population. It was the duty of
the prince, he declared, to promote public welfare and to hinder its deterioration by proper police ordinances. This ordinance applied only to
the cities of the Neumark on the east side of the Oder River. It detailed the
various categories of police regulation by the state, extending into areas
not properly, by definition, sumptuary.

Under the broad category of sumptuary legislation, Margrave John included a moral concern about the evils of blasphemy and profanity and
about proper observance of the Sabbath and holy days. Restrictions were
placed on festive occasions such as weddings, baptisms, or the first churching of a confined woman. All the various aspects of the life cycle from
birth to death and the celebrations attendant to them came under sump-

---

1. Kent R. Greenfield, *Sumptuary Law in Nürnberg;* John M. Vincent, "European
Blue Laws," *Annual Report of the American Historical Association,* 1897, pp. 355-373.
2. Adolf Riedel, ed., *Codex Diplomaticus Brandenburgensis,* supp. vol., no. 11, pp. 227-
228, "The city councillors of Berlin and Köln issue a Police and Sumptuary Ordinance
[*Polizei- und Kleiderordung*] for both cities, 24 September 1334" (cited hereafter as *Cod.
Dipl. Brand.*).
3. Christian Otto Mylius, ed., *Corpus Constitutionum Marchicarum,* vol. 5, pt. 1, sec.
1, no. 1, col. 1 (cited hereafter as *C. C. March.*).

tuary regulation. One of the earliest and most persistent forms of regulation of private life had to do with the habits of clothing and personal decoration. In this area are to be observed not only the moral concern over luxury but a deliberate effort to preserve the traditional pattern of social stratification. The prince, by legislation, determined the external symbols of social status by establishing varying standards of consumption, expenditure, and extravagance.

Sumptuary legislation, perhaps more than any other regulatory acts of a welfare state, affects the subject or citizen in a direct, personal sense. This fact lends significance to the question of the attitude of those subjected to regulation and the degree of effectiveness of such regulation. The first question offers no great difficulty, so long as human nature is what it is. People in all eras of history resent and evade efforts to regulate personal eating, drinking, and clothing habits, to restrain the festive or sportive spirit in man or the desire to flaunt affluence. The relative lack of success in enforcement was due, in large measure, to public evasion of this type of intrusion into private life. Enforcement was left to local city and rural officials who had no greater zeal for this assignment than their neighbors had for obedience. Except where such legislation is linked with religious ritual, no state legislation is ever met with less enthusiasm than that which intrudes directly into personal habits. Prohibition, threats of fines, the enforcement machinery of a strong, central government gained only a partial success in the never-ending battle between the moral and personal behavior of the individual and the prevailing "social standards" of morality and decency.

2

Moral Behavior

Blasphemy and Profanity

The fundamentally moral aspect of the paternalistic police legislation of the sixteenth century is patently observable in the provisions that had to do with violations of divine command. Joachim I, in 1515, directed the city council of Berlin (composed at this time of four *Bürgermeister* and twelve councillors), as well as the judges and jurymen of the city court, to punish those who were guilty of blasphemy and lascivious conduct.[1]

Some years later Margrave John of the Neumark and his brother, Elector Joachim II of Brandenburg, sought to protect the moral life of their subjects by simple prohibitory edict. In 1540 Margrave John forbade blasphemy and profanity in the towns of the Neumark and required the mayors and town councillors to announce this prohibition to the congregations from the town pulpits.[2] A decade later, in 1550, Joachim II repeated this prohibition of blasphemy and profanity in the central territory of the Hohenzollern princes, Brandenburg.[3] The elector was moved to issue this ordinance because the electoral diet (*Landtag*) had complained about the lack of adequate police regulation on this matter and pointed out the need to safeguard the public welfare. What had been a church concern during the later Middle Ages now became a secular concern. The basic motive, however—after, as before, the Lutheran Reformation—remained the same: concern for the moral welfare of the individual and the community. This moral concern of the Brandenburg princes extended itself to the social vices conducive to profanity, such as drinking, dancing, ribaldry, card playing, and dicing. There is little evidence, despite sixteenth-century intensification of the ban against profanity, that there was ever more than a perfunctory restatement of the ban. Any serious effort at enforcement or punishment in succeeding centuries by a secular government concerned with moral welfare increasingly acquired social or economic association. Police ordinances issued by the Great Elector in 1687 and 1688 for the benefit of the newly acquired cities of Halle and Magdeburg included the traditional prohibition of cursing, and profanity.[4] The moral welfare of these cities was also to be protected by forbidding gam-

---

1. "Police Ordinance for the Cities of Brandenburg of Elector Joachim I, 1515," *C. C. March.*, vol. 6, pt. 2, no. 1, col. 3.
2. "Police Ordinance of Margrave John of Custrin," *C. C. March.*, vol. 5, pt. 1, sec. 1, no. 1, col. 3.
3. "Ordinance Concerning Police and Public Welfare in the Mark Brandenburg, 1550," *C. C. March.*, ibid., no. 2, col. 19.
4. *C. C. Magdeb.*, pt. 6, no. 1, "Revised Administrative Ordinance [*Regiments Ordnung*] of the city of Halle" (20 Dec. 1687), and pt. 3, no. 1, "Police Ordinance for Magdeburg of 1688."

bling in public houses (1711) and by forbidding the sale and public singing of obscene songs (1712).[5] Under the first two kings of Prussia, moral
misbehavior in the form of profanity, gaming, card playing, and carousing
was still serious in itself but seemed to come more under the province of
disturbing the peace on earth rather than paving the road to hell. By 1735
the only concern about card playing in the beer taverns was whether or
not the stamp tax had been paid on the cards in use.[6]

Observance of the Sabbath

Just as the state based its injunction against blasphemy on the biblical
command found in the Mosaic code, so similarly the scriptural enjoinment
to remember the Sabbath and keep it holy was enforced by the sixteenth-
century prince as it had been during the Middle Ages. In 1457 an ordinance of the Brandenburg diet had required that all persons practice
observance of the Sabbath according to the Holy Roman Church and
that no one haul wood or manure, or plow, or do anything normally done
on a workday.[7] Suggestive of the police regulations for two centuries after
was the ordinance of Margrave John of the Neumark of 1540[8] His requirement for the proper celebration of Sundays and holy days was twofold.
First, there was the simple requirement of attendance at church; second,
the daily activities that seemed inappropriate to the Sabbath were forbidden. Markets were closed down, no business of any kind was transacted,
the town gates were closed to discourage the local citizens from unnecessary travel or other outside activities which would keep them from attending public worship. The brewing of beer and the carrying of wood and
water were also forbidden. These last items applied particularly to the
peasants in the countryside. Entertaining guests in one's home with beer
or wine was forbidden; the public inns and taverns could not serve
drinks.[9] At the end of the seventeenth century, Pietist influence resulted in
an intensification of the requirement to keep the Sabbath sacred and to refrain from the temptations of the tavern and coffee houses during the hours
of church services.

5. Ibid., pt. 3, no. 229 (28 Jan. 1711); ibid., nos. 240, 248 (8 Sept., 25 Nov. 1712).

6. *C. C. March.,* vol. 5, pt. 1, sec. 1, no. 27, col. 126, "Instruction for Police Superintendents in Berlin" (23 May 1735).

7. Georg W. von Raumer, ed., *Codex diplomaticus brandenburgensis continuatus,* pt. 1,
no. 106, p. 239, "Ordinance of the Diet on Keeping the Sabbath" (cited hereafter as *Cod.
dipl. brand. cont.*).

8. See note 2 above.

9. In June 1969, the governor of the state of Connecticut vetoed a bill extending hours of
public drinking on Sundays by arguing that "the ruling question must always be whether the
proposed change will further the public good. The question becomes of special significance
when the proposed change affects the observance of the Sabbath."

There is no reason to believe that this type of moral legislation in a Lutheran territory reflected a more zealous interest in the moral life and security of the citizen than had existed under medieval ecclesiastical authorities. This type of legislation was a product of the religious and paternalistic nature of sixteenth-century government. It was more than a police regulation to maintain peace and order. The prince felt a genuine sense of responsibility for the moral behavior of his subjects. The line between desire for peace and order (or, later on, economic motives) and concern for the effects of improper moral behavior was perhaps a thin one in determining police regulations of a sumptuary character. The mixed nature of princely motives was rather distinctly revealed in the efforts to regulate luxury, extravagance, sumptuous living, social uppishness. The rationale behind this sumptuary legislation was that it was the duty of a prince to control personal extravagance and to curb personal habits that would endanger the moral welfare of the individual.

3

The Life Cycle

Sumptuary legislation, whatever its motivations and purposes, was curiously linked to the human cycle of life from birth to death. It was concerned with curbing sinful display of luxury, immoderate celebration, and wasteful expenditures, either for the moral or economic protection of the individual. The legislation tended to be ad hoc in nature, occurring whenever there seemed to be flagrant abuses of extravagance or waste. Christenings, betrothals, weddings, and funerals as ritualistic social events provided occasions for personal extravagance.

Christenings

By the sixteenth century, at least in Germanic Europe, it had long been the practice to celebrate births and baptisms with the offering of gifts and refreshments. After the birth, relatives and friends naturally wished to visit and congratulate the confined mother. And at the time of the christening of the child or the first churching of the confined woman (six weeks after the birth), there was another occasion for celebrating. As early as the ordinance of 1334, the city fathers of Berlin and Cölln had placed limitations on expenditures to celebrate the first churching. A police ordinance of 1515 declared that *Kindel-Biere* should be conducted in the traditional manner. In north Germany *Kindel-Bier* referred to the celebration either after the baptism of the child at the home or after the mother's first churching. The nature of the limitations on such celebrations was made clear in the ordinance of 1540 for the Neumark.[1] For the christening ceremony not more than twelve women and their husbands were to be invited to attend the church service. To prevent excessive celebration after the child and godparents were escorted home, the guests were limited to an hour's visit. There was to be no sitting down; cakes and ale were to be distributed for taking out for home consumption. The intent here was not to protect the mother but to prevent idleness. This regulation applied to towns and villages throughout the Neumark. A later ordinance of 1551 for the Mark Brandenburg limited the number of invited participants at the christening or first churching to ten women and their husbands.[2] Afterward a light

1. *C. C. March.*, vol. 5, pt. 1, sec. 1, no. 1, cols. 8-9. A police ordinance issued in 1502 for the city of Soldin in the Neumark (*Cod. dipl. brand. cont.*, pt. 2, sec. 2, no. 14, pp. 218-221) may well have served as a model for the 1515 ordinance for Brandenburg. It restricted the *Kindelbier* to a *Kollation* for the women who took the newborn child to church for baptism or who went with the mother for her first churching. For a definition of *Kindelbier* see *Deutsches Wörterbuch*, ed. Jacob and Wilhelm Grimm, 5 (1873): 730.

2. *C. C. March.*, vol. 5, pt. 1, sec. 1, no. 3, col. 30.

lunch of cheese and butter with cakes, fish, and domestic wine and beer was permitted.

By 1580 the social and economic motives were distinctly revealed in an ordinance effective in the twin cities of Berlin and Cölln.[3] This ordinance was issued because of a shortage of goods and food and because of the desire of each man to emulate or surpass his neighbors, which led to a lack of moderation in the celebration of baptisms, betrothals, and weddings and in wearing apparel. Although the city fathers wished to avoid these evils in general, they first found it necessary to distinguish in the ordinance four social classes, for which different standards of celebration and dress were allowed. There entered here a new emphasis that was to recur persistently during the next two centuries: a desire to conserve domestic resources and a desire to maintain social class distinctions by regulation. The first class consisted of doctors, clerical superintendents, burgomasters, eminent advocates, city councillors, scribes, judges, and jurymen. The second class included chaplains, prosperous burghers, guildsmen, and retailers. The common burghers and craftsmen were assigned to the third class. Tenants, journeymen, servants, and maids made up the fourth class.

This class distinction immediately restricted the number of guests who might be invited to christening services and celebrations. Fines from two to a half *thaler* were to be assessed for each person in excess of the allowable quota. Members of the first class were allowed eight to ten married couples. The second, third, and fourth classes were allowed respectively six, four, and two or three pairs of guests.

No meal could be provided after the baptismal ceremony, although the godparents and the invited women might be offered light refreshment of cheese, butter, wine, and beer. When the mother made her first churching at the end of six weeks of confinement, the invited women who accompanied her might be treated to a meal of roast meat, butter and cheese, pastries, wine and beer. Those who wished could invite the godparents for an evening meal. But immoderate offering of food and cheeses was forbidden. The number of godparents was to be limited to three, at the most five, because the practice of asking as many as seven to nine was only for the sake of the money gifts.

In 1604 Elector Joachim Frederick reduced the four classes to three and used much the same language and provisions as contained in the ordinance of 1580 in prescribing the number of sponsors and the kind of meals allowed for christening celebrations.[4]

---

3. "A Police Ordinance for Berlin and Cölln, 13 July 1580," ibid., no. 7, cols. 66-67. This was issued by the two city councils and approved by the elector. Berlin and Cölln were twin cities on the Spree River but had separate city administrations.

4. Ibid., no. 8, col. 78, "A Police Ordinance for Berlin and Cölln of 1 January 1604."

2. Kindelbier: Celebration after Christening

3. A Bridal Couple

By 1655 there was evidence that on festive occasions the peasants in the villages were equally guilty of immoderate eating and drinking or of trying to impress their neighbors. The Great Elector limited the number of godparents for a peasant's child to three.[5] Only five heads of households could be invited to a christening. The celebration afterward could last only one day, with the amount of refreshment allowed varying according to the social status of the peasant. A *Hüfner* (one who owned a hide of land) was allowed two tuns of beer, while a cotter was restricted to one tun. A small party, to which only six or eight women could be invited, was permissible on the occasion of the confined woman's first churchgoing. Food but no heavy drinking was allowed for this occasion.

It is apparent that from reign to reign the concern of the Hohenzollern princes for the moral conduct of their subjects had an increasingly economic basis. Elector Frederick III in 1696 expressed his sorrow at the "luxury, uppishness and lavishness [*Luxus, Üppigkeit und Verschwendung*]" which ignored the shortage of food and money of that war-ridden year.[6] There is little indication that by the end of the seventeenth century the prince was as much moved by a genuine concern for the moral welfare of his subjects per se as he was for the economic welfare of those who spent extravagantly on celebrating christenings and similar events. A mercantilist concern about consuming domestic resources or imported foreign goods became increasingly predominant in the eighteenth century.

Betrothal Celebrations

Traditionally, the ceremonies of betrothal and marriage have been occasions for happy celebration and have provided the major participants and their guests with opportunities for displaying their material prosperity. This prosperity manifested itself in the abundance of food and drink and of musical entertainment, the size of the betrothal or wedding party, and the expenditure on gifts, clothes, and adornment. From the Middle Ages on, these celebrations readily invited regulation by sumptuary legislation. The effort to control extravagance was generally motivated by economic considerations: to prevent the impoverishment of those involved or to protect the community welfare against excessive consumption of resources. Such legislation emerged gradually on an ad hoc basis to meet the evils or dangers as they developed. In time the regulating ordinances tended to take on a universal language and a stereotyped form, which was passed on from generation to generation.

5. "Ordinance and Constitution on the Proper Conduct at Betrothals, Weddings, Christenings, and Funerals in the Case of Peasants in the Villages of the Altmark, Prignitz, the Mittelmark, and Ruppin, 20 March 1655," ibid., no. 9, col. 87.

6. "Constitution and Ordinance Regarding Clothes and Livery, Banquets, Weddings, Christenings, and Burials in the Mark Brandenburg of 28 May 1696," ibid., no. 10, col. 89.

At least as early as 1465 the elector of Brandenburg showed concern about the excessive consumption and extravagance that threatened to impoverish burghers in the cities of the Uckermark. Accordingly, he restricted betrothal celebrations to a maximum of sixteen persons for one day.[7] The same concern about the lack of moderation in betrothal celebrations was expressed by the city government of Berlin and Cölln in 1580. A police ordinance of that year stated that because on the occasion of betrothals in the past there had been an immoderate and lavish consumption of food and drink, enough to furnish half the need for a wedding, such celebrations in the future would be limited in accordance with a formula reflecting class distinction.[8] This ordinance defined the four classes mentioned above. For members of the first class the number of guests invited was limited to three tables. Food was restricted to four or five main courses not including butter, cheese, and pastries. One kind of wine (not sweet) and one foreign beer were allowed. The second and third classes were allowed no more than two tables of invited guests, not more than three or four main courses, no wine, and only one kind of beer. The fourth class of journeymen, servants, and maids was limited to one table. The celebration could not begin until four o'clock in the afternoon and had to end by nine or ten that evening.

A generation later, in 1604, Elector Joachim Frederick renewed the complaint about immoderate betrothal celebrations, "das keine Masse gehalten wird [that there was no moderation]." To achieve this moderation he once again tabulated the number of allowable guests, the number of courses, the kinds of wine and beer as they had been described in 1580.[9] Similar provisions were extended to the peasants in Brandenburg by the Great Elector in 1655, when betrothal celebrations were limited to one day in the villages.[10]

Betrothal celebrations took on special significance, because in old Germanic custom betrothals were equivalent to marriage. Under Christian influence the wedding ceremony was placed between the betrothal and the fulfillment of the marriage. Although the wedding thus acquired greater significance, the custom of celebrating betrothals almost as lavishly as weddings lingered on.

Weddings

In the police legislation affecting weddings and banquets in general, the festive spirit was granted considerably greater latitude than it was for

7. Hans Bahr, ed., *Quellen zur brandenburgischen-preussischen Geschichte,* vol. 2, no. 31, pp. 65-68, "Ordinances for the Cities in the Uckermark," of 12 July 1465 (cited hereafter as *Quellen brand.-preuss.*).

8. *C. C. March.,* vol. 5, pt. 1, sec. 1, no. 7, col. 60.

9. "Police Ordinance of 1 January 1604," ibid., no. 8, col. 73. This ordinance was effective in the electoral capital cities of Berlin and Cölln.

10. Ibid., no. 9, col. 84.

christenings and betrothals. At the same time the area of restriction by legislation was much more inclusive. Essentially all sumptuary legislation, aimed at whatever festive occasion, had the common denominators of restraining the natural human impulse to put on a good show, curtailing the wasting of local supplies of food and drink by excess consumption, and preventing undesirable idleness (and therefore unproductiveness) by prolonged celebration.

The police ordinance of 1334 had permitted eighty guests for a wedding dinner held in Berlin. But about the year 1460 a city ordinance put out by the Berlin city council reduced this number to sixty, requiring a "limitation of luxury at weddings."[11] A few years later, the ordinance of 1465 for the cities of the Uckermark permitted no more than sixty-four guests at wedding dinners.[12]

In 1515 Elector Joachim I told his subjects in the towns of Brandenburg that banquets and wedding celebrations should be moderate according to each person's affluence.[13] They should not be more than two days in duration, the wealthy burghers should not have more than five tables of invited guests (fifty guests in all) and common folk not more than three tables. It was urged that celebrations be planned with the approval of the city council to avoid the sudden consumption in a short time of food which was meant to last for the year.

The general pattern of regulating wedding celebrations in terms of moderation, as suggested in 1515, was spelled out in more specific detail in 1551 and 1580. The ordinance of Joachim II of 1551 regulated the number of guests who could be invited, the number of persons who could be fed, how long the celebration might last, how much could be spent on musicians.[14] Not more than ten tables of twelve guests each were permitted, although an extra table for out-of-town guests and one extra table for small children might be added. The maximum number of courses at each meal was not to exceed four; white and red wine and one foreign beer were allowed. Local guests could not be fed on the third day, thus implying a two-day celebration.

By 1580 the issue of class distinction appears again in an ordinance affecting Berlin.[15] The total number of guests who might be invited to wedding celebrations among families of the first class was eighty (specifically, eight tables of ten persons each), except that at the table for maidens there was no limit. Strangers from outside the twin cities of Berlin and Cölln could be invited in addition to the eight tables. Exclusive of cheese,

11. *Quellen brand.-preuss.*, vol. 2, no. 30, p. 64, "Ordinance of the Berlin City Council on Limitation of Extravagance at Weddings."

12. See note 7 above.

13. *C. C. March.*, vol. 6, pt. 2, no. 1, col. 4.

14. "Ordinance for the Cities of Brandenburg Concerning Costs and Expenses of Weddings and Christenings," *C. C. March.*, vol. 5, pt. 1, sec. 1, no. 3, cols. 27-29, revised the ordinance of Joachim I of 1515.

15. Ibid., no. 7, cols. 60-66.

butter, and pastries, the noon meal was to consist of no more than five courses, the evening meal of four. A Rhenish and a domestic wine as well as two kinds of foreign beer might be served.

Families of the second class were allowed only six tables of invited guests, and the number of courses for noon and evening meals was restricted to four and three courses. Only domestic wine and Bernauer and Ruppin beer were allowed. More important was the fact that the maximum number of tuns or barrels of wine or beer was specified. The third class of common burghers and craftsmen could have but four tables, and no outside guests. No wine was allowed, and only one barrel of Bernauer beer was permitted. The families of journeymen, servants, and maids of the fourth class were restricted to a one-day celebration consisting of two tables of guests, three-course meals, no wine, and no foreign beer.

Concern was expressed about the duration of wedding celebrations. The first two classes were allowed two days and were permitted to attend church twice, "as has been the custom." Strangers, that is guests from outside the city, were allowed to stay over for a third or fourth day, and not more than one table of local friends was permitted to join them for food and drink. Wedding parties of the third and fourth classes were granted only one churchgoing, the marriage ceremony occurring on Monday morning at ten o'clock. Celebrations were to last but that one day, except that the bride and groom could invite their young friends to a dance on the second day, before the evening meal. Out-of-town guests and immediate relatives could celebrate one additional day.

The city ordinance expressed concern about other aspects of wedding ceremonies and celebrations. It ordered an end to what was called disorders attending church services, such as the practice of being late for the wedding service or prolonging the service beyond one hour. The ordinance further prescribed or forbade various practices or standards of conduct. The carrying of wedding torches in procession before the bride enroute to the church was to cease, on the ground that this practice no longer had any significance and was only a waste of money. This torch-carrying tradition survived from the superstitions of an earlier age and was designed to ward off evil spirits that might endanger the happiness of the bride. Two torches were allowed, however, when weddings occurred in the winter evenings. The two upper classes were allowed to schedule weddings at four o'clock on a Sunday or Monday afternoon. Mondays were preferred for weddings, because in traditional superstition the omens of this day of the week were most propitious for a happy and fertile marriage. As wedding celebrations were often held at the local town hall with music and dancing, certain precautions were ordered. There were to be chaperons on the dance floor to assure that all conducted themselves with propriety. Limitations were placed on sending food out of the dining area to uninvited guests, on the fees paid to singers, organists, and musicians, as well as on the payments made to cooks, butchers, sausage-makers, and dishwashers. Instructions were issued on the procedure for inviting guests to the wedding (young men customarily went from house to house extending the invitations). The value of wedding gifts was likewise subject to sumptuary restriction.

It is apparent that the primary concerns of the police ordinance of 1580 were the excessive consumption of food and drink—a concern which was economic as much as moral—and the preservation of class distinction, so that the upper classes were allowed greater extravagance than were the lower ranks. Elements of moral propriety and preservation of peace and order on the dance floor by town police officers, who were responsible for enforcement of the provisions of the ordinance, may also be detected.

A quarter of a century later, in a police ordinance of 1 January 1604, again confined to the capital cities of Berlin and Cölln, Elector Joachim Frederick, desirous of "furthering the common or public welfare [*der gemeine Nutzen*]," took note of the poverty and the diminution of the cities' food supply and attributed this state not only to immoderate eating and drinking but to the immoderate or unseemly pomp expressed in consumption of foreign or expensive items of apparel and decorations.[16] For this reason he issued an ordinance on food and clothing that retained the previous emphasis on class distinctions. The number of classes was reduced to three. The first class was to include the provost, deacons, and preachers of the Elector's court church as well as those of the parish churches, physicians, public officials, privy councillors, tax collectors, eminent merchants. The second class was composed of jurymen, members of the four crafts, beer-brewers, craftsmen in general, and the common propertied burghers. The third class was made up of persons not resident in the cities, tenants, journeymen, and domestic servants. Many of the regulative provisions of 1604 were identical to those of 1580. The procedure for inviting guests to a wedding was described. Four inviters *(Hochzeitsbitter)* were to be sent out on the day before the wedding to invite guests to the wedding party. Each had a list of names and were to write down whether or not those invited planned to attend, so that the allowable number of tables could be filled. These inviters had in the past been gaily decked out with garlands and golden braids and feathers in their hats. Now only flower wreaths were permitted. Wedding gifts were to be presented to the bride and groom on the Tuesday after the wedding and before the noon meal. But *Brauthäne* were forbidden. The *Brauthahn,* perhaps, can be most closely identified with a charivari. Originally gifts were brought by invited guests on the eve of the wedding. This was accompanied by much hullabaloo, noisemaking, and singing. After a time only

16. Ibid., no. 8, cols. 71-77.

4. *Wedding Dancers and Costumes of the Sixteenth Century by Hans Schäuffelein*

6. *Peasant Dancers of the Sixteenth Century by Albrecht Durer*

5. *Wedding Dancers and Costumes of the Sixteenth Century by Heinrich Aldegrever*

the latter survived as a sort of playful, sometimes ribald, harassment of the bride. In old Germanic custom a cock had been sacrificed to ward off evil spirits and to assure a fertile marriage. Perhaps this explains the term *Brauthahn*. At any rate, the need for electoral banning of the practice suggests that it had gotten out of control.

To prevent overgenerous fees, the ordinance also prescribed the wages that might be paid to the church organist, singers, cooks, and dishwashers. Fifers and drummers could be hired to furnish music at the dinners and at the dances. The dance was an integral part of the festivities. Traditionally the bride, groom, and wedding guests went to the town hall for dancing after the noon and evening meals. This practice was permitted only on the second day and only for the first two classes. Dancing in the home was permitted, but the ordinance insisted on proper behavior on the dance floor, frowning on bodies pressed too close together. The bride and groom were required to be at the church for the wedding service on a Monday punctually at two o'clock at the risk of having the church doors closed and being fined two *thaler*. The number of guests at the following celebration was again determined by classes. The first two classes were allowed a two-day celebration from Monday through the evening meal on Tuesday, and three main meals were permitted. The third class was granted one day and one banquet meal on Monday evening. So that there would be no evasion of the ordinance in respect to the number of tables, the number of persons per table, and the number of courses at each meal, the ordinance ordered the city council to appoint a reliable person to attend the celebration and to count tables and heads and to report back to the council if the prescribed maximums were exceeded.

Rural weddings came under consideration in 1655.[17] Frederick William showed the greatest concern over the expense incurred by the peasants in the villages of Brandenburg. He remarked that a man with several children could hardly survive the successive expenditures for celebrating betrothals, weddings, and christenings, because each peasant tried to impress his neighbors. The most serious problem was the incurring of a beer-debt. He therefore not only limited peasant weddings to three tables of guests and one tun of beer per table per day during the three-day celebration, but he forbade the burgher retailers in nearby cities to extend credit for beer to the peasants in excess of these provisions. Peasants had in the past evaded restrictions by buying beer on credit in the city and thus placing themselves deeply in debt. The village magistrate was ordered to observe if the maximum number of wedding guests was adhered to, and whether or not uninvited guests came to the party.

As late as 1696 Frederick III was still trying to control huge wedding banquets at a time when food and money were scarce.[18] He protested the

17. Ibid., no. 9, cols. 85-87.
18. Ibid., no. 10, col. 92.

serving of food in heaping quantities, and he limited wedding celebrations both in the towns and villages to one day, from the afternoon ceremony to the following noon, thus permitting only two main meals.

Funerals

It is not until 1604, in the police ordinance of Elector Joachim Frederick, that one finds legislative regulation of burials and the associated mourning practices.[19] This particular ordinance concerned itself with one aspect of funerals, that having to do with expenditure for mourning clothes. It had been customary for a bereaved family to provide mourning clothes or other apparel at the time of burial. But "since the dead cannot profit from this," the elector ordered certain restrictions. Those of the first rank, who could afford to, might provide armbands and veils for parents, brothers, sisters, and pallbearers. The other two ranks were forbidden to provide armbands, veils, or aprons. The guilds, brotherhoods, and craftsmen were allowed to continue the traditional practice of carrying the corpse to the grave but were not allowed to give armbands to the guild bearers. Since some women were accustomed to going to funerals with veils just to gain precedence over those who were unveiled, "we order that no woman will attend a funeral wearing a veil unless she is a close friend of the deceased." Widows were to cease wearing a mourning veil after three months.

One of the principal occasions for mischief in connection with funerals was provided by the wake. Traditionally those who stayed the long hours of a wake had been given refreshment. In 1655 Frederick William took note of the abuses among the village peasants of Brandenburg. There were large gatherings at wakes, much frivolity and feasting and even superstitious doings. The elector ordered this mischief to cease and directed that only those who were invited to a wake by housefather or mother could attend. It was and long remained a traditional practice for those attending a funeral to return to the home of a deceased after the burial for food and drink. The elector forbade post-burial meals, directing that in the future only those who carried the corpse to the burying ground or those who came from a distance were to be given refreshments.[20]

After the turn of the century, greater attention was directed toward regulating funeral and burial practices. In 1707 the Lutheran Consistory of Berlin issued a rescript, effective in the Mark Brandenburg, forbidding the playing of music at evening burials.[21] The upper classes were allowed no more than twenty torches, the lower classes no more than ten to light the way.

19. Ibid., no. 8, cols. 71-73, 81. This ordinance established three social ranks.
20. Ibid., no. 9, col. 88.
21. Ibid., no. 13, cols. 95-96, of 14 March 1707.

A year later an entirely new element was introduced, reflecting the growing size of the population of Berlin and a concern for finding adequate burying space within the city. In 1648 the population of Berlin has been estimated to have been between 6,000 and 8,000. By 1708 the capital city had a population of over 50,000. King Frederick I in 1708 approved new regulations concerning graves and burying places in Berlin.[22]

In the year 1616 a cemetery belonging to the St. George Hospital and located in the suburb outside the St. George Gate on the east side of Berlin was converted into a general public cemetery. Already there was concern over the growing lack of burial space in the cemeteries attached to the churches in both Berlin and Cölln. The declining population during the Thirty Years' War presumably reduced the pressure of this problem.[23] The regulation of 1708 permitted citizens and natives of Berlin as before to choose a burial place within the city, but servants were to be buried in the new cemetery (presumably this refers to the cemetery outside the St. George Gate). A burgher was free to choose the new cemetery for burial if he wished. All strangers without class standing who died in Berlin were to be buried here. To keep the churches and the churchyards within the city from being filled with corpses, there was to be a charge in the future, payable to the churches, for a burial place within the city. For burial in the two churchyards of St. Nicholas and St. Mary parishes, there was to be a charge of 30 *thaler* for an adult and 15 for a child under fifteen years. For burial in the churchyards of the cathedral (the Dom) and of the Church of the Holy Ghost, only half these charges were to be made.[24] Resident nobles were to pay the churches 50 and 25 *thaler* respectively, while nonresident nobles were to be assessed as much as 80 and 40 *thaler* by the several churches. However, if anyone so qualified wished to be buried in a church vault at St. Nicholas or St. Mary churches, the fee was 100 *thaler;* for the Dom and the Church of the Holy Ghost, 50. As had been the practice before, deceased burgomasters were to get free burial places, but not vaults.

For burial in the remaining cemeteries within the city of Berlin, all adult burghers without distinction were to pay a charge of 3 *thaler* (1½ for children), and nobles were to be charged twice as much. Free burial places, in accordance with tradition, were to be granted to preachers, deacons, schoolteachers, and church servants. Indigent persons would pay according to ability or would be buried free in the new cemetery.

Frederick William I made several efforts to regulate the length of

22. Ibid., no. 15, cols. 95-98, of 25 July 1708.
23. See Eberhard Faden, *Berlin im Dreissigjährigen Kriege,* p. 119.
24. The Dom was located in Cölln adjacent to the royal castle. It had been the church of a Dominican monastery, and after the Reformation it had been reserved for members of the court. In 1610 it was made the chief parish church of Cölln, open to all citizens. Hohenzollern princes had been buried in its vaults. The other three churches referred to were located in Berlin, across the Spree River.

7. *Funeral Procession of the Sixteenth Century by Hans Burgkmair*

mourning periods. His concern was primarily economic—not the economic interest of the individual, however, but that of the textile industry. In 1716 this practical-minded king declared that the traditional period of mourning was too long and only entailed additional costs for those who had to wear special mourning clothes.[25] Besides, in what was really more than an afterthought, Frederick William asserted that the wearing of mourning clothes for too long a period was injurious to the manufacturing and sale of colored garments. Accordingly he prescribed fixed and shorter periods of mourning throughout his territories for the children, the parents, husbands, wives, brothers, sisters, and in-laws of a deceased person. Four years later Frederick William reissued the edict of 1716 because it was "not properly obeyed."[26] This time he enjoined the fiscal agents to look for violations of the prescribed length of the mourning period and ordered heavy fines to be levied against violators.[27] This attempt to interfere in private life was not successful. In 1734 the king issued another renewed edict concerning mourning.[28] Because the edict of 27 July 1720 was not properly observed, the king issued this new edict of 20 May 1734 and ordered wide publicity. Once again he set limits to the

25. "Edict and Regulation on Mourning Periods" of 25 Aug. 1716, *C. C. March.,* vol. 5, pt. 1, sec. 1, no. 18, cols. 101-104.

26. "Renewed Edict on Mourning" of 27 July 1720, ibid., no. 19, cols. 103-106.

27. *Fiscals* were royal agents or spies appointed to supervise observance and enforcement of the king's edicts and ordinances. See Reinhold A. Dorwart, *The Administrative Reforms of Frederick William I of Prussia,* pp. 190-191.

28. *C. C. March.,* vol. 5, pt. 1, sec. 1, no. 25, cols. 119-122.

mourning period for various categories of relationship and restricted the use of mourning clothes. The *fiscals* were again instructed to watch for violations which were to be punished with fines ranging from 100 to 1,000 *Reichsthaler*. The severity of the impossible fines revealed not only the heavy hand of Frederick William but the degree to which by the eighteenth century sumptuary legislation was diverted toward serving the mercantilist interests of the state.

One of the most interesting edicts of Frederick William I placed the whole business of funerals on a state-regulated basis and at the same time described the various traditional practices associated with funerals.[29] By this edict of 1725 the whole funeral business for the city was granted to an undertaker named Hauschke in return for an annual payment of 400 *Reichsthaler* to the *Hofstaatskasse*.[30] The licensee was instructed to conduct the undertaking business without overburdening the public financially, particularly the poor, and to keep funerals as inexpensive as possible.

Each parish in the city was allowed two inviters and twelve bearers. Anyone who needed inviters for funerals (or for weddings) or bearers or the funeral hearse was to apply to the undertaker Hauschke and pay the established fees. The undertaker was allowed a commission for furnishing these persons, receiving one-quarter of the inviters' fees and one-eighth of the bearers' fees. The fees for inviters and bearers were fixed by this edict, which forbade the licensed undertaker to charge more than this statutory sum. But the actual fees varied according to social rank, and Frederick William I recognized four ranks for this purpose. The first rank was composed of ministers of state and important councillors of the principal administrative offices. Lesser government officials were placed in the second rank: for example, ordinary councillors, secretaries, and commissaries. The third rank comprised prominent citizens, including professional persons. The fourth rank was made up of the common citizens or other inhabitants of Berlin. The fees to be paid by class rank for the use of an inviter were respectively graded from 3 *Reichsthaler* to 16 *Groschen*. For the use of a funeral bearer, the charges varied from 1 *Reichsthaler* to a minimum of 4 *Groschen*. But Frederick William's constant concern for the poor freed the impoverished from any fees. He ordered that they be carried to their graves free, if affidavits from the city government or from their parish preachers were furnished to prove their poverty.

Hauschke, the undertaker, was required to keep a diary or log in which he would enter all weddings and funerals. The clerks of the exchequer were to furnish Hauschke with a weekly list of all deaths in Berlin. The

---

29. "Royal Regulation Concerning Funerals in the City of Berlin," of 25 May 1725, ibid., no. 21, cols. 105-110.

30. This was a household treasury which by 1725 was no more than a disbursing office to pay the expenses of the royal household.

parish inviters were to obtain this same information weekly from the church sextons.

One of the requirements imposed upon the official undertaker was the maintenance of the city hearse or funeral wagon. This official hearse had to be used by all citizens. The edict specifically forbade the use of any other wagon or cart except for children under the age of four. There was, of course, a charge for the use of the hearse, varying according to whether it was to be drawn by two, four, or six horses. A major exception to this requirement deferred to tradition. The edict recognized that certain guilds traditionally had carried the bodies of their deceased members to the burying ground. Frederick William permitted guild masters to carry masters or members of their families as before, without using the undertaker's facilities and without paying his fee.

4

Clothing and Personal Decoration

The primary purpose in regulating the festivities or events associated with betrothals, weddings, christenings, and funerals was to restrain immoral, extravagant, wasteful consumption of food and drink. From ancient times, however, such occasions had not only provided an opportunity for feasting, dancing, and gaiety but had invariably required special costumes, gowns, decorative apparel. The clothing may originally have been ritualistic, but in time it became another form of displaying personal pomp and affluence. Girdles, garlands, jewels, colorful and expensive materials, furs and feathers, fancy boots all offered an irresistible form of sumptuous display.

It is not surprising, then, that the Christian and paternalistic princes of German territories as well as city governments during the late Middle Ages attempted to restrain extravagance in wearing apparel. The police ordinance of 1334, the oldest in Brandenburg history, was really a *Kleiderordnung* (sumptuary ordinance) aimed at the beginnings of urban ostentation. Women were limited in the cost of jewelry and garlands and were forbidden to use gold-striped cloth or sable borders on dresses and cloaks.[1] The cities of Germany in the fourteenth century first undertook a systematic regulation by statute of the style, quality, and material of the clothes and accessories worn by German citizens. In part this appeared to be a reaction to the introduction of French styles and clothes. These municipal ordinances gradually developed a uniform type or form used in many German cities.[2] In the late fifteenth century the Imperial Reichstag took cognizance of the problem of luxury in clothes and attempted restraining regulation. In the sixteenth century, territorial *Kleiderordnungen* were modeled on imperial police ordinances. These territorial ordinances were uniform in content and purpose. They sought to preserve class distinctions in determining the degree of luxury permitted the citizens. They attempted to preserve traditional costume against innovations, particularly of foreign origin. And, in regulating cut and style, there was a moral purpose of preserving decency.[3]

The Protestant reformers, Luther and Calvin, added their support to this type of sumptuary legislation. In his *Address to the Christian No-*

1. *Cod. Dipl. Brand.,* supp. vol., no. 11, pp. 227-228.
2. See, e.g., Joseph Baader, ed., *Nürnberger Polizeiordnungen aus dem XIII bis XV Jahrhundert;* and Vincent, *Costume and Conduct,* pp. 42-52.
3. See Albert Richter, *Bilder aus der deutschen Kulturgeschichte,* pt. 2, pp. 372-381; and the recent work of Liselotte C. Eisenbart, *Kleiderordnungen der deutschen Städte zwishen 1350 und 1700.*

bility of the German Nation (1520), Luther argued, "We require a general law and consent of the German nation against profusion and extravagance in dress, which is the cause of so much poverty among the nobles and the people . . . It cannot be necessary to spend such enormous sums for silk, velvet, cloth of gold, and all other kinds of outlandish stuff."[4]

Efforts to regulate luxury in clothing throughout Germany continued until the eighteenth century with little success. A statement of 1682, quoted by Richter, summed up the efforts to deter the individual from wearing forbidden styles, colors, and luxury items: "An Kleiderordnungen mangelt es nicht, sondern nur am Halten [There is no lack of sumptuary laws, but only of observance]."[5]

Just when the Hohenzollern princes of Brandenburg first included clothing regulation in their police ordinances is not certain. It apparently was not until the important and inclusive police ordinance of 13 July 1580, issued by the city governments of Berlin and Cölln, that authorities concerned themselves with immoderateness in clothing.[6] There was precedent among the Brandenburg police regulations, the earlier regulations of this kind in Nuremberg and the Swiss cities, and in the imperial police ordinances. The stimulus seemed to come from extravagance in clothes worn at wedding celebrations. At any rate, this ordinance took note of the fact that many burghers bought clothes beyond their means, and after weddings these clothes were sold in the secondhand market. It then proceeded on the basis of the four social ranks to prescribe the kinds and prices of materials which were proper for festive dress for each class. Women in general were not allowed to wear golden brooches or pearl garlands, unless they were inherited. Women of the first rank were permitted to wear gold lace or a gold chain worth at most 60 Rhenish *gulden*. Except for the most distinguished men, the use of sable as a border on hats was forbidden. The women of the second and third ranks were not to make use of velvet or satin, except that velvet could be used for trim. The serving girls of the fourth rank were denied silk, pearl, or even gilt trim. A bridal dress could have a wisp of velvet trim. For head decoration, it was proper as of old to wear a coronet with brooches and velvet border. Neckpieces made of dyed squirrel skins but not of marten were allowed these domestic servants, but they were completely forbidden to wear a silk garment even if it was a gift to the maid by her lady of the house. By 1604 this earlier dual concern for personal economy and preservation of social distinction was joined by a desire to protect the local market (industrial and financial) against the consumption of imported foreign apparel.[7] Elector Joachim Frederick charged that the

---

4. Martin Luther, *First Principles of the Reformation,* p. 88.
5. Albert Richter, *Bilder,* p. 380.
6. *C. C. March.,* vol. 5, pt. 1, sec. 1, no. 7, cols. 67-70.
7. Ibid., no. 8, cols. 71-73, 78-80.

poverty and unhealthy economic condition of Berlin and its inhabitants was due not just to immoderate eating and drinking at festivities but also to the unseemly pomp of the burghers in using expensive foreign clothing and decorations. The greatest extravagance in clothes was found among women because "keine der andern etwas zuvor gehen wil [none will let another be first in style]." The result was poverty and the selling of expensive gowns at half price in the secondhand market, gowns which the seller bought to impress others but really could not afford. The complaint was made that "even serving maids step out with such pride and fashion style that one can hardly distinguish them from burghers' daughters, so that such insolence and pride not only angers God but the whole city will lose its money as the foreigners get it." This is a curious but historically interesting mixture of motives for regulating the kind of clothes a citizen might wear. To what degree was there still a genuine moral concern for the sinful pride which would anger God and perhaps endanger salvation? Was the prince in 1604 terribly disturbed over the perennial problem of the uppishness *(Üppigkeit)* of servant maids who acquired the cast-off gowns of milady and tried to ape her? Or can one as early as this date find the beginnings of a mercantilistic alarm about the *"thaler*-deficit"? It is not merely a matter of which motive in itself was uppermost in the paternalistic policy of a Hohenzollern prince. What can be detected here is a slight shifting of emphasis from the concern for the welfare of the individual (essentially moral, partly economic) to the general welfare of the community. In fact, the elector stated that he was issuing this police ordinance of 1604 "for the promotion of the general good." Primarily, this meant both a concern for the draining off of domestic bullion to pay for the new expensive fabrics and textiles which were appearing on the

8. Costumes of the Sixteenth and Seventeenth Centuries

European market and a desire to protect the domestic textile fabricators.

Specifically, the members of the first social rank—the city clergy, professional people, civil servants, and eminent merchants—were forbidden to use velvet, satin, sable, marten, or more expensive furs for whole coats, mantles, cloaks, jackets, or trousers or to wear silk stockings. They were to be content with damask, tobines (twilled silks), taffeta, and soft silk cloth. Pearl fringes or garlands of gilded roses to decorate hats were forbidden. Dress gowns and cloaks for women could be made of damask, tobine, and taffeta. Velvet was allowed for bodices, jackets, collars, and hats. Jeweled and gilded decorations were forbidden. Unmarried maidens of first-class families could wear dresses made of taffeta, sarsenet (a soft silk lining), jacquard, camlet, and damask, but until their marriages they were not allowed dresses of velvet and satin. For those who could afford it, gold chains of no greater value than 50 Rhenish gold *gulden,* bracelets worth no more than ten crowns, and pearl brooches worth no more than thirty *thaler* were permitted.

Members of the second rank—craftsmen and propertied burghers—were allowed various items of clothing made of sarsenet, camlet, or *Lündisch* cloth (a soft silk). Fox fur but not velvet trim was allowed. The women of this class were denied gold chains, bracelets, velvet hats, and silk cloth. The third class persons—tenants, journeymen, and domestic servants—were forbidden to wear silks or *Lündisch* cloth. Serving maids specifically were forbidden to wear silk dresses, to use velvet trim, to wear gold brooches or garlands, as the ordinance took particular precaution against the maids' acquisition of these items from the ladies whom they served.

To make this ordinance more effective at a lower level, tailors and craftsmen were forbidden to make up clothes or do decorative work except as provided in this ordinance for the several class ranks. Heavy fines were designed to assure observance.

Restrictions on the wearing of mourning clothes, including veils and armbands, as well as limitations on the mourning period observed by widows, may well have been designed in 1604 to protect the individual against unnecessary expense. At any rate it was not until 1716 that Frederick William I openly admitted that the prolonged wearing of the dark mourning clothes was not beneficial to the textile industry.

At the end of the century, in 1696, Elector Frederick III renewed this *Kleiderordnung* and extended its applicability from the cities of Berlin and Cölln to the whole Mark Brandenburg.[8] He was filled with sorrow, he said, at the sight of the luxuriance and extravagance manifested in the sumptuous clothing and wearing apparel which ignored the hard times

8. Ibid., no. 10, cols. 89-92.

and shortage of money. Not only was this contrary to God's word, but many families became impoverished. So out of "treu-väterlicher sorgfalt" ("paternal concern") he sought to restrain this luxury. The use of all cloth and material, ribbons and border trim that contained gold and silver was forbidden. Except when appearing in the electoral court, no one was to wear precious stones or jewelry in their hair or on their heads. No jeweled brooches were to be worn in church. Silver and gold edges, fringes, and galloons were forbidden, except that cavaliers were permitted gold and silver buttons and buttonholes done with gold or silver thread. The daughters of burghers could use only silk or wool trim. Satin and silk garments were still restricted to the upper rank. Except for the elector himself or members of his house, no one was to use gold or silver on his livery. Generals, privy councillors, and the highest public officials might use silk braid. Only the highest officials were allowed to use satin or silk furnishings in new carriages.

If the achievement of salutary effects for the individual and society were merely a matter of issuing sumptuary and regulative legislation, all would be quite simple. The frequent renewals and reissues of police ordinances, the threat of severe fines, the requirement that local officials attend festivities to prevent violations indicated a tendency to ignore or evade legislative efforts to restrain the normal human proclivity for ostentation, pomp, and outdoing one's neighbors. Within six months of his becoming king in Prussia and elector of Brandenburg, Frederick William I issued a general instruction (15 September 1713) intended to put some teeth into enforcement procedures.[9] "Since a number of ordinances issued by previous rulers concerning police matters have not been observed, to the harm of the common good, so that the well-being of the residents of cities be protected," the king directed that special mounted gendarmes *(Ausreuter)* should be appointed in the administrative circles *(Kreise)* who would be dependent for their orders on the General War Commissariat.[10] These rural police officers were subordinate to the district tax commissaries as well as the local magistrates and were responsible for enforcing observance of many ordinances which were becoming increasingly mercantilistic rather than sumptuary. For example, while forbidding the making or selling of whole wool cloth in the villages (in competition with the towns), this ordinance allowed the rural poor to clothe themselves in linen or linsey-woolsey. An example of persistent evasion of clothing regulations is seen in the edict of 6 November 1731.[11] Frederick William

9. "General Instruction Concerning Various Police Matters," ibid., no. 17, cols. 97-102. This instruction was the first issued by the new king and was countersigned by the General War Commissary, Frederick William von Grumbkow.

10. See Dorwart, *Administrative Reforms,* pp. 138-148.

11. *C. C. March.,* vol. 5, pt. 1, sec. 1, no. 22, cols. 109-110.

forbade, after a period of six months' grace, the further wearing of silk dresses, camisoles, and bodices by serving girls and common womenfolk, Christians as well as Jews. Violators after six months were threatened with having these banned clothes taken away publicly on the streets. The king explained this action by stating simply, "To wear silk is in violation of previous ordinances regulating wearing apparel according to classes, and besides it does not help our wool-industry." As late as 1735, Frederick William was still protecting his wool industry when he directed the city police to be alert against the wearing of calico and cotton goods.[12] However, by 1735 this type of regulation of certain dress materials was in no way related to the sumptuary legislation of 1580. It was avowedly mercantilistic—designed to increase the consumption and thus the manufacturing of wool cloth.

12. "Instruction for the Superintendents of Police of the Royal Residences in Berlin" of 23 May 1735, ibid., no. 27, cols. 121-130.

Part II
Urban Affairs

II

Urban Affairs

The care of the city and the regulation of the multifarious aspects of city life historically have come under the police jurisdiction of the state. The rise of towns, the increase of population, and the expansion of commerce after the later Middle Ages created problems for which the medieval feudal-ecclesiastical institutions were inadequate. City councils and territorial princes, of necessity, responded to the new historical contingencies by police regulations that sought to protect the welfare of the community as well as that of the individual. Areas of city life inviting action and regulation included: the maintenance of urban peace and order; supervision of streets, buildings, and public facilities; regulation of the marketplace in the broadest sense; urban development; fire protection; public sanitation and anti-pollution efforts; and the care of the poor, the infirm, and the unfortunates.

5

The Marketplace

The regulation of trade and commerce and the preservation of an environment conducive to the peaceful exchange of goods originated in Western Europe with medieval guilds but soon passed under the regulative control of city council and territorial prince. Protection, regulation, supervision by the state extended to consumer protection, establishing uniform systems of weights and measures, protection of the marketplace against undesirable practices, and protection of the shopkeeper or market against hawkers and unlicensed traders.

The commercial activity within the Brandenburg-Prussian state, as elsewhere, developed out of the Middle Ages in several forms. The annual fairs for wholesale purposes; the weekly market to satisfy the daily needs of towns and cities for items of food; the urban shops that dispensed consumer goods like food and drink, spices, drugs, clothing, apparel, and hardware; the itinerant hawker or peddler; all combined to provide a general marketplace for buyer and seller. Much of the regulative legislation designed to protect the buyer, the seller, the citizen-consumer grew out of medieval practices. However, neither guild nor city council was capable of exercising regulatory control over the marketplace beyond city walls. Wholesale trade in annual fairs, uniform standards of weights and measures over large economic areas, protection of natural resources, and subsistence for a territory required state regulation.

Uniform Weights and Measures

Trade and commerce emerged in the later Middle Ages handicapped by a great variance in standards of weights and measures. This was a product of the urban origin and control of trade. The problem, not wholly solved even by 1700 throughout Europe, was enormously complicated. Standardization of units was lacking not only between national states but within these states. The Holy Roman Empire, with its several hundred particularistic political atoms, was in many ways the worst offender and greatest victim. The territories of the Hohenzollern, extending after 1618 from the Memel to the Rhine rivers, offered tremendous variation in standards. The problem was twofold. First, standard units of bulk measure (dry and liquid), of linear measure, and of weight had to be determined. Then it was necessary to establish a standard unit for all the Hohenzollern territories.

As early as 1515, Margrave Joachim I attempted to standardize the Berlin ell as the linear unit of measure in the cities of Brandenburg and to make the Berlin unit of bulk weight (e.g., of meat, copper, lead) the standard.[1] For small wares (e.g., spices, grocer and retail trade) the Erfurt unit of weight was declared standard. Discrepancies in liquid measure were attacked by declaring a tun (used for beer, wine, brandy) equal to 24 *Stübchen* (about 3.6 liters per *Stübchen*) or about 20 U.S. gallons per tun.

The problem of uniformity of units can be observed in the legislation of the brothers Margrave John of the Neumark and Elector Joachim II of Brandenburg. In 1540 John established the uniform units of dry and liquid measurements in the Neumark cities as the Soldin bushel for corn, the Soldin tun, barrel, and quart for wine, beer, honey, and fish, and the Soldin ell for linear measure (in textiles, e.g.).[2] Products that crossed the Oder River to enter the Frankfurt market, however, were to be measured and weighed according to Frankfurt standards.

In Brandenburg in 1550 Joachim II recognized four standard bushels in the several provinces of the electorate, while trying to establish as uniform for all his provinces the linear and weight measurements decreed in 1515.[3] In the sixteenth century the great need was to define a standard of measurement or weight. Without it, normal trade activity and meaningful prices and values would be difficult to establish.

The seventeenth century made no great progress either in establishing standard units or in making a given standard uniform in all the territories held by the Hohenzollern dynasty. The acquisition of new territories after 1648 complicated the problem. A police ordinance of 1688 attempted to introduce standard units in the Duchy of Magdeburg.[4]

Increasingly the tendency was to achieve standardization and then uniformity by placing official seals on measuring instruments used in trade, wholesale and retail, and in public taverns.[5] Coopers were not allowed to sell barrels and tuns prior to testing and branding with the official seal of certification.[6] By 1713 it was decreed that the Berlin units for bushel, ell, and weights were to become the standards throughout the Mark Brandenburg.[7] This effort to establish uniformity was extended to the adjacent Duchy of Magdeburg in June 1714.[8] A year earlier Frederick William I had ordered the use of the Berlin bushel and quart throughout all his lands

1. *C. C. March.,* vol. 6, pt. 2, app., no. 1, cols. 1-6.
2. *C. C. March.,* vol. 5, pt. 1, sec. 1, no. 1, cols. 4-7. Margrave John acquired the Trans-Oder Neumark in 1535 while his older brother, Joachim II, became Margrave of Brandenburg. This separation of the provinces of the electorate ceased after 1571.
3. Ibid., no. 2, cols. 23-24.
4. *C. C. Magdeb.,* pt. 3, chap. 24, pp. 96-97.
5. Ibid., pt. 3, no. 26, pp. 354-355, "Government Patent on Standardization of Beer Measure on the Basis of the Magdeburg One," 20 Sept. 1686.
6. *C. C. March.,* vol. 5, pt. 2, sec. 8, no. 2, cols. 531-532, of 13 March 1693.
7. Ibid., no. 5, cols. 535-536, of 16 June 1713.
8. *C. C. Magdeb.,* pt. 3, no. 277, pp. 725-726.

in buying grain for the cavalry and for measuring daily rations for horses.[9]

It was not until 1722 that Frederick William took the next logical step aimed at establishing a uniform standard bushel (the Berlin bushel) for the grain trade in all his territories, with the major exception of East Prussia.[10]

The various efforts to establish uniform standards for weights and measures in Brandenburg and a uniform bushel for grain in practically all of the Hohenzollern territories not only were designed to benefit Prussian commerce, particularly the grain and cloth trade, but likewise were meant to protect the buyer or consumer against fraud, short weight, and short measure. Pots and pitchers in the taverns, heavy weights and small retail scales, cloth merchants' ells, barrels and bushel baskets were all to be inspected and stamped as approved. Town officials, the king's local tax commissaries, police officers *(Ausreuter)*,[11] and Berlin police inspectors[12] were all ordered and used to enforce the edict of May 1722 and other edicts decreeing uniform standards. Weekly markets, street hawkers, butcher, baker, grocer, and craftsmen shops were all to be inspected annually.[13]

Much progress was made by 1740 in establishing uniform standards. Nevertheless, resistance to governmental efforts, persistence of local variations, tendencies of fraud by false weight or measure denied complete success to two centuries of effort.

Annual Fairs

The Mark Brandenburg was an inland territory intersected by the Elbe River in the west and the Oder River in the east. It had a most favorable economic-geographical potential, sprawling across the North German plain from Slavic Poland and Silesia to the fringes of western Germany. It could have been the profit-taking middleman between the hinterland and the great Hanseatic seaports. It was not, in fact, until the later seventeenth century that any of this potential was achieved. Brandenburg cities were overshadowed commercially by the great trading centers of Hamburg, Lübeck, Magdeburg, and Leipzig in the west, Stettin, Posen, and Breslau in the east. Prior to 1500, no Brandenburg city was the scene for annual fairs with their free-trade privileges.

9. *C. C. Magdeb.*, pt. 4, no. 3, p. 41, "Rations Ordinance, and Regulation for Quartering Cavalry and Dragoons," of 18 May 1713.

10. *C. C. March.*, vol. 5, pt. 2, sec. 8, no. 7, cols. 537-540, "A Regulation Concerning Standard Bushels," 5 May 1722.

11. Ibid., vol. 5, pt. 1, sec. 1, no. 24, col. 118, Instruction to Neumark Police, 1733.

12. Ibid., no. 27, col. 125, Instruction to Berlin Police, May 1735.

13. "Edict Concerning Various Points of Police Functions [for the city of Berlin]," of 1 July 1735, ibid., no. 28, cols. 129-134.

About the turn of the century, the electors attempted to establish such fairs. The lower Elbe was not fully developed for river traffic until the sixteenth century. Grain and timber as bulk items were floated downstream, but, the greater portion of moving goods was carried on land routes, particularly the foreign goods moving inland from Hamburg. In 1496 John Cicero granted the privilege of an annual fair to Salzwedel in the Altmark, west of the Elbe River. The purpose was to improve the prosperity of its citizens by attracting foreign merchants away from Luneburg and Brunswick highways as they moved from Hamburg to Magdeburg and Leipzig. The Salzwedel burghers apparently did not respond vigorously to the opportunity. In 1570 Joachim II reaffirmed the privilege and allowed two fairs of three days' duration.[14] Improvement of river navigation by 1600 presumably negated some of the advantages hoped for, and the Salzwedel fairs did not prosper.

In the sixteenth and seventeenth centuries, Berlin likewise enjoyed an annual fair. Lasting only one day, it apparently did not attract the attendance of foreign merchants. After the opening of the Friedrich Wilhelm Canal linking the Oder River with the Spree, Havel, and Elbe rivers via Berlin, the Great Elector, in 1672, extended the period of the two Berlin fairs (beginning August 10 and November 1) to fourteen days.[15] This extension did not result in immediate full utilization by foreign merchants of the Berlin opportunities, although Berlin's importance as an entrepôt between Hamburg and Silesian merchants did increase. In 1706, King Frederick I again extended the duration of the Berlin annual fair of November 1 to fourteen days.[16] This time success was immediate, as the act created facilities for foreign merchants to buy up Berlin manufactured goods as well as badly needed raw materials. The following year, Frederick extended the mid-Lent fair to fourteen days also.[17] From this time on, Berlin was to be more than a political capital. It became the pivotal link between east and west in Prussia's economic expansion.

More important than either the Salzwedel or Berlin fairs were the Frankfurt fairs on the Oder River. By mid-seventeenth century, or shortly after the Thirty Years' War, there were three annual fairs, each lasting about two weeks.[18]

The three Frankfurt fairs were established in 1516, but they gained no real commercial significance until the seventeenth century. These fairs began on a Monday and continued through the second Friday.[19] The welfare of the city was enormously enhanced by them, as the volume of

14. Ibid., vol. 5, pt. 2, sec. 9, no. 1, cols. 557-558.
15. Ibid., no. 5, cols. 563-564.
16. Ibid., no. 9, cols. 565-568, patent of 1 Oct. 1706.
17. Ibid., no. 10, cols. 567-570, edict of 31 Jan. 1707.
18. See the ordinance of 14 Jan. 1723, ibid., no. 14, cols. 573-574.
19. Hugo Rachel, *Die Handels-, Zoll-, und Akzisepolitik Brandenburg-Preussens bis 1713*, pp. 233-234.

imported goods and the toll income during the fair weeks far exceeded the total volume during the rest of the year.

The various patents or edicts after 1496 that granted to three cities of Brandenburg the right to have annual fairs reflected the fact that by the early sixteenth century the economic life of the electoral towns had come under the regulation of the territorial prince. Prior to the Hohenzollern entry into Brandenburg in 1411, the towns of the Altmark particularly, as well as the cities of Brandenburg and Berlin, had joined the Hanseatic League or had otherwise on their own initiative extended their trade beyond the local market.

The assumption of princely responsibility extended beyond granting the privilege of holding fairs. As early as the fifteenth century, the Brandenburg electors began to concern themselves with the security and the usability of the main highways. Brandenburg joined with neighboring states and some Hanseatic cities to guarantee peace and safety on the main highways and either the recovery of or compensation for goods lost by highway robbery. Merchants who used the highways and enjoyed this protection were required to pay a *Schutzgeld,* a protection fee. Elector Joachim I (1499-1535) was most effective in winning transit trade by making the roads safe against robber barons. This was the real purpose of the convoy system and highway patrols, to attract the transit trade into the Mark Brandenburg, away from Brunswick. A principal highway for trade purposes passed from Hamburg and Lübeck south to Nuremberg or to Leipzig. This highway passed through the Altmark, giving importance to the Salzwedel fair. The idea of convoys on the highways was not new in the sixteenth century, but under Joachim I they were systematized with regular rates.[20] In the east, as early as 1514, Joachim I established the convoying of freight wagons from Frankfurt to the Polish border. This enhanced the value of the Frankfurt fairs. By 1585 the ending of highway robbery by this electoral police escort made the system dispensable, and it was replaced by customs inspectors.

The only other respectable high road that Brandenburg had ran north from Leipzig through Wittenberg, Saarmund, Berlin, and Frankfurt on the way to Posen in Poland. Merchants preferred, however, to go from Silesia to Hamburg via Leipzig. It was not until the Friedrich Wilhelm Canal was completed in 1668 that Berlin emerged as an important inland port. This explains, if not wholly, why the Great Elector in 1672 and Frederick I in 1706 and 1707 extended the two annual Berlin fairs to fourteen days.

The primary purpose of the Hohenzollern economic policy of the six-

20. Between the twelfth and fourteenth centuries the Counts of Champagne attracted foreign merchants to the prosperous fairs of Champagne by providing security on the highways through paid police officers. John F. Benton, in a paper read before the American Historical Association in December 1965, entitled "Comital Police Power and the Champagne Fairs," discussed the protection of the public highways as an attribute of sovereignty.

teenth century was to attract transit trade into Brandenburg by means of safety on the highways and by the establishment of fairs at Salzwedel, Berlin, and Frankfurt. From the middle of the seventeenth century on, there was increasing interest in the growth of internal commerce and development of domestic manufacturing.[21]

Weekly Markets

In addition to the fairs and of greater local importance was the weekly town market. This was a local market and preceded the fairs in origin as well as differing from them in function. The weekly market served to supply the daily needs of a local population in and around a town nucleus. It provided an outlet for the surplus goods of the agricultural producer and a source for the hardware and textiles, for example, that the town offered. Unlike the fairs, the local town market offered a retail trade between the rural supplier of food and raw material and the urban buyer.

In Brandenburg, the first cities to be chartered and to be granted the right of weekly market were the episcopal cities of Havelberg and Brandenburg. They received these rights about 1170 from Albert the Bear. Sometime later the Wendish village of Cölln on an island of the Spree River, and a German town opposite on the north side, Berlin, were granted status by the margrave as cities with market privileges, Cölln in 1232, Berlin in 1242. Cölln and Berlin were located at the crossroads of colonial expansion eastward through the Mark, and they became an important way station for trade between the Elbe and Oder rivers. These two cities became the capital and principal residence of the margraves of Brandenburg. By 1253 Frankfurt was granted city status and market privileges. Throughout the thirteenth century, the margraves of Brandenburg extended town rights and market privileges to many old and new towns from Salzwedel and Stendhal in the west to Soldin and Landsberg east of the Oder.[22]

After 1500 the town and city markets in Brandenburg, as well as the annual fairs, became subject to increasing regulation by the electors. Market inspectors, either as local town or electoral police agents, were appointed to maintain peace and order, to enforce edicts and ordinances of the electors, such as those regarding weights and measures, forestalling, priority rights of purchase of townspeople, fair prices, sanitation,

21. The comments on Brandenburg trade policy in the sixteenth century are based primarily on Rachel, *Handelspolitik*, pp. 3-12.

22. By the year 1540 there were over 100 towns in the entire Brandenburg Mark, some directly under electoral jurisdiction, some located within the holdings of noble or clerical estates, some rather large, some little more than oversized villages. See Berthold Schulze, *Brandenburgische Besitzstandskarte des 16. Jahrhundert: der ritterschaftliche, geistliche, städtische und landesherrliche Besitz um 1540.*

even protection of the market square cobblestones torn up and used by the merchants for their booths.[23]

When towns were small in size, one general market sufficed for the needs of the residents. With the growth of population in towns or cities such as Berlin or Frankfurt, it became necessary to expand the number of available city markets. Some continued to be general, serving sections of the city. Others were specialized. There were separate grain markets, bread and meat markets, dairy and fish markets, and firewood markets. Markers were sometimes erected to identify the locations; and in 1735 a Berlin weekly newspaper was used for public advertising of these locations.[24]

Retail Shops, Hawkers, and Peddlers

In addition to the annual fairs and weekly markets, the marketplace was also served by retail shops in the towns, by street hawkers, and by itinerant peddlers. The shops were specialized retail stores permanently established in the towns for satisfying the daily needs of the residents. There were bakeries and confectionary shops, butcher shops, dry grocers, green grocers, clothiers, drapery shops, tailors, cobblers, hardware shops, apothecaries, and spice merchants as well as shops for selling the products of various other craftsmen in the town.[25] Street hawkers were unlicensed competitors of shopkeepers, selling cheap in the streets and in the market square. The itinerant peddler was usually a packman or pushcart trader who dealt in dry goods and hardware. He traveled in rural areas, performing a retail service when he was honest, and always constituting a threat to the urban guild monopoly.

During the fifteenth century, the Brandenburg nobility developed an active commercial competition with the towns and helped to ruin them economically. Because of the serious decline in the volume of trade participated in by the towns and cities, many of them withdrew from the Hanseatic League (Berlin and Cölln in 1452, Brandenburg in 1476). The competition of the nobility affected the value of the local weekly market, the livelihood of the local shopkeeper and craftsmen, as well as the foreign

23. "Circular Ordinance Issued to *Steuerräte,* 22 Aug. 1727," *C. C. March.,* vol. 5, pt. 2, sec. 9, no. 15, cols. 573-574.

24. "Ordinance Concerning Various Weekly and Annual Markets in Friedrichsstadt in Berlin, 22 June 1735," ibid., no. 18, cols. 575-578.

25. Perhaps the earliest granting of guild privileges to craftsmen or shopkeepers in the Mark Brandenburg occurred in 1310 in the city of Havelberg, which had been given *Stadtrecht* as early as 1151. In 1310 the margrave granted hereditary right to city butchers to have 22 butcher shops at an annual payment of 22 Brandenburg schillings. These shops could sell fresh meat, fish, and herring, but not salted meat or jellied meat (*Sultze*) (*Cod. Dipl. Brand.,* pt. 1, vol. 1, no. 4, p. 27). In the same year a guild of drapers (*Gewandschneider*) was established at Havelberg (*Cod. dipl. brand. cont.,* vol. 1, no. 19, pp. 15-16). In 1326 reference was made to the guild of clothmakers of Berlin (*Cod. Dipl. Brand.,* supp. vol., no. 8, p. 226).

9. *Buying Jewelry*

10. *Market Scene in the Sixteenth Century*

11. *A Vagrant Family*

12. *The Quacksalver Makes His Pitch*

trade with Lübeck and Hamburg. By the sixteenth century this competition between the aristocratic landholders and the towns became one of the primary concerns of the elector, as the economic life of the Brandenburg towns and cities came under the police regulation of the territorial prince.

In a report to the Brandenburg *Landtag* on 10 August 1536, Elector Joachim II expressed concern that, contrary to previous ordinances and to traditional usage, nobles and clergy were getting involved in merchandising (merchant's trade) and were causing injury to the peasants in the villages and to the town merchants as well.[26] Eager to preserve the traditional structure of social status and dignity, the elector ordered each person to remain within his social caste and economic occupation. This statement to the *Landtag* stipulated that no prelate, nobleman, clergyman, or peasant who did not live in a town and had no burgher rights and duties should conduct either wholesale or retail business. All were granted the traditional right to sell those farm products which they themselves produced. Two specific grievances of the towns were charged against the nobles and clergy. Under the cloak of their special privileges, they brewed beer on their estates beyond their own needs and then sold to taverns and inns, thus competing with town breweries. Nobles, sometimes using duress, bought up the farm products produced by peasants on the nobles' lands (wool, grain, cattle, poultry, e.g.) and then sold these items in the foreign market. Thus, in 1536, Joachim II forbade illegal brewing of beer for sale by nobles and clergy and required that all selling and buying of local farm products be done in the local town markets. The intent was not only to preserve the weekly market, but to protect the needs of the local consumers, both housewife and craftsman. Foreign merchants were forbidden to buy up farm products (wool, butter, cheese, eggs) in the weekly market at the expense of the local residents. The local town craftsman was also to be protected against encroachment upon his guild privilege. No craftsman was to be allowed to set up a shop in rural areas within a mile of a town. One of the frequently expressed motives for requiring the use of the local town markets was to protect the peasant-seller and the urban-buyer against false measure. Joachim II, in 1538, made the town councils responsible for assuring that all sellers used correct weights and measures. To accomplish this goal, all goods—wool, grain, and other agricultural products—had to be brought to the towns and sold in the weekly market.[27]

After 1540, a new pressure force exerted considerable influence upon the elector's interest in the economic welfare of the towns, namely, the in-

26. Walter Friedensburg, ed., *Kurmärkische Ständeakten aus der Regierungszeit Joachims II,* vol. 1, no. 9, pp. 31-40 (cited hereafter as *Kurm. Ständ. Joach.*). Also in C. C. *March.,* vol. 6, no. 18, cols. 33-40.
27. *Kurm. Ständ. Joach.,* vol. 1, no. 12, art. 34, p. 57.

creasingly severe fiscal situation of the prince. On 14 March 1540, Joachim II, in return for the towns' agreeing to assume 450,000 *thaler* of the electoral debt, renewed the privileges and prohibitions which he had granted on 10 August 1536.[28]

The year 1549 was one of the most significant years of the sixteenth century in the relations between the elector and the Brandenburg Estates. Joachim II was heavily in debt and was forced to ask the Estates to grant him taxes sufficient to meet his debt obligations and to balance his current budget. For this purpose Joachim summoned a meeting of the *Landtag* for 24 June 1549. This session of the *Landtag* was taken so seriously that it was attended by almost a total representation of the three Estates (nobles, clergy, and towns). The nobles and towns eventually agreed to certain taxes in return for concessions by the elector. The fiscal problems, the struggles between Estates and prince and between nobles and towns, and the details of the fiscal solution are of no immediate concern to this study. The concessions that were obtained to mitigate the various grievances of the towns in so far as they affected the economy and livelihood of the townspeople are germane to this examination of the police power of the state applied to the marketplace.

The one tax that caused considerable difficulty was the new beer tax, which yielded eight times the old one, that is, eight *Groschen* per tun of beer consumed in the land. Negotiations between representatives of the Estates and of the elector in June, July, and August led to the submission of grievances and requests for redress by the representatives of the towns. The grievances centered around two problems affecting the economic welfare of the towns: the illegal brewing of beer by nobles, clergy, and peasants, and other practices which harmed the sale of city-brewed beer; and the competition with town craftsmen and shopkeepers by rural shops and retailers.[29]

The towns of the Prignitz submitted their complaints in August.[30] They complained that the clergy and the peasants illegally brewed beer in the villages for their own consumption and that the nobles brewed beer and sold it to the peasants for weddings and christenings or sold it to taverns. They petitioned that the buying up (forestalling) of wool and hides by nobles and peasants be forbidden, that these items be sold in the town markets so that clothmakers and leather-workers in the towns would not lack raw materials for their shops. Items like building timber, firewood, and grain were being shipped out of the electorate, thus increasing the cost to city residents. They wanted these items brought to the town markets for sale.

28. Ibid., no. 16, pp. 81-85.
29. The electoral proposal of new taxes was presented by Joachim II to the *Landtag* on 24 June 1549. See ibid., no. 121, pp. 356-362.
30. "Complaints of Towns of the Prignitz and of Their Craftsmen Concerning Beer-brewing and Protection of the Crafts and of Trade," ibid., no. 141, pp. 409-411.

The complaints of the Prignitz towns were typical of the complaints presented during July and August to the elector by many towns. The most common grievance referred to the illegal competition from rural areas in beer-brewing and retailing.[31] Other towns complained about evasions that limited the usefulness of the town markets.[32] There were also grievances against illegal competition from rural, unprivileged craftsmen.[33]

When the *Landtag* reconvened on 17 August 1549, all the towns of Brandenburg submitted a collective statement of their grievances and petitioned for a confirmation of their privileges.[34] The towns agreed to a new beer tax to be collected over a period of eight years (later extended to fourteen years). In return, Joachim II issued an ordinance on 14 September 1549 designed to protect the economic interests of the towns.[35] This ordinance of 1549 based itself on an earlier ordinance of his father (1513) and directed that wherever beer-brewing in villages had previously not been allowed, it was not to be allowed now; that nobles, lords, and clergy were not to be allowed to sell their own brew to innkeepers; and that no one in the villages was to be allowed to brew beer (the peasants were accustomed to brewing a so-called *Kesselbier* [a home brew]). And then, with an eye to preserving class dignity and occupational caste status, Joachim ordered that no noble, lord, or prelate should engage in commerce or burgher trade (*Kauffmannschaft oder bürgerlicher Narung*).[36] Neither peasants nor unpropertied persons in the towns were to engage in forestalling in the villages or in secret commerce, and thus neither peasant nor merchant would be cheated by false weight or measure. Peasants had to sell farm products in the free weekly market in the towns, but prelates and nobles were free to sell in any market the goods that they themselves produced on their own estates.

31. E.g., Neuruppin (ibid., no. 142, p. 412). Prentzlau in the Ukermark (ibid., no. 143, pp. 413-415), and Bernau (ibid., no. 144, pp. 415-416) protested that innkeepers in the villages brewed beer for sale; Müncheberg complained against the Bishop of Lebus (ibid., no. 145, pp. 416-417); Wrietzen complained about the illegal competition in selling beer in inns by a nobleman who acquired a convent and used its facilities to set up a brewery (ibid., no. 151, pp. 427-428); Trebbin protested that peasants and innkeepers brewed and sold beer to thirteen village inns around the town (ibid., no. 154, pp. 430-431).

32. E.g., Neu-Angermünde protested the injury to the livelihood of its burghers from illegal buying up of wool, tallow, grease, and hides in the villages, items which then did not enter the local free market (ibid., no. 146, pp. 418-421). Wrietzen complained of the violation of its privilege to buy for fuel wood passing the town on the river. Fishermen and riverpeople bought it up and then sold it down-river (Stettin, e.g.) at higher prices (ibid., no. 151, pp. 427-428).

33. E.g., Strausburg complained that tailors of the nobles made and sold clothing to village peasants (ibid., no. 149, pp. 424-426).

34. Ibid., no. 155, pp. 431-441.

35. "Electoral Ordinance against Illegal Brewing and Sale of Beer, against Forestallers and Craftsmen in the Villages," ibid., no. 165, pp. 481-488; also *C. C. March.,* vol. 4, pt. 4, no. 4, cols. 11-18.

36. "ob auch wol in gemeinen rechten und guter policeiordnung zu erhaltung eines jeden stands gebüre, narung und notdurft . . . ," *Kurm. Stand. Joach.,* no. 165, p. 482.

The elector took note of the fact that many nobles engaged in mercantile practices that were unbecoming to their social standing—buying up grain and wool from their peasant tenants, for instance, and selling these products outside Brandenburg. Many persons also illicitly bought up rural products and then smuggled them out of the land, to the harm of the electoral toll revenues and the livelihood of the townspeople. Not only did the elector order all clerics and nobles to refrain from all bourgeois business, but he also forbade burghers, craftsmen, and townspeople to go out into the countryside to buy up the peasants' wool, hides, waxes, and other products. The peasants were required to bring their products into the weekly markets of nearby towns. Local officials were ordered to enforce these provisions and to confiscate all goods of violators as well as their boats, wagons, and horses. City and town craftsmen in turn were forbidden to set up shops in the villages.

Underlying this attempted regulation of economic activity affecting the towns was an electoral concern for the common welfare (*gemeine Nutze*). The forbidden practices decreased the supply of goods to the towns and thus increased prices, injured the livelihood of merchants and craftsmen, and caused an economic decline in the towns. The peasant was expected to sell his surplus products in the weekly town market and to make his purchases of hardware, clothing, textiles, spices, and so forth, from the retailers in the towns. The peasants were specifically forbidden to practice crafts in the villages. The great concern for illegal brewing and sale of beer in the rural areas was motivated by a desire to protect the town breweries so that the beer tax could be collected to meet the towns' quota of the electoral debt.

With the social and economic interests of various groups involved, it was difficult to obtain acceptance of or to enforce the articles of the police ordinance of 14 September 1549. The second half of the sixteenth century was filled with complaints and grievances by the Brandenburg towns about rural practices which injured the occupational and economic conditions of townsmen. In 1551, a "Committee of the Towns" submitted a list of grievances to the elector.[37] The violations which they protested included the illegal brewing of beer on nobles' estates, the grinding of malt by the peasants, the selling of illegal (and untaxed) beer to taverns in the villages, and the connivance of the police authorities (*Landreiter*) with violators.[38] They also found fault with the nobles' engaging in the grain trade—buying up grain in the country and diverting it from the local town markets, thus increasing the cost of bread grains. The same grievance was expressed with regard to building-timber and firewood. Later in the same

37. Ibid., vol. 2, no. 303, "Grievances Submitted to the Elector by a Committee of the Towns," 5 April 1551, pp. 5-8.
38. On 4 February 1551, Joachim II had issued an order to his *Landreiter* to enforce the edicts against illegal beer-brewing among the villagers. The rural police were appointed by local nobles and were not effective in enforcing electoral police regulations in the rural areas. *Kurm. Ständ. Joach.*, vol. 1, no. 302, 848-850.

year the towns petitioned the elector to enforce his police regulations affecting the towns' economy in order to preserve "our prosperity and welfare [unser aller gedeig und wolfhart]".[39] The townspeople about whom they were concerned constituted at least one-third of the population; about 100,000 persons lived in the towns of Brandenburg at this time.[40]

The problem of protecting the town market, the livelihood of the townspeople, and the monopoly of the guild craftsmen and shopkeepers against the competition of non-burgher classes continued for over a century, despite frequent issues and reissues of police ordinances attempting to regulate economic functions according to class status. Enforcement was feeble or ineffective; evasion persisted. Between 1572 and 1682, successive electors were compelled to issue and reissue edicts attempting to prevent nobility, clergy, and peasants from engaging in trade and commerce that involved forestalling or circumventing the function of the town weekly markets.[41] The format and the purpose of the ordinances remained unchanged after the ordinance of 1549. Protection of class interests as well as promotion of the common welfare of the towns through an effective weekly market was basic. Toward the end of the seventeenth century, the purposes were to prevent scarcity of goods and speculation in commodities, and to maintain fair and cheap prices. Equally important was the fiscal purpose of assuring the collection of tolls and excise duties by using the towns and town markets as a focus of trade. The regulative provisions remained the same as they had been for almost two centuries, but the goals became increasingly economic and fiscal.

During the war years (the War of the League of Augsburg, 1688-1697), the shortage of food encouraged speculative buying, and Elector Frederick III (1688-1713) was forced to issue a number of edicts designed to protect the interests of town consumers, particularly in Berlin. In 1688, the burgomasters and city councilmen took the initiative of forbidding the speculative buying of food products brought into the city markets.[42] This was followed by a series of edicts to protect the availability in a free market of bread grains, mutton, fish, beef, and other victuals.[43] Numerous complaints reached the elector about the high cost of food because of the speculative buying by greedy merchants, cattle dealers, butchers, bakers, brewers, hawkers, officers and soldiers, women, and Jews, who all ran out to meet the farmer as he approached the city and bargained for his pro-

39. *Kurm. Ständ. Joach.,* vol. 2, no. 306, p. 13.

40. A tabulation made in 1564 by Thomas Matthias (a close adviser to Joachim II) estimated the population of the Mark at about 300,000 with 99,000 in the towns. Ibid., vol. 2, no. 412, "Tabulation of 1 Nov. 1564," p. 311.

41. See, e.g., electoral edicts of 1572, 1583, 1607, and 1682 in *C. C. March.,* vol. 5, pt. 2, sec. 1, nos. 4, 5, 6, 14 (cols. 7-26); and vol. 5, pt. 2, sec. 2, no. 17, cols. 85-88, edict of 1664 against forestalling.

42. *C. C. March.,* vol. 5, pt. 2, sec. 2, no. 38, cols. 105-108, edict of 28 July 1688.

43. Edicts of 16 Jan. 1693, 21 Sept. 1694, 25 Sept. 1694, 3 Jan. 1695, 7 June 1695, 3 Jan. 1698, 28 Aug. 1898, ibid., nos. 44, 47, 48, 50, 51, 55, 56, cols. 115-132.

ducts. This practice was forbidden. All food products were to be taken to the public marketplaces and there sold to the needy householders. No sales to dealers or peddlers were to be allowed so long as the market pennants were flying. Foreign merchants were to make purchases for export only in the towns and only after the local residents had been satisfied.

Protection of the town retailers and shopkeepers was again sought by means of forbidding clergy, nobles, peasants, and unauthorized townspeople to engage in commerce. Dealers in drugs, pots, ironware, and other goods were forbidden to peddle to peasants, who were expected to make these purchases in town shops or markets.[44] Compliance with these directives would, of course, lead to effective collection of tolls and excise duties on goods moving through the city gates.

In 1713, King Frederick William I issued a candid and revealing statement. He said that in spite of the many edicts issued since 1557 against illicit trading and speculative forestalling in the rural areas and forbidding the avoidance of town market facilities by peasants, these practices still persisted, not only among Brandenburgers but among foreign merchants as well.[45] A major target of Frederick William was the Hamburg and Stettin merchants plying the Elbe, Oder, and subsidiary rivers of Brandenburg. In an effort to protect the town markets and to prevent a loss of excise income from these illegal sales, a patent of 1714 forbade shippers and merchants to sell or buy wares and victuals to or from the villages along the Elbe River and ordered them to do business only in the towns.[46]

The persistent electoral legislation, edicts, and police ordinances of the sixteenth and seventeenth centuries which sought to preserve the economic viability of the free, weekly town market were concerned with keeping the town the focal point of buying and selling for a given area. This meant (1) keeping the townspeople supplied with victuals at a fair price and the craftsmen supplied with raw materials, (2) establishing a center where merchants could purchase surplus rural products for export trade, (3) protecting the craft guilds and retail shopkeepers, and (4) assuring the collection of tolls and consumption and excise taxes.

While all this protective police legislation assumed the general existence of weekly markets in all electoral towns, an act of Frederick William I suggests the probability that not all towns enjoyed the privilege and utility of a town market. This, of course, would encourage those malpractices of trade against which so many edicts and ordinances had been promulgated. Recognizing the perennial problem of forestalling and

44. Edict of 10 Oct. 1697, *C. C. March.,* vol. 5, pt. 2, sec. 1, no. 17, cols. 27-32.
45. "Edict on Trade in Grain, Wool, Victuals, to Whom It Is Allowed, Speculative Buying and Trading Forbidden," 24 Aug. 1713, ibid., no. 22, cols. 41-44.
46. Ibid., no. 26, cols. 47-48.

of withholding victuals from the market to enhance the price, and moved by a concern for the development of internal commerce between town and country, Frederick William, in November 1713, authorized the establishment of weekly markets in all towns throughout the Mark Brandenburg, wherever markets did not already exist. These were to be held twice weekly (Wednesday and Saturday), and all farmers were obliged to bring their products to market on these occasions.[47] This ordinance also placed the burden of local supervision and policing of the weekly markets on the town councils. The magistrates were to appoint out of the council two market inspectors and two town commissioners, whose mission it was to enforce market regulations and ordinances. They were to assure that all goods were sold at a fair market price, that forestalling was suppressed, and that no false weights or measures were used. They were to provide a clean and convenient place for the grain, wool, and other retail carts and booths and were to keep the passageways between market booths free of carts. In accord with the market ordinances issued on 28 July 1688 and on 9 February 1693, the market inspectors were to designate where particular kinds of wares and victuals were to be sold so that without confusion the farmer, merchant, or consumer would know exactly where to set up his cart or booth and where to buy desired items. Smaller towns were allowed a general, common marketplace and a separate cattle market. Larger cities would have specialized markets. Berlin, for example, in the time of Frederick William I, had a number of firewood markets along the Spree River outside the city limits on both sides of the city, east and west. There was a dairy market (*Molckenmarkt*) near the St. Nicholas Church and adjacent to the Berlin fish market. There was also a Cölln fish market near the *Mühlendamm,* where the Spree River entered the city from the east. For the convenience of the city residents (over 60,000) marketplaces were located at the Frankfurt Gate, the Oranienburg Gate, and the Potsdam Gate, and a New Market was established near St. Mary's Church and the synagogue.

To maintain order and establish priority in buying and selling, the market inspectors were to restrict the markets to burghers and town residents until 10:00 in the morning. Until then they could buy for their households or craftshops the food, raw goods, and wares they personally needed. After this hour, a special pennant was to be raised opening up the market to all buyers, foreign or domestic. The purchase of raw wool was restricted in the morning hours to town clothmakers and local fabricators. Wool dealers were permitted to buy only after midday.

Hawkers were not to be allowed on the market square, only on the corners of the streets or at the ends of bridges. Hawking in the towns and cities was carried on by peasants with their own victuals and goods,

---

47. Market ordinance of 16 Nov. 1713, effective in Brandenburg, *C. C. March.,* vol. 5, pt. 2, sec. 2, no. 71, cols. 153-156.

by burghers and Jewish peddlers. Because of complaints about this competition, Frederick William ordered the cessation of house-to-house peddling of victuals and other items on pain of confiscation of the goods and a money fine levied on both buyer and seller. To deprive the peddlers of their source, forestalling at the town gates by "townies" was forbidden. All goods were to be taken directly to and sold in the appropriate marketplace at a fair market price.

Despite all royal efforts to prevent *Entgegenlaufen* (the practice of burghers and their servants, soldiers' wives, and others of running out on the highways to intercept the farmers on market days in order to buy up their products and sell them through house-to-house peddling or at the marketplace at a higher price), the violators continued to defy the king's efforts. The king threatened violators with confiscation of food, whipping with cat-o'-nine tails, and imprisonment at Spandau.[48] The persistence of those who evaded the prescribed monopoly of the town market suggests that either the profit urge was too powerful or that the privileged system of retailing was inadequate and antiquated.

After the Thirty Years' War, there appeared other threats to the security of the town retailer and shopkeeper, namely, the itinerant peddler in rural areas and the street hawkers in the cities and towns. This problem seems to have been either nonexistent or not serious in the sixteenth century. Sixteenth-century complaints against Jews made to the elector by the representatives of the towns usually referred to their money-lending rates or competition in wholesale trade.

By the middle of the seventeenth century, however, perhaps because of the large number of footloose persons after the war years, there was a growing concern about this problem. Immediately after peace was concluded in 1648, foreign peddlers moved into an obvious market vacuum. The retailers of the Altmark and of the city of Stendhal complained as early as 1649 of the violation of privileges granted by Elector George William (1619-1640) and confirmed by his son. The guilty ones, probably coming from Hamburg, were foreign peddlers and pushcart hawkers who traveled about the towns and villages of the Altmark peddling wares of all kinds that had probably been long absent in wartorn Brandenburg. The charges were that these peddlers brought harm to the simple peasant by adulterating goods, by light weight and short measure. Of course, they also deprived the native retailers of their livelihood. Since these persons were nonresidents and paid no civil obligations or taxes, Elector Frederick William, by an edict of 23 October 1649, forbade itinerant peddlers except at the time of the annual public fairs.[49]

48. "Edict Concerning Repression of the Often Forbidden Forestalling," 26 Sept. 1720, ibid., no. 79, cols. 161-166; "Edict on Forestalling," 27 Feb. 1722, ibid., no. 81, cols. 165-166.
49. "Edict against the Foreign Traveling Salesman of All and Sundry Wares," 23 Oct. 1649, *C. C. March.*, vol. 5, pt. 2, sec. 3, no. 8, cols. 173-176.

In the next decade, the problem spread across the Elbe River and caused increasing grievances among the Brandenburg retailers, forcing Frederick William to take action again in 1663.[50] "We have had complaints from grocers, sellers of pins and needles, and of tinware, that for some time now peddlers with pushcarts, Jews, wayfarers who have learned no honorable trade, often runaway apprentices, who possess no property and pay no taxes, have been peddling all kinds of wares, such as lace, ribbon, linen, serges, stockings, cloth covers, hatbands, Meissnerware such as needles, knives, saws, pliers, drills, and padlocks, other than at the time of the public fairs, in towns and villages to the harm of merchants, retailers, and craftsmen who make or sell these items." To stop this illegal selling, Frederick William directed his toll officials and rural gendarmes to warn these foreign interlopers and pushcart peddlers to sell their goods only at public fairs; on second offense, all their goods would be confiscated. The edict was to be posted at all toll stations, and arresting officials were to receive one-quarter of all proceeds from confiscated goods.

This edict against illegal peddling was no more effective than the 200 years of police ordinances against profiteering noblemen, clergymen, and peasants. Repeated edicts were issued by the Great Elector and during the reigns of the first two Prussian kings in the eighteenth century. Jewish peddlers, unable to acquire property or guild rights in the towns, were a frequent target.[51] In 1692 the Jews were accused of peddling their wares in rural areas, thereby hurting trade between villages and towns and defrauding the elector of excise payments.[52] In 1687 other noncitizen groups —Savoyards, Italians, quack pill-peddlers—were accused of peddling goods in Berlin, Cölln, and Friedrichswerder, thereby injuring commerce and taking money out of the land.[53]

Early in the eighteenth century, the privileged hardware iron-dealers in Berlin complained of losing their livelihood to so-called *WasserBrenner* (shoddy dealers, literally "water-distillers") who sold their ironware around the countryside. Such peddling was forbidden in 1702.[54] A few years later, in 1708, the sievemakers of Berlin complained of similar unlawful competition from peddlers, and the peddlers were forbidden to sell sieves except at annual fairs. The sale of fly and rat poisons by peddlers was also forbidden.[55] A mandate of 25 April 1712 reveals how ineffective were the various bans of fifty years. Once again peddling and unlicensed retailing were condemned and banned, and all law enforcement

50. "Edict against Peddling of All Sorts," 21 Sept. 1663, *C. C. March.,* vol. 5, pt. 2, sec. 7, no. 1, cols. 507-508.

51. Ibid., no. 2, cols. 507-510, edict of 11 April 1665.

52. "Edict against Peddling by Jews," 17 Aug. 1692, ibid., no. 4, cols. 509-510.

53. "Ordinance against Peddling by Savoyards and Italians in Capital Residences," 18 Aug. 1687, ibid., no. 3, cols. 509-510.

54. "Mandate against Peddling of Iron, Brass, Steel, and Cheap Jewelry Wares," 20 Oct. 1702, ibid., no. 5, cols. 509-512.

55. Ibid., no. 6, cols. 511-512. The edict actually repeated a similar ban of 27 May 1699.

officers were urged to be on the lookout for violators, of whom the mandate confessed there were large numbers, particularly in the streets of Berlin.[56]

The first edict of this nature in the reign of King Frederick William I, dated 24 August 1713, forbade pack-merchants from moving about the countryside retailing various goods, apothecary items, hardware, tinware, and so forth. The king abolished all passes of any kind permitting such peddling.[57] A year later, in August 1714, Frederick William not only forbade Jewish peddlers to go from house to house, but, on the complaint of German and French merchants in Berlin that craftsmen were illegally engaging in trade, he had to forbid tailors, lacemakers, and buttonmakers from trading in dry goods.[58]

Obviously, constant prohibition against the illegal retailing practices of town and country peddlers, who either sold more conveniently or more cheaply than the licensed town retailers, was without significant effect. Frederick William I was sufficiently realistic to recognize that peddling persisted because his citizens supported it. A mandate of 8 March 1715, which reaffirmed the ban on house-to-house peddling in Berlin by both Jews and Christians, admitted that the burghers encouraged the practice by buying rather than reporting it to the *Fiskal* agents of the General War Commissariat. This king used his whole enforcement officialdom—the city military government, the General War Commissariat, the excise office, the city council, and two police officers specially appointed to enforce the regulations against peddling.[59] Public reaction both to prohibition and enforcement was manifested in the roughing-up of rural gendarmes who tried to enforce the edicts and in the illegal buying up of rural products. Commanders of cavalry units quartered in the countryside were forced to lend protection and support to local police officials.[60]

Another form of peddling, illicit retailing, and evasion of excise tax originated on the riverboats and canal barges. In April 1716, Frederick William found it necessary to warn that no ship's company was to violate the edict of 21 December 1713 against peddling victuals and other goods in the villages.[61] Two mandates of the following year, 1717, reveal that selling or hawking goods from riverboats continued, infringing on the rights of towns as trading centers.[62] The grocers of Berlin complained that boatmen sold cheeses, dried fish, other victuals, and dry goods from Ham-

56. Ibid., no. 7, cols. 511-514.
57. *C. C. March.,* vol. 5, pt. 2, sec. 1, no. 22, col. 43.
58. Ibid., no. 25, cols. 47-48.
59. *C. C. March.,* vol. 5, pt. 2, sec. 7, no. 8, cols. 513-514.
60. "Ordinance Concerning Military Support for Gendarmes," 25 Dec. 1716, ibid., no. 9, cols. 513-516.
61. "Regulation for Shipmasters' Guild," 18 April 1716, *C. C. March.,* vol. 5, pt. 2, sec. 1, no. 27, col. 53.
62. "Patent of 24 March 1717," ibid., no. 29, cols. 550-558.

burg. These were sold not only in Berlin but along the rivers in villages and hamlets where sales of wines, cheeses, herring, tobacco were made without paying excise or tolls. Equally annoying was the fact that the stopover at river villages for illegal peddling caused delays of as much as eight days in delivery time. Frederick William I for the moment could only storm, restate previous edicts, and demand stricter enforcement with more severe punishment.[63]

By April of 1718, however, Frederick William lost all patience with the repeated efforts and constant failure to get enforcement of the ban .against peddling. He listed the many police ordinances and edicts from 1557 to 24 August 1713 that had attempted to end the problems preventing the successful functioning of the town markets and town retailers and concluded "dennoch der davon gehoffte Effect nicht erfolget [still the hoped-for effect does not follow]." He found that the only result was constant complaint that in town and country the livelihood of his subjects was impaired. As a result, in his characteristic fashion of meeting administrative problems head-on, he undertook to revise completely the last ordinance concerning peddling and trading in rural areas in accordance with the requirements of good police administration and the territory's welfare. This meant still another edict, a "New Revised Edict on Peddling in the Mark Brandenburg" of 25 April 1718.[64] The first six articles of the edict redefined the obligation of farmers or rural property owners to carry their products to weekly town markets. The nobles, officials, clergymen, peasants who lived in the villages or on the land were forbidden to engage in commerce or burgher trading and were to refrain from buying up the peasants' products for sale. They could purchase seed corn or livestock to fatten up on their fields for later sale. This practice would increase the available livestock and would be beneficial for field and meadow. Foreign merchants, native merchants, burghers, craftsmen, and Jewish traders were not to drive about the countryside to buy up from the peasants grain, cattle, flax, hemp, tallow, wax, hops, and other such items. These products were to be brought by the farmers into nearby towns where they could be sold to foreign as well as native dealers (except for wool, hides, flax, and hemp, whose export was forbidden). What the farmer himself needed for his own use he was to buy in the towns. However, if sufficient food and raw materials were not brought into towns by the farmers, then cattle dealers, merchants, butchers, craftsmen, and city dwellers were allowed to go out into the country to buy such items as tobacco, hides, cattle, and grain from the nobles if the sellers would deliver these goods to the town. Fresh fish could be sold either in town or village, but dried or pickled fish had to be brought to town market.

63. "Mandate That Boatmen Should Not Engage in Trading and Peddling," 27 March 1717, *C. C. March.*, vol. 5, pt. 2, sec. 7, no. 10, cols. 515-518.
64. Ibid., no. 11, cols. 517-522.

Fats, hams, sausages, butter, and cheese had to be sold in weekly markets, but again, when quantity was insufficient to meet the needs of the towns-people, dealers were permitted to make purchases directly in the rural areas.

Next, Frederick William required that all nonfarm products were to be sold in the towns by regular retailers either in the market or in the shops. No one coming up the Elbe or Oder rivers from Hamburg or Stettin by land or riverboat was to sell in villages or along the river banks victuals or other retail items. These were to be sold or bought only in towns. House-to-house peddling by persons going from village to village with grocer or draper's goods in wagons or back-packs was forbidden. Bakers living in excise towns, after paying the required tax, could sell their rolls and pretzels in the country. Sievemakers were allowed to sell their products in the villages. All foreign iron-merchants, potters, and victual dealers were to lose their passes or licenses, so as to eliminate illegal trading. All wine, foreign or domestic, was to be sold only in the towns.

To achieve enforcement of this revised edict, Frederick William decreed that in all cases of illegal trading both the seller and the buyer would suffer confiscation of goods and a fine of ten *Reichsthaler* for each *thaler* of traded goods. The zeal of informers was to be whetted by receiving one-third of the fines.

With the more efficient administrative machinery of Frederick William I, with a more effective enforcement officialdom (the *Landrat* [district commissary] in rural areas and the *Steurrat* [tax commissary] in towns), there may have been some improvement in protecting the livelihood of townspeople and the tax receipts of the king. Later edicts, however, make it clear that the forbidden practices persisted. In fact, the types of persons and the goods involved increased in variety. Illegal trading thrived on the desire and support of the populace and the failure of enforcement of existing legislation.

In 1733 Frederick William found that there was much illegal trading and merchandising in victuals, brandy, coffee, tea, tobacco—on land by coachmen and post riders, by freighters, by Jewish peddlers, on water by riverboat and canal barge personnel—to the great loss of toll and excise receipts. The king ordered his many local officials and civil servants to be on the lookout for such peddling and retail evasions in the villages and rural areas, and to prevent such goods from being smuggled into the towns at night. Violations were to be punished by confiscation of goods, horses, carriages, boats, and even with imprisonment.[65] Mere issuance of police regulative edicts for the control of illegal peddling was in effect no solution. Actually, between the edict of 1718 and a revision and re-

65. "Edict against Merchandising in Wares, Victuals, and Beverages in the Villages," 15 July 1733, *C. C. March.*, vol. 5, pt. 2, sec. 1, no. 33, cols. 65-68.

issue of it in 1737, there were any number of edicts against peddling in pots and pans, linens, spices, drugs, by itinerant peddlers. There was increasing emphasis on violations by Jewish dealers, traders, and peddlers.[66]

Enforcement of Police Ordinances

In 1737, as all during his reign, Frederick William I recognized that the basic issue in preventing peddling, illegal retailing outside the framework of the town market, unauthorized craftsmen, and illegal beer-brewing was enforcement of existing police ordinances and electoral and royal edicts. Early in his reign, in September 1713, he had tried to face up to this problem.[67] "Since a number of ordinances, issued by previous rulers, concerning police matters had not been observed, to the harm of the common good, and so that the welfare of the residents of towns and cities be protected, the king has directed that mounted gendarmes [*Ausreuter*] be appointed in the local administrative districts [*Kreise*], dependent for their orders on the General War Commissariat." These police officers were to be sworn in and subordinated to both the central tax commissaries and the local magistrates. Then, the king issued a general instruction for the guidance of these *Ausreuter*. They were to be on the lookout for the illegal consumption of foreign beer or brandy in the countryside, assure that nobles, officials, and clergymen did not sell beer or brandy from their households, that rural brewing of beer for peasant weddings, christenings, and banquets was prosecuted, and that the edict of 24 August 1713 against peddling goods in rural areas, whether by Christians or Jews, was enforced. "Since it would be to the disadvantage of towns to increase the number of craftsmen in the villages, only those tailor or smithy shops that were originally allowed to the villages may continue." In order to prevent domestic competition with guild production, no additional shops of these crafts and no other crafts were to be allowed in the villages. All unauthorized craftsmen in the villages were to be moved to the towns by the police authorities.

Recognizing that the quality of enforcement depended upon the honesty of his officials, and brought up as Crown Prince in an atmosphere of ministerial and bureaucratic corruption, the suspicious king warned the *Ausreuter* that if they connived with peddlers, illegal brewers, and others to violate police ordinances, they would be bodily punished and dismissed from royal service.

This instruction of 1713 takes on special significance because it applied

66. "Renewed Patent against Peddling in Rural Zones," 27 March 1737, *C. C. March.*, vol. 5, pt. 2, sec. 7, no. 20, cols. 527-530.

67. "General Instruction to *Ausreuter* [Gendarmes]," 15 Sept. 1713, *C. C. March.*, vol. 5, pt. 1, sec. 1, no. 17, cols. 97-102.

to all Frederick William's lands and territories, not just the electorate of Brandenburg. It reveals that the police ordinances were applicable throughout the centralized state [*Gesamtstaat*] and were under the jurisdiction of the central General War Commissariat and the provincial commissariats and were to be enforced by the local and royal *Kreiskommissare* (district commissaries).

Twenty years later, in 1733, in an instruction for *Polizei-Ausreuter* in the Neumark and Sternberg (provinces east of the Oder River), we find that the rural gendarmes were subordinate to the *Landrat* and were directed to enforce the brewing edict of 5 February 1714, the edict of 25 April 1718 against hawking and peddling, as well as the edict of 24 April 1720 against the hawking of pills, medicines, and drugs.[68] They were to prevent foreign kettle-menders and tinsmiths from passing through the country. They were to be alert to the presence of unauthorized craftsmen in the villages, including furloughed soldiers. Frederick William's concern for limiting the number of craftsmen in the villages was perhaps less for the purpose of protecting the town guilds than to get maximum return from the excise tax levied on materials used by the craftsmen. Better control was possible in the towns.

The zeal which Frederick William I first displayed in 1713 for enforcing police ordinances throughout his royal territories with effective police officers remained undiminished to the end of his reign. As late as 1735 he showed continued interest in policing the Berlin marketplaces. Berlin was an active inland port for transit trade from the Oder to the Elbe rivers, and it was a city with a large population. The king insisted upon a strict policing of the city's markets for protection of the consumer, the craftsman, and the retailer. In an instruction to the superintendents of police (*Polizei-Meister*) for Berlin on the functions of their office, the superintendents, as officials of the city council, were held responsible for executing and enforcing all city and royal ordinances concerning police matters of all kinds.[69] Among these police matters was the duty of inspecting and supervising the city's special market inspectors. The latter were expected to appear with the break of dawn at the opening of the city gates, on the highways and streets, in order to keep a watchful eye on attempted market forestalling, particularly with respect to grain and other victuals. Purchases by female hawkers and peddlers of food and victuals in the weekly food markets were forbidden until the market flag was lowered, indicating that the city residents had had time to provide themselves with food. The market police were responsible for stationing the farmers' wagons of grain, straw, and hay in their allotted stalls, for keeping the streets open for traffic by requiring the empty carts be parked

---

68. Instruction of 30 Sept. 1733, ibid., no. 24, cols. 111-120.
69. "Instruction for the *Polizei-Meister* of the Royal Residences (Berlin), of the Functions of the Office, etc.," 23 May 1735, ibid., no. 27, cols. 121-130.

in the street gutters close to the street houses. Hawkers and street-criers were to take their places on the corners of the marketplace, streets, or bridges and were not to clog up the passageways between stalls or carts. Peasants and others were to be kept from driving their wagons, carriages, chaises at reckless speeds through the streets. An effort to curb the Berlin jehus, particularly on the crowded streets of market days, had been made in 1732 with little effect.

One of the major concerns of the market police was to prevent peddling and hawking in commodities that competed with local craftsmen or retailers, exceptions being made during the annual fairs. Forbidden hawkers included Jews, Italians, druggists, all hawkers of handcraft goods such as chandlery (small wares), tobacco, tea, brandy, pastries and bread, cheeses and confectioneries. Items that could be peddled included milk, butter, French bread, poultry, game, fresh fish, crabs, fresh vegetables, mops, brooms, quills, shoe polish, old shoes, hats, stockings and clothing, and mousetraps. Scissor sharpeners were permitted to offer their services at the weekly market, as were those in general who cried out their wares in the streets for the convenience of the residents or who did no harm to retailers and craftsmen.

The provisions of the May 23 instruction against hawking apparently were rigidly enforced by the Berlin police. They had been instructed to stop people in the streets if they were carrying wares or goods or appeared to offer services and discover if such persons were licensed. Many Jewish merchants, having legal shops, were being annoyed by zealous police inspectors. So, three months after the instruction was published, the Jewish elders of Berlin asked for a definition of "hawking." It was defined simply as the carrying on or practice of unlicensed trade and exchange. The police were instructed to wait until they saw a suspicious person actually going from house to house peddling and only then to seize the culprit. This, it was argued, would save many innocent persons from annoyance and complaint and would protect shopkeepers who were conducting legitimate trade.[70]

70. "A Declaration Concerning Arts. 9 and 10 of the Police-Superintendents Instruction of 23 May 1735," 19 Aug. 1735, ibid., no. 30, cols. 135-136.

6

Public Works and Urban Development

The chartering of towns and cities in the later Middle Ages created problems of municipal administration, regulation, safety, sanitation, security, and construction which in modern practice would come within the jurisdiction of public works and urban development. The nature of these problems and areas of electoral police regulation were suggested as early as 1515 in the police ordinance of Joachim I for the towns of Brandenburg. The elector imposed upon the magistrates the supervision of town or city walls, bridges, streets, dams, and moats. They were also required to check the administration of poor houses and hospitals as public institutions.[1] In 1540 Margrave John of the Neumark warned all residents of the towns of that territory that those who neglected their houses and yards, or who failed to build on or improve their lots of land within the towns, would be deprived of them.[2] The mayors and town councils were instructed to maintain in good repair the town gates, surrounding houses, walls, moats, wells, and other town buildings.[3]

After the year 1540 the general police ordinances issued by the Brandenburg electors conspicuously omit any provisions concerning town walls, streets, and wells, or houses. Either such provisions were put into separate and distinct directives during the sixteenth century or, one may assume, they were made the complete responsibility of city and town councils and no longer needed specific electoral edicts. It was not until the reign of Elector Frederick William (1640-1688) in the years after the Thirty Years' War that we find a lively and vigorous interest in urban development, house construction, and public works improvements on the part of the Brandenburg rulers. This was as much a matter of the necessity of reconstruction after 1648 as it was an expression of electoral paternalism. Brandenburg had suffered devastation in town and country during most of the war. The troops of Wallenstein, Gustavus Adolphus, the Saxons, and her own undisciplined mercenary troops had pillaged, looted, and seized recruits, not only during campaigns, but also during long periods of military occupation and quartering or garrisoning of troops. Villages, hamlets, towns, and cities had been ruined, much manpower was lost, and many areas had become deserted and overgrown. Reasonable estimates suggest that in 1648 Brandenburg had a population of 200,000, a decline from the 300,000 or more estimated by an electoral adviser in 1564. Berlin

1. *C. C. March.,* vol. 6, pt. 2, app., no. 1, col. 6.
2. *C. C. March.,* vol. 5, pt. 1, sec. 1, no. 1, col. 7.
3. Ibid., col. 18.

declined from a population of approximately 25,000 in late sixteenth century to at most 8,000 in 1648. Frederick William had ambitious plans for the political future of Brandenburg, and he was a product of the age of mercantilism. He was thus moved to rebuild his state, its population, its towns and villages, its wealth and strength by princely regulations.

Frederick William's most urgent desire after the war was to restore devastated areas in town and village. This meant persuading people to settle depopulated areas and restore old or build new houses, and making both rural and urban land once again economically productive. In 1661 he offered various inducements to any persons who would settle permanently and restore certain devastated rural areas, particularly electoral domains and villages. The inducements took the form of exemption from civic burdens for six years: for instance, the land-tax *(Schoss, Kontribution)*, quartering of troops, military service, taxes, and tithes. In addition, those who had served Brandenburg in war (there had been two wars since 1648) would receive free building timber.[4]

In 1667 the elector sought to encourage urban house construction and resettlement. People had been reluctant to take over vacant land or houses because of the high asking price, and because of the demand by city officials for the payment of back taxes on the land. Frederick William now ordered that persons building new houses on vacant city land or repairing vacant houses for permanent residence were to be given such land and houses free of cost and of previous tax delinquency, plus the six years of exemptions granted in 1661.[5] City magistrates were reluctant to grant the proffered exemptions. In a patent of 1669 Frederick William not only ordered the magistrates to honor the exemptions granted in 1661 and 1667, but extended the period of freedom from obligations to ten years.[6]

The efforts of the elector were further impeded by those who tried to abuse the offered exemptions by chicanery or profiteering. Some persons already living in town houses sold these and then erected small shacks on vacant lots, claiming exemption from taxes. Those guilty of such evasion were forced to build good houses along the city street.[7] Others sold the free building timber for a profit. They were forced to pay double and triple the current cost of lumber.[8]

To encourage construction of new houses of good quality, an electoral ruling of 1683 ordered tax collectors to refund 15 percent of each 100 *thaler* of actual cost. This was intended as compensation for payment of excise taxes on building materials. The excise and consumption tax had been introduced into the electoral cities after the edict of 1661, and there

---

4. "Edict on Granting of Six Years' Freedom and Exemption to Those Who Rebuilt Devastated Areas," 19 Jan. 1661, *C. C. March.,* vol. 5, pt. 1, sec. 4, no. 1, cols. 367-368.
5. A patent of 12 April 1667, ibid., no. 2, cols. 367-370.
6. Patent of 4 Oct. 1669, ibid., no. 4, cols. 369-372.
7. Edict of 16 Feb. 1670, ibid., no. 5, cols. 371-374.
8. Edicts of 19 Sept. and 30 Sept. 1670, ibid., no. 6, cols. 373-376.

was a dispute about their inclusion in the tax exemptions for new construction.[9] In 1693 tax exemption was further extended to those who tore down old, unusable houses and replaced them with new houses.[10] In the Duchy of Magdeburg, the police ordinance of 1688 prescribed fireproof building materials (e.g., brick and roof tile) for new construction.[11] It also provided that those who built on deserted building lots or rehabilitated old houses were to be protected in their proprietary rights.

It is not surprising that electoral directives permitting the takeover of vacant building lots or houses by persons who would build on the lots or rehabilitate and live in such town houses would produce conflicts of proprietary interests. In 1709, fifty years after the initial edicts of 1661 and 1667, King Frederick I became concerned about the numerous complaints that litigation over such proprietary claims frequently cost more than the real estate was worth and ruined the burghers who were seeking to make good use of the unoccupied spaces in the towns. Seeking to eliminate or terminate such legal proceedings, the king ordered all town councils in all his provinces to make a register of all built up and all waste (unoccupied) areas in the towns and cities, and to specify, after exact measurement, the width of a lot along the street, its depth, and who the neighbors were.[12] Then, when a person claimed a vacant lot for new construction, he would receive an assignment certificate with the seal of the town council specifying the exact dimensions of the lot and the neighbors bounding that lot. Prior to the granting of the certificate, the neighbors were to be forewarned, and if they made no claim, there would be no basis for suit after the certificate was issued. This patent also noted that in the smaller towns certain burghers or craftsmen undertook to build beyond their means by claiming large lots and building big houses. The king, therefore, ordered that in the lesser towns the larger vacant lots were to be subdivided into two or three lots, except when they were to be used for breweries or inns.

The city which attracted the greatest interest and energy of the Great Elector and his immediate successors was the capital city of Berlin/Cölln. The direct intervention of the sovereign in the sphere of urban development and construction was best exemplified in the growth of the twin cities after 1648 in size, population, number of public buildings, and grandeur. An excellent description of the physical plan of the cities before 1648 is found in Eberhard Faden's study of Berlin during the Thirty Years' War.[13]

9. "Edict Concerning Privileges of Those Who Produce New Construction in the Towns," 2 July 1683, ibid., no. 7, cols. 375–378.
10. Ibid., no. 9, cols. 377–378.
11. *C. C. Magdeb.,* vol. 3, no. 1, chap. 13, pp. 72–73.
12. "Patent on the Assignment of Vacant Places in the Cities—How It Should Be Done," 3 Dec. 1709, *C. C. March.,* vol. 5, pt. 1, sec. 4, no. 19, cols. 387–390.
13. *Berlin im Dreissigjährigen Kriege,* pp. 3–22. Included is a reproduction of Memhardt's plan of Berlin of 1648.

Faden offers a description of the buildings, churches, city halls, the electoral castle, gates, streets, hospitals, and cemeteries. Although the monks of the thirteenth century had introduced the use of brick in Berlin and Cölln, most of the houses constructed prior to 1648 had been built of wood. Major buildings such as St. Nicholas and St. Mary churches of thirteenth-century origin and the electoral castle of the fifteenth century had been built in large part of stone or brick. The second Hohenzollern elector, Frederick Irontooth, laid the cornerstone for the electoral castle in Cölln on 31 July 1443 and occupied it in 1451. This was built of brick. Close by was the Dom, of monkish origin, then serving as the electoral cathedral before becoming a parish church for Cölln. Under Joachim II the castle of Frederick II was completely modified, expanded, and beautified under the influence and direction of Caspar Theiss, the first Renaissance architect of Berlin. The castle received further improvements in the sixteenth century through the efforts of an Italian architect, Count Lynar, and the apothecary wing was added by a Saxon architect Peter Kummer.

During the Thirty Years' War the castle fell into disrepair and had to be rebuilt by Frederick William. It was converted into a grand baroque edifice by Andreas Schlüter, the great architect of Frederick I.

The damage to Berlin is better illustrated by the decline of population and the number of vacant houses. As a result of the war, in 1640, of 845 houses in Berlin 200 stood vacant, and in Cölln 150 of 364 houses were unoccupied as the total population dwindled to about 6,000.[14] Frederick William had been deeply influenced by his three-year stay in Holland (1635-1638). Dutch influence manifested itself in architecture, gardens, parks, and in the building of Oranienburg on the Havel River for his first wife, Louise Henrietta of the House of Orange. With the aid of Johann Georg Memhard, Berlin was converted into a fortress city, was expanded to the West with the Lustgarten, new suburbs, such as Friedrichswerder (1660), Dorotheenstadt (1678), and Friedrichsstadt (planned by Elector Frederick III in 1688). An avenue, Unter den Linden, running west from Cölln across the Hundebrücke (later Castle Bridge) linked the new suburbs of Dorotheenstadt and Friedrichsstadt.

The physical expansion of the city reflected the growth of population. By 1688 there were 18,000 residents in Berlin/Cölln, of whom 4,000 were French Huguenots. By 1713 the population had grown to 60,000. This growth would not have been possible without city planning, without legal provision for taking over vacant houses and for the construction of new houses on vacant lots. New settlers, immigrants who had technical, professional, and intellectual skills, were persuaded to settle in Berlin and other cities by the offer of houses and favorable building terms. Much ef-

14. Edwin Redslob, "Die Städtebauliche Entwicklung Berlins," *Jahrbuch für Geschichte des Deutschen Ostens* 1 (1952): 203-224.

fort was expended to make Berlin clean, safe, and healthy by various police regulations concerning water supply, fireproof construction, street sanitation, and so forth.

Early in the eighteenth century the rapid growth of Berlin/Cölln and the great expansion of both public and private construction created problems which invited royal intervention to prevent urban growth without planning. In May and July of 1710 royal patents forbade absolutely any new construction or alteration of old buildings in the capital cities or their suburbs without the express permission of the building commissioners.[15] And before a license to build was issued by a building commissioner, the commissioner was first to look over the building site, indicate the precise line of the building along the street, and lay down principles of regularity and uniformity in accordance with the architectural characteristics of the city.[16] The prior approval of both the governor and the military commandant of the city was also required. This requirement had to be renewed in 1716 and again in 1717, which suggests that its provisions were not being fully observed.[17]

Under Frederick William I, there was less indication of gentle persuasion or coaxing to fill in open spaces. The rigid control of a centralist government acting through royally appointed officials manifested itself in the area of urban development. This was forcefully expressed in 1720 in a set of instructions issued by the king for the guidance of royal city building inspectors in the middle provinces.[18] These inspectors were assigned to the administrative districts *(Kreise)* established for supervision of city government by the royal *commissarius loci (Steuerrat).*[19] The tax commissary *(Steuerkommissar* or *Steuerrat)* had broad administrative functions associated with tax collection and auditing of town treasury accounts as well as with enforcement of all police ordinances in the towns of his district. The building inspector had a parallel function in the same district, but his responsibilities were limited (as the title suggests) to the problems of building, repairing, and maintaining all treasury and public city buildings, churches, schools, town halls, excise buildings, barracks, toll houses, city walls, bridges, dams, paving, and wells. Whether it was a question of repairing public buildings or erecting new ones, the building inspector was to confer with the tax commissary and with the local town magistrates before preparing an accurate estimate of costs. These estimates for public works in each of his assigned towns were to be forwarded at the end of each year to the local commissary for inclusion in his annual

15. Patent of 14 May 1710, *C. C. March.,* vol. 5, pt. 1, sec. 4, no. 20, cols. 389-390.

16. Patent of 16 July 1710, ibid., no. 21, cols. 389-392.

17. Patents of 4 July 1716 and of 23 Jan. 1717, ibid., nos. 28 and 30, cols. 399-402.

18. "Instruction for the City Building Inspectors Appointed by the King in the Electorate and the Neumark, the Duchies of Magdeburg, Pomerania, and the Principality of Halberstadt," 26 Sept. 1720, ibid., no. 36, cols. 407-410.

19. See Reinhold A. Dorwart, *The Administrative Reforms of Frederick William I of Prussia,* pp. 132-134, 148-150.

report to the General War Commissariat in Berlin. His report explained the necessity of each building and the expected source of the money to defray the cost. Each of these projects was then submitted to the *Oberbaudirektor,* the chief building director, for his opinion. Finally, judgment was made within the General War Commissariat.[20] If the commissariat approved the project, both the chief building director and local tax commissary were notified so that they could cooperate with the building inspector who had originated the recommended project.

In the building of private houses in towns and suburbs, the building inspectors were to assure that established principles and regulations were followed with regard to the architectural or structural uniformity of houses, the landscaping of streets, and fire protection. In essence, they enforced a uniform building code in the royal towns. They were required to check the professional qualifications of the master masons and carpenters and assist the town council in fixing daily wages in the building trades for the protection of the burghers.

The building inspectors in 1720 were further required to complete a plan of each city within their districts. This was to consist of a map of each town or city within the walls, its division into quarters, and the laying out of house plans. They were to survey the fields, meadows, and woodlots outside the town walls. To obtain the required city plans and field sketches, the building inspectors each year were to prepare such maps for at least two cities, with a copy to be deposited in Berlin with the chief building director, to whom all building inspectors were subordinate, making monthly reports of their activities.

It could be said of Frederick William I that he abhorred a vacuum, either of space or of people. Not inappropriately is he called the *Baumeister,* the building master, of the Prussian state. People were the key to all his efforts to build his state. People filled the open spaces with houses, furnished labor for new or expanded city industries or for the reconstruction of villages. People furnished recruits for his army and paid taxes. To encourage the flow of immigrants into his territories, he offered a variety of exemptions and immunities from normal civic burdens and responsibilities. He also offered positive inducements or rewards. In 1719 he offered to foreigners who wished to settle in Prussian cities as bankers, merchants, manufacturers, artists, or craftsmen a 10 percent cash return for either building a new city house on a vacant lot or for rebuilding on the site of an old house torn down for that purpose.[21] So intent was he on

20. In origin the General War Commissariat was an electoral-royal central office concerned with matters of military administration and military revenues. Increasingly it became an office of financial (excise tax) and police administration and supervised municipal administration. It was the principal bureaucratic office for promotion of commerce, industry, and immigration, and also acquired responsibility for city planning, city development, and public works construction. See Dorwart, *Administrative Reforms,* pp. 138-152.

21. "Patent on Privileges for Foreigners Who Settle in Prussia and Practice a Trade," 16 March 1719, *C. C. March.,* vol. 5, pt. 1, sec. 4, no. 34, cols. 405-408.

increasing the number of houses in his cities, particularly the capital cities, that in 1721 we find him complaining that the intention of previous commissions to fill up the empty house lots in the new suburb of Friedrichsstadt was not being achieved. To stimulate new construction in this city, begun by his father in 1688, Frederick William offered inducements to those who would build in Friedrichsstadt.[22] He offered to distribute 10,000 *thaler* in cash to those filling in the vacant lots, in proportion to the value of each house. He further offered the necessary wood, stone, and lime free of cost, and agreed in this case to permit the construction of one-story houses. At the same time, the king served warning to the owners of vacant house lots that if they themselves did not soon begin construction on these lots, he would grant them to others who would build.

A few months later, the king pursued this threat with legislative action.[23] Acting in behalf of his electoral cities, desirous of advancing new construction on vacant places, and eager to provide a sufficient number of skilled craftsmen of all kinds in these cities, Frederick William in late 1721 directed that the owners of vacant house lots who had ignored all previous edicts urging new construction were to lose these lots and all their appurtenances, such as gardens and meadows outside the city walls, and that such land would become public property. This action of the king was less an exercising of the right of eminent domain by compulsory purchase for public use than it was an eighteenth-century anticipation of Henry George's concept of the utilization of undeveloped land for the public interest.

Those who desired to build on these conficated lots were to make a claim with the burgomaster, the excise collector, or the local commissary. They would be given free burgher's and master's rights, if they did not already possess them, and free building timber. To encourage speedy action, further provision for cash rebates of 15 percent, 12 percent, and 8 percent, respectively, were offered if the tile roof was up on the new house by the end of 1722, 1723, or 1724.

The patent of 1721 publicized a long list of towns and cities, listing under each the number of vacant lots available for building as well as the specific type and number of craftsmen lacking in each. Foreign craftsmen who wished to improve their social and economic status by moving into the towns of Brandenburg would of course have motivation to build houses on the vacant lots because of the benefits offered.

The king's goals and objectives were not achieved, as he desired, by a mere waving of his legislative wand. Those interest groups which had failed to respond to electoral and royal prodding about building on vacant spaces were not likely to accept loss of those spaces by royal edict

22. "Patent Concerning the Benefits for Those Who Provide New Buildings in Friedrichsstadt," 23 May 1721, ibid., no. 37, cols. 409-412.

23. "Patent on Furthering of Construction, in the Electoral Cities, of Houses on Vacant Lots . . . ," 20 Nov. 1721, ibid., no. 39, cols. 411-418.

without contest. In October 1722, Frederick William recognized that the surrender of unimproved lots to the public for claiming was being hindered by litigation over titles by the current owners against the new claimants. By a new edict, the king ordered that all transfers of land and title were to be made by proper legal means and that the courts should not accept legal suits or appeals deriving from such change of ownership.[24] Further, any vacant land not claimed by the end of 1722 by private builders was to become public property, and after 1 January 1723 such land was to be leased for cultivation on one-, two-, or three-year contracts, with the rent to be paid into the town treasury. If anyone subsequently claimed a lot under lease, he would be given the house lot, but the lessee would retain the use of all other portions until his contract expired.

Frederick William's building program was made more difficult by the profiteering instincts of his subjects. By 1722 there were numerous complaints about price-gouging by the suppliers of building bricks, roof tiles, and lime; construction costs had risen sharply since 1720. Sometimes prices were actually increased. At other times suppliers delivered short quantities of tiles and bricks while collecting full payment. By a series of edicts between 1722 and 1725, attempts were made to fix prices for roofing tiles, building bricks, and lime.[25]

Royal interest in the improvement of towns and cities, in population expansion, and in house construction continued unabated into the last decade of Frederick William's reign. In 1732 the king was still inviting foreigners to settle down and build houses in Friedrichsstadt.[26] In 1734 he attempted to attract foreign manufacturers and craftsmen to Berlin by offering free grants of a portion of the building materials to those who would build. And if whole colonies of immigrants were interested in settling in one community, he offered to give them an entire street on which to build their houses, while building church and schools for them out of the royal treasury.[27]

After 75 years of encouraging citizens and foreigners to build houses in the towns and cities of Brandenburg-Prussia by three Hohenzollern princes, Frederick William I, by a patent of 29 July 1734, placed a royal seal of legality on all titles and benefits that had accrued to those who had responded by adding to the new construction of buildings in Prussian towns. The patent assured all those who had put up new homes, and had accordingly received titles to the land thus improved, and had benefited by cash rebates and free building materials, that their titles were secure and safe and that all the moneys paid out of the royal treasury to them were gifts and not cash advances to be repaid.[28]

24. Edict of 24 Oct. 1722, ibid., no. 43, cols. 423-424.
25. Ibid., nos. 38, 40, 42, and 46, cols. 411-426.
26. Ibid., no. 52, cols. 431-434.
27. Ibid., no. 54, cols. 433-435.
28. Ibid., no. 53, cols. 433-434.

7

City Sanitation—Streets and Wells

At the same time that Frederick William began to concern himself with building up his devastated and depopulated towns by encouraging the building of new houses on vacant city lots, he expressed an equal interest in improving the internal conditions of his towns, particularly in matters of street sanitation, cleanliness, security, and city wells. His primary interest, like that of his two successors, was in the capital.

In 1660 Frederick William vigorously condemned the conditions he found in Berlin and Cölln. He complained that the wells and streets in the two cities were in sad and dangerous condition. Wells had been dug by his predecessors to supply water in case of fire, and now so much rubbish had been allowed to accumulate around them that they were frequently inaccessible. Wood, lumber, sand, and manure piles clogged the streets so that wagons could hardly pass through, let alone the fireladders and fire-fighting equipment. The city air and streets were polluted by decaying organic matter, animal manure, and free-running pigs, and this might also affect the wells and thus the health of burghers.

Prompted or goaded by this electoral criticism, the burgomasters and city councillors of Berlin and Cölln drew up an ordinance concerning the improvement of wells and streets in their cities and submitted it to Frederick William for approval. He apparently was satisfied with its provisions and merely confirmed it and published it as an electoral ordinance for his capital.[1]

It was estimated in 1660 that there were about 380 private wells in the two cities. The owners were required to keep them in good repair and cleanliness, with a threat of a ten-*thaler* fine for failure to do so. In addition there were a number of public street wells, to furnish domestic water and a source for fire-fighting. The water needs of the electoral castle and household were supplied from a tall water tower located west of the castle in Cölln and filled by pumping from the Spree River. Gravity feed thus supplied running water to the castle.

The public wells were to be kept clean and provided with equipment for drawing water, and each well was to be supplied with a sled and tub ready for use in case of fire. Throwing foreign matter or refuse into the wells was made a crime punishable by jailing, pillorying, and assessment for the costs of cleaning. Anyone caught stealing or tampering with any parts

---

1. "Ordinance Concerning Wells and Streets in Berlin and Cölln," 14 Aug. 1660, *C. C. March.*, vol. 5, pt. 1, sec. 3, no. 1, cols. 313-334.

of the wells (chains, ropes, buckets) would be jailed and punished according to the criminal (*Halsgericht*) ordinance.

Well wardens, appointed for each public well, were responsible for cleaning the well when the water level was low and for checking the condition of the well structure, apparatus, fire tub, and sled.

A required listing of the public wells by streets, and of the houses responsible for maintaining each well, revealed that there were in Berlin and Cölln in 1660 some 52 public street wells. To keep up with the water needs of a growing city, the ordinance required the digging of new wells. To meet the costs of digging, building the masonry structure, and maintaining the public wells, those houses which relied upon a public well for domestic water or for fire protection were to be assessed quarterly at a rate of two *Groschen* (or one if they possessed private wells). The net effect was to increase the supply of potable water within the city limits and to introduce measures of sanitation affecting the water supply and measures of maintenance important to fire-fighting.

Proper maintenance of city streets—their physical condition, cleanliness, sanitation, and usability for city traffic—was also regulated by the ordinance of 1660. Individual property owners were assigned responsibilities, and public officials such as street wardens, street cleaners, market police, dog wardens were all assigned specific tasks aimed at achieving the basic goal of well-ordered streets. Houseowners were required to pave the street (i.e., the walk) the length of their houses up to the street gutter. Each houseowner was expected to keep this area fronting his house clean; no rubbish was to be swept into the gutters. If it was necessary to pile up rubbish, debris, or manure in the streets, the street warden was to be notified immediately so that such material could be carted away without delay. Lumber and other building materials were not to be left lying in the public streets overnight. Heavy planks and beams were not to be dragged through the streets and across pavement. Wagons were to be used for such hauling, and building timber would be confiscated if they were not. Carpenters were forbidden to square beams in the public streets unless the task could be completed in two days and the beams removed from the street. Guards at the city gates were not to permit planks and lumber to be hauled into the cities unless assured that it would not lie in the streets more than two days. Lumber which had been cut and squared outside the gates was not to be brought in until the building was ready for erection. Building contractors were then, as now, frequently guilty of obstructing the streets with lumber and piles of brick or sand and of littering the streets with the debris resulting from construction. This was an important necessary precaution in anticipation of the building boom which Frederick William hoped would fill vacant city lots in the succeeding decades.

The capital cities of Brandenburg in 1660 were little more than oversized agricultural communities. Cattle and sheep were not kept within the city walls because little pasture was available. However, poultry, pigs, and horses were housed. Pigpens often were set up on the streets in front of the houses. The ordinance of 1660 ordered the removal of such odoriferous installations as pigpens and stables from public streets.

The several city marketplaces and the areas around the two city halls also had become a problem. Except at the time of the annual fairs, held twice a year, no one was to erect a permanent retail booth or market stall in these locations. Stalls already erected were to be torn down or removed within three weeks of publication of the 1660 street ordinance. Those who needed stalls or booths for their livelihood during the day were to remove them to their homes at night. But no booths were to be erected immediately in front of or against the *Rathaus* (city hall). Only in the marketplaces were street stalls to be permitted. The erection of unrestricted, permanent retail booths in the free square of the marketplace not only threatened to clutter up the area with unsightly competitors of regular retail shops but would make it difficult for the peasants to set up their wagons at the weekly market.

The elector was also concerned about clean streets and city squares. House servants who cast rubbish, manure, or any kind of dirt in the market squares, in the churchyard, or in the public streets before their house doors on the grounds that the street wardens would clean it up were to be punished with a jail sentence for the first offense, and the pillory for the second. The householder responsible for the guilty servant was to be fined six *thaler* and assessed the cost of cleaning up. It was not uncommon to dispose of rubbish by dumping it on the marketplaces or near the city halls. The market police and the night watch were ordered to apprehend any persons with rubbish to dispose of who were found in the streets leading to such public places.

Each Saturday the city dog warden was to sweep and pile manure, straw, and rubbish in the area before the city halls. Private houseowners were to do the same in the areas before their houses, piling rubbish in the gutters. In the afternoon the street cleaners would collect such piled-up rubbish, ringing a warning bell as the collecting wagon made its rounds. Houseowners paid a fee to the street warden for picking up rubbish. In return for a horse and feed furnished by the elector, the street warden was required to keep the streets clean in front of the royal residence and the city halls. All accumulated rubbish and waste collected by the city street-cleaning department was disposed of outside the city limits.

Frederick William displayed a rather harsh interest in beautifying the cities. Mere cleanliness was not enough. He wanted to preserve the little greenery which could be found in the form of trees and grapevines planted in front of the city houses. Any person caught in an attempt to cut down such trees was to have his fist cut off. This was the man who later in his reign planted the linden trees and laid out the avenue famous in Berlin history as "Unter den Linden."

Not all citizens met the responsibilities described in the 1660 street ordinance. Those who neglected to keep the area of the street fronting their houses free of rubbish and unclean matter were threatened with military compulsion. Fear was expressed of the danger of unclean air and contagious disease resulting from accumulated filth in the streets.[2] By 1676-1680 the initiative was taken not by the city magistrates but by the privy council of the elector. The responsibilities of property owners to keep the streets clean in front of their houses and to leave no rubbish in the gutters overnight was given renewed emphasis in a street ordinance of 1 May 1680.[3] Some of the problems of street sanitation derived from the unclean if convenient habit of the citizens of relieving themselves in the streets or against the city walls or emptying night pans in the streets. Guilty persons were threatened with being placed in the city pillory. It was still necessary to forbid builders and craftsmen using lumber in their shops to store this material in the streets. Proprietors who failed to pave half the street in front of their houses would find it done at public cost with these costs collected from the proprietor by military force.

To the end of the century it was necessary to repeat the street ordinances requiring houseowners to keep the streets clean and swept. An edict of 1691 required the removal of privies from the passages between houses.[4] In the earliest form of city house construction, narrow passages existed between houses, and rain water drained from the gabled roofs into these passages, thus creating a health problem if privies were located here instead of in the backyards. Later construction eliminated these passages; houses along a street were built against each other, with the roofs sloping into the streets.

Another area of uncleanliness and pollution that attracted royal attention was the Spree River and canals passing through Berlin/Cölln. Ordinances of 1704 and 1707 forbade the throwing of rubble and rubbish into the river and canals by persons with houses along these waterways.[5] Wood lying in the water of the canals before the various water-driven mills was to be removed to safeguard the mills. Washing benches put up along the banks of river and canals without written permission were ordered removed. These benches were utilized for washing clothes but frequently interfered with commercial use of the waterways. A *Strohm-Meister* (river inspector) was made responsible for compelling proprietors facing the river area to clean out the obstructing fill. Various craftsmen, tanners, butchers, and fishmongers frequently polluted the river.

2. Ibid., nos. 2 and 3, cols. 335-336, edicts of 24 Sept. 1676 and 15 Sept. 1679.

3. "Ordinance on Keeping the Streets of Berlin Clean," 1 May 1680, ibid., no. 4, cols. 335-338. On 20 November this ordinance was extended by edict of the privy council to the suburb of Friedrichswerder.

4. Ibid., no. 10, cols. 347-348.

5. Patent of 16 July 1704, ibid., no. 12, cols. 349-352; ordinance of 27 Oct. 1707, ibid., no. 14, cols. 355-356.

Dissatisfied with the state of street cleanliness, in 1707 King Frederick I issued a new street ordinance for his capital cities.[6] He published a schedule according to which the city streets were to be kept clean. On Mondays and Thursdays the whole of Berlin, including the dairy market (*Molken-markt*), the nearby fish market, and the mill dam area, was to be swept down by houseowners or assigned street cleaners; on Tuesdays and Fridays the cities of Cölln and Friedrichswerder were to be swept; on Wednesday, the suburb cities of Dorotheenstadt and Friedrichsstadt; and on Saturday, the avenues and squares around the royal residence. In the summer, with dry weather causing the raising of dust, the ground was to be sprinkled before sweeping. Market areas near the river could easily be washed down and scrubbed. Accumulated rubbish was to be piled up in front of the houses, but not in the gutter, and only on rubbish-collection days. Negligent private owners who failed to sweep their areas were to be fined six *Groschen* and pay the cost of one *Groschen* for a prisoner who came to sweep. Persons who were serviced by vendors' wagons and carts at their doors were responsible for cleaning up any debris left in front of their houses. If there was room, horses and oxen were to be tethered in house yards and not in the streets. Those who kept horses stabled in their yards and carried away the manure and straw were to make certain that enroute from the city they did not litter the streets. Market police were to keep the marketplaces clean by requiring the fishwives and sellers of vegetables to clean up their refuse at the end of the day.

An increasingly serious problem with the growth of the capital cities was the disposal of human filth. To avoid the stench of emptied nightpans and pots, city authorities were directed to install more privies or to assure that night soil was carried off regularly at night by "night women" who received a fee from each house so serviced. These "sanitation women" were also responsible for removing any filth dumped into the streets or marketplaces and were paid for this by the city council. Various designated areas of the Spree River were assigned as disposal places for the collected night soil.

For a quarter of a century the provisions of the ordinance of 1707, including its schedule of sweeping and collecting, were the basis of keeping the Berlin streets clean. However, in 1735 Frederick William I complained that the city streets were not clean enough. While retaining many of the 1707 provisions, he modified or expanded the former ordinance to include other areas of regulation. His first concern was to order a daily sweeping routine and the purchase of more collection carts. As a result, twenty-eight trash-collection carts were made available with an increased number of street cleaners to pick up the sweepings and the rubbish put out each morning by the houseowners. A special commission,

6. "Street Ordinance for the Capital," 3 May 1707, ibid., no. 13, cols. 351-356.

the *Gassen-Fuhrwercks-Commission* (Street Sanitation Carts Commission), was attached to the city government to supervise the task of keeping the streets clean. With almost military organization, the several cities making up the capital were divided into eight districts. The twenty-eight sanitation wagons and their crews were assigned to specific numbered districts. All the streets were numbered 1 to 8, and the number painted on the street sign or a corner lamp post. The carts were assigned numbers 1 to 8, so that carts numbered "1" collected rubbish in all streets numbered "1," and so on. Berlin and NeuCölln were assigned one street superintendent, eight carts, eight carters, and four loaders. Numbers "1" to "3" were assigned to streets and carts in this municipal area. Cölln (the old city) and Friedrichswerder were assigned the same number of carts and personnel, and the numbers "4" and "5." Dorotheenstadt and Friedrichsstadt were assigned two street superintendents, twelve carts, twelve carters, six loaders, and the numbers "6," "7," and "8."

These street carts were used in winter months to haul away snow and ice. But when they were unable to cope with this task, the individual property owner was made responsible for snow removal in front of his house.

Other responsibilities were assigned. The public hangman was to dispose of any carrion reported lying in the street. Police and market and street inspectors were to check for damaged siderails and chains on all bridges. The night watch were to protect wells, street lanterns, and the linden trees against vandalism or other damage. Concerned about the personal injuries suffered by the city residents, particularly children, who were frequently run over by recklessly driving peasants (primarily on market days), the king made reference to his edict of 12 February 1732 which ordered all sentries, road police, and market and street inspectors to arrest such rustic jehus and to deliver them to the military government for punishment.[7]

7. "Street Regulation Concerning Keeping the Streets Clean in the Royal Residences," 3 Sept. 1735, ibid., no. 16, cols. 357-366.

Part III

The Unprivileged and the Underprivileged Society

III

The Unprivileged and the Underprivileged Society

Long before (and for that matter long after) it became a "self-evident truth" that all men are born free and equal, another truth equally self-evident had determined the structure of Western society. Society in the feudal-manorial world was corporately organized, and each individual acquired legal status according to the corporate group of which he was a part. He owed obligations, he performed duties, he was entitled to privileges, services, exemptions, according to his social status. In the later Middle Ages, changing historical conditions introduced social groups that were not associated with a landed economy, but which acquired corporate recognition and legal status. By the sixteenth century the older traditional society composed of the clergy, landholding nobility, and peasants (free or serf) acquired the addition of townspeople engaged in commerce, trade, banking, and industrial crafts as well as those identified with university life and professional activities. Church, fief, manor, university, merchant and craft guilds, all gave social status with legal or traditional definition of the privileges or disabilities of each corporate group. This was evident, for instance, in princely efforts to preserve social distinctions through sumptuary legislation or to protect burgher economic interests against encroachment by nobles and clergy.

However, there were social elements or groups which did not enjoy corporate or legal existence, which had no status. These groups lived in a world of shadows, sometimes tolerated, sometimes prosecuted, generally representing an unprivileged or underprivileged segment of European society, in the Middle Ages and in the early modern period. There were the wayfarers, vagabonds, beggars, lawless ones. There were the pilgrims, unemployed soldiers of the new armies, gypsies, and Jews. Runaway serfs, unruly apprentices, and university students often added to the problems created by this social mélange. The public welfare, preservation of peace and order on highways, in villages and towns, and the social welfare of unfortunate individuals all required the exercise of the police power of the state or of the paternalistic prince.

8

Wayfaring Life in Electoral Brandenburg

There probably is no better general term than that of "wayfarer" to describe the great variety of mobile persons who wandered about the countryside with no apparent legitimate purpose or function. Some were innocent and harmless; most of them had a tendency to be knavish, thieving, or violent. There were rogues and vagabonds, paupers and beggars, mendicant friars, highway robbers, quacks of all kinds, unemployed common soldiers. Practically all of them were mischief-makers. All of them sought to keep alive without honest work and thus became a burden and a menace to the peaceful and privileged portions of society. There were, of course, the legitimate traveler, the merchant, those on the prince's business. With these wayfarers we are not here concerned.

Closely associated with the problems created by the wayfarers was a basic social problem of poverty. Not all of the poor were shady characters living on the edge, at best, of the law. There were widows, orphans, the aged, the infirm, the maimed, the innocent victims of war and economic change who had a legitimate claim on the charity of local communities. These frequently became beggars but rarely itinerant beggars. Poor relief as such was distinct from the concern for those who were too lazy to work, who were vagrants and knaves by preference and profession. The latter relied upon thievery, treachery, and deceit and were guilty of preying upon the gullibility of both peasants and burghers. The police power of the state was exercised both to protect the individual citizen against the knavery and quackery of vagabonds, rogues, and professional beggars, and to provide some form of poor relief.

The early sixteenth century produced a most interesting and revealing literary mirror of vagabondage in the later Middle Ages and at the time of the Lutheran Reformation. The *Liber Vagatorum: Der Bettler Orden* first appeared about 1509, under an Augsburg imprint, and ran through eighteen editions before Martin Luther wrote a preface for it in 1528.[1] It offers illuminating information about the types, the manners, and the customs of the vagabond population of Central Europe before the Reformation. It presents a useful glossary of the special jargon used by German vagrants, not always a respectable vocabulary. This *rotwelsche Sprache* (beggar welsh or rogues' cant) was partly derived from wandering, mendicant monks and wandering students. Latin and

---

1. *The Book of Vagabonds and Beggars: With a Vocabulary of Their Language,* ed. Martin Luther, trans. John C. Hotten; also *The Book of Vagabonds and Beggars with a Vocabulary of Their Language, and a Preface by Martin Luther* (1528), ed. D. B. Thomas.

Hebrew supplied most of the strange, outlandish words of the German beggars' lingo. The vocabulary peculiar to the vagabonds of this period reveals the great variety of rogues who wandered about Central Europe. There were *stabeylers* (professional beggars with families), *kleuckner* (who sat at churchyards and fairs with broken legs and limbs, sometimes self-inflicted or merely feigned), *grantner* (claiming to be affected by falling sickness, using soap to froth at the mouth), *kammesierer* (young students "working their way through college" who became tramps and beggars using forged licenses), *schlepper* (*kammesierer* who pretended to be priests begging for the support of their nonexistent churches or altars), *vagierer* (beggars in yellow garments who claimed to know the black art which enabled them to exorcise the devil who brought hail and storm or by witchcraft could produce rain; they preyed upon the farmer). Some of this class were simply cheats and deceivers (quack doctors and peddlers of charms and pills), some were thieves (the gypsy type), and some were not above violence on the highways or in the villages.

Vagabondage has a long history in Western Europe. Charlemagne (789) legislated against the "mangones et cogciones qui sine omni lege vagabundi vadunt [waremongers and hucksters who went about freely as vagabonds]" practicing their deceptions on all men. It was not until the centuries following the Crusades, however, that there was a significant increase in a footloose, mobile population which sought to live by its wits on the fringe of respectable society. By 1250 vagabondage was already organized on a large scale, and by 1400 it had become a regular business east of the Rhine. Since individual charity had been regarded as a religious obligation, unregulated almsgiving (as distinguished from organized care of the poor by monasteries, e.g.) was shared by crusaders, pilgrims, wandering students, and mendicant monks. This in turn encouraged imposters and deceivers who fattened on the "credulous charity of country-folk." In the fifteenth century large numbers of gypsies began to appear in Germany; they were to attract penal legislation in Prussia as late as the eighteenth century.

Germany in the sixteenth century was the scene of considerable violence manifested in various forms. Social unrest erupted violently on several occasions, culminating in the Peasants' Revolt of 1525. The frequent wars (political, religious, social) produced unemployed soldiers and thousands of war victims who turned to begging and to violence. The Reformation spawned a form of radical Christian socialism which in turn engendered a violent reaction from conservative Reformers. The spirit of violence found outlets in anti-clericalism, anti-Semitism, anti-feudalism, and anti-modernism. There were many types of uprooted, dislocated, itinerant persons from robber barons, "emancipated" monks, runaway serfs, and war veterans to innocent victims of social and economic distress. The latter were forced to turn to begging.

In the fourteenth and fifteenth centures, German towns first took notice of the social problems created by vagabonds, beggars, gypsies, and
medicant monks. Municipal legislation was particularly aimed at those
vagrant wayfarers who turned into felons. The author of the *Liber Vagatorum* purposefully bared the vagabond as a rogue and deceiver. Luther's
preface to the 1528 edition marked the real starting point of systematic
legislative measures directed against vagrancy and vagabondage in Germany. He argued that "every town and village should know their own
paupers . . . and assist them. But as to outlandish and strange beggars
they ought not to be borne with."[2]

By midcentury the problems of vagrants, vagabonds, and beggars assumed such grave proportions that both national and territorial legislative efforts were made to suppress criminous wayfarers. The Augsburg
Reichstag of 1548, in an imperial police ordinance, took cognizance of
the problem of regulating the behavior of mendicants, vagrants, gypsies,
and *ociosis* (the idle and unemployed).[3] However, there was no imperial
enforcement machinery to make this *Polizeiordnung* effective. Its real
significance was in serving as a legislative model for territorial ordinances.

As early as 1540, the brothers Joachim II and Margrave John were
forced to take action. John was disturbed by the felonious activities of
gypsies and foreign beggars in the Neumark. The strange ways of the
gypsies, as much as their traditional reputation as thieves, made them
targets of abuse. They and foreign beggars were to be driven out of the
Neumark, presumably into Poland.[4] Only the native poor were allowed
to beg, and then only on Sundays in front of the local churches.

In Brandenburg proper, Elector Joachim II issued a penal mandate
"Ordinance against Violence [Ordnung wider die Plackerei]" of 22
March 1540 against beggars in general but in particular against the begging and violence of discharged *Landsknechte* (unemployed soldiers).[5] All
law enforcement officers in Brandenburg were warned to prevent disturbing of the peace by blackguards, robbers, and other suspicious evildoers. This 1540 mandate was primarily directed against the more dangerous and violent type of wayfarer. This was spelled out more distinctly in an "Edict against Strange Beggars and Vagabonds" of July
1565.[6] Joachim II particularly singled out the *Landsknechte*. When these
soldiers were not occupied in the wars of Charles V against the king
of France, or the Pope, or the Turks, they frequently moved about in

2. I am indebted to the Introduction to Thomas, *Book of Vagabonds,* for some of these
thoughts.

3. "Charles V. His Imperial Majesty's Reform of the Empire, published for the public
good in the Imperial Meeting, A.D. 1548 [Caroli V. Imperatoris Augusti Reformatio Politiae
Imperialis, Pro bono publico edita in Comitiis Augustanis, A.D. MDXLVIII]," *Collectio
Constitutionum Imperialium,* ed. Melchior Goldast, pt. 2, chaps. 26 and 27.

4. *C. C. March.,* vol. 5, pt. 1, sec. 1, no. 1, col. 13.

5. *Kurm. Ständ. Joach.,* vol. 1, no. 15B, pp. 78-81.

6. *C. C. March.,* vol. 5, pt. 5, sec. 1, no. 1, cols. 1-4.

small groups causing mischief or violence. Thieving, begging, and coercing peasants were among their lesser crimes. On other occasions they engaged in highway robbery using their numbers and military weapons to victimize merchants and highway travelers. The edict of 1565 ordered local, noble landowners to arrest troublesome soldiers. If they were unable to do this alone, then they were to ring the church bells, raise hue and cry in neighboring villages, set up roadblocks, and hunt down the criminals until they were caught and punished.

Under the guise of begging, many strangers had entered the lands of the Hohenzollern elector, committing deeds of violence. Local authorities were ordered to halt the begging and to drive the strangers out of Brandenburg. Possession of muskets by wayfarers, other than legitimate merchants and travelers, was forbidden. Nevertheless, near the end of his reign, in 1567, Joachim II complained that violence and lawlessness continued to prevail because the criminous wayfarers were sheltered and aided by the local populace.[7] This would be a frequent deterrent to effective enforcement of penal laws.

In the following reign, Elector John George, in 1572, again made it clear that violence on the Brandenburg highways continued unabated and undeterred by previous edicts of electors and emperors.[8] The greatest danger still came from the unemployed *Landsknechte,* armed as they were with muskets. To combat this widespread danger more successfully, Elector John George and neighboring princes agreed on common security measures and cooperative efforts to suppress the increasing wave of violence and robbery. The edict of 1572 published the Nordhausen agreement in Brandenburg.

Essentially the edict attempted to enforce a close surveillance of all strangers and travelers. It sought to achieve the kind of police control over travelers and strangers registering in public places which later passport or domestic identification papers would expedite. Overnight guests taken into a private home had to be reported to local police officials, with names and descriptions provided. Identical requirements were made for strangers who stopped at public inns and inquired about wagons, carts, and horses. Saddlers and musketmakers were to report any strangers bringing in work for them. Footloose soldiers and masterless servants were to be denied accommodations in villages. At times of fairs and markets or in the vicinity of major trading centers, river passes, fords, and bridges were to be guarded against the passing of suspicious persons.

When an act of violence occurred on the highways or villages, hue and cry was to be raised in all surrounding villages, and immediate pursuit

7. Ibid., no. 2, cols. 3-6.
8. "Edict against Highwaymen, Incendiaries, Suspicious Loiterers, and Unemployed Servants," ibid., no. 3, cols. 5-10.

on horse and foot was to follow until the criminals were captured. If the latter crossed territorial boundaries, hot pursuit was to be continued, with the aid of local personnel. The provision for hot pursuit, agreed on at Nordhausen, must be judged in the light of Germany's atomized political structure.

Between 1572 and 1624 a series of princely edicts and mandates, promulgated to curb violence and mischief, only emphasized the failure to combat crime among the various types of violent wayfarers. Vagabonds and beggars,[9] *Landsknechte,* extorters, beggars, and loose rogues,[10] soldiers and gravediggers,[11] gypsies,[12] incendiaries,[13] unemployed servants, all attracted the legislative attention of the elector. There was much evidence that those criminals were aided, concealed, and fed by local people —whether out of fear or sympathy is not clear. The gypsies were defined as a thieving, robbing people to whom all evil persons attached themselves and who joined in preying upon the helpless peasants. The legislation was always aimed at the wandering, unemployed, idle elements who lived by violence and extortion, abusing the village people or the innocent travelers on the highways.

During the Thirty Years' War, at least after 1624, Brandenburg, despite weak efforts to follow a policy of neutrality, was exposed to a more organized form of violence in the form of armies living off the land. Edicts against vagabonds, beggars, and marauding soldiers would have been empty gestures.

Not until after the war did the new elector, Frederick William, resume the penal legislation against unlawful wayfarers. An edict against gypsies of 3 January 1663 took note of the fact that since 1648 many unemployed servants, passing themselves off as gypsies, had formed in packs attracting the scum of the countryside, and armed with muskets they intimidated the people and extorted wealth from them.[14] This edict again referred to the law of the Holy Roman Empire which declared gypsies to be a thieving, robbing people who were not to be tolerated within the empire and were to be driven out wherever they might be found. It is reasonable to assume that "gypsies" was an inclusive term referring as much to domestic evildoers as to genuine gypsies. Edicts against vagabonds, beggars, and gypsies coming into Brandenburg and causing considerable mischief continued to be issued by Frederick William in 1670, 1672, 1682, and 1684. The rural gendarmes were ordered to take these people to the borders of the Mark and to evict them. But there always seemed to be more, even pushing into the capital cities of Berlin and Cölln.

9. Ibid., no. 4, cols. 9-12, edict of 1573.
10. Ibid., no. 5, cols. 11-16, edict of 1574.
11. Ibid., nos. 6 and 7, cols. 15-20, edicts of 1584 and 1589.
12. Ibid., no. 8, cols. 19-20, mandate of 26 April 1590.
13. Ibid., no. 9, cols. 19-22, mandate of 1 Aug. 1590.
14. Ibid., no. 19, cols. 37-40.

A new policy was adopted in 1687. Loiterers, beggars, and the suspicious idle, capable of working and spinning, were put to work. Those who resisted were to be placed in prisons or houses of correction for the benefit of manufacturers.[15] The elector referred to his manufacturing edict of 30 March 1687 which recognized that the advancement of wool weaving was held back mostly by the lack of spinners. Perhaps influenced by the French efforts under Mazarin and Colbert, the electoral edict of 1687 established in the central Hohenzollern provinces of Brandenburg, Pomerania, Magdeburg, and Halberstadt, prisons, spinning houses, and houses of correction to which all idle, loose, and unmarried women as well as beggars capable of work were to be driven and taught how to spin. Widows and other unemployed women were not to be allowed "to sit on their hands" but were required to spin yarn for the wool weavers. Wages of spinners were fixed by law, and both spinners and wool manufacturers were forbidden to evade the fixed wage scale. This mercantilistic effort to put the idle to some useful work may have alleviated the problem of poverty and begging, but it did not affect the criminal wayfarer on the highways.

Perhaps as early as 1648, the strong and effective leadership and administration, particularly the military reforms, of Frederick William had solved one serious problem which had plagued Brandenburg as well as most of Germany since the early sixteenth century—that of the bands of unemployed, mercenary soldiers who turned into brigands. The founding of the Prussian standing army, with better discipline, regular pay, and efficient administration, reduced this nuisance.

The problem of gypsies and beggars remained, however. Elector Frederick III in 1691 admitted that in spite of all past edicts against the presence of gypsies in the land, many were still to be found who broke into the homes of peasants and stole goods, who somehow acquired passes and certificates of their good conduct while being guilty of much thievery. The elector's subjects were forbidden to give shelter or food or to issue passes to gypsies, and they were called upon to assist in driving these undesirables out of the land.[16] This edict, applicable in Brandenburg, was extended to Magdeburg in 1698.[17]

By the end of the seventeenth century, the Hohenzollern electors began to follow Luther's admonition of 1528 to distinguish between local or domestic paupers and the foreign beggars. The former were to be cared for by some means of state poor relief, while the latter were not to be tolerated in Hohenzollern lands. The increasing concern for the care and support of the poor, on the part of the first two Prussian kings, Fred-

15. Ibid., no. 25, cols. 43-46, edict of 2 June 1687.
16. Ibid., no. 26, cols. 45-46, "Edict against Gypsies," of 12 Jan. 1691.
17. *C. C. Magdeb.*, pt. 1, no. 16, ". . . auch die Ziegeuner im Lande nicht zu dulden [gypsies are not to be tolerated in the land]."

erick I (1701-1713) and Frederick William I (1713-1740), may well have reflected the growing influence and example of the Pietists of the city of
Halle. As poor relief became better organized and state controlled, a distinction was made between those who were poor in spite of themselves
and those who were beggars by preference. This distinction appeared clearly in an electoral edict of 1696 which was designed to curb unbridled
begging and the growth in the number of idle persons.[18]

The need for distinguishing between idle beggars and the genuine
paupers was a sad reflection on the existing system of poor relief.[19] Prior
to the Reformation, begging had not been considered dishonorable.
Churchmen, for example, engaged in the practice. The Church and the
guilds had offered alms and relief to the poor, the sick, and the old. But
there was no program for the care of the poor, only distribution of alms.
After the Reformation, with the property and pious foundations of the
Roman Church confiscated in Brandenburg, poor relief was made a parish
responsibility, with poor boxes placed in each church to collect contributions from the pious.

The inadequacy of the poor boxes led to an ordinance for the poor and
beggars of 1596 which was the first serious effort at regulating poor relief
for all the various sorts of impoverished persons. Effective for a century, it
in part solved the poverty problem by permitting begging by destitute
persons, while attempting to control abuse of begging by vagabonds,
rogues, and cheats. In reality, the poor and the beggars were placed on the
same plane.

In the second half of the seventeenth century, the numbers of the poor
and of beggars increased. The fast-growing capital of Berlin/Cölln
acquired more than its share and was unable to cope with the problem,
particularly with the aggressive beggars who were little more than thieves.
This situation led to a series of legislative acts by Frederick III designed to establish a state-supervised anti-poverty program, and to separate permanently the basic issue of poor relief as social welfare from
the criminal issue of vagabondage and "professional" beggars. The problem was first attacked in Berlin. On recommendation of an electoral investigating commission of 1693, a "General Poor Fund" was established
for Berlin in 1695. The needy would receive charity or welfare grants, according to established need, by reporting weekly to the Berlin city hall.
Weekly collections were expected to keep the General Poor Fund (distinct from the parish poor boxes) solvent. The elector made a large contribution to establish the fund. Equally important was the electoral ap-

18. *C. C. March.*, vol. 5, pt. 5, sec. 1, no. 28, cols. 47-50, "Edict against Gypsies and
Foreign Beggars, as well as Care for the Poor in the Land, and That One Should Distinguish
between Refugees and Exiles on the One Hand and Malicious Beggars on the Other," of
10 April 1696.

19. See Felix Stiller, "Das Berliner Armenwesen vor dem Jahre 1820," *Forschungen
zur Brandenburgischen und Preussischen Geschichte* 21 (1908): 175-197, for a fuller
description of poor relief in Berlin and Brandenburg after the Lutheran Reformation.

pointment, in April 1699, of a Permanent Commission for Poor Relief, to organize and supervise a poor relief program for Berlin.[20] The city government was unable to handle the large number of homeless vagrants, beggars, orphans, invalids, and poor roaming the streets of Berlin. This commission of seven, including the Pietist preacher Philip Spener, was to direct the anti-poverty program, while city officials administered the actual poor relief.

Further legislation in 1703 converted the Commission for Poor Relief into a Directory for the Poor, with its functions and responsibility detailed in separate ordinances for family welfare, for orphans, for the old, sick, and infirm, for treatment of prisoners in jail, and for the mentally sick.[21] The legislation of 1703 determined the pattern of poor relief for Berlin and Prussia until the nineteenth century. It required the poor, who wanted aid, to register with the Poor Relief Directory. The applicant was then investigated by the directory staff to determine his personal and economic circumstances, and thus the extent of his need for poor relief. The problem was to screen out the frauds who claimed public charity. The goal was to provide family welfare aid, for those not cared for in orphanages and hospitals, out of the General Poor Fund. In this manner, it was hoped, a direct attack would be made on begging and the evils associated with it, by establishing a state-controlled poor relief program of a more humanitarian nature.

The edict of April 1696 made the first serious effort to combat the growing number of beggars by introducing a program of aid to the poor and work or exile for the beggars. Those who applied for poor relief from the General Poor Fund were to be offered work, if they were capable. Most of the applicants offered all kinds of pretexts, or feigned illnesses, to avoid work. Young and strong women covered themselves with rags and brought small children with them to prove their need. Many of these women preferred to run out into the countryside and there join up with unemployed servants. They preferred to beg rather than earn an honest living. Not only were they molested by the villagers, but they frequently engaged in shameful activities in the local inns. Faced with this situation, Elector Frederick III, acting out of "paternalistic concern" for the welfare of his subjects, prescribed a number of statutory remedies. As Luther had suggested, and as English poor relief required, the edict of 1696 placed the responsibility upon each local, rural (village) authority to provide poor relief for those beggars who were born within such jurisdiction and who were unfit for any work, so that such social unfortunates would no longer have to beg. If by chance the number of poor in a given governmental unit was too large, then several neighboring villages and

20. *C. C. March.*, vol. 1, pt. 2, no. 67, cols. 127-130.
21. "Interim Poor Ordinances for the Royal Residences of Berlin, Cölln, Friedrichswerder, Dorotheen- und Friedrichs-Stadt," ibid., no. 73, cols. 133-146.

towns were to combine their resources and cooperate. Almsgiving as a Christian obligation, while still urged and practiced, was now really replaced by public charity and state-supported poor relief.

Foreign beggars were not to be allowed to cross Brandenburg's borders but were to be turned back with a *viaticum* (handout). Those who resisted were to be threatened with prison and forced labor. However, those foreigners who were obviously victims of war and fire should be given public relief. Traditionally, the borders of Hohenzollern territory were open to refugees and exiles, except that the edict noted that refugees from the Palatinate (victims of the wars of Louis XIV), from France (Huguenots), from Switzerland and Silesia seldom included paupers and beggars.

In the cities, the magistrates were ordered to make adequate provisions in hospices for the care of beggars so that these persons would not be compelled to seek alms by begging in the countryside. The preachers were to make reports to electoral inspectors of any failure by city magistrates to provide this poor relief, and the inspectors in turn made regular reports to the Berlin consistory.

Strong and healthy beggars as well as mature children who were capable of earning their bread by spinning or other work were to be taken off the city streets and put to work. They were to be placed in the spinning house at Spandau or similar establishments for spinning wool yarn or other manufacturing.

Local governments which were responsible for the care of beggars in their jurisdictions were forbidden to evade this responsibility by giving passes to beggars to go elsewhere. Since gypsies belonged to the world of the idle and beggars, no passes issued to them for travel through Brandenburg were to be honored by local authorities.

Innkeepers and publicans were not to put up strangers for more than one night without reporting them to the local authorities.

The basic purpose of this edict, the elector stated, was to prevent idleness (and mischief) among all beggars who were fit to work by putting them to work, thereby eliminating, it was hoped, all the evil which stemmed from begging and wandering around the land.

Local law enforcement agencies in town and country were ordered to see that the provisions of this edict were enforced. In turn the elector's representatives, the district commissaries (*Kreiskommissare*) in the country and the tax commissaries (*Steuerkommissare*) in the cities, were to consult regularly with the local magistrates to see if this was being done.

Only two years later, in 1698, the elector complained that the provisions of the edict of 1696 were not being carried out at the local level, that no steps had been taken to care for the poor, and that the number of beggars in Brandenburg had increased. Frederick III, after many decades of failure, took a realistic legislative approach to the problem of vagabondage, criminous or otherwise. He separated the paupers and beggars from the footloose rogues, and then he separated the beggars who could work but would not from those who would but could not. Genuine poor relief for the latter would take them off the streets and highways, and workhouses would diminish the opportunity for mischief among the vagabond beggars. But these legislative efforts got mired in the indifference or neglect of enforcement (*ins stecken gerathen*). Poor relief for the unfortunate and police enforcement for the criminal sector cost money. The police power of the state when exercised for the good of the individual by coercing society in general to achieve sanitation, to relieve poverty, to foster economic welfare, and so on, almost consistently in history fails or falters, because the state in the abstract attempts to do things which the more affluent society in reality feels is not its burden. Recognizing that the failure of his program to care for the poor and to keep out foreign sturdy beggars and gypsies stemmed from improper enforcement of his 1696 edict by local magistrates, Frederick issued a new edict in November 1698.[22] He decreed that as often as they failed to observe the 1696 edict, the magistrates in the cities should be fined 5, 10, 20, or more *Reichsthaler*. They must, he ordered, in proper time make sufficient provision for the care of their poor. And so that the alms would be paid out properly both in amount and on time and the need of the poor be properly met, he directed that in all his Brandenburg towns, inspectors should be appointed on a rotating basis to serve for a year or two at a time without pay, so that the commission would have one Lutheran preacher, a representative of town government, and one representative of the burghers. The central agents, the *Steuerkommissare,* in turn were to watch over the local inspectors. The edict likewise decreed that the nobles and the *Kreiskommissare* in the rural areas should be penalized with the same fines as the city magistrates if they failed to provide care for the poor in their jurisdiction.

The elector further stated that since experience had shown that beggars, even when they received relief in the cities, would still go out into the country to beg, monthly announcements forbidding this practice were to be made from the pulpits. Rural gendarmes, when they met up with such beggars, were to pick them up and take them for punishment to the location from which they had received their alms. They were to be punished by jail or other similar penalty or transferred to the elector so that they could be sent to the spinning house at Spandau. If any runaway apprentices were found among the itinerant beggars, they were to be returned to their guilds, or, if they resisted, were to be turned over to the local militia for military service.

The new edict (1698) again directed that no foreign beggars were to be allowed to pass the borders, except for war refugees or those who had

22. *C. C. March.,* vol. 5, pt. 5, sec. 1, no. 29, cols. 49-52.

been burned out. However, since some of these fugitives or exiles used their certificates for three or four years to collect alms, and even sold such documentary evidence of their need, issuing authorities were ordered to limit the validity of such certificates in Brandenburg to one year.

As for gypsies, "the worst of the lot," who were to be arrested on sight, they roamed about unmolested. So villagers were forbidden to permit these people to stop overnight but instead were to drive them to the borders. Militia commanders were ordered to assist in this whenever the villagers requested aid.

Whether or not the edicts concerning poor relief were more actively enforced (and in Berlin there did seem to be a good relief system), the number of paupers in Berlin/Cölln continued to grow, the General Poor Fund was insufficient to meet the need, and by the end of 1700 it was clear that a new means to increase the fund had to be found. Hitherto the poor fund was sustained by monthly passing of a collection box in the churches of the cities. It was suggested to Frederick (and he approved) that poor boxes should be placed at all city gates, and that those who wished to enter or leave at night after the gates were closed would have to pay a fee to the poor box.[23] Thus, when the evening bell for closing the gates rang at dusk, the drawbridges were raised, but neither bridges nor gates were actually locked until ten or eleven o'clock. Late comers or departers could enter or leave by payment of six *Pfenning* per person on foot and one *Groschen* for each horse for those who traveled in chaise, coach, wagon, or on horse. The night watch was instructed to wait until three or four persons or coaches gathered before lowering the bridges. Those who were impatient could get immediate service by paying double. Not even the elector was exempt from this payment.

The collected fees were placed in locked poor boxes which were then delivered quarterly to the agents in charge of charity at the Berlin *Rathaus*.

While some improvement in the cities may have resulted from the edict of 1698, the problem remained serious, mostly because local authorities neglected enforcement of the edicts concerning paupers and beggars. In 1701 the elector complained that children eight to fifteen years old swarmed over the countryside as beggars, increasing the burden of the villagers.[24] Beggars who received charity in the cities still went out begging on the highways and in the villages. Again the elector ordered charity systems to be established by local magistrates and nobles, local pastors were instructed to report failures to do so, and rural gendarmes, dragoons, inspectors, electoral agents were all again ordered to arrest vagrants and beggars for imprisonment or assignment to spinning houses. Agents of the

---

23. Ibid., no. 31, cols. 53-56, "Patent Concerning Poor Boxes at the Berlin City Gates," of 3 Dec. 1700.

24. Ibid., no. 32, cols. 55-64, "Pauper and Beggar Ordinance" of 18 March 1701.

commission for the poor in Berlin were required to visit inns frequented by beggars and loose women, with the aid of the militia if necessary, and to drive such idle persons out of Berlin and out of the country if they were foreign beggars.

The measures taken by Elector Frederick (king after 1701) did not meet with noticeable effect. The poor laws were not observed, poor relief was inadequate, beggars were on the increase. In fact, in the capital, beggars, paupers, and vagrants were described as bold and insolent and made life unsafe for the city police (*Gassenmeister*) who patrolled the streets and were supposed to arrest beggars. In a renewed effort in 1706, the king ordered that no beggar, man or woman, young or old, was to approach anyone on the streets, in their homes, in church or at church doors, at the royal castles, or at pleasure houses.[25] Violators were to be apprehended by the street police, brought to the city hall, examined there by the poor commission, and if found guilty were to be flogged (if they were sturdy) and then expelled from the city. The frail and the sick were to be denied alms and also expelled. Young boys and girls were to be turned over to the work and spinning houses, flogged, and made to work on a bread and water diet.

Innkeepers who failed to report to the poor relief commission beggars or suspicious persons who stayed more than one night were to get jail sentences. Guard units were forbidden to permit beggar youths to bunk in at the barracks for the night. No beggars were to be allowed to pass through the city gates. And anyone who hindered the street police in their duties or sought to assist the escape of an apprehended beggar was, without trial, to be punished with prison or hard labor in a fortress. The lack of success in ending the social problem of beggars was manifested in the growing irritation of the king and the severer penalties which were threatened.

The same frustration was felt in the failure to solve the problem of gypsies and similar wayfaring, thieving elements who made the highways unsafe. Despite the many previous edicts banning gypsies from Brandenburg, a substantial number of them were to be found in the electorate making their way in from Saxony and Mecklenburg. The gypsy bands attracted various unsavory elements of the native population such as footloose servants, fugitive apprentices, military deserters, and itinerant beggars. These lawless bands fell upon travelers, robbing and plundering them. A patent against gypsies of January 1707 claimed that if any of these gypsies were captured, the record revealed that the bailiffs and village authorities did not punish them, out of fear of having their houses and barns burned down by others of the same ilk.[26] This in turn

25. Ibid., no. 35, cols. 65-68, "Mandate on What to Do about Beggars and Paupers in the Capital," of 8 Dec. 1706.
26. Ibid., no. 36, cols. 67-70.

encouraged the disreputable element to quarter itself in village taverns which they used as bases for carrying on their highway robbery. Shielded by this blackmail shelter, the gypsy menace could not be easily eradicated. Proper enforcement of royal edicts was lacking. In addition, a segment of both the urban and rural population was unfriendly to the efforts of police officers to enforce the penal legislation against the lawless or classless elements.

The problem of beggars, vagrants, and vagabonds which was faced by the Hohenzollern princes as early as the first half of the sixteenth century was inherited by the second king of Prussia, Frederick William I.

In two edicts of 1715 he, too, attempted to solve this social problem by legislative means. He observed that in spite of what he called "a well-ordered system of charity," the practice of begging in Berlin had increased and gotten out of hand. Natives and foreigners, soldiers and burghers, young and old, loose, able-bodied women, boys and girls unashamedly ran about the streets approaching all respectable citizens, even the king, bothered people in their homes, and under the pretext of begging engaged in thievery. As a result, in a "Mandate against the Increasing Begging in the Capital," Frederick William ordered all beggars to be picked up off the streets by the *Gassenmeister* and brought to a designated secure place for interrogation.[27] Those who were genuine residents and really indigent were to be given relief out of the poor fund. The vagrants from other lands were to be escorted to the borders. Soldier and citizen alike who came from other towns and villages of the king's provinces were to be given aid to return thence, and able-bodied beggars born in Berlin were to be put to work.

Innkeepers in and out of Berlin were forbidden to take in beggars or other suspicious persons without first getting permission from the commissioners of the poor fund. Those who neglected to do this were to be fined or given a jail sentence. Refugees of war, religious persecution, or disaster were allowed to travel freely with proper certificates, but when they arrived in Berlin they were to be taken directly to the poor commissioners by a member of the city guard for examination.

Revealing of public attitude was the king's forbidding of any mob action which abused the *Gassenmeister* or sought to take away their prisoners. Officers of the guard were instructed to assist and protect the street police when necessary.

A few months later Frederick William tried to put teeth into previous edicts against gypsies, footloose wayfarers such as jugglers, gamblers, and so-called "lucky-bag operators," and swindlers in general. No one was to be allowed to cross borders, travel on highways, or put up at inns unless he could produce evidence that his business was legitimate. Ap-

27. Ibid., no. 44, cols. 73-74, of 10 Feb. 1715.

prehended thieves were to be given quick justice to forestall the possibility of escape.[28]

Less than a year later, in January 1716, the king found a new target of idle persons to legislate against—quacks, mummers, jugglers, rope-dancers, cardplayers, conjurers, marionette and puppet masters.[29] These persons posed a problem particularly at the annual fairs in Brandenburg and other territories. They were offensive to the king not only because of their supposed thieving habits, but because they represented an unproductive social group who consumed hard cash. He accused these various entertainers of setting a bad example for the youth of Brandenburg who were thus encouraged to live loose and idle lives. Furthermore, the king charged this quick-fingered, glib-tongued, unproductive fringe of society of depriving gullible spectators of their money with their legerdemain, and of sending pickpockets into the crowds around excise and toll stations, and of stealing the property of foreign merchants stopping at the inns during the fairs. Pious Frederick William felt it was his Christian duty as king to protect his people against such deceit, trickery, and thieving and to assure a wholesome, moral, and honest life for all.

To this end he directed his attention against quacks and mountebanks. Those not licensed by the Board of Medicine of Berlin were not allowed to peddle their remedies at the fairs. Those who were certified were to sell only those remedies which were approved by the board and without the aid of any merry-andrews. No actors, unless royally privileged as they had been in the previous reign, no jugglers, tight-rope dancers, cardplayers, puppeteers were to be allowed in any town or village even during the annual fairs, but were to be shown directly to the borders. There was probably as much puritanical Calvinism in this action on the part of Frederick William as there was concern for the loss of hard cash. To protect his citizens from the evils of this group of entertainers at the fairs, the king ordered all gates in the cities where fairs were held to be manned by local militia or armed citizens from the day before the fairs opened for the duration, in order to turn away from the city this source of moral evil, economic danger, and social pleasure.

Early in his reign Frederick William was faced with a problem somewhat reminiscent of the sixteenth and seventeenth centuries, when the wars of Charles V and the Thirty Years' War had left a wartime heritage of former mercenary soldiers, the *Landsknechte* and the *Soldatesca* (mercenary soldiers), who lived as vagabonds, beggars, and robbers. Prussia had been involved in two great wars between 1688 and 1713. There were many invalided and discharged soldiers, and many who posed as such, who wandered about the countryside of Brandenburg as

28. Ibid., no. 45, cols. 75-78, edict of 26 July 1715.
29. Ibid., no. 46, cols. 77-80.

13. *Landsknechte: Soldiers of the Sixteenth Century*

14. *A Natural History Collection*

beggars. In a patent of 1718 the king directed that such beggars should be arrested and sent to the fortress of Colberg.[30] A few months later this patent was extended to all the territories of the king.

The legislative efforts of the second king were more vigorous, more threatening, and just as ineffective as those of his predecessors in eliminating the problem of foreign and domestic beggars (even in Berlin), of gypsies, and of other types of itinerant vagrants. In December 1720, he complained that, in spite of all previous edicts, the number of beggars and gypsies and other idle persons in his lands seemed to increase. Discharged and invalided soldiers, thieves, gypsies, wayfarers of all kinds infested the highways, towns, and villages. Once again he tried to achieve expulsion of this vagabond element.[31] He ordered the *Landpolizei* (rural police), the mounted gendarmes, and highway officials to take vigorous action to keep all foreign beggars, gypsies, and the like away from his borders, to inspect inns, taverns, suspicious places, and particularly ferries across the rivers and to seize all vagrants. These were then to be turned over to the nearest garrison for examination, and then imprisoned or used for cleaning the streets and other manual labor. Female vagrants were to be imprisoned on a bread and water diet. All were subsequently to be banished from Prussia.

Innkeepers who harbored such vagabonds overnight without reporting them and ferrymen who gave them transportation were to be punished by heavy fine (half to go to the poor fund) or in some cases by corporal punishment (flogging) and were to be deprived of their business permits.

Gypsies and their thieving confederates were to be given no shelter or aid. As soon as they were observed near the borders they were to be hunted down with the aid of the nearest garrison. The able-bodied men were to be sent to fortresses for construction work, and then with their hair cut off were to be put back across the borders. The women and other useless trash, particularly if they were guilty of stealing, were to be flogged, branded, and expelled.

All other vagabonds and rogues who were guilty of thievery were to be summarily punished by flogging without further approval. Discharged soldiers and war and religious refugees with proper certificates were to be given alms for a limited period of time. If they exceeded this period without obtaining gainful employment, they could expect to be treated like other beggars.

Henceforth, almost impatiently, the king decreed that no beggars were to be tolerated in the cities on the streets, or on the highways in villages, but were to be seized immediately. Those born in Brandenburg were to be returned to their places of origin; foreigners were to be expelled.

The problem was not a simple one of thieves, beggars, and vaga-

30. Ibid., no. 47, cols. 79-80.
31. Ibid., no. 50, cols. 83-86, edict of 10 Dec. 1720.

bonds who were idlers or mischief-makers. It frequently became a problem of arson, robbery, and violence. Particularly in the border regions
near Poland, there were large bands of robbers and gypsies who fell on the
peasants, beat and robbed them, plundered them, and burned their houses
and villages. In 1723 Frederick William offered a reward of 100 *Reichsthaler* to anyone reporting an arsonist.[32] A year later he offered a reward
of 10 *Reichsthaler* to anyone giving information about the hideout of a
band of robbers, gypsies, or thieves.[33] After a report no time was to be
lost in hunting down such a band. If gypsies or robbers were caught red-
handed, be they men or women, they were to be hanged without further
inquiry, and if they resisted they were to be shot.[34] Children who were
seized were to be taken to the house of correction (*Zuchthaus*) at Spandau.
If a robber band was reported in an area, a military detachment, aided by
surrounding villages, was to beat the bushes until the band was flushed
out.

Frederick William was determined to provide security for his subjects
against the violence committed by robbers, thieves, and arsonists. However, despite informers, flogging, branding, banishment, imprisonment at
hard work in the fortresses, or forced labor in the spinning houses, the
problem persisted.

In 1730 the king planned a general inspection and roundup of all
vagabond and knavish elements in an effort to suppress the robber bands,
beggars, and gypsies. He issued a general instruction in November of
that year elaborately detailing the procedure to be followed both in
rural areas and in the towns.[35] In the rural areas village magistrates,
when directed by civil government officials, were to make a house-to-house
inspection for the purpose of discovering any undesirable persons. The
visitation was to begin after sundown. Village magistrates and their assistants were first to inspect village taverns, then the houses of peasants,
cottagers, and laborers, and then the mills, smithies, tar-kilns, brick-
yards, and dairy and sheep farms. In short, all places in a village where
a person might hide were to be inspected. All suspicious persons who did
not pursue an honest trade, all beggars were to be seized and brought
before the local governing authority, noble landowners, *arrendatori*
(lessees of royal domains), or royal officials for immediate examination. In
towns and cities the burgomasters, working with the town council and garrison commanders for military assistance, were to inspect inns and all
suspicious places. Visitations were to be scheduled by royal officials
without warning.

The interrogation of all persons rounded up in this manner was pre-

32. Ibid., no. 54, cols. 91-92, patent of 14 Oct. 1723.
33. Ibid., no. 55, cols. 91-94, edict against robbery of 24 Nov. 1724 issued by the new
General Directory of Berlin.
34. *C. C. March.*, vol. 2, pt. 3, no. 54, cols. 141-144, edict of 5 Oct. 1725.
35. *C. C. March.*, vol. 5, pt. 5, sec. 1, no. 58, cols. 95-102, instruction of 20 Nov. 1730.

scribed in procedure and type of questions: name, place of birth, marital status, profession or trade, means of support during the previous two years. A foreigner was to be asked to show a valid pass, how long he had been in the area, from where he had come, how long he planned to stay, what he had been doing during the previous six weeks.

If interrogation revealed that any of the arrested persons were beggars, tramps, vagabonds, jugglers, conjurers, gypsies, or itinerant rogues, the type of punishment was prescribed with increasing severity for repeat offenders. Foreign, nomadic beggars and vagabonds who were able-bodied but who preferred to live by begging were to get six months hard labor in fortresses for the first offense. Those who possessed forged passes were to receive three years to life sentences at hard labor. Wandering apprentices were to be returned to their guilds, but if they were caught begging they were to get four months in prison. Discharged soldiers capable of working but who preferred to beg were to be treated like foreign beggars. Women who were apprehended and punished were to be sent to spinning houses or houses of correction rather than to fortresses or prisons. All local officials were required to provide work or alms to beggars returned to their jurisdiction, on pain of being fined for neglect of proper poor relief. The local rural districts (*Kreise*) and towns were made liable for transportation costs of prisoners and for advancing subsistence money to fortresses and workhouses for prisoners sentenced by them.

Subsequent edicts to the end of Frederick William's reign in 1740 make it clear that the problem of vagabonds and beggars persisted in acute form. There was no lack of statutory prohibition; the failure to eliminate begging and vagabondage was due to ineffective enforcement of royal edicts. The crossing of Prussian borders by foreign rogues, beggars, and gypsies was not prevented by border guards, highway patrols, or local officials. No effort was made to hunt down those who did illegally enter Prussian lands. And despite efforts to set up a good system of poor relief to end begging by the king's subjects, poor funds were inadequate or exploited by persons who were unwilling to earn an honest living. To a certain extent the royal efforts were rendered nugatory by a popular opposition to the coercive measures of a bureaucratic government. Evasion by local authority of its responsibility to the genuine poor and failure to support police legislation by effective coercive measures demonstrated over two and a half centuries that the public good could not be achieved by legislative means alone.

9

The Jews in Brandenburg

There can be little doubt that the Jews in German and Brandenburg history from the Middle Ages to the eighteenth century were an underprivileged segment of society. Whether or not they were an unprivileged or privileged group is a matter of legal technicality. They were privileged only to the extent of specific, retractable privileges granted to them by imperial or territorial charters, edicts, or letters patent. For example, the most fundamental of all privileges was that of admission to a territory for the purpose of settlement. The Jews were an alien group, outsiders, set apart from the basic population socially and spiritually because of their persevering adherence to their religion and customs.

The history of the Jews as underprivileged members of European and German society began with the Roman Emperor Constantine who, in the fourth century, limited the rights of Jews as citizens of the Roman Empire. Christian influence in the following centuries with both Roman Emperors and Germanic kings contributed further to a limitation of the civil and political rights of the Jews. Noting that the Justinian Code (534) firmly established the second-class status of citizenship of the Jew in the Roman Empire, Jacob Marcus states that "as early as the sixth century the Jews were already laboring under social, economic, political, and religious disabilities."[1] The latter affected intermarriage, the building of synagogues, the holding of public offices. In feudal Europe, the Jews emerged as masterless men, barred from the land, beyond the law, and under the protection of the Holy Roman Emperor.[2]

The Jews came to the area of Europe later called Germany as early as the second or third century A.D.; they came as traders to the Roman garrison cities on the Rhine. Surviving the fall of the Roman Empire in the West, the Jews became international carriers of trade in the era of the Frankish Kingdom. They served a purpose (that of trade) and were welcome to Germanic kings and princes. The German *Drang nach Osten* was accompanied by Jews who moved east across Germany all the way to Poland. As they had followed the Roman legions to the Rhine, Jewish merchants and traders as early as Carolingian days and certainly in the tenth century traded in Transelbian regions among the Slavic peoples.[3]

---

1. Jacob R. Marcus, *The Jew in the Medieval World: A Source Book, 315-1791*, p. 4.
2. Marvin Lowenthal, *The Jews of Germany*, pp. 5-15.
3. Werner Heise, *Die Juden in der Mark Brandenburg bis zum Jahre 1571*. I am indebted to Heise's thorough examination of the history of the Jews in Brandenburg to the sixteenth century. This work includes an extensive and useful bibliography consisting, however, only of books in German.

By the end of the tenth century they were working out of the great archiepiscopal city of Magdeburg on the Elbe. By the eleventh century they were well established in Poland and were the principal commercial links between Poland and Germany for many centuries, primarily through Brandenburg.

The increasing number and distribution of Jews in Germany after the tenth century and their lack of legal status necessitated regulation of their presence, economic activities, social and religious relations, and their legal or political status by legislative means. As successors to the Roman Emperors, the medieval Holy Roman Emperors had looked upon Jews as their property and under their protection. In 1157 an "Edictum in Favorem Judaeorum" of Emperor Frederick I placed all Jews in the Holy Roman Empire under imperial protection, granted them the privilege to move about, to own property, and to engage in trade and commerce and forbade the exacting of tolls or tribute by anyone in the Empire.[4] But by the thirteenth century, particularly after the Imperial Interregnum, this right passed to territorial princes, bishops, and cities. The Jews lived under the protection of *Schutzbriefe,* letters of protection, issued by emperors, kings, or princes. Such letters granted the privilege of admission and residence, permitted the Jews to engage in wholesale and retail trading, to build synagogues and schools, forbade them the right to carry arms, and above all placed the Jews under princely protection and court jurisdiction. One of the earliest charters was that of Emperor Henry IV, granted to the Jews of Worms about 1090. Another early example was a charter for the Jews of the Duchy of Austria of 1244, which placed the Jews under the protection of the duke to encourage their settlement as traders and moneylenders.[5]

By the eleventh century, competition from Italian merchants forced the Jewish traders to turn increasingly to moneylending. Their supplies of hard cash were in demand by princes, bishops, and cities. Their settlement, therefore, was encouraged by territorial princes, who offered protection because the Jews were "useful citizens and indispensable to the common man." Withal, however, the Jews paid a heavy tax (*Schutzgeld*) for the privileges granted to them, in addition to the normal tolls, rents, and property taxes.[6]

The number of Jews who spread throughout Germany and settled down under imperial and territorial protection before the twelfth century was surprisingly large, large enough to be an important factor in the economic, financial, and tax structure of the German territories. Just how large the total number may have been can be judged from a grisly by-product of the religious fanaticism stirred up by the First Crusade. In 1196 the

4. *Monumenta Germaniae Historica, Legum Sectio IV,* vol. 1, no. 163, pp. 226-228.
5. Marcus, *Jew in Medieval World,* p. 28.
6. See Lowenthal, *Jews of Germany,* pp. 38-65.

pilgrims passing through Germany struck out at the European Jews in their crusading fervor, almost wiping out the Jewish communities. "The First Crusade cost the Jews of Germany close to 12,000 lives."[7] The heaviest blows were struck in the towns of western and southern Germany on the route to Hungary. It was significant for the future history of the Jews in the German territories that city governments and territorial princes were helpless to protect the Jews against the religious superstition and economic resentment of the masses of the people.

The first important appearance of Jews in Brandenburg probably occurred with the German colonization of Brandenburg under the Ascanian margraves in the twelfth century. They came from older German cities in the west. Persecution and murder in the Rhineland and south German cities caused many to seek security in the new frontier regions of Brandenburg. The development of towns and markets encouraged settlement. By 1300 documentary evidence indicates that Jewish communities had settled in a number of Brandenburg towns, in the Altmark west of the Elbe between the Elbe and Oder in the Mittelmark, and east of the Oder in the Neumark. They were usually directly under the protection of the margraves, representing an important source of revenue in the form of the annual tax paid in return for the letters of protection. They engaged in trade and moneylending and were active in the cattle and butcher trades. The Jews were found only in towns; they did not settle in the countryside.

In the early fourteenth century, Jews were granted civic rights *(Bürgerrecht)* in Brandenburg towns, and were permitted to own town houses, even to acquire property by foreclosure on unpaid loans. Heise claims there was no indication of hatred of Jews in Brandenburg before 1319.[8] This attitude changed in the fourteenth century, although the electors and towns generally adopted a friendly and protective attitude towards the Jews because of their financial indispensability. But among the general Christian population of town and country, in the course of the fourteenth and fifteenth centuries, the status of the Brandenburg Jews became that of a harassed, oppressed, hated, despised, and persecuted minority group.

The official, princely attitude may be learned best from the *Schutzbrief* of 24 December 1334[9] issued by Margrave Louis the Elder (of the Wittelsbach dynasty) and the Great Privilege of the Neumark Jews of 9 September 1344.[10] The Privilege is the most important source for the medieval *Judenrecht* (law for Jews) of the Mark Brandenburg next to the *Judenrecht* of the Berlin *Stadtbuch* (municipal law code). Originally effective only in the Neumark, it would be extended to cover all Jews in the

7. Ibid., p. 47.
8. Heise, *Die Juden,* pp. 9-38.
9. Ibid.. pp. 53-56.
10. Ibid., pp. 67-68.

whole territory of Brandenburg as it was renewed repeatedly between 1350 and 1440.

Aside from personal freedom, right of settlement, and protection, the privileges granted by Margrave Louis included freedom to buy and sell meat and other food items, established the right of Jews to engage in moneylending and pawnbroking with protection against defaulters or false accusations, and gave the Jews guarantees of just treatment in the town and electoral courts. Jews were to be judged only in the courts of the towns in which they resided. Village magistrates were denied any jurisdiction over them. To assure justice the Jews could ask for the right of an electoral hearing. The principal purpose of the Privilege of 1344 was to protect the economic functions of the Jews. Since the resident Jews engaged primarily in *Kleinhandel* (retail trade), they aroused ill will among the Christian butcher's guild. In some towns (as in Berlin in 1343) their right to slaughter and sell meat was restricted.

By the end of the fourteenth century, on the eve of the first arrival of the Hohenzollern princes in Brandenburg (1411), the Jews were a distinct part of the Brandenburg population. They were not without rights, but these rights were granted by letters patent or contracts valid only in the towns. In rural areas Jews, in effect, were without rights and were help-less. The *Berlinische Stadtbuch* of the late fourteenth century established the Jews in Berlin as a class with rights protected by law, similar to the Christian population. There is no evidence of a residential separation of Jew and Christian in the Mark Brandenburg as late as the fifteenth century. Jews and Christians lived on the same streets, in the center of towns and cities. Although there was reference to *Judenstrasse* or *Juden-hof* (Street of the Jews) in nine towns between the fourteenth and six-teenth centuries, there is no indication of any Jewish quarter or ghetto prior to the late seventeenth century. Jews often lived on the same street, close to their synagogues. But there were Christian churches nearby. Until at least the fourteenth century Jews owned their own houses or rented from Christians, even lived in with Christian families. In the fifteenth century they ceased acquiring title to property and were assigned houses (*Judenbuden*) which were town property, for which they paid rent.

Jewish synagogues, schools, and cemeteries existed from an early date in Brandenburg towns. Synagogue and school were usually one, a town house on which a regular house tax had to be paid. Not all towns had cemeteries, which, with one exception, lay outside the town walls. The old-est cemetery, located in Arnswalde in the Neumark, dated back to 1321. Fees were exacted for transporting the dead to cemeteries and for burial.

While in general the official attitude towards the Jews, expressed in charters and privileges, was friendly and protective in the period before 1400, it was in sharp contrast to an attitude of hate which developed in the fourteenth century among the general public (frequently encouraged by the clergy). This popular attitude became increasingly intense, even ferocious on occasions, in the fifteenth and sixteenth centuries, and led to persecutions and expulsions.

Whatever latent hostility existed in the Christian mind against the Jew (at least since the external flare-up at the time of the First Crusade) broke out into the open again at the time of the epidemic of the Black Death after 1348. Religious superstition, fear, greed, resentment of the trading and usurious practices of the Jews seized upon the dreaded plague to produce charges against the Jews throughout Germany of poisoning wells, engaging in black magic, and practicing ritualistic murder of Christian boys. All forms of accusations, persecutions, and violence were suffered by the Jews in Germany, including Brandenburg. The worst enemy of the Jew in Brandenburg was the urban mob. This was a time of weak territorial government because of conflict over the title of margrave. Towns usurped the prince's function of protection, regulation, and legal jurisdiction with a deterioration in the status and treatment of the Jews in Brandenburg.

The Jews under the Hohenzollern Margraves

In the fifteenth century, the new margraves and electors of Brandenburg of the Hohenzollern dynasty succeeded in bringing the Jews back under the territorial prince's exclusive protection and jurisdiction, as part of the electoral victory over the towns. The very first Hohenzollern, Frederick I, in 1420 renewed the *Judenprivileg* of the Neumark of 1344, and extended its economic and juridical provisions to cover all the Jews in Brandenburg. By the Privileges of 1420 and 1440 (both really renewals of that of 1344 with additions), the Jews in fifteenth-century Brandenburg were given the free right to engage in retailing of slaughtered meat and other food commodities, were free to sell items taken as security or pawns for loans, were to be protected in the collection of interest and capital as well as against unjust accusations relative to loans, interest, and items put up as security or pawns (that they were not stolen goods); they were to be protected against imposition of tolls heavier than those paid by Christian traders and against taxes beyond those owed to the elector. Jews paid to the elector an annual tax fixed in the Privilege in return for electoral protection. Wherever they still owned town houses, they paid to the towns a *Budenzins* (house tax). Judicial jurisdiction over the Jews was delegated to town judges but was also personally administered in the elector's chamber on appeal of the Jews. More Jews were allowed to settle in Brandenburg towns under the first two Hohenzollern electors, after 1430.

Despite this favorable change of status and treatment by the prince, the Jews suffered two serious setbacks between 1440 and 1446. About

1440, perhaps beginning earlier, the whole Jewish community in the Mark seemed to suffer financial and economic decline and poverty. Heise believes that this was probably due to the prevalence of a contagious disease which produced a high death rate.[11]

The second catastrophe occurred on 17 December 1446. By order of the elector all the Jews in the Mark Brandenburg were suddenly seized, incarcerated, their goods and property confiscated, and then were driven out of the Mark. This was the first expulsion of Jews out of Brandenburg of which there is historical record. Even so, the expulsion was not completely executed against all Jews, many of whom stayed on in areas of Trans-Oder Neumark near the Polish borders. And in the following year, 1447, Jews were again admitted to Brandenburg.

The expulsion of 1446 certainly met with the approval of towns and citizens who resented the Jews primarily for religious reasons. It is clear, however, that the elector did not take this action freely. It represented a substantial loss of revenue, and the decline of Jewish wealth in the preceding decade meant there was no great profit in the confiscation of Jewish property. The cause was external. It seems to lie in a letter of Emperor Frederick III to Elector Frederick II of 14 October 1443 ordering him and all German princes to drive all Jews out of their territories. The elector was finally forced to take reluctant action in 1446.[12]

After the events of 1446, the Privilege of 1440 (a renewal of the Great Privilege of 1334), which established the contractual basis of Jewish status in Brandenburg, gradually ceased to have meaning and was not again renewed. This necessarily raises the question: Were the Jews in Brandenburg after 1447 an unprivileged group? Their return in 1447 was on a different basis from that of the previous centuries. Jews were now admitted to Brandenburg for a limited number of years (usually no more than four years) and paid *Schutzgeld* semiannually for these years. They were completely under electoral protection and were admitted to towns frequently over the resistance of the towns. Essentially the legal position of the Jews and their privileges after 1447 remained the same as before 1446, but they no longer enjoyed *Bürgerrecht*. They were a resident, alien group with a limited stay (although the period of stay was renewed regularly). The elector had to maintain a constant resistance against the whole Christian community to protect the Jews. The whole population was determined to expel the Jews permanently, with the Brandenburg Estates, consisting of prelates, nobles, and cities, serving as the voice of the opposition.

There could be only one reason why the electors of Brandenburg would so bitterly oppose public opinion as to make a political issue of the Jews and to expose to attack the prince's sovereign authority (*Herrschafts-*

11. Ibid., pp. 131, 145.
12. Ibid., pp. 148-153.

recht). They were convinced of the economic and financial indispensability of the Jews. During the second half of the fifteenth century the Jews gained an increasing influence over the economic life of the territory. This was achieved by their role as moneylenders and by their ability to furnish silver bullion for the electoral mint. The very nobles, clergy, and towns who opposed their presence in Brandenburg borrowed heavily from them. And the special taxes paid by them to the electors gave the latter some freedom from complete financial dependence upon the Estates. Without them there would exist no credit system for trade and commerce. The extensive borrowing at high interest rates and the increasing affluence of the Jews naturally led to attacks upon Jewish usury. For a short time Frederick II after 1461 banned the Jews from moneylending, only to find that Christian moneylenders were even more usurious. After 1467 the Jews were allowed back into the money market and flourished until their second expulsion in 1510.

Although the increasing economic influence of the Jews, and the growing wealth of the creditor Jew, would naturally cause resentment among the Christian population, this alone does not explain the greater popular urge to evict the Jews from Brandenburg. There emerged in the second half of the fifteenth century and in the first half of the sixteenth century an increasingly intense and dominant religious hatred of the Jews on the part of the Christian population. In statistical terms this emotion is almost inexplicable. According to Heise's study, in 1473 there were only 40 Jews plus families in Brandenburg, scattered in small numbers among many towns. In 1510 there were about 100 Jews (heads of families) with a maximum population of 400 to 500, including families.

Throughout Germany at the turn of the century there existed a hostile environment for the Jews. Social unrest and dissatisfaction with the pre-Reformation religious structure may have contributed to making the Jews scapegoats to satisfy the fear and superstition of the Christians. There was a strong anti-Semitic undercurrent in the recurring peasant rebellions, such as the *Bundschuh* revolt of the 1490's. The Dominican monks in the early sixteenth century made a great effort completely to expel the Jews from Germany or to burn them all as heretics, an effort culminating in the Pfefferkorn-Reuchlin controversy. After the Reformation, Protestantism was as abusive in its Jew-hating as the Dominicans had been. Martin Luther's vitriolic treatise of 1543, "Concerning the Jews and Their Lies," gave credence to Christian propaganda of ritual murder, well-poisoning, and black magic. He urged the burning of synagogues, depriving the Jews of their passport and traveling privileges, the burning of Hebrew books, the closing of business and professions to Jews. This harsh attack seemed to justify violence against and expulsion of Jews during the sixteenth century.[13]

13. Marcus, *Jew in Medieval World,* pp. 67-69; Lowenthal, *Jews of Germany,* p. 162.

In Brandenburg by 1510 the religious hatred of the Christian population reached an explosive point, producing the catastrophe of that year. A terrible and bloody persecution of the Jews, and the execution of thirty-eight innocent Jews by burning, was followed by the expulsion of all Jews from Brandenburg. The cause that was seized upon to produce these events was the stealing of the host from a church by a Christian who later confessed he sold it to a Jew. Charges of defamation of the host were followed by a general attack on the Jews. One hundred Jews were accused, with torture producing confessions and statements of the involvement of other Jews. False charges of ritual murder of Christian children flowed fiercely as the criminal procedure was driven on by Christian hatred, abetted by the clergy. Thirty-eight Jews were found guilty and were executed in a mass burning on 19 July 1510 on Newmarket Square in Berlin. Others probably died under torture. The property of the condemned was confiscated. After the execution, all remaining Jews in Brandenburg were ordered driven out of the territory. This really affected only the sixty Jews still in prison; most all other Jews had already fled the territory.[14]

The expulsion edict of 1510 was strictly enforced for twenty years. There were no Jews in Brandenburg between 1510 and 1532. After 1532 some Polish Jews were allowed to attend annual fairs in the Neumark for trade purposes, particularly in cattle. Joachim II opened all of Brandenburg in 1539 to Jews for trading purposes. He showed a more tolerant attitude and during his reign, after 1543, Jews were again allowed to settle down in Brandenburg.

The blood bath of 1510 did not satisfy the popular hatred of Jews. For thirty years elector and diet were in constant conflict over the issue of the admission of Jews, and Joachim successfully resisted the Estates and protected the Jews to his death in 1571. He even appointed two Jews, Michael (1543-1549) and Lippold (1556-1571), to high positions. Joachim II was convinced that the procedure against the thirty-eight Jews burned in 1510 was unjust. And he needed the credit and financial support furnished by the Jews. In 1564, for example, for an additional annual payment of 800 *gulden,* the Jews were given permission to build a synagogue in Berlin. In 1554 the Jews were required to deliver silver to the electoral mints at Berlin and Stendal.

For most of his reign Joachim II was financially embarrassed and was constantly negotiating with the Estates for new taxes, as at the Great *Landtag* of 1549. Between 1549 and 1562 the towns repeatedly petitioned him to expel the Jews as his father had done, accusing the Jews of blasphemy, usury, and unfair trade practices.[15] Joachim in 1554 replied

---

14. The chief description of the criminal procedure is found in Friedrich Holtze, *Das Strafverfahren gegen die märkischen Juden im Jahre 1510.*

15. See *Kurm. Ständ. Joach.,* vol. 1, no. 155 (1549), p. 434; vol. 2, no. 303 (1551), p. 7; no. 325 (1554), p. 67; no. 327 (1555), p. 70.

to the towns that there were not many Jews in the electorate, and since they had agreed to supply silver for his mint it was better to tolerate them. In regard to their unfair trade practices, he evasively promised to investigate.

The public deeply resented the presence of the Jews, and despite Joachim's protection there were disturbances against them, even violence in Berlin. The resentment which was generally contained by Joachim II erupted violently on the very day of his death, 3 January 1571. On the same day his successor son, John George, ordered the arrest of all Jews in Frankfurt. Joachim's confidant, Lippold, was arrested in Berlin. Under torture, he confessed to the charges of sorcery brought against him.[16] He was executed on 28 January 1573 with a brutality which exceeded that of the mass burning of 1510.

As soon as Joachim II died, the Berlin mob attacked the Jews, desecrated the new synagogue in the *Klosterstrasse,* and plundered the homes of the Jews. John George ordered all Jews to leave his territory by 15 April 1571. Most of them went to Poland and Bohemia. Although Jews soon after were allowed to attend the annual fairs as transients, they were not allowed to settle down as residents again for 100 years.

The year 1571 ends a chapter of Jewish history in Brandenburg which began in the twelfth century. For 400 years the Jews struggled to survive within a hostile environment of Christian resentment and religious hatred. Always an underprivileged portion of the population, they enjoyed only specific and restricted privileges as granted by the margraves of Brandenburg in special charters. Their right to reside, to earn a living, to worship in their own way, to have a synagogue, a school, their own cemeteries, and the right to burial were all contractual privileges extended under electoral protection in return for special taxes. *Judenrecht* and *Judengeld* were reciprocal parts of an equation which was balanced by the regulatory power of electoral sovereignty. The electors were not necessarily any more tolerant than their subjects, but the privileges which they extended to the Jews were designed to exploit the economic usefulness of the Jews for the welfare of the territory. At no time before the seventeenth century was the police power of the prince used for the personal welfare of the Jews except out of self-interest.

The Jews in Brandenburg, 1650-1740

The second chapter of Jewish history in Brandenburg began in the reign of Frederick William, the Great Elector (1640-1688). Just how significant the Jew was or could be in stimulating commerce, in providing

---

16. A six-month study of all his books as collector of Jewish taxes, penalties, and fines produced no evidence of malfeasance, only that the elector owed Lippold a large sum of money.

financial leadership and improved financial administration, is quickly discerned from the almost desperate recruiting of Jews by German princes to aid in recovering from the commercial ruin caused by the Thirty Years' War, in obtaining the financial resources needed by the German princes for reconstruction and to support the new armies. Money was the essence of mercantilist doctrines, the sine qua non to establish the power of the baroque state. And for this purpose the Jew was as useful in the seventeenth century as he had been in earlier centuries.

After 1648, the *Hof-Jude,* a court Jew, made his appearance at many German courts. His function was to furnish loans to the rulers, direction to their finances, and as court purveyors to provide supplies for the new standing armies. Court Jews had wide international connections both in commerce and finance. Jewish peddlers and traders reappeared, reviving commerce. Increasing numbers appeared at the leading German fairs, introducing foreign commodities wanted by princes and nobles. They were often used to obtain jewelry or works of art, as for example by the first king of Prussia when he wanted impressive gifts for a Duke of Marlborough or an Eastern European king. Because of the favored position won by a few, many Jews filtered back into German states from Poland, old communities increased in population and new communities appeared in many German cities. In an age of intra- and interdenominational religious tension, the Jews still lived in great danger from Christian Jew-haters. For example, public feeling in Brandenburg against the Jews was so strong that in 1640 the new elector, Frederick William, for fear of public wrath had to turn down an offer of 20,000 *thaler* by Jews for permission to reenter Brandenburg, despite his great financial need.[17]

Elector Frederick William belonged to a new breed of political figures that appeared in the seventeenth century. He was dedicated to the transformation of his state from a patrimonial, feudal, *Ständestaat* (corporate state) to a modern, absolutist, administrative state. A Calvinist by preference, he adopted a policy of religious toleration as much out of intellectual conviction as from political expediency. Calvinist Huguenots, Dutchmen, and Rhinelanders, Lutherans, Catholics, and Jews were all welcome in his territories for their manufacturing, agricultural, commercial, and financial contributions. The new elector was a child of the age of mercantilism; he believed in a well-regulated state. His concern was for the promotion of the wealth and strength of his territories and the welfare of his subjects. To achieve his ends he had to

17. On 1 July 1641 Margrave Ernst, the Statthalter of Brandenburg, informed Elector Frederick William, then in Königsberg, Prussia, of a proposal from a Jewish representative to make a 20,000-*Reichsthaler* payment to the elector for permission for Jews to enter the electorate. The reply from Frederick William, of 30 July 1641, stated that he did not see how it could be done, since the Brandenburg Estates were sure to make objections. His own position was still too insecure for him to risk antagonizing the Estates. See *Urkunden und Actenstücke zur Geschichte des Kurfürsten Friedrich Wilhelm von Brandenburg, Politische Verhandlungen,* vol. 1, ed. Bernhard Erdmannsdörffer et al., p. 479.

overcome the legislative opposition of the several Estates in his territories, as well as the narrow, bigoted religious attitudes of his subjects.

The greatest need of the ruler of Brandenburg in the decade from 1640 to 1650 was money. His territory was impoverished, plundered by friendly and hostile troops, occupied by the Swedes. The population of Brandenburg and Berlin had shrunk alarmingly. He needed money to pay off a Swedish indemnity and to build the nucleus of a standing army. His electorate was fundamentally an agrarian state. During an involuntary visit of three years in the Netherlands (1635-1638), the young prince had acquired an awareness of the value of commerce as a means of obtaining the needed bullion. Uncertain of himself and not yet master of his inheritance in 1640, he did not risk granting permission to Jews to enter Brandenburg. Ten years later, however, he showed his hand more boldly. He granted a general charter on 1 May 1650 to the Jews of Halberstadt, a bishopric recently acquired by the terms of the Peace of Westphalia. The charter placed the Jews under his protection and established their right to engage in commerce and trade. And on 20 August 1650 he issued an edict exempting Polish Jews from arrest in Brandenburg and granting them the privilege of visiting the annual fairs in Brandenburg for a period of seven years. Toll collectors were forbidden to levy extraordinary tolls on the Jews, and all local magistrates were directed to allow Polish Jews to pass into and through the Mark.[18] Since the thirteenth century Jewish merchants had been the principal commercial link between Brandenburg and the Slavic regions of Poland and Silesia. Poland was a principal source of cattle, grain, and other natural products. With the mouth of the Oder River in Swedish hands, reopening trade directly with Poland could be a useful function of the Jewish merchant.

The Brandenburg diet was suspicious of the elector's plans, and it was not until 1671 that he dramatically ended the one-hundred-year exclusion of resident Jews from Brandenburg. By an edict of 21 May 1671, Frederick William admitted fifty Jewish families into Brandenburg under his electoral protection.[19] He stated frankly that they were admitted for the purpose of "furthering trade and commerce." According to Mylius, the provisions and conditions of admission and activity were borrowed to a large extent from the general charter of 1650 issued on behalf of the Jews of Halberstadt. The opportunity and the timing of this admission resulted from the expulsion of these families from Vienna. Once the doors were opened, the number of Jews who came to Brandenburg increased rapidly until sixty years later there were some 6,000 Jews in Hohenzollern territory.[20]

18. *C. C. March.,* vol. 5, pt. 5, sec. 3, no. 1, cols. 121-122.

19. Ibid., no. 2, cols. 121-126, "Edict Concerning the Admitted Fifty Families of *Schutz-Juden."* An English translation may be found in Marcus, *Jew in Medieval World,* pp. 75-79.

20. In 1956 the total number of Jews in Berlin was reported to be only 4,200.

The edict of 1671 is of such major importance in the history of the Brandenburg-Prussian Jews that its provisions and terms require a close analysis. Jews were allowed to settle in Brandenburg and in the Duchy of Krossen (adjacent to Poland and Silesia) in those places and towns where it was most convenient for them, and to rent, buy, or build houses and places of business. The elector directed that these Jewish families were to be permitted to engage in trading throughout all of Brandenburg and Krossen, and were specifically granted the right to have retail stores and shops, to sell dry goods by the piece or yard, to sell bulk goods by weight, to deal in old and new clothes, to butcher in their own homes and to sell the surplus meat, and in general to sell their goods and wares at the weekly markets and annual fairs.

The laws of the Holy Roman Empire as they applied to Jews in carrying on trade were to be observed, forbidden business such as dealing in stolen goods was to be avoided, and Jews were warned not to treat any of the elector's subjects unjustly in trade or practice usury, but to be content with the interest rate permitted the Jews in Halberstadt.

Resident Jews were to pay tolls and excise and grain taxes like all other subjects, but were declared exempt from the head tax which transient (nonprivileged) Jews had to pay.

The fifty families admitted in 1671 were known as *Schutz-Juden,* and as resident Jews under the elector's protection they were required to pay an annual protection tribute for each family of eight *Reichsthaler,* and as often as a Jew got married he had to pay one gold *gulden.* As for other civic dues, the Jews were to arrive at a just agreement with the town magistrates; lacking this, they could appeal to the elector.

Although the elector had taken the fifty families under his special protection, they were to be subject, in civil cases, to the local burgomasters' jurisdiction and courts. Criminal cases involving Jews, however, were to be reported to the elector at once.

So as not to annoy his Christian subjects, the fifty families were not permitted to have a synagogue. But they could meet in their homes for prayer and religious ceremonies. They were permitted a kosher butcher and a schoolmaster for instruction of their children.

The merchants were forbidden to take good mint pieces out of the land to bring back depreciated coins, and they were to sell all silver and gold bullion only in the elector's mint at a fair price.

The town magistrates of all places where these families settled down were ordered to accept them gracefully, to help them settle down, show them good will, and allow no one to slander or curse them. They were to treat them like other citizens and burghers and allow them to have a place for the burial of their dead.

The elector extended to these fifty families his protection for twenty years, and according to circumstances beyond this point. In the event of war they were to be permitted to take refuge in the territory's fortresses.

The privileges and conditions granted in 1671 were in many respects similar to those of the privileges granted in the fourteenth century. Jews were allowed to engage in trade, to sell in the market surplus meat slaughtered for their own use, to lend money, supply silver for the mint, pay annual protection money plus fees for marriage and burial, were to have a special cemetery, were under local jurisdiction and courts for civil cases but subject to the elector's justice for criminal cases. To a large extent the future occupational pattern of many Jews in Germany, Eastern Europe, and the United States was suggested by the edict of 1671. They would be shopkeepers, dry-goods dealers, secondhand and clothing dealers, cattle and poultry dealers, moneylenders, pawnbrokers, jewelers, diamond cutters, and lens-grinders. A hundred years after 1671 they began to appear in the arts and literature.

Less than a year after readmission, on 20 February 1672, at the request of the Jewish community, Frederick William granted a privilege to a Rabbi Cain to serve as rabbi throughout the Mark Brandenburg. As rabbi he would also serve as judge among the Jews in problems concerning ceremonies, rites, and customs, and he was to have the power to pass judgment and to levy fines (two-thirds of which would go to the elector). If necessary he was authorized to call on the local magistrates or militia to coerce delinquents.[21]

The edict of 1671 had fixed a specific number of families to reside permanently and each family was to pay an annual tax. During the next twenty years many unlicensed families had entered the territory and settled, and others had neglected to pay the annual protection tribute. Civil authorities in 1695 were directed by Elector Frederick III to collect the *Schutzgeld* from the protected families and to expel all others without protection letters. No foreign Jews were to be housed or harbored for more than three nights, on pain of payment of one ducat for each night thereafter.[22]

In 1696 the shopkeepers' guild of Berlin complained that Jews were setting up an increasing number of shops and stalls and were crowding them out of the retail business, in spite of an edict of 1693 which had closed many of their booths. There was hardly a street in Berlin, they complained, where a Jew's shop was not to be found, loaded with all kinds of retail wares. In response, the elector ordered that all shops and booths of the protected Jews which had been opened since 1690 were to be closed.[23] Those who had special concessions were not affected and were to be protected. Since many Jewish retailers were given their shop concessions on the understanding that they would sell only old clothes and

21. *C. C. March.,* vol. 5, pt. 5, sec. 3, no. 3, cols. 125-126.
22. Ibid., no. 6, cols. 127-128, edict of 14 Dec. 1695.
23. Ibid., no. 7, cols. 127-130, "Patent Concerning Jewish Stores and Shops in the Capital," of 16 Oct. 1696.

pawn pledges, these concessions were not to be expanded. Those found in violation were given four weeks to dispose of all forbidden goods on pain of losing their concessions altogether.

When the fifty families were first admitted in 1671 they were allowed to buy or build their own houses. A change of attitude occurred in the 1690's, under pressure, one may assume, from the elector's Christian subjects. Jewish moneylenders accepted mortgages on the security of private homes, and sometimes foreclosed. As early as 1694 Frederick, as Duke of Magdeburg, decreed for that territory "that Jews will not take possession of houses or real estate."[24] In 1697 the elector forbade the Jews of Berlin in the future to acquire houses and real estate.[25] Property already owned by Jewish families could not in future be inherited by agnates or friends but only directly by children. If there were no children, the property of the deceased was to be sold to the highest Christian bidder and the proceeds paid to the heirs.

The complaints about Jewish retailers, competition, and the denial of the right of Jews to acquire real estate undoubtedly were directly related to the large increase of the Jewish population in Berlin and Brandenburg, most of it unauthorized. The economic value of the Jews to the territory may very well have led to the elector's ignoring this influx, except when it was officially brought to his attention. Early in 1700 the elector received such a report of the Jewish Commission on the status of the Jewish community in his territory. From this he learned that the 50 families authorized in 1671 had increased considerably: 28 families had no formal confirmation of their protection, 47 were new families with letters of protection, and 33 or more had no letters and were illegally resident. What was more upsetting was the revelation that the electoral treasury was being defrauded of protection and marriage payments, head taxes for transients and improper harboring of foreign Jews, and had suffered various other abuses.

In an ordinance of January 1700, Frederick III stated that because of the neglect of previous ordinances, brought about by deceit, treachery, and misdeeds, the Jews had really forfeited his protection, and it would be within his rights to levy a heavy fine on the whole community and then to drive them all out of Berlin and the Mark.[26] When the elector said he would be merciful and not drive them all out, he was doing no more than admitting his financial dependence upon the Jews, and he took this opportunity to blackmail the whole Jewish community into a large payment in return for the privilege of a protected status. Those families who had letters of protection were required to pay a double tribute; the unpro-

---

24. *C. C. Magdeb.*, pt. 3, no. 76, of 6 March 1694. This was repeated in December of the same year, no. 82.

25. *C. C. March.*, vol. 5, pt. 5, sec. 3, no. 8, cols. 129-130, ordinance of 24 Sept. 1697.

26. Ibid., no. 10, cols. 131-134.

tected ones who had entered illegally not only had to pay the doubled fee for each year of residence, but then were to be expelled. However, the elector immediately modified this threat. The unprivileged families, upon humble petition, could obtain the precious *Schutzbrief,* if they were of good reputation and made the required payment. Those of bad reputation would have to leave his lands. This often meant the impoverished Jews who had little to offer the elector or his territory.

It was intended, the elector declared, that the total number of Jewish families in Brandenburg would return to the fifty fixed in 1671, by the dying out of excess families and by not admitting any new families until the total fell below fifty.

For the future, the amount of annual protection payment was increased. The first families after 1671 had been required to pay 8 *Reichsthaler* annually and had been exempt from payment of a head tax. But this had been valid for only twenty years. Now, all exemptions were lifted and the annual protection payment was fixed at 3,000 *Reichsthaler* for the entire community. This collective responsibility, which had been assigned in earlier centuries, would make it impossible for individual families to default by deceit since the community would either enforce payment or make up the lacking contributions. The elector estimated that there were 1,000 Jews in his territory in 1700, earning at least 52,000 *Reichsthaler* annually, and that the levied 3,000 *Reichsthaler* was less than a 6-percent assessment for his protection. This had to be paid in gold ducats in one sum at Michaelmas by the Jewish elders into the *Schatulle* (privy purse of the elector). Each year, four weeks before payment was due, the elders aided by the rabbis were to divide the Jewish families into three classes, according to their means, and then to assign proportionate shares to each class. No defaulters were to be permitted—this, however, was really a problem for the community to solve. Anyone who tried to evade these requirements was threatened with loss of electoral protection and expulsion.

Further, no protected Jew was allowed to join in business with an unmarried and unprotected Jew nor to take such a person into his house to live. The required payment of one gold *gulden* for a Jew who married was to be collected by the elders. The number of synagogues in Berlin was to be reduced to one, selected by the community from its several such buildings. This would be in addition to the one previously granted as a special concession to David Ries, a wealthy member of the Jewish community.

Finally, Frederick III promised to issue an ordinance which would clarify the extent of electoral protection for Jews and set forth how they should conduct their lives and carry on trade and business with the Christians.

It was not until the end of the year, in December 1700, that the elector issued a "Regulation for the Jews Living in Berlin."[27] At this time there

27. Ibid., no. 12, cols. 135-142.

were supposedly seventy protected Jewish families living in Berlin and Cölln. The city *Hausvogt* (civilian governor or chief bailiff, an electoral rather than a burgher official) and the Jewish elders were to examine and expel those Jews whose conduct was not honorable or who could not earn a living. The *Hausvogt* was to keep an accurate list of all Jewish families in the capital cities, with a record of the year and day when their letters of protection were issued, and to record the deaths of any holders of such letters. As for the unprotected families, whose numbers had increased, the elector noted, if they would pay their doubled protection money in fourteen days and provide character references of their honorable conduct and ability to earn a living, they would be granted protection. Otherwise, they would have to leave his territory within four weeks. Obviously the edict of January had not been complied with, many families had not yet paid the fine, nor had they been evicted. One can only conclude that the elector had no desire to expel Jewish families, but was interested in their tribute. Referring to his edict of 16 October 1696, Frederick reminded the Berlin Jews that they were not to establish new retail shops but were limited to those existing in 1690 or to those whose business was selling old clothes or pawnbroking. Peddling in city or in country was forbidden to Jews.

The annual protection tribute of 3,000 *Reichsthaler* was increased to 1,000 ducats in gold, and to ease the burden of paying it, Frederick offered to extend letters of protection to ten more well-to-do foreign families chosen by the Jewish elders.[28] The new letters patent would be issued in return for a payment of 50 ducats. The community payment was in future to be paid semiannually at Easter and at Michaelmas. The *Hausvogt* was to assist the elders in collecting from delinquents.

No marriages were to be performed by a rabbi unless the marriage fee had first been paid and a receipt from the *Hausvogt* was presented.

The Jews of Berlin were now allowed to have three synagogues, one general and two private.

The interest rate which Jewish moneylenders could charge was fixed by an edict of 26 November 1700.[29] Jews and Christians were placed on an equal basis with respect to interest rates charged. The ban against owning real estate was renewed, except that property already owned could be inherited by children, but collateral heirs were required to sell to Christians.

Although Jews were permitted to engage in business under certain re-

---

28. The Imperial Mint Ordinance of 1559 had made the gold ducat an imperial mint with a value of 3.44 grams of gold. A *Reichsthaler* was worth about 20 grams of silver.

29. Ibid., vol. 2, pt. 1, no. 93, col. 219. The edict of Nov. 1700 modified an earlier "Edict on the Amount of Interest Jews and Chrisitians May Exact on Loans" of 27 Nov. 1695, ibid., no. 82, cols. 205-206. Now, a maximum rate was established of 12 percent for short-term and of 8 percent for long-term loans to be paid equally by Jew or Christian, whichever was the borrower.

strictions, all trade and business was denied to schoolmasters, teachers, musicians, gravediggers, and similar persons who lived by the support of their fellow Jews.

The Jews were to have elders and community headmen who were to be elected by majority vote, every three years, by the whole Jewish community, in the presence of the *Hausvogt* and the rabbi. Their names were then to be presented to the elector for confirmation.

The elected elders were to enforce the Regulation of December 1700 among the whole community, and were to allow no foreign Jews to settle or be housed for more than three days. The elders were to give testimony concerning the character of those who applied for protection, and were to report any who, because of their conduct, should be deprived of electoral protection. The leaders were authorized to settle controversies within the synagogue with the collaboration of the rabbi and to settle civil disputes among the Jews not exceeding six *Reichsthaler* in value.

In marriage cases, where civil and provincial law forbade marriage within certain relationships but the Mosaic Code permitted it, the Jews were to conform to the civil law, except that the elector could grant a dispensation.

Aside from the Jewish elders, this ordinance regulating the activities of the Jewish community was to be enforced by the *Kammergericht* (supreme civil court in Brandenburg), the Lutheran consistory (chief ecclesiastical office), and the electoral *Hausvogt* for Berlin.

That the granting of electoral protection to all recipients of letters patent was not an empty formality was demonstrated on several occasions after 1700. Perhaps the most precious privilege enjoyed by the Jews was the right to worship freely according to their ancient customs. But it was precisely this privilege which placed them outside of and in a way opposed to the Christian community. Christian religious hostility threatened the Jews, and on two occasions in 1703, King Frederick I was forced to intervene. In 1702 there had been complaints by the Jews to the king that Christians, on the grounds that the Jews slandered the Christian faith in their daily prayers, threatened and even attacked the Jews. An investigation conducted by the General *Fiskal* (the king's chief law enforcement official), with the collaboration of leading Lutheran theologians found the charge of slander to be unfounded. As a result, the king ordered that all Jews were to be protected against harm.[30]

A few months later, because Christians believed that Jesus Christ was slandered by certain words and acts in the Jewish prayer "Alenu leschabbeach," the king ordered certain words deleted from the prayer. This prayer dated from Joshua, there was no slander contained in it,

---

30. *C. C. March.*, vol. 5, pt. 5, sec. 3, no. 14, cols. 141-142, "Patent Not to Harm the Jews," of 4 Jan. 1703.

and the king recognized this. But he apparently wanted to eliminate a basis for suspicion and bad feeling between Christian and Jew.[31]

In 1712, the Jewish community was adversely affected by circumstances requiring royal protection both of the Jews legally resident in Brandenburg and of the territory itself. Because of the dangers from the bubonic plague prevalent in surrounding territories (essentially in the east), commerce had been severely restricted, and the Jews were hard pressed to earn a living. Many had to be supported by public charity. However, foreign Jews (from Poland mostly) made their way across the borders from infected areas and resorted to begging, thus putting a strain on local charity facilities. By an edict of October 1712, the king ordered all his law enforcement agencies in towns and villages to guard against the crossing of frontiers of any beggar-Jews who came to the border villages.[32] They were to be driven back with the threat that if they stubbornly persisted they would be seized and put to work either in fortresses or in cleaning streets, and would be fed only bread and stale beer.

Further—and this had to be passed on to their foreign correspondents by the Jews living in Königsberg, Frankfurt, Landsberg, Halle, Cleves, Stargard, Halberstadt, Minden, and other trade centers—no foreign traveling Jew would be admitted to royal territories who did not have valid evidence from his local government that he was a resident Jew in good standing, conducting an honorable trade or business which was the reason for his travel, and that therefore he did not come for the purpose of begging.

To prevent Jewish beggars from entering his territories in the guise of rabbis, schoolmasters, or musicians, no such persons were to be allowed to enter unless the Jewish community first applied to the Jewish commission in Berlin or to provincial governments.[33] These authorities, according to their findings as to need and character, would issue the necessary passes without which rabbis and teachers were not to be admitted.

To prevent deception in the matter of certificates carried by traveling Jews, these were to give a detailed description of the bearer: stature, color of eyes, hair, beard, any peculiar features, and the kind of business he would pursue at his destination. In addition each Jew possessing a certificate or passport which would allow him to enter and pass through Prussian territories was to take an oath, at the first toll station in the presence of a magistrate, on the Torah, if available, or on the book of

---

31. Ibid., no. 15, cols. 141-146, "Edict Concerning the Jewish Prayer 'Alenu'," of 28 Aug. 1703.

32. Ibid., no. 30, cols. 151-158, "Edict That Jews Who Are Not Protected and Who Beg Are Not to Be Tolerated," of 17 Oct. 1712.

33. The Jewish commission was established on 23 Nov. 1708 as a judicial commission. See Reinhold A. Dorwart, *The Administrative Reforms of Frederick William I of Prussia,* p. 61.

devotion, called the Tefellin, which each Jew carried on a leather strap. In the oath he swore that he was the one to whom the certificate was issued, and that he would not beg for a living or he would be cursed by God.

Once the traveler had been admitted into royal territories, it was the responsibility of the Jewish elders to report the migrant Jew to the local government if he resorted to begging. Special alertness was to be extended at the times of Jewish holidays, such as the New Year and Passover, so that Jewish beggars trying to take advantage of wealthy Jews would be apprehended.

Ferrymen, fishermen, and others living near the borders were warned against helping beggar-Jews enter the land illegally because of the danger of introducing the plague from across the borders. The impoverished Jewish families who had lived in Brandenburg for a long time and who were now too old to move were to be supported by alms from other Jews.

Frederick's motives obviously were mixed. He was, of course, concerned about the spread of the plague into his lands by Jews entering from Poland. Nevertheless, he did seek to protect his own Jews from being burdened by foreign Jews who attempted to enter Brandenburg-Prussian lands for the purpose of begging. It was important, after all, to keep his Jewish community, despite restrictions of commerce, financially capable of paying its annual protection tax. Because of his own foolish extravagances, King Frederick I was personally involved in staggering debt. He was humiliatingly dependent on foreign subsidies during the War of Spanish Succession. Prussia, between 1707 and 1713, was faced with constant financial crisis. Contemporary gossip in 1709 had it that the king since 1701 had spent 3½ million *thaler* on jewels. The Court Jewess *(Hofjüdin)* Liebmann was a constant source of new pearls and diamonds. Because of the enormous debt owed her, in 1707 Frederick yielded to her demands and gave her the right to mint 150,000 *Reichsthaler* worth of 6-*Groschen* pieces and to place them in circulation. The estimated cost to her was reputed to be a mere 4,000 *Reichsthaler*.[34] Frederick had good reason for protecting the Jews and their financial stability.

Under the second king in Prussia, Frederick William I, the status of the Jews in Brandenburg-Prussia remained much as it had been under his father and grandfather. Frederick William's attitude toward the Jews was a begrudging tolerance because of their economic value to his mercantilist program. He detested them on religious grounds and took delight in humiliating them. Fundamentally they were simply a convenient source of hard cash and should expect to pay heavily for the privilege of residing in his kingdom and earning a living. If they did not contribute to the financial and economic welfare of the kingdom, the tradi-

34. Carl Hinrichs, *Friedrich Wilhelm I* (Hamburg, 1941), pp. 322-323, 430.

tional Hohenzollern policy of religious toleration would not protect them against expulsion.

And yet there was another factor, peculiar to Frederick William's attitude of reverence for the office of king. He felt it to be a matter of honor to respect the promises of his ancestors. He could not, as Elector John George had done in 1571, violate privileges previously granted by the edicts of 1671 and 1700, privileges which lapsed at the death of his father. In the first year of his reign, the new king renewed and confirmed all letters of protection, residence permits, and other concessions granted by his father to Jewish families.[35]

Listing 113 families (107 from before 1713, and 6 added since 1713), Frederick William granted his royal protection to wives, children, and servants, so that they would remain resident in Berlin and carry on their trade and commerce, their buying and selling. They were to retain the old privileges and liberties "granted by our grandfather and father." Particularly, they were to be permitted, in accord with the Potsdam Privilege of 21 May 1671, to have open shops and booths for the purpose of their trade and retailing, and to sell their cloth goods at weekly markets and annual fairs, either by the whole piece or by the yard. They could engage in the grocery business and in retailing all other kinds of wares and goods. Peddling in the countryside or hawking in the towns (except at fairs and markets) was forbidden. They were not knowingly to loan money on or buy spiritualities or stolen goods. Pawn pledges on which the Jews loaned money could not be sold for one year, but in turn, after a year, pledges could not be redeemed.

The edict of 1671 permitted Jews to buy or build their own homes so long as what they bought would again become purchasable. This provision was renewed in 1714, except that each purchase had to be confirmed by the king.

If a protected Jew desired to earn a living from a craft or an honorable profession, this would be permitted in accordance with the Privilege for the Jews of Halberstadt (1 May 1650) or as was permitted by the laws of the Holy Roman Empire. Jews apparently were interested in higher education, as seen in a royal letter of 1707 which forbade the University of Halle to admit Jews. If Jews wished to study at Halle, their applications had to be submitted first for royal approval.[36]

To protect the privileged Jews in Berlin from being overburdened with too many poor Jews, the edict of 1714 forbade the entrance into Berlin of any Jews other than those whose names were attached at the end of the edict (113 families). A widow of a protected Jew was permitted to marry again if she received a certificate of good conduct from the elders, if she

---

35. *C. C. March.,* vol. 5, pt. 5, sec. 3, no. 31, cols. 157-168, "Confirmation of the Privilege of the Local Jewry," of 20 May 1714.
36. *C. C. Magdeb.,* vol. 1, no. 36, of 25 Jan. 1707.

and her husband had regularly paid their protection money, paid their civic taxes, and owed nothing to the Jewish community. On payment of 30 *Reichsthaler* the widow was allowed to enjoy the privileges granted to her deceased husband. So long as she remained a widow she was required to pay only half the annual *Schutzgeld* (i.e., 4 *Reichsthaler*). If a privileged Jew had faithfully met all his financial obligations in the past, the king now allowed such person to include under his privilege one of his children, boy or girl, when he got married, and provided further that the father's privilege would be transferred to (i.e., inherited by) this child on the father's death. Obviously, this is a revealing two-way street. Not only were the privilege and protection passed on to the son, but Frederick William and his kingdom would be assured of retaining that particular family's economic or business interests on a continuing basis. As for the other children in a protected family, if the father wished to keep in Berlin more than one of his children in permanent residence and in business, the second child must have a capital of 1,000 *thaler,* the third child 2,000 *thaler.* The second child had to pay 50 *thaler* for this concession, the third child 100 *thaler.* The expressed purpose of this requirement was to keep the Jewish community in Berlin from becoming impoverished by having to support its own poor. In reality, in Frederick William's view, the Jews were to be permitted the privilege of permanent residence in his territories only if they were capable of paying for the privilege. The Jew was a golden goose to be kept fat so he could continuously furnish golden eggs.

If a child married elsewhere than in Berlin, he was allowed to live with his parents in Berlin for one year, but then had to leave Berlin. No betrothals or marriages were to be permitted without the foreknowledge and approval of the elders and of the rabbi.

Any family which desired to leave the royal territories was free to do so after paying two years' protection money. No privilege or letter of protection would be granted to a Jew, no matter how much he was recommended, unless he could put up bond that he was worth at least 10,000 *thaler.* All Jews were obliged to remain part of the Jewish community, which was subject to the supervision of the elders and rabbi, and could not separate themselves from it. The king confirmed the right to have a synagogue and assured the Jews he would protect their right to religious worship according to their cult, rites, and ceremonies. The right of free election of elders and of rabbi was granted, subject to royal confirmation. All officials, schoolteachers, cantors, and butchers were granted the king's special protection. Conflicts over ceremonies and rites were to be settled by the elders and rabbi, acting as a judicial commission.

The Privilege for the Jews of Berlin of 20 May 1714 was the basic guideline in regulating the existence and the doings of the Jewish population under Frederick William I for most of his reign, until a modification in 1730. The status of the Jews as a protected class with special privileges, however favorable or unfavorable it might appear in 1714, declined in succeeding years as subsequent legislation nibbled away at the "generous" provisions of 1714.

Frederick William was determined that the Jews would remain Jews, a special class or group given legal status by royal privilege, and would not become integrated with the Christian subjects of the king. In a letter to the Elders of Berlin of 1715, the king resolved that none of the protected Jews should be allowed to separate from the Jewish community.[37] On pain of losing his protection, each Jew must work in common with all Jews in all things, share his responsibilities proportionately, and accept the decisions of the rabbi and elders in matters of school and faith. Frederick William ordered the private schools which had been conceded to the Liebman family and to David Ries to be abolished. There would now be no Jewish school other than the newly built synagogue. All Jews in Berlin were required to attend the one synagogue and to hold their religious services together. With the threat of confiscation of all property, no Jew in the future was to hold private religious services.

Each person was to be responsible for making his contribution, proportionate to his means, to the community with an annual payment to the elders. If any Jew wished to leave Berlin with his family, he was not to leave until he had paid his share of the 3,000 *Reichsthaler* (collective *Schutzgeld*), as well as his community contributions. Each three years the assessment to meet general expenses was to be presented for royal confirmation.

The Privilege of 20 May 1714 was to be observed in all points, and the Jewish community was not to be injured in any way concerning their buying and selling or in their freedom of religious exercise. The Berlin *Kammergericht,* the city burgomasters, and the Jewish commission were made responsible for protecting the Jews in all their privileges.

Some Jews in the kingdom failed to pay their protection money for several years, while enjoying their privileges. To remedy this situation, in 1716 Frederick William ordered city and town officials to require the delinquent Jewish families in their jurisdiction to pay up within fourteen days through the Berlin *Hausvogt* or their schools would be closed, their cattle slaughtering would be forbidden, and soldiers would be quartered in their homes until they paid their protection money. Local officials were ordered to carry out these punishments unless receipts from the *Hausvogt* were produced.[38]

The new king's first interest had been with the Jews of Berlin and of Brandenburg. But in 1717 he recognized the fact there were about 100

37. *C. C. March.,* vol. 5, pt. 5, sec. 3, no. 33, cols. 167-170, "Resolution for the Elders of the Jews in Berlin Concerning Abolition of All Private Schools and Separation from the Community," of 20 March 1715.

38. Ibid., no. 34, cols. 169-170, "Order That Delinquent Jews Must Pay Their Back Protection Money within Fourteen Days," of 3 June 1716.

Jewish families living in the Neumark, east of the Oder River, who had no letters of protection but who were born in his lands and had lived in the Neumark for 20, 30, or more years. He decreed that of these 100 families, 47 should be granted *Schutzbriefe* and, with 7 other families already protected, should be allowed to live in some twenty-one towns of the Neumark. In a Privilege of 30 October 1717, the usual conditions were laid down for buying and selling various goods, peddling was forbidden, pawnbroking permitted, moneylending at a maximum 10-percent interest allowed.[39] The Neumark Jews were allowed to buy or build homes to assure their permanent residence. They were to be free from payment of a head tax, were allowed to butcher in their homes according to their custom, and were to have the same inheritance rights by sons of the father's privilege and the same widows' and children's rights as had been granted in Brandenburg.

In four towns (Landsberg, Königsberg, Friedenberg, Züllichow) where schools already existed, the king's protection was extended and the Jewish communities there were allowed to have schoolmasters, sextons, and gravediggers. These individuals could not engage in business and were required to pay only half the usual protection money. Disputes among Jews about rites and ceremonies were to be settled by the rabbi resident in Frankfurt. Other disputes and disputes between Jews and Christians were, in first instance, to go before the local town court, with right of appeal to the Neumark regency. Community affairs for the Jews of the Neumark were to be supervised by four elected elders. These elders were also to make the necessary assessment upon members for the annual protection money and were required to present the assessment and division of burden to the senior tax commissary of the Neumark for approval.

In those places where the Jews had already purchased land for a cemetery, they were granted continued ownership. However, in those towns where they had no special cemetery, they were required to pay into the town treasury for each burial place 6 *Groschen* for a small child, 12 *Groschen* for a child over ten years, and for an adult 1 *thaler*.

In return for the king's promised protection, as soon as the letters of protection were issued, the forty-seven families listed in the Neumark Privilege agreed not only to pay 6,000 *thaler* in half-florin pieces to the king, but also agreed jointly to take as their share 8,000 *thaler* worth of the wool cloth which the Brandenburg Jewish community had been forced to purchase from the Berlin *Lagerhaus,* with a value of 25,000 *thaler*.[40] The Jews thus became an instrument in the economic success of the wool production plans of Frederick William. The Neumark Jews also agreed to purchase at the Frankfurt fair 2,666 *thaler* worth of merchan-

---

39. Ibid., no. 35, cols. 171-178.
40. The *Lagerhaus* was a royal wool factory established in 1714 for the purpose of making Brandenburg self-sufficient in wool cloth production and to process the raw wool, export of which was forbidden.

dise, which they could sell in or out of the land. If any one of the forty-seven protected Jews could not handle his share of the goods or of the protection money, the king decreed that such person was to lose his privilege and his place was to be assigned to another of adequate financial means.

In addition, each of the forty-seven families was required to make the usual annual payment of protection money of 8 *thaler* plus 1 *thaler* for the silver trade. The export of good minted coin or of silver in any form was forbidden.

Finally, the king demanded that the Neumark Jews refrain from any blasphemy or slander of Jesus Christ, and that "they shall act in regard to the prayer *Alenu* as prescribed by the edict of our blessed father." Frederick William, in his own Christian intensity, was capable of suspecting the worst of the Jews.

In the decade between 1719 and 1730, Frederick William became concerned over the increasing number of Jews in his kingdom, attempted to curb this increase, and restricted some of the privileges previously granted. In 1719 he renewed the ban against beggar Jews entering from the east.[41] The contagious plague was still a threat in Russia, Hungary, and Siebenbürgen, and these beggar Jews frequently came from infected areas. Not only were they a possible threat, but they would be a burden on the Jewish community and had no economic value to the king.

Because of many young marriages, the number of Jews increased considerably by natural means. In an effort to curb these marriages, an ordinance of 1722[42] ordered that no Jew was to get married until he had presented himself to the *Rekrutenkasse,*[43] proved his age, paid his marriage fee, and received a marriage permit. Severe penalities were threatened to individuals concerned and to officiating rabbis for any secret marriages. This ordinance was effective in all the territories of the king.

In a state and society in which the Jew did not possess normal legal status and the privileges of a citizen but was admitted to residence and the right of a livelihood only by the specially granted privilege of a letter of protection from the ruling prince (which could readily be withdrawn or terminated), the Jews of Europe were constantly faced with a dilemma. The natural increase of protected families created the problem of a Jewish population in excess of that intended. Some Jews did not receive letters of protection. The number of unprotected Jews in any territory

41. *C. C. March.,* vol. 5, pt. 5, sec. 3, no. 40, cols. 179-184, of 13 Nov. 1719.
42. Ibid., no. 43, cols. 185-186, of 18 Aug. 1722.
43. The *Rekrutenkasse* was a special treasury out of which Frederick William I paid for his one extravagance, the tall grenadiers, *die lange Kerle,* the Potsdam Giants. This treasury replaced the *Marinenkasse,* which, as in the ordinance of 24 January 1700, received payments of *Schutzgeld.* Since the Jews traditionally were treated as princely property, special wards of the king, their various financial payments and taxes were received by special treasuries for the king's own disposal, e.g., the *Schatulle,* the royal privy purse. Some taxes, such as burial fees, were allocated to town treasuries.

where Jews were tolerated tended to increase as the result of illegal entries. When Jews were expelled from a territory, it was natural that they should migrate to the places of least resistance. The peculiar political structure of the Holy Roman Empire, composed of hundreds of small and large territories, was a boon for the wandering Jew. There was always a nearby border to cross. By 1724 the number of unprotected Jews in Prussia had grown considerably, particularly in electoral Brandenburg and in the Duchy of Magdeburg, to the prejudice of Christian retailers and traders. The king claimed that the Jews were carrying on forbidden trade and were dealing in stolen goods (a claim, if valid, resulting from the pawnbroking business). As so many times before, the Christian cry of unfair competition and the apparent illegal practices of some Jews led Frederick William to issue a general edict in January 1724 directing that all unprotected Jews should be driven out of the land.[44] The Jewish community was made responsible for ferreting out any Jews without letters of protection. If any deception was uncovered (i.e., concealing an unprotected Jew), the whole community would be fined, and any individual guilty of such deception, if he himself enjoyed the king's protection, would lose this privilege.

One of the illegal practices which disturbed the king was that of peddling in the villages. Many young Jews moved about the countryside selling retail goods needed by the peasants. This resulted in a loss of the excise or consumption tax which was collected within the town walls. An edict of 1727 threatened the loss of *Schutzbriefe* to any Jew who himself or through his sons engaged in the forbidden peddling.[45]

A month after Frederick William had published his edict concerning the expulsion of unprotected Jews, he forwarded, in February 1724, an order to his General *Fiskal* Durham that Jews no longer were to be permitted to buy Christian houses outright or to acquire them through forfeited mortgages. Further, in Christian houses where mostly Jews lived as tenants, at least one Christian family was to be given a rental.[46] Although Jewish families to a large extent lived fairly close to each other, in part to be near the synagogue, this edict seems to suggest the absence of a Jewish ghetto in Prussia as late as 1724. This act was, perhaps, the first serious abridgment of the privileges granted to the Jews in 1671.

In 1728 Frederick William took another step in this direction. Whether out of religious motivation or because the Jews had already adequately served his mercantilist policy of economic development, Frederick William began to show signs of wanting to wipe out the presence of Jewish families in all his lands as well as in his capital. By patents of 27 January and 15 September 1723 he had announced that no new letters of protection were to be issued for his territories, and that further, when a

44. *C. C. March.,* vol. 5, pt. 5, sec. 3, no. 44, cols. 185-190.
45. Ibid., no. 50, cols. 189-192, of 12 Dec. 1727.
46. Ibid., no. 45, cols. 189-190, of 19 Feb. 1724.

protected Jew died, his *Schutzbrief* was to be destroyed. The king now, in 1728, ordered the same treatment for the Berlin Jews, thus abrogating his earlier concession (of 1714) that one child could inherit his father's privilege.[47] Theoretically, of course, upon the father's death, the children were without a letter of protection and thus liable to expulsion. However, in practice, the threatening decrees of the king against the Jews, as in so many other areas of his personal rule, were not vigorously enforced.

By 1730, presumably after some serious soul-searching, Frederick William decided to retain the Jewish community in his kingdom. However, he redefined the conditions and privileges under which the Jews could exist in a "General Privilege and Regulation of How to Treat the Jews in Royal Lands," issued 29 September 1730.[48] This replaced the Privilege of 1714 and was effective until the end of his reign in 1740, in fact until 1750 when Frederick II issued a new, less favorable charter. Frederick William claimed that this new regulation was necessary because of the many abuses of their privileges by the protected Jews, and because many unprotected Jews continued to enter his lands.

First, he declared that no letter of protection would be valid in his lands unless it conformed to this regulation of 1730. Next, he dealt with the economic privileges and limitations. Those Jews who had previously received special concessions from the king, in those towns where they resided, to have open shops or booths to sell their goods there or at markets and fairs were still permitted to do so. They were not, however, to operate in either home or market more than one shop or booth, nor were they to open a shop in any other town than that of residence (except for the annual fairs). Jews were now forbidden to retail groceries and spices, to deal in raw cow and horse hides, to brew beer or distill brandy. Those who were allowed to have shops could sell jewels and silverware, silk, gold and silver braid, cloth of gold and cloth of silver, ribbons, embroidered clothes and caparisons, Brabant and Saxon lace, muslin, cannequin, feathers, dressed leather, raw calf and sheep skins, perukes, camel and horse hair, cotton, foreign yarn, talc, wax, furs, Polish goods not subject to import restrictions, and also tea and coffee. They could deal in wool cloth but only that which was manufactured in Prussia. Trade in domestic and foreign linen was also permitted. Primarily they were limited to luxury goods or goods the purchase or sale of which their connections with international Jewry would facilitate. Clearly, they were to promote the mercantilistic program of Prussia.

Other Jews, not so privileged as those above, were allowed to deal in old clothes and other secondhand goods. They could deal in the exchange of financial notes and in horse trading. Peddling, that is back-peddling in rural areas, was strictly forbidden. All Jews were forbidden to deal

47. Ibid., no. 51, cols. 191-194, of 31 Aug. 1728.
48. Ibid., no. 53, cols. 193-200.

in stolen goods, either buying or pawning such items. Pawned items could not be sold for a period of two years, and when sold the excess over capital, interest, and costs had to be refunded to the pawnee. To avoid overcharging and other deceit, each pawnbroker was required to keep a register or pawn book in which the pledger was to record in his own hand what he pawned, how much money he received for it, and on what day and year the transaction occurred. Pawnbroking was susceptible to abuse, and there is reason to believe that this was one of the areas where shady practices existed.

Moneylenders were restricted to a maximum interest rate of 12 percent, but for loans of 500 *Reichsthaler* or larger, for a period of a year or longer, the maximum was set at 8 percent. For small pledges and loans under 10 *Reichsthaler* the lender could charge a *Pfennig* per *thaler* weekly, for more than 10 *Reichsthaler* only 12 percent.

No Jew was allowed to buy a house for his own ownership without special royal permission. This appeared to be a retreat from the complete prohibition of 1724. Royal permission presumably was purchasable.

All burgher crafts were forbidden to Jews except seal engraving. But before a Jew could engage in this craft, he had to swear before the provincial War and Domain Chamber that he would make no counterfeit excise, toll, or other royal seal or mint stamp. Gold and silver engraving and the fining of gold and silver were not granted as a specific privilege but the king decided that the Jews would be allowed to pursue this activity until it was specifically forbidden.

One of the oldest privileges granted to the Jews since their entry into medieval Brandenburg had been that of slaughtering cattle for their own use and then selling the surplus meat in their butcher shops. This was now radically altered. Slaughtering of cattle, calves, or wethers for their own use by their own butchers according to Jewish ritual was still allowed, but this now had to be done in a Christian abattoir. The Jews could take what they needed for their own use, but the remainder had to be left for the Christian butcher to sell to Christians. This was the identical royal "cleverness" which led Frederick William to compel wealthy Berlin Jews to buy some of the wild boars which he bagged on his frequent hunting trips. The Jews, in turn, donated the unwanted meat to local hospitals.

The number of Jewish families permitted in Berlin by the regulation of 1730 was fixed at 100, while that in the provinces was fixed at the existing number. Again, by fixing the allowable number of Jews in Berlin or in his provinces, the king thought he could control any further growth and keep the protected Jews from bringing in foreign Jews. This limitation of numbers in 1714 had not been effective, nor would that in 1730. As an illustration of the difficulty in keeping the numbers within the fixed maxima, the king once again permitted a Jew in good standing to include one or two of his sons under his letter of protection. These sons were also granted permission to marry, provided that the first son had a capital of 1,000 *Reichsthaler* and the second of 2,000 *Reichsthaler*. From the day of marriage each son had to pay the annual protection money, and before transferring the privilege of the father to the son, each son had to make payment to the *Rekrutenkasse, 50 Reichsthaler* for the first son, 100 for the second. Daughters were not included. But, with all this, the king would not permit the number of protected families to be increased by these sons. There is no evidence to suggest that this restraint was successful.

The king of Prussia was confused in his attitudes and policy toward the Jews. He detested them for religious reasons, he found them useful for the advancement of his financial and economic welfare; he permitted them to stay and do business, but he tried to keep the number of permitted Jews to a fixed number. Two provisions of the regulation of 1730 perhaps offer insight into his mixed feelings. He would have preferred fundamentally to have his kingdom free of Jews, and he provided that no Jew who wished to leave for another territory would be hindered, but instead he would receive a refund of the current year's protection money. As for new admissions, no application for a letter of protection was to be considered unless the petitioning Jew had a capital of 10,000 *Reichsthaler.* While holding open the exit door with one hand, with the other, in 1730, Frederick William welcomed the capital of the Jews into his lands as eagerly as had his grandfather in 1671.

For the last ten years of Frederick William's reign, the General Privilege of 1730 determined the conditions under which the Jews of Brandenburg-Prussia were allowed to live in the kingdom. To the end of his reign, the king continued to show concern over the illegal entry of beggar and unprotected Jews into his lands. The number increased, nevertheless, and they earned their religious and economic privileges by the contributions they made to the financial and commercial development of Prussia. However, for over 400 years the Jews were essentially an unprivileged segment of Brandenburg society, an alien group not enjoying a normal legal status. They existed from 1300 to 1740 and beyond only under the letters of protection which made them the special wards of the ruler, a privilege for which they paid an annual *Schutzgeld*.

Part IV
Education, Schools, and Culture

Die Furcht Gottes ist der Weisheit Anfang.
—*Elector Joachim Frederick, 1607*

10

The Reformation and Education in Germany

For almost 1000 years before 1500, education and schools in Western Europe were part of a universal Christian culture supported, maintained, and dominated by the Roman Christian church and serving primarily the needs of the church. Schools were church schools, universities were staffed by clerics, the purpose and philosophy of education were determined by the church. Latin was the language of instruction.

In the later Middle Ages new elements were introduced with the rise of towns and a new business class and with a revived and intensified interest in classical civilization. Secular and humanistic influences modified the curriculum and purposes of education, but the system of schools remained unchanged from parish school to university.

The German lands were part of this universal system and Christian culture. The church played a major role in education, schools were church schools, and clerics were the teachers. It was thus that Martin Luther, an Augustinian monk, first came to the new university at Wittenberg in 1508 and in 1511 became Professor of Holy Scriptures. The Reformation of the Christian church which began shortly after had a revolutionary effect upon the school system and educational concepts of Germany, at least of Protestant Germany.

The Influence of Martin Luther

In 1524 Martin Luther published a "Letter to the Mayors and City Councillors of All the Cities of Germany in Behalf of Christian Schools,"[1] and in 1530 he sent to Lazarus Spengler, a councillor of the city of Nuremberg, a "Sermon on the Duty of Sending Children to School."[2] In the first of these publications Luther proclaimed the principle that education is a responsibility of public authorities, and in the second he essentially declared a principle of compulsory education for children. These two principles are complementary; one is meaningless without the other. The two were the guiding principles of at least the Protestant states of Germany and became infused in the theory of the welfare state of the Hohenzollern rulers of Brandenburg-Prussia. Educational philosophers of the seventeenth and eighteenth centuries were guided by these principles. As a result of Luther's urging, German Protestant territories were the

1. For a translation of this letter see F. V. N. Painter, *Luther on Education.* pp. 169-209.
2. Ibid., pp. 210-271.

first to establish a system of public schools. Efforts were made in the following centuries to require attendance at these public schools of all children, rural as well as urban, at least to the extent of acquiring skill in the basic elements of reading and writing.

In stressing public and secular responsibility for schools and a popular education, Luther not only denounced the deficiencies of existing church schools. More positively and constructively, he identified education for all with individual fulfillment, the welfare of the church, and the needs of the state. In his letter of 1524 Luther wrote, "The welfare of a city does not consist alone in great treasures, firm walls, beautiful homes, and munitions of war. . . . The highest welfare, safety, and power of a city consists in able, learned, wise, upright, cultivated citizens. . . . In all the world even among the heathens, schoolmasters and teachers have been found necessary where a nation was to be elevated."

Since civil government needs educated men, since a knowledge of ancient languages is necessary to understand the Scriptures, and "society for the maintenance of civil order and the proper regulation of the household needs accomplished and well-trained men and women," Luther stated that it was the duty of city fathers to establish schools where languages (Latin, Greek, Hebrew), history, and mathematics could be taught. He wanted both boys and girls to be educated. While all children should receive a minimum of education, "the brightest pupils who give promise of becoming accomplished teachers, preachers, and workers, should be kept longer at school, or set apart wholly for study."

Luther was moved to appeal to public authorities because "the schools are deteriorating throughout Germany," and since the existing monastic and cathedral schools turn out "asses and blockheads," the city authorities must build schools and assume the responsibility of educating children. Not only schools were needed in Luther's judgment. He pleaded that "no cost nor pains should be spared to procure good libraries in suitable buildings, especially in the large cities, which are able to afford it."

The idea of universal compulsory education may properly be attributed to Luther, as the result of his sermon or discourse of 1530 addressed to the evangelical preachers on their duty of admonishing parishioners to send their children to school. The very principles of the Protestant Reformation, which declared the Scriptures to be supreme, required a literate population. Luther argued that the world needed preachers and schoolmasters and that they could come only from the boys who needed to be sent to school for education. But not all boys were to become preachers and teachers. "Society needs men for secular authority and social order." If justice, wisdom, and reason were to guide civil government, then men must be educated. And, "since more wisdom is required in civil office than in the ministry, it will be necessary to set apart for it the brightest boys." Luther not only wanted some elementary education for all, but promoted the idea that promising children, those of unusual quality, "especially the children of the poor," should be kept in school for a longer time, at public expense if necessary. Luther put the charge in his forthright manner by stating, "I maintain that the civil authorities are under obligation to compel the people to send their children to school, especially such as are promising. If the government can compel citizens who are fit for military service to serve for defense in time of war, how much more has it a right to compel the people to send their children to school, since children are educated for their own and the general good."

The influence of Martin Luther and of the Protestant Reformation in general upon the development of education in the following centuries is almost incalculable. His two major contributions were to make the establishment, maintenance, and supervision of schools a public responsibility and thus an aspect of the public welfare to be promoted by the state, and secondly to urge not only that schools be available to all social classes but that attendance at schools be made universally compulsory for all children, according to qualification. The latter goal, particularly in rural areas, was achieved slowly, but the acceptance of the principle of public schools at all levels by city councils and territorial princes was almost immediate.

Pre-Reformation Schools and Education

As early as 1520, in his "Address to the Christian Nobility of the German Nation," as well as in his letter of 1524, Luther had urged a reformation of the schools of Germany. To appreciate the post-Reformation development of schools, it may be profitable to look at the scholastic heritage of the Middle Ages.

The origin of medieval, continental schools is usually associated with Charlemagne's capitulary of 789 which required that in each monastery and cathedral chapter there should be schools in which the young boys could learn singing, the Psalms, and grammar. Under the influence of this edict, in the ensuing centuries, there appeared throughout the former Carolingian Empire *Klosterschulen* (monastic schools) and *Domschulen* (cathedral schools), conducted by the monks and cathedral canons respectively. To these were added parochial schools under the supervision of the parochial priest. Education was an exclusive function of the church, and was essentially, if not exclusively, religious in scope and nature. The laity had no special schools until the late Middle Ages. The church schools not only provided professional education for the clergy but also satisfied the needs of the middle class. However, the growing economic prosperity of the new burgher class led to the establishment of city schools or Latin schools for the sons of the middle-class burghers. The origin of these city schools probably was in the parish schools run by the priests. They now offered a higher level of education, in addition to the former elementary level, in order to meet the needs of the commercial, urban community and to prepare burghers' sons for the new universities (sixteen were established in the Holy Roman Empire between 1349 [Prague] and 1506 [Frankfurt]). The city schools were administered by municipal authorities who employed the schoolmasters, built, maintained, and inspected the schools, and sometimes paid the salaries of schoolteachers. Luther's later appeal for publicly supported schools was something less than an innovation.

In order to prepare the sons of shopkeepers and craftsmen for business or trade, private writing schools appeared. These were elementary schools, called German schools, because German was the language of instruction. The goal was to provide a practical education rather than a classical one, to serve the needs of an urban, business class.

Church schools suffered from dissolution during the Reformation. Monastery schools were completely abolished in evangelical territories; in many cases cathedral schools became city schools. The property of the Roman Catholic church, monastic and episcopal, was secularized and became the property of the state. The princes not only converted convents to schools, but granted the income from former church lands to the support of the new state schools. At any rate, whatever the state of deterioration in the pre-Reformation schools of Germany, educational facilities declined after the Reformation began. It was fortunate, indeed, that Luther and the Reformers were interested in the advancement of education and of schools. Much of the credit for the practical organization of a new educational system in Protestant cities and territories must be given to Philip Melanchthon, Johann Bugenhagen, and Joachim Camerarius.

Influence of the Reformation on German Schools

The Protestant Reformation with its emphasis on personal religion and a literate populace, as well as by its dissolution of church institutions, created a challenge to traditional education in form and content. After 1524 the teachings of Luther on education, and the organizational influence of Melanchthon, the Preceptor of Germany, would combine to restructure the school systems of the German Protestant cities and territories. The principal organizational feature of the Reformation era was the intrusion of the state into the field of education and schools. The evangelical cities were the first to respond, already having a tradition of *Stadtschulen* (city schools). The former parish schools and cathedral schools were replaced by city Latin schools, and the former city schools were converted or transformed into intermediate-level grammar schools. There was necessarily some confusion at first in nomenclature and levels of instruction. But essentially they were city schools, whether called

Klosterschule, Partikularschule, or *Stadtschule.* Some were elementary, some became humanistic, preparatory schools for theological studies or for training in public service. They were established by action of the city council, which hired the teachers, paid them, and supervised the instruction. These schools were intended for the sons of native burghers. Parish churches, cathedrals, and former cloisters (Augustinian and Franciscan) were used as locations of the city schools. The plan of study was humanistic, all instruction was in Latin, and most schools had three divisions on the basis of level of achievement from elementary to fluency in Latin.

Most of these city schools were continuations of the medieval church or city Latin schools. Responding to Luther's appeals, the city magistrates founded more schools; new humanistic studies and new methods were introduced. Classical literature, the writings of Erasmus, classical Latin, Greek, and some Hebrew, and improved grammar prepared the student for theological or classical studies. The principal textbooks used in the Latin schools were written by Melanchthon.

The first institutional innovation resulting from the Reformation was introduced in the 1540s, with the establishment of *Fürstenschulen* or *Landesschulen* (princes' or territorial schools). These princes' schools, as secondary-level grammar schools, were intended to serve the needs of the students of a whole territory. In turn, the products of these territorial schools were expected to serve the religious, educational, and public needs of the state. The establishment of these schools resulted from a more energetic intervention of territorial princely power in both ecclesiastical and educational affairs. As the prince replaced the hierarchy of the church in his evangelical territory, he took over the property of church foundations, cathedral chapters, and cloisters, and assumed responsibility for schools and education.

Fürstenschulen were public schools, established by the state with public funds and placed under the supervision of the secular, territorial church administrative office, the consistory. As grammar schools they served as an intermediate step between the city Latin schools and the universities, receiving their students from the Latin schools between the ages of 11 and 15. Usually for six years they offered a free education and support, preparing young men for the university. After completion of university training, students were required to serve either state or church.

The first *Fürstenschulen* were established by Duke Maurice of Albertine Saxony on 21 May 1543, "an epoch-making date in the history of the schools," Friedrich Paulsen calls it. Three grammar schools were established in the towns of Meissen, Pforta, and Grimma in former Cistercian cloisters and were endowed with the secularized buildings and properties. The Saxon *Fürstenschulen* became the model for many similar *Landes-*

schulen in northern Germany. The cloister life, cloister discipline, the black clerical robes of the cloister likewise became a model. The course of instruction to the middle of the seventeenth century was rather uniform, consisting of grammar, rhetoric, and dialectic in the Latin tongue, Greek and elementary Hebrew, religious instruction and music.

Thus, after the Reformation, a school system began to emerge in the Protestant territories with two school forms existing side by side: the city Latin schools and the state grammar schools. The Latin schools at the elementary level prepared pupils to master Latin so that they might enter intermediate-level schools. In some instances city Latin schools, by addition of higher levels of instruction, expanded into *Gymnasien.*

The *Fürstenschulen* or state grammar schools in turn prepared the student for university. With expanded curriculum in arts and sciences, these schools sometimes approached the level of universities. The distinction between school and university lay in possession of the right, granted by public authority, to award an academic degree. *Fürstenschule* or *Landesschule* came to be called *Gymnasium* or in some instances *Paedagogium* (when boarding facilities were included).

The former German writing schools survived the Reformation and in town and village became public elementary schools, attached to parish or village church, to teach reading and writing, catechism and singing. The village schools were called *Küsterschulen* because the school teacher was most often the *Küster,* the sacristan or parish clerk. The origin of the *Volksschule,* the common elementary school, can be found in the German schools and *Küsterschulen.*

The system of schools in Protestant territories from the elementary levels of city schools (by whatever name) through the intermediate, territorial, state-supported *Gymnasien,* to the universities was rather clearly delineated by the end of the sixteenth century and remained almost unchanged to the age of Frederick the Great. The only significant institutional development would occur after the Thirty Years' War with the establishment of the *Ritterakademien* (cadet academies) in the seventeenth century, and a fuller emergence of the *Volksschule* in the eighteenth century.[3]

Within the framework of this system of schools, certain principles or

3. The most useful description of schools and education in Germany in the period from the Middle Ages to the nineteenth century, relied on heavily here, is that of Friedrich Paulsen, *Geschichte des Gelehrten Unterrichts auf den deutschen schulen und universitäten vom ausgang des mittelalters bis zur gegenwart,* 2 vols., 3d ed., rev. An English version of Paulsen is found in *German Education, Past and Present,* trans. T. Lorenz (originally published as *Das Deutsche Bildungswesen in seiner geschichtlichen Entwicklung*). Other useful references include Fritz Blättner, *Das Gymnasium;* Heinrich Lewin, *Geschichte der Entwicklung der Preussischen Volksschule und der Förderung der Volksbildung durch die Hohenzollern;* Thomas Woody, *Fürstenschulen in Germany after the Reformation.* Printed school ordinances affecting city and territorial schools beginning with the Saxon School Ordinance of 1528 are made available in Reinhold Vormbaum, ed., *Die Evangelische Schulordnungen des 16en - 18en Jahrhunderts,* 3 vols.

features emerged in the sixteenth century which characterized German education for at least two centuries with varying intensity. All evangelical reformers insisted upon education for all classes according to ability, for boys and girls, for rich and poor. A corollary of this basic principle was the insistence on free, compulsory education for all children in town and village, free education including stipends for needy and deserving students for the complete sequence from elementary school to university, with emphasis on religious education. Compulsory attendance at schools was attempted in some territories, such as Saxony and Württemberg in the sixteenth century, but neither schools, teachers, nor public attitude were adequate to support such efforts. Paulsen declares that "The principle of compulsory school attendance was proclaimed, as far as I know, for the first time in the School Regulations issued for Weimar in 1619."[4] In 1642 the *Schul-Methodus* issued by Ernest the Pious of Gotha adopted and enforced this principle of compulsory attendance. But not until the eighteenth century did Luther's appeal begin to win general acceptance.

A feature of all school ordinances in Germany beginning in the sixteenth century was the division of schools into classes or grades according to achievement. In the Latin schools, for instance, the distinction would be: Class 1 was for those who were learning to read and write (Latin); Class 2, for those who had mastered elementary reading, offered basic Latin grammar, Aesop's Fables, Erasmus' Colloquies, music (singing), and Christian education; Class 3 was for those who had finished grammar and were intellectually qualified to go on to reading Virgil, Ovid, Cicero, dialectics and rhetoric and were capable of writing essays and poetry in Latin. They were now ready for promotion to *Paedagogium, Gymnasium, Landesschule* at the intermediate level.[5] The 1528 Saxon ordinance may well have set the pattern for a class or grade division throughout the history of German education, eventually influencing even American schools. The number of grades varied, and sometimes there was an overlap in the level of work in the several schools.

Although there were some schools at the elementary level which remained German schools (in the villages, girls' schools, the old writing schools), the real emphasis, decreed by Martin Luther and the Reformers in general, and the whole weight of the Christian Renaissance, was on developing a system of Latin schools, with Latin the exclusive language of instruction. This remained true through the seventeenth century. Only at the end of the seventeenth century did the German language gain increasing importance through the influence of Thomasius and the Pietists as a language of instruction.

---

4. Paulsen, *German Education,* p. 136.
5. See, e.g., the Saxon School Ordinance of 1528 drawn up by Philip Melanchthon, in which, taking his cue from Luther, he admonished the schoolmasters that the children must be divided into groups or grades according to achievement. Vormbaum, *Schulordnungen,* vol. 1, no. 1, pp. 1-8.

The spirit of the Reformation deeply influenced educational development in the sixteenth century. Education was essentially religious based
on a classical foundation. Latin was indispensable. Luther extolled the
value of ancient languages for the training of theologians. After Latin
was mastered in the city Latin schools, Greek and Hebrew were introduced at the *Gymnasium* level. However, Luther the practical man and
Melanchthon the classical and Christian humanist recognized the value
of a humanistic education for the training of public servants as well as of
preachers and teachers. In his sermon of 1530, Luther asserted that the
temporal life also needed educated men. In a letter to Elector John of
Saxony in 1526 Luther wrote, "There is nothing more necessary than to
educate men who are to succeed us and to govern."[6] The general mission
of schools was defined by Melanchthon in the Saxon school ordinance
of 1528 when he urged that children be sent to school, "so that one can
bring up a generation which can teach in the church and which is capable
of governing." For most of the seventeenth century the *Gymnasium*
remained a preparatory school for theological studies, with emphasis on
languages. The humanistic schools, although their curricula expanded,
were not sufficiently flexible to adopt the new sciences, natural, economic,
political, and legal, to fill the need for educating the sons of nobles
for military and state service. After 1650 new schools appeared, particularly
the *Ritterakademien*.

6. Painter, *Luther on Education*, p. 136.

11

Education in Brandenburg-Prussia, 1540-1650

The Hohenzollern electors of Brandenburg responded to the new intellectual, religious, and educational influences permeating Germany in the sixteenth century. There was little, if any, originality in their actions. They were creatures of the age, usually carried forward by the tide of events elsewhere or influenced by the new climate of secularism and Reformation thought. The founding of the first Brandenburg university in 1506 at Frankfurt, the establishment of *Gymnasien,* the intervention of princely authority in the promotion of schools at all levels, educational principles, were all patterned after other German models, particularly those of Saxony.

It was not until 1540 that Elector Joachim II concerned himself with the conditions of the schools in Brandenburg. Even then it was not a direct concern for the educational welfare of his subjects so much as it was an afterthought prompted by the necessity of providing a new church administration after the formal adoption of Lutheranism in Brandenburg in 1539.[1] A church ordinance of 1540 established a board of visitors to investigate the condition of the churches, schools, and other affiliated charitable foundations being taken over by the state. One paragraph, entitled "Schools," expressed the electoral realization that the Brandenburg schools were in serious need of reform and restoration ("because for some time the schools have fallen into marked decline").[2] The only schools surviving in Berlin and Cölln were the two attached to St. Nicholas Church in Berlin and to St. Peter's Church in Cölln. Perhaps because of the action of 1540 the old church school at St. Mary Church was restored in 1552.

The effort to establish or improve schools in Brandenburg in 1540 was not too effective. In Berlin, for instance, there were fewer schools between 1540 and 1573 than in the period before the Reformation. The inspiration of the Reformation, however, moved Joachim II to concern himself with the condition of schools in his lands. He emphasized the need for education in order to preserve the Christian religion (Lutheran style) and to maintain good order (*guter Polizei*).[3] Schools were to be associated with

1. See Reinhold A. Dorwart, *The Administrative Reforms of Frederick William I of Prussia,* pp. 96-98.
2. *C. C. March.,* vol. 1, pt. 1, no. 2, col. 246, "weil die Schulen etliche Zeit her in mercklichen abfall kommen."
3. "Zu erhaltung Christlicher Religion und guter Pollicey auffs höchst von nöten. [For the preservation of the Christian religion and good order is of the highest necessity]." This is probably the first documentary use of *Polizei* in Brandenburg and occurred ten years after the first use of the word in an Imperial *Polizeiordnung. Polizei* refers here to the keeping of good order in a well-regulated state.

parish churches, so that instruction in the Christian religion could be offered. In the towns, parish schools usually had their own separate buildings. In the villages, the parish house or the home of the teacher was usually the location for catechism classes conducted by pastor or *Küster* (sacristan). The latter was seldom well educated, was normally a local craftsman who had acquired the rudiments of reading and writing and had some knowledge of Luther's catechism and of music.[4]

Elementary Schools

The church ordinance of 1540 was primarily concerned with establishing Latin schools. Where there was any measure of success it was in the cities. The only concern about the education of the lower classes, particularly in the villages, was for religious instruction. Parish preachers were to give catechism lessons on Sunday afternoons. This task was frequently delegated to the preacher's assistant, the *Küster.*

Elementary education received no significant boost from the Reformation emphasis on education for all children until 1573. In that year a Visitation and Consistorial Ordinance"[5] required that all children in the electorate should be sent to school to get Christian instruction and good discipline. It further required that local governing authorities of all localities should build schools where they were needed. The school ordinance concerned itself with three types of elementary schools: city Latin schools, German schools for girls, and village schools.

In the Latin schools the curriculum included religious instruction as well as the secular arts. But Latin grammar and syntax was fundamental, and teachers were urged to drill the students hard and faithfully in this subject. The development of good handwriting and the inculcation of a knowledge and fear of God were also desirable goals.

Although the parish preachers in cities were directed, in 1573, to warn parents to send their children to these city schools, too many of the children were not qualified for or interested in these Latin schools. Thus, one finds other elementary schools for boys and girls, which carried on the tradition of the German schools. The ordinance of 1573 declared that schools for girls were useful and that the burghers should send their daughters to learn reading, writing, prayer, and Christian hymn singing. An instruction of 1574 refers to two schools for girls established at St. Nicholas and St. Mary churches in Berlin.[6] As early as 1551, a German

4. Detailed information on the development of a school system in Brandenburg-Prussia may be found in the following useful works: Lewin, *Preussischen Volksschule;* Kurt Wöhe, *Die Geschichte der Leitung der preussischen Volksschule von ihren Anfängen bis zur Gegenwart;* Ferdinand Vollmer, *Friedrich Wilhelm I und die Volksschule;* Friedrich E. Keller, *Geschichte des preussischen Volksschulwesen;* and Vormbaum, *Schulordnungen,* vols. 1-3.

5. *C. C. March.,* vol. 1, pt. 1, no. 7, cols. 305-311. The school ordinance contained within the Brandenburg visitation and consistorial ordinance of 1573 may also be found in Vormbaum, *Schulordnungen,* vol. 1, no. 20, pp. 226-230.

6. *C. C. March.,* vol. 1, pt. 2, no. 5, cols. 11-30, "Visitation Instruction Concerning Schools and Churches in Berlin, 1574."

school was established at Stendal to teach German, writing, and arithmetic. Similar schools appeared in Berlin and other towns to satisfy the needs of a burgher society and the children of the lower classes. Priests, former monks, wandering students, and laymen served as teachers in the German schools.[7] In 1596 a free school was established in Berlin where the children of the poor were to receive instruction in prayer, reading, and writing.[8]

The visitation ordinance of 1573 made the members of the Lutheran consistory responsible for general supervision of all Brandenburg schools. In addition, in a monthly inspection of the city schools carried out by the parish clergy, two city councillors, and two lay members of the congregation, the students were to be examined on their knowledge of Christian doctrine and church music.

The ordinance of 1573 was primarily concerned with city schools and recognized that "in rural areas there still were no schools [auf dem Lande gibt es noch keine Schulen]." In lieu of formal schools in the villages, the local sacristan was required to instruct the villagers, particularly the children, on Sunday afternoons or on one day during the week, in Luther's *Small Catechism,* was to teach them to pray, and was to teach the children to sing Christian German hymns. The method of teaching was for the sacristan to read from the catechism and then make the children repeat the words. By learning the hymns, the children would lead the adults in church singing. In many instances the village priest and sacristan served mission chapels outside the village, and catechism instruction was extended to these hamlets. To Kurt Wöhe, the Sunday catechism classes were the *Urform* (prototype) of the rural *Volksschule* or elementary school. Village schools would grow out of these weekly catechism sessions and would offer elementary instruction in German reading and writing as well as singing, although religious education would remain the primary purpose.

Kurt Wöhe sees the year 1573 as the birthyear of the Brandenburg *Volksschule,* because the visitation ordinance of that year for the first time established the principle of a universal or common education.[9] This conclusion is even less valid than Wöhe's later designation of Frederick William I as the father of the Prussian *Volksschule.* There is, of course, a broken line of descent from the Sunday catechism classes and *Küsterschulen* to the later village German schools where reading, writing, arithmetic, singing, and religious instruction were taught. Elementary schools and universal education in the villages were, however, over a century away. Whatever beginnings were made after 1573 to improve schools in city and village were sadly interrupted by the Thirty Years' War. Lack of teachers, inability to pay teachers, parental resistance to

7. Wöhe, *Geschichte der Leitung,* pp. 12-14.

8. "Poor and Beggar Ordinance of 13 June 1596," cited by Vollmer, *Friedrich Wilhelm I,* p. 3.

9. Ibid., p. 6.

sending children to school, and lack of school buildings served to deprive Brandenburg of a fulfillment of the electoral decree for elementary schools made in 1573.

The Gymnasium

Elector John George (1571-1598), who issued the ordinance of 1573 to establish Latin schools, German schools for girls, and *Küsterschulen* in the villages, also established the first intermediate school or *Gymnasium* in Brandenburg territory. The last Franciscan in the Graue Kloster ("Gray Cloister") in Berlin died in 1571. On 13 July 1574, some buildings of the cloister having been granted to the city for this purpose, the *Gymnasium* of the Gray Cloister was established in Berlin, under city administration. In 1579 a school ordinance for this *Gymnasium* prescribed a curriculum consisting of religious education and Latin and Greek languages. Use of the German language for instruction was forbidden.[10] This was an effort to provide intermediate instruction and preparation for admission to the University at Frankfurt. However, the Berlin *Gymnasium* was established by combining the older Church schools, the St. Nicholas and St. Mary schools. The result was little more than a Latin school. The new creation had seven grades, the first two of which were really elementary. As Eberhard Faden put it, "The *Gymnasium* takes pupils without any basic education."[11] There was no other elementary Latin school in Berlin, according to Faden. Of the 600 students reported attending in 1586, the greatest number passed only through the first two grades to learn elementary reading and writing. The *Gymnasium,* nevertheless, continued to serve as both an elementary and an intermediate school and functioned adequately until the plague struck Berlin in 1637. The school was closed for most of 1637-1638, and it did not regain importance until restored by Frederick William after the Thirty Years' War.

A more significant effort to establish an intermediate school occurred in 1607 when Elector Joachim Frederick established a *Fürstenschule* at Joachimsthal, northeast of Berlin in the Uckermark.[12] The Elector's first concern in founding a territorial *Fürstenschule* was that it should offer to the children of his subjects instruction "in rechter reiner und unverfelschter Lehre [in pure and unadulterated doctrine]." Upon completion of studies at the new *Gymnasium,* Joachim Frederick then intended these students to continue their education at the University of Frankfurt so that these people could be used in future to fill Lutheran pulpits or secular offices.

10. See Keller, *Volksschulwesen.*
11. *Berlin im Dreissigjährigen Kriege,* p. 120.
12. "Ordinance for the electoral Brandenburg *Gymnasium* at Joachimsthal, 24 Aug. 1607," Vormbaum, *Schulordnungen,* vol. 2, no. 2, pp. 62-70.

In founding this school Joachim Frederick clearly expressed his conception of the office of prince and the responsibility he felt for the welfare of his people. It was a duty imposed upon him by God to provide churches and schools as well as a *Fürstenschule* for the lands of the Mark Brandenburg.[13]

In fulfillment of this responsibility he endowed his *Fürstenschule* rather generously. He granted a house which he had built for himself, plus the local church, and the buildings formerly used by a glass factory. A new garden and a fish pond were assigned to provide food and income for the school.

A library was established with circulating or borrowing rights for both teachers and students. The elector further authorized the spending of 5 *thaler* at each Leipzig Fair for the acquisition of new books.

Out of his own capital he granted an endowment of 40,000 *Reichsthaler* to provide an interest yield of 2,400 *Reichsthaler* to pay the salaries of teachers and other servants. A newly established paper mill at Zedenick was to contribute 300 *Reichsthaler* annually and furnish thirty reams of paper (*drei Ballen*) to be distributed among the poor students. From certain designated electoral domains he assigned annual gifts of food (2,400 bushels each of rye and barley, 600 bushels of hops, 72 bushels each of peas and buckwheat grits, mutton, and pork), and 20 tuns each of red and white wine from the electoral wine cellar at Cölln. He also directed the annual delivery from Ruppin of 36 bolts of black cloth to provide clothing for the students.

In the previous reign, the nobility of the Neumark had agreed to support twenty girls at a school located at the Kloster Zehden. This had not been done. Now, Joachim Frederick required the nobility to support ten needy sons of the Neumark nobility at Joachimsthal, ten who could meet the entrance requirements. The overseers of the Zehden cloister were required each year to furnish to the *Gymnasium* either 50 oxen or 500 *thaler* out of the Neumark domain chamber.

The school further was endowed with a number of electoral domains whose income would be used for the support of the school and to furnish free building timber and firewood. The elector in addition indicated his intention to purchase a nearby village for 6,000 *Reichsthaler* so that the villagers would be able to furnish transportation labor and other servants for the school.

The charter of establishment for the new princely school, so richly endowed, assigned an original enrollment of 120 free students: the 10

13. ". . . we are reminded that our highest and chief duty imposed by God is to provide, multiply, and maintain churches and schools, to establish princes' schools in our Electorate of Brandenburg, so that our subjects' children, brought up in correct, pure and unadulterated doctrine, get a good foundation of learning and then usefully continue their studies at our University of Frankfurt, and we, or our successors, may then make good use of them as preachers or in some other position." Ibid., pp. 63-64.

needy sons of Neumark nobility, 80 from the towns and cities of the Altmark, Mittelmark, Uckermark, Ruppin, Prignitz, and Neumark, 10 sons of poor court servants, and 20 indigent sons of clergymen. Each town was to nominate 4 candidates, and 1 or 2 of the best qualified were to be selected. Each student would furnish his own bed linen, personal clothes, and books. Otherwise he would get free education for four to five years. Those who neglected their studies or were guilty of misbehavior were to be dismissed and replaced by others more appreciative. In addition to the 120 free students, 50 more who could pay their own way were to be taken in at an annual fee of 25 *thaler*. The elector directed that any surplus from fees, gifts, and sale of domain products was to be invested and the income used either to support more free students or to increase the stipends of the existing free students.

In endowing the school so generously and in offering a free education to so many young men who were competitively selected, the elector made it clear that the school was established for the welfare of the electorate. Those who received stipends would in the future be obliged to serve in some public capacity, religious or civil, in the electorate. The students were to be native children of poor parents from the towns and villages of Brandenburg who were the best qualified academically and who were selected by examination. Some students were to be selected on the basis of proficiency in the Wendish or Polish languages, so that they could serve the churches of those areas where these languages were spoken. All students were required to have basic skill in Latin acquired in the city Latin schools. The minimum age was set at twelve, and the course of study was not to exceed four or five years.

A second part of the establishing ordinance detailed the administrative organization, the duties and responsibilities of the rector, instructors, and students, as well as the course of study and the daily schedule of classes.

The head of the school was the rector, who "should be a learned man in humanities, arts, Latin, and Greek." He was to assign each student according to ability to his proper class or grade. He was to see that all instruction was given as scheduled, and was to consult frequently with his colleagues on the means of improving instruction and discipline. The first rector was a Carl Bumann (1607-1610).

Below the rector there was to be a curator or administrator, primarily responsible for discipline—personal, pedagogical, and confessional. All members of the administration and instruction staff were to adhere to the Augsburg Confession. Instructors were to prevent students from having exposure to sectarian teaching, particularly Calvinism. The elector felt that students should not read heretical books. The business management and administration of the property and income of the school were placed under the jurisdiction of a *Vorwalter* (comptroller). All nonacademic servants were placed under his supervision.

The subjects of instruction at this intermediate level included grammar, Latin, Greek, Hebrew, dialectics, rhetoric, ethics, physics, arithmetic, geometry, and astronomy. The pastor assigned to the school was to give lectures in theology. No instructor was to absent himself from class without permission of the rector and curator. His colleagues were expected to teach his classes in his absence. A precise schedule of classes by the day and hour for each grade was laid down.

All dismissals, resignations, and new admissions were to be reported to and approved by the elector.

This was an enlightened and necessary effort to give to Brandenburg a link in the system of schools which was lacking despite the establishment of the *Gymnasium* of the Gray Cloister in Berlin in 1574. The need for preachers, teachers, and public servants, the promotion of the general welfare of the subjects and territory of the elector required a well-endowed intermediate school which could produce useful graduates or serve as preparation for further university study. The whole plan and design of the school fitted in with Luther's exhortations almost a century earlier. The best minds of Brandenburg were to be selected by competitive examination for education according to merit. Free education was to be offered to the poor but deserving students so that Brandenburg would not lack educated leaders. Unfortunately, the school was founded on the eve of the Thirty Years' War and suffered extinction because of it. In 1636 the buildings of the school were burned by the Swedes. Students and teachers were dispersed, and the school ceased, temporarily, to exist.

Frederick William (1640-1688) restored this *Fürstenschule*. A commission appointed by him to advise on the restoration recommended that the Joachimsthal *Gymnasium* should be moved to Berlin. This was done in 1650, and the school at first existed in private houses. In 1667 the elector gave the school its own building, but this was soon outgrown. King Frederick I in 1707 laid the foundation for an addition to the school which was not completed until 1717 under Frederick William I.[14]

The University

Between 1500 and 1694 Brandenburg had only one university, that of Frankfurt. Other universities existed or were established in the several territories inherited or acquired by the Hohenzollern electors in the seventeenth century.[15] Frankfurt, however, had the distinction of being the oldest university in Hohenzollern lands. Albert Achilles (1470-1486) conceived of the idea of founding a university and willed the idea to his

---

14. See Vormbaum, *Schulordnungen,* vol. 2.
15. E.g., the University of Königsberg was founded by the Duke of Prussia in 1544. Prussia was inherited by the Hohenzollern of Brandenburg in 1618.

successor John Cicero (1486-1499). John Cicero collected funds for this purpose and took the first steps. As early as 1493 the city of Frankfurt put in a claim for location. In 1495, at the Diet of Worms, Emperor Maximilian urged the electors of the Holy Roman Empire to establish universities in their lands—having Brandenburg and Saxony in mind particularly. Brandenburg was in need of domestically trained university men for public service and diplomacy, but Elector John died before he could fulfill his inherited mission or carry out the imperial urging.

It was Joachim I (1499-1535) who achieved success. From Emperor Maximilian he received a Privilege dated 26 October 1500 to establish a university for the purpose of introducing the teaching of Roman law and humanistic studies. The university was established at Frankfurt on 26 April 1506, with the Bishop of Lebus serving as the first chancellor.[16] The university consisted of the traditional four faculties: arts, theology, medicine, and law. The university was immediately endowed with certain privileges, including exemption of students from civil authority. Students involved in violations of law were to be turned over to the rector, who would send them to the Bishop of Lebus for trial.

The normal procedure for those admitted to the University of Frankfurt was to enter the faculty of arts (after 1574 and 1607 from the two Brandenburg *Gymnasien*) where a course of study in general liberal arts for about four years led to a master's degree. Then for some came a period of professional training of another four years leading to a doctor's degree in theology, law, or medicine. Of the professional faculties, that of law was perhaps the most distinguished and most useful. It trained men who then were appointed to various municipal or territorial administrative offices. It became the principal means for the introduction of Roman law into the Brandenburg territories. It served as a decision-making court for criminal cases tried in municipal courts. The faculty of theology was for a time a conservative Catholic body which resisted the Lutheran Reformation. Until the late seventeenth century, the Saxon Lutheran university at Wittenberg furnished more theologians, preachers, and teachers for Brandenburg than did that of Frankfurt. The medical faculty as late as the eighteenth century was small and not particularly distinguished for the quality of its medical teaching.

The University of Frankfurt from the beginning was a territorial university, a creation of the elector of Brandenburg and an instrument of the *Polizeistaat*. It was established to serve the needs of the state for educated and professional servants in church and state, to promote the general welfare of the state. The university was financially supported by the elector; students were given stipends to enable them to complete their studies. In 1564 Brandenburg citizens were forbidden to study at

---

16. "First Privilege of the University of Frankfurt, 1506," *C. C. March.,* vol. 1, pt. 2, no. 1, cols. 573-576. See Gustav Bauch, *Die Anfänge der Universität Franckfurt a. Oder,* pp. 1-6.

outside universities, and city magistrates were ordered to fill public vacancies with graduates of the domestic university.[17] The ban against foreign study and the requirement to employ native sons were ineffective. Wittenberg continued to be more attractive for theological studies until the University of Halle was established in 1694. Nevertheless, the university which was founded at Frankfurt in 1506, for two hundred years after its founding, served in many ways as an institutional expression of the interest of the Hohenzollern electors in the welfare of their lands. Founded in an era of universal Catholic unity, it became, until eclipsed by the new University of Halle, the highest educational institution in the system of schools which included the elementary city Latin schools and the intermediate *Fürstenschulen*.

17. Paulsen, *Gelehrten Unterrichts*, 1:258.

12

Ideas and Writers Influencing Education
in the Seventeenth Century

The heritage of ideas about education and schools in seventeenth-century Germany and Brandenburg derived essentially from the Protestant Reformers. The desire for universal literacy inspired the principles of universal and compulsory education. Religious instruction was fundamental to all instruction both for the salvation of souls (i.e., personal welfare) and to promote *guter Polizei* (general welfare). Despite complete secularization of responsibility for the establishment and maintenance of schools, there was still a close association of church and school. Clergymen and theologians served as teachers and inspectors in schools at all levels. Supervision of schools was placed under the secular administrative office of the Lutheran consistory, in effect a "Bureau of Ecclesiastical Affairs."

The framework of a school system from the elementary to the university level was well defined by the seventeenth century. On a religious-humanistic foundation this system was designed to produce public servants for school, church, the marketplace, and city and territorial government. Intrinsic to this Protestant school system were the ideas of free education, supported by stipends to indigent students, schools for girls, selection for admission to higher schools by examination and merit, and certification of teachers.

In the seventeenth century new ideas were introduced by a great variety of writers. Some were theologians, some political philosophers, some were protophilosophers of education. Some of these ideas were closely attuned to the ideas of the previous century, some were radically different and more attuned to the changing circumstances or demands of the early modern state. And it must be recognized that some ideas of the seventeenth century were no more successful of realization than were some of the sixteenth century, for instance, the idea of compulsory, universal education.

Some of the notable personalities and writers on schools and education included Johann Justus Winckelmann (1620-1699), Wolfgang Ratichius (1571-1635), Johann Amos Comenius (1592-1671), Veit Ludwig von Seckendorff (1626-1692), and Johann Joachim Becher (1635-1682). Probably the most effective influence upon the Brandenburg-Prussian school system was that of Pietism, and more particularly the ideas and model schools of August Hermann Francke (1663-1727) at Halle.

The men of the seventeenth century concerned themselves with methods of instruction more than their predecessors had. Ratichius and Comenius both urged the use of the German language for instruction, although it was not until the end of the seventeenth century that Thomasius took this revolutionary step at Halle. Ratichius in 1612 urged a new method of teaching languages, a method which would be endorsed in the mid-twentieth century. He, like his contemporary Francis Bacon, wanted to free the higher schools from the tyranny of "the vain pagan Aristotle," in a reaction against the pagan humanism introduced by the Renaissance. Both Comenius and Ratichius, like Luther, were convinced of the necessity of knowing the ancient languages as a tool, something which could be acquired rather quickly and which served the cause of Christianity. Comenius particularly was concerned with the use of German through the age of twelve, which was roughly half the time he would devote to education. The period of study for him was divided into four stages of six years each. The first six years were the time of the *Mutterschule* where the child learned from the mother the elements of the German language and of virtue and piety. After infancy, from six to twelve years, the child should enter a public vernacular school, a German school. From the ages twelve to eighteen, those who were qualified should attend a classical Latin school; and finally the student should go to the academy or university from the ages of nineteen to twenty-four. He believed in compulsory attendance for both boys and girls to the age of twelve. But he recognized, writing in 1633, that there were no schools to achieve this purpose and urged a reformation of the school system to establish elementary schools everywhere. He believed in a broad, inclusive curriculum which would expose the child in the second and third stages to elements of physics, optics, astronomy, geography, chronology, history, and home economy. He suggested new methods and devices to aid in easy learning, relying upon experience with nature, identifying the thing with the word for quick learning.[1] Actually, Comenius and Ratichius had little influence on elementary schools, which were lacking, but they exerted considerable influence in many territories on the upper school system.

In the seventeenth century, political philosophers increasingly emphasized the legal responsibility of the state for education, and educational writers urged placing school supervision entirely under secular officials of the prince. Most of the writers on schools wanted professional supervision (with the exception of Althusius, who would leave it with the church).[2] Winckelmann, in a pedagogical treatise of 1649, wanted to

1. See Vormbaum, *Schulordnungen,* vol. 2, app., for J. A. Comenius, *Informatorium der Mutterschule,* part of his *Didactica Magna* (1633). See also Paulsen, *Gelehrten Unterrichts,* 1:472-481, for the ideas of Ratichius and Comenius.
2. Wilhelm Kahl, "Zur Geschichte der Schulaufsicht im 16., 17. und 18. Jahrhundert: V Die Schulaufsichtsfrage bei den deutschen Rechtsphilosophen und Nationalokönomen des 17. Jahrhunderts," in *Monatsblätter für Schulaufsicht* 8 (1907): 129-136, as reviewed in *Historisch-pädagogischer Literatur-Bericht Über das Jahr 1907* (Berlin, 1908).

divorce the state's school officials from the consistory. He urged a general inspector for each territory who would hold regular visitations and inspection of territorial schools (rural and urban), but he would leave responsibility for weekly checks on the elementary schools and teachers with the parish clergy.[3]

Much the same secular view was held by Johann Joachim Becher, forerunner of the German cameralist school. In his *Methodus Didactica* (1668), he stressed education as the means by which the fundamental goal, the welfare of the state, would be best advanced. To make education contribute to the general welfare of the state with greatest efficiency, Becher advocated complete separation of church and school and urged establishment of a separate administrative bureau for education.[4]

One of the most interesting and significant writers of mid-seventeenth-century Germany on schools and education was Veit Ludwig von Seckendorff. Like Winckelmann, he wrote after the conclusion of the Thirty Years' War and was concerned with the restoration of schools and the advancement of education. He was influenced not only by the Reformation heritage of ideas but by the writings of Ratichius and Comenius. Like his contemporary Becher, but more from the viewpoint of a political philosopher than of a cameralist, he approached education and schools in terms of their promotional significance to the welfare of the state. Seckendorff published his views on schools and education in his *Teutscher Fürsten-Staat* in 1655, and reviewed the whole system of schools which had developed in Protestant Germany since the Reformation.[5]

Seckendorff maintained that schools must have two basic functions: necessary instruction in Christian doctrine, and instruction in those skills and arts which are generally useful to all classes, namely, reading, writing, and arithmetic. He was thus in agreement with Comenius and Luther that the elementary level of schools was indispensable. But he found that in the German nation very few parents recognized how important it was to bring up their children in the Christian religion, no matter what else they were educated for. It was not enough, he argued, to expose children to public sermons to learn the true faith, since sermons were for adults. Only schools could do this properly. He recognized that for almost a century, in Lutheran lands, the establishment of schools had been urged and that school ordinances had been issued to further schools and educational standards. These ordinances had required qualified teachers of good religious standing, had laid down principles and methods of teaching and conduct, had standardized books, had divided students according to ability and progress into grades, and had given

3. Wöhe, *Geschichte der Leitung,* pp. 18-20.
4. Ibid., p. 28.
5. Veit Ludwig von Seckendorff, *Teutscher Fürsten-Staat,* 9th ed., ed. Andres Simson von Biechling. First published 1656. See pt. 2, chap. 4, "Concerning Schools," pp. 329-349.

priority to religious education in the German language. Like Comenius, he felt that children at the elementary level should be taught certain virtues: honesty, obedience, humility, and moral behavior. Comenius had written that all misbehavior and delinquency among men were to be found rooted in the neglect of education of children. Seckendorff argued that the kind of upbringing and education which a child had would determine the kind of adult he would be. However, where to Comenius "the goal of life is the achievement of salvation," Seckendorff, perhaps, was equally concerned with the benefits to the welfare of the state to be derived from a literate population brought up in the Christian virtues of obedience, honesty, hard work, and good behavior. He agreed with his predecessors that parents should be required to send children to school at age five and that truancy was not to be permitted.

He called for regular inspections and examinations by ministers and official inspectors, to see that the school ordinances were obeyed. Seckendorff further deplored the universal fact that poor salaries for teachers at the elementary level attracted the incompetent rather than those who were most suitable for teaching.

These elementary schools, which Seckendorff described, were German schools "such as are found in practically all villages and in towns." This is a surprising statement to find in Seckendorff. Elementary German schools may have existed in villages in some German territories; there were very few in Brandenburg. The Thirty Years' War had certainly had a disastrous effect on village life and on elementary schools in many parts of Germany. Teachers were not available. At the most, one might have found *Küsterschulen,* essentially catechism schools. However accurate or inaccurate his assessment in 1655 was, the jurist Seckendorff made a good case for the necessity of a universal *Volksschule* and for compulsory education through the elementary level.

Next in sequence he found Latin schools, which were mostly limited to towns and cities. Here, he stated, Latin, Greek, and Hebrew were taught. This had been the sixteenth-century goal and plan. In fact, few Latin schools offered instruction in Greek and Hebrew.

Too often parents were eager to terminate the education of their children after elementary school. But Seckendorff felt it was important to persuade parents whose children were intellectually apt and who could profit from higher schools to send those children on to the Latin schools and beyond. Not all children, however, should get the same kind of education after age twelve. Some should follow a course of languages and humanities to prepare them for service to church and state. For these the classical course in the Latin school was right. But others should be trained in crafts and business, since "the general welfare required all kinds of people, and not all similarly educated." The common welfare required all kinds of trained people, some in the humanities, some in what would later be called the *Realen* (the sciences), some in crafts and trades.

Seckendorff opposed sending to higher schools those who lacked the proper aptitude, "so that the world would not be endangered by half-educated people."

From the Latin school the student moved to the *Gymnasium,* where he was expected to have a usable knowledge of Latin and some elementary Greek. The curriculum consisted of advanced reading in theological and religious literature, in Latin and Greek classics, the study of Hebrew, logic, physics, mathematics, and secular and church history. Finally, he would complete his studies at a university or academy, in one of the four professional faculties.

Seckendorff offered no novel ideas about the school systems of the Protestant territories, but he did describe the system as it had evolved since the days of Luther. For our purpose, perhaps the most valuable aspect of Seckendorff's writing was the identification of a good school system, and a population educated according to ability, with the general welfare and progress of a state.

None of the writers of the seventeenth century—Ratichius, Comenius, Seckendorff, among others—had any real influence on elementary education or on teacher training. It would be difficult to find any direct influences on the school system resulting from their writings.

There was one powerful source of influence which did, however, have a practical, direct, and immediate impact on all levels of schools and upon education in general. This was Pietism, and particularly the ideas of August Hermann Francke. The influence of Pietism on education was felt most in the Hohenzollern territories of Brandenburg-Prussia, and manifested itself in the schools established at Halle by Francke. This influence was not effective until the end of the seventeenth century, and then, through the model schools at Halle and the graduates of the new University of Halle, it was the single most powerful influence on Prussian schools and education throughout the eighteenth century. Pietism did more for the development of the Prussian *Volksschule* than all previous admonitions about the need for elementary schools. That it achieved enormous success in the school system of Prussia, shaped the philosophy of education, and contributed to a systematic effort to improve the methods and quality of teaching was due less to anything intrinsic in Pietism than it was due to the close alliance between the leaders of Pietism and the first two kings in Prussia. Elector/King Frederick III/I (1688-1713) and Frederick William I (1713-1740) offered royal protection and support to the Pietists and to Francke and were themselves deeply influenced in their legislative efforts to improve schools and education by the Pietists of Halle.

Until the late seventeenth century, Brandenburg and Brandenburg-Prussia had reacted, in terms of educational ideas and institutions, to the developments elsewhere in Germany. Under Pietist inspiration, the flow of ideas and influence on educational development was reversed. Prussia became a leader and a model generally, and a pioneer in a realistic *Volksschule.*

Pietism as a religious movement is not the primary concern here, but rather its impact on education. Yet it is impossible to divorce the two, since the religious goals and objectives of Pietism can only be reached through the medium of education. Pietism was part of the Second Reformation, which sought to restore the ideals of Luther to a living reality. Primarily and basically it was concerned with a spiritual-moral regeneration, an uplifting of the life of the people, a rejection of the rigid dogmatism of Lutheran orthodoxy. The means for this was through the advancement of universal popular education. This in turn produced the idea of a universal, legal, compulsory school attendance (*Schulpflicht* or *Schulzwang*). To the Pietist, life on this earth should be dedicated to the glorification of God. The world and life have meaning only in terms of God's purpose. And education was the principal instrument to discover God's purpose, to fill man with a proper religious spirit. Religion was an individual experience of consciousness; it was a religion of the heart not of mind or reason. Intellectual confession of faith and external worship do not make the Christian man; it is the inner man who receives God into his heart. Piety thus is a moral fulfillment which releases the individual from concern only for the "I." Education will emphasize development of personality, of moral character, to the end of improving public life. Pietism did not seek to flee the world in ascetic fashion but to live in and to improve the world by improving the personality and moral character of the individual through religious education. Preaching the Golden Rule and emphasizing the Christian doctrine of "Love your neighbor," Pietism became social welfare and social teaching, as the individual achieves fulfillment morally by his service to the community. In the development of individual personality there was a fundamental law of the community: concern for one's fellowman. "All wisdom and learning is vain and foolish if it is not founded on true and clear love of God and one's fellowman."[6] The education of Pietism was education by and for the community. All human differences of person, estate, profession, and education disappear before the commonality of community welfare and the glory of God. This opened the door for education for all men, a Christian popular education. The Pietists were concerned with *Volksbildung* (popular education). Writers like Comenius and Seckendorff had emphasized secondary education. The Latin schools were isolated from a concept of popular education.

6. Quoted by Elisabeth Gloria, *Der Pietismus als Förderer der Volksbildung und sein Einfluss auf die preussische Volksschule,* from the enabling ordinance for the orphanage schools of Francke. This work of Gloria is an exceptionally able examination of the influence of Pietism upon Prussian education.

The Pietist influence on Prussian education manifested itself after 1690 in several forms. Schools for orphans and schools for the poor set a pattern for elementary schools taught in German. The emphasis on social welfare meant that education was not only religious but useful in the form of technical training. The need for teachers was met with schools designed to train teachers and develop improved methods of teaching. Thus, through the influence of Pietism, some of the basic teachings of Martin Luther were finally realized. Religious instruction was fundamental to all education. The catechism, fallen into neglect during the Thirty Years' War, was again made basic in Christian education. Education was made universal through obligatory attendance at elementary schools. The fulfillment of this goal meant more schools and more teachers. And the Pietist schools at Halle, including the university, made a major contribution towards supplying teachers from teacher-training seminaries. Francke was perhaps a pioneer in revealing that education is a technical profession requiring training.[7]

7. For a general study of Pietism as a religious movement as well as its promotion of education, see Klaus Deppermann, *Der hallesche Pietismus und der preussische Staat unter Friedrich III. (I.),* a recent and thorough work. A brief summary may be found in Wöhe, *Geschichte der Leitung,* pp. 30-34.

13

Development of a School System, 1650-1740

During the seventeenth century two major factors (or events) placed a severe strain on the efforts of the Hohenzollern electors to develop a complete school system for Brandenburg. One was the catastrophic effect of the Thirty Years' War on education. The other factor was the acquisition of German territories from the Rhine to the Memel River, territories with their own distinct educational and school traditions. Inheritance and the terms of peace treaties added to Brandenburg the territories of East Prussia, East Pomerania, Magdeburg, Halberstadt, Minden, Cleves, Mark, and Ravensberg. The multiplicity of possessions with varying traditions and institutions made it difficult to establish a uniform school system and uniform administration for Brandenburg-Prussia. However, this factor did not diminish the interest of the Hohenzollern princes in furthering the welfare of their subjects or of their lands through the promotion of educational institutions, schools, universities, libraries, museums, academies of science and arts, an astronomical observatory, and so on.

A much greater problem facing the Hohenzollern in the seventeenth century was that produced by the great religious war. Friend and foe, confessional allies as well as Roman Catholics, all ravaged the land, destroyed its prosperity, reduced its population. Many schools in Brandenburg were forced to close or ceased to exist. They suffered a loss of students and teachers because of the disorders of the time. Teachers could not be paid and turned to other activities. The first to suffer were the elementary schools which at best had had a precarious existence. The Latin schools, the *Gymnasien,* and the universities were closed or drastically reduced in numbers and activity. In 1650 the electorate of Brandenburg was not much better provided with schools than it had been in 1573. It did have a tradition of schools, a tradition of princely establishment and endowment of schools; it had learned the practical value of these princely schools in furnishing educated public leaders; it would be encouraged to reestablish schools by the writings and influence of the great German minds of the seventeenth century.

Brandenburg-Prussia in the ninety-year span from 1650 to 1740 was fortunate to have three rulers who were seriously concerned, among their other interests, with the general welfare of their subjects and particularly with the advancement of education, schools, and intellectual development in their lands. An interesting source of information on this personal concern about schools on the part of the Brandenburg electors is provided in the series of political testaments which the princes published for the guidance of their successors. Thus an instruction of John Sigismund of 24 October 1619 exhorted his son and successor to concern himself with the growth and prosperity of the academies and princely schools "which are the territory's most precious treasure."[1] A formula for the protection of churches and schools began to evolve in the second testament of Frederick William of 25 August 1655.[2] For himself and for his successors, the elector was primarily concerned with protection and preservation of the schools of the Reformed church (e.g., Joachimsthalschule and the University of Frankfurt) as well as with assuring the continuance of the positions of Calvinist teachers.

Not until the first testament of Elector Frederick III, of 3 July 1690, was any constructive reference made to improving the school system of Brandenburg: "The church and school system in all territories, where it cannot be improved, must at least preserve the status quo."[3] This identical language was adopted in the testament of King Frederick William I of 1 July 1714.[4] The testament of the first king, of 9 May 1705, perhaps best expressed the Hohenzollern policy concerning schools when he urged his successor not to be content with maintaining Reformed schools as he found them on his succession, but to seek to increase the number of schools and churches.[5]

These testaments were more than pious formularies paying lip service to the cause of education. Constructive, legislative action and personal intervention to promote the building and expansion of schools and to increase the supply of educated men in Brandenburg filled the century between 1640 and 1740.

Elector Frederick William, called the Great Elector, not only concerned himself with the restoration of schools and the addition of new schools but also was determined to establish a uniform, state educational system in all his many territories. He did little for elementary education, but he made a considerable contribution to the secondary and university levels of schools. He laid the foundations for the later *Staatsbibliothek* (State Library) in Berlin and established the first *Ritterakademie* in Brandenburg for the sons of nobles. Frederick III came under the influence of the Pietists, established the University of Halle, offered his protection to the Pietist schools, and established the Academy of Sciences. Frederick William I, also deeply influenced by the Pietists, did more for elementary schools than any previous Hohenzollern, and out of practical considerations he significantly advanced cameralist and medical education during his reign.

1. Hermann von Caemmerer, *Die Testamente der Kurfürsten von Brandenburg und der beiden ersten Könige von Preussen,* app., no. 3, p. 410.
    2. Ibid., no. 15, pp. 185-186.
    3. Ibid., no. 29, pp. 293-295.
    4. Ibid., no. 39, pp. 359-360.
    5. Ibid., no. 35, pp. 328-329.

Elementary Schools

Frederick William (1640-1688)

The Thirty Years' War had destroyed the promising beginnings of an elementary school system in Brandenburg, particularly in the villages. Elector Frederick William, between 1650 and 1688, evidenced a great interest in schools, in education, and in the advancement of cultural institutions, but he did practically nothing to promote elementary education. The area of elementary education too intimately involved the interests of corporate groups which Frederick William was unable to or unprepared to resist; there were other considerations of greater immediate concern to him for which he needed the cooperation of these groups: the granting of taxes, the increase of his army, the pursuit of an aggressive foreign policy. The Estates of his several territories asserted their constitutional rights to be involved in church and school affairs. In rural areas the noble landholders exercised the rights of patrons in appointing village preachers and teachers. They were financially responsible and were not interested in improvements which would be a burden on them. The towns, for obvious reasons, were more interested in elementary schools, both German and Latin.

However, even if there had been a more favorable attitude towards elementary education, there was a great lack of pastors and teachers as a result of the havoc of the Thirty Years' War. Those who did serve as teachers and preachers at the elementary level were forced to support themselves with other remunerative activities.[6]

That Frederick William was aware of the need for restoration and expansion of schools, that he recognized the need for state initiative and direction was best illustrated by his decision and effort to establish a uniform, state educational system in the Mark Brandenburg. In 1654 he called upon Johann Raue to serve as the first professional state school inspector in Brandenburg. He carried the title of "General Inspector of All Schools" in Brandenburg. He had previously served as Professor of History at Erfurt, and had been a collaborator of Comenius in Danzig. In January of 1654 Raue had submitted to Frederick William a plan for a State School Board which would be independent of the Lutheran consistory. It would be composed of a number of *Schulräte* (school commissioners), including privy councillors, members of the nobility, and members of the Estates who were interested in advancing the cause of education. The board was not to involve itself with religious matters; it was to supervise the plan of instruction in all schools, visit the lower and upper classes of schools, participate in annual general examinations,

6. *Urkunden und Actenstücke Zur Geschichte des Kurfürsten Friedrich Wilhelm von Brandenburg,* vol. 15: *Ständische Verhandlungen,* vol. 3 *(Preussen,* vol. 1), ed. Kurt Breysig (1894), p. 257 (cited hereafter as *UA*). The Prussian Diet at Königsberg of 1640 heard complaints about clerics who brewed beer and distilled brandy for sale.

make recommendations on methods of teaching and on discipline, enforce all measures legislated by the board, and have the right of approval of all books used in the schools. Raue's plan pleased Frederick William to the extent that on 26 July 1654 he appointed Raue "General-Inspector of All Schools of Our Electorate and Head of Our New Board."[7] The hopes attached to the appointment of Raue by the elector never achieved realization because the diet failed to provide collaborators and because of opposition to a state board with exclusive jurisdiction over schools. Five years later, in 1659, Raue was appointed director of the new electoral library in Berlin. It is not clear why Raue failed, but presumably it was because the Lutheran church feared the loss of control over schools and the nobles feared loss of the right of patronage. Brandenburg was not ready for a complete separation of church and school administration.

In the decade after the Peace of Westphalia, the Estates of Brandenburg and of the Duchy of Prussia were concerned with improvement of school affairs, but their grievances were directed primarily at restoring the universities of Frankfurt and of Königsberg as well as the several *Fürstenschulen* which had suffered from the war.[8] Elementary schools did not evoke a similar concern on the part of the several diets.

In Brandenburg, the Visitation and Consistorial Ordinance of 1573 was still the basic law for elementary education and remained so until 1713. Frederick William could do no more than his predecessor of 1573 in ordering that elementary schools be established by towns and rural parishes. The latter were responsible for building schools, requiring attendance, and supporting the schools. The effectiveness of the order was dependent upon the interest and initiative of noble patrons, village preachers, or town councils.[9] Rural elementary schools were little more than cathechism schools. Local and church control precluded any uniform regulation, supervision, and enforcement by a state board of education.

Frederick William had the problem of establishing a uniform school administration not only in electoral Brandenburg but also in the several territories which passed into the hands of the Hohenzollern between 1614 and 1680. To attempt to establish a centralized department of schools and education for all his territories would have been foolhardy. This was achieved only in the eighteenth century. In 1614, at the time of acquisition of the essentially Calvinist Rhineland territories of the Duchy of Cleves and the County of Mark, there already existed a number of Latin and German schools in the towns and some *Küsterschulen* in the villages. About fifty years later, in 1662, a report of the General Synod of the Calvinist Church in Cleves-Mark, based on a church visitation,

---

7. See Alfred Heubaum, *Geschichte des deutschen Bildungswesen seit der Mitte des 17. Jahrhunderts,* 1:349.

8. E.g., the diets of Brandenburg of June-November 1641, *UA,* vol. 10: *Ständische Verhandlungen,* vol. 2 (Mark-Brandenburg), ed. Siegfried Isaacsohn (1880), pp. 99-100; diet of 24 April 1652, ibid., p. 233; the Diet of Prussia of July 1661, *UA,* 15:523.

9. See Wöhe, *Geschichte der Leitung,* pp. 20-25.

suggested that there was need for improvement of schools. In the same year, Frederick William as Duke of Cleves published a church ordinance (which had been drawn up and submitted to him for approval by the general synod) which included a school ordinance.[10] Churches and congregations were urged to establish schools in villages and towns and to furnish qualified teachers. The primary qualification was adherence to the Reformed Church; the Heidelberg catechism was prescribed as the basis of religious instruction. The ordinance had effect mostly on town schools, but in general it made no more major contribution to expansion of elementary schools than similar legislation had in Brandenburg. Not until 6 August 1687 was a similar church and school ordinance published requiring the Lutheran parishes in Cleves and Mark to establish elementary schools.[11]

In the Duchy of East Prussia the oldest schools had been established by the Teutonic Order as early as 1300. There were cathedral and parochial schools in Elbing, Königsberg, and other towns. All were burgher schools in the trading towns; there were no village schools. After the Lutheran Reformation was introduced in 1525, some improvement was attempted. By an edict of 1568, church schools were attached to the larger town churches or parishes, and catechism instruction was required in the villages once a week. Not until 1638 did an official document speak of true elementary schools in East Prussia. During the winter months each village was to send one boy to school so that he could learn to pray and teach others. This weak beginning was disrupted by war, the Tartar invasion (1656-1657), and a plague (1709-1710). Thousands of persons were killed or died, villages were destroyed, and education for the young suffered. There were few churches and few teachers. As many as twenty to forty villages were served by one church and one school. The first Prussian *Landtag* meeting at Königsberg in 1640 petitioned their new duke to take measures to restore elementary schools in the towns. They made a surprising request for introduction of a uniform method of instruction with standard textbooks and lessons in all schools of the duchy.[12] In response to their complaint that preachers were neglecting their duties and no longer inspected parish schools Frederick William ordered on 19 November 1640 that church visitations, including inspections of schools, were to be renewed.[13] Nevertheless, no real progress in elementary education was made in East Prussia until the time of Frederick William I.[14]

The Duchy of East Pomerania, acquired in 1648, had made a good be-

10. Vormbaum, *Schulordnungen,* vol. 2, no. 28, chap. 4, pars. 49-52, "Schulordnung aus der Cleve-Märkischen Kirchenordnung."

11. Ibid., no. 42, pars. 89-102, "Schulordnung."

12. *UA,* 15:258.

13. *UA,* 15:276-277.

14. Lewin, *Preussischen Volksschule,* pp. 14-17. See also Jürgen Petersohn, "Wissenschaftspflege und Gelehrte Bildung im Herzogtum Preussen im letzten Viertel des 16. Jahrhundert," *Jahrbuch für die Geschichte Mittel- und Ostdeutschland* 11 (1962): 75-110.

ginning in developing an elementary school system in the sixteenth century through the influence of Johann Bugenhagen, who had been one of the first to respond to the teachings of Martin Luther. In 1534 he had been invited by the Pomeranian *Landtag* of Treptow to take charge of reforming the Pomeranian school system. The church ordinance of 1535, drawn up by him, included significant provisions for schools. He based his provisions on the "School Plans for Saxony" authored by Melanchthon in 1528. His ordinance attempted to provide schools, teachers, and a curriculum for the whole territory. His plans extended only to towns and town schools, however. City councils were to establish Latin schools, German schools, and girls' schools. The last two types of schools offered only catechism instruction and the learning of Bible verses and a few psalms. By 1600 schools had been established in half the Pomeranian towns and cities, but there was no evidence of schools in villages. The church ordinance of 1535 did not even mention them. As late as 1700 there were only a few village schools. The *Küster* gave catechism lessons, but there was a scarcity of village *Küster* in the Hohenzollern portion of Pomerania.[15]

By the terms of the Peace of Westphalia, the former Archbishopric of Magdeburg was acquired by the Hohenzollern dynasty in 1680. Prior to that time the Duchy of Magdeburg had been administered by August of Saxony. He was more enlightened and more successful in school reform than any other Protestant prince immediately after 1648. Magdeburg and Halberstadt thus were more fortunate in their school systems than any other Hohenzollern territory under the Great Elector. The city of Magdeburg had suffered total disaster during the great war, and the territory had been devastated. Administrator August lost no time in reviving and reforming the school system. A church ordinance of 1652 made the sacristans responsible for teaching boys and girls reading, writing, catechism, and church singing. A visitation of 1656 revealed the deplorable condition of schools, however, and this led to the publication of the Magdeburg school ordinance of 1658.[16] This ordinance was concerned with both the city Latin schools and the village German elementary schools. Reflecting the influence of Comenius, August prescribed a sequence of education which left the child in the *Mutterschule* until the age of six. From six to twelve he attended the elementary and grammar schools of town or village, and then went on to the public *Landschule* or *Gymnasium* until the age of eighteen. The Latin schools were divided into classes according to ability and achievement. The village schools were expected to teach rural children at least elementary reading and writing

15. Martin Wehrmann, *Die Begründung des evangelischen Schulwesens in Pommern bis 1563*, in *Beiträge zur Geschichte der Erziehung und des Unterrichts in Pommern,* no. 7.

16. Vormbaum, *Schulordnungen,* vol. 2, no. 25, pp. 486-518. The *Schul-Ordnung* of 14 October 1658 was first published (1673) in *Sämpliche Fürstliche Magdeburgische Ordnungen/ und vornehmsten Mandata . . . ,* pp. 271-325.

along with catechism instruction and Bible verses. The local village authorities were directed to enforce school attendance but, as was true elsewhere, this directive was ineffective because of the resistance of peasants who undeniably needed the farm labor of their children.

The most significant aspect of the Magdeburg school ordinance of 1658 was that it made school attendance compulsory, at least legislatively, between the ages of six and twelve. This requirement remained in effect after Frederick William became the Duke of Magdeburg in 1680. In 1685 the Magdeburg church ordinance was confirmed by Frederick William.[17] It detailed the duties, functions, and conduct of the village *Küster* who were to provide instruction in reading, writing, and catechism. As late as 1698, however, Elector Frederick III complained about poor school attendance in many ducal villages.[18] Six school laws (part of the 1698 edict but known only from an ordinance of 14 May 1716) proclaimed universal school attendance from age five until excused after catechism examination by the village pastor.[19] School attendance was required in summer and winter. Parents were threatened with a fine of six *Groschen* for each week of classes missed by their children.[20]

During the forty years after the Peace of Westphalia, the general situation regarding elementary education in the several territories which came under Hohenzollern rule presented much the same disappointing and futile picture. The Great Elector had a genuine and earnest interest and desire to further the general welfare by reestablishing elementary schools in town and village. The selfish corporate interests of the established Calvinist and Lutheran churches as well as the landed noble patrons negated any effort of the prince to establish a school administration completely under public control. Legislative requirements for compulsory attendance were frustrated by the noncooperation of rural parents. The war, in most territories, had destroyed schools and reduced the number of qualified teachers. In the villages, *Küsterschulen* were attempted as a means of providing instruction in reading and in catechism. Elementary schools were successful or effective only in the towns and cities to the extent that they were supported by town councils. The Great Elector, despite his concern for education, accomplished practically nothing in elementary education. Diplomacy, war, struggles with the territorial diets, economic development absorbed most of his energies. And yet, it would be at the risk of neglecting a fundamental cleavage in the historical nature of the seventeenth-century state to attribute Frederick William's lack of success in furthering elementary education to his involvement with other problems. Frederick William belonged to the new breed of "statist" rulers who subordinated all corporate group interests

17. *C. C. Magdeb.*, pt. 1, p. 29.
18. Ibid., pt. 1, p. 109, edict of 15 Oct. 1698.
19. Ibid., *Continuatio*, p. 231.
20. Vollmer, *Friedrich Wilhelm I*, pp. 15-16.

to the overriding purposes and general interests of the state. Education and a literate population were useful to the state. The purposes and values of education required state or public control, administration, support, supervision. The higher levels of schools made greater advances in the century after 1650 precisely because they were princely or territorial schools. So long as elementary schools remained essentially church schools or catechism schools, so long as the purposes of elementary schools were to teach "the pure faith," to inculcate a "fear of God," so long as teachers in elementary schools were church-sponsored, so long as elementary education was supervised by ecclesiastical consistories, in short, so long as elementary schools were under the control of the church and noble patron, it would be impossible to establish a uniform regulation of schools in Brandenburg or the other territories and to redirect the aims and purposes of elementary education. Legislative efforts to require compulsory education were conspicuous in all school ordinances of the seventeenth century. But this was neither a modern nor an innovating step. Luther and the Reformers had urged this. What was urgently needed was a complete separation of church and state in the field of education. Johann Raue had urged this in 1654. Similar ideas were expressed in the writings of J. B. Schupp, court preacher in Hesse-Darmstadt and later serving in Hamburg. In two important pedagogical works (*Der teutsche Lehrmeister,* 1658, and *Vom Schulwesen,* 1660) Schupp argued the need for separation of German schools from the church if Germany was to have good schools. The principal concern of the state, he further pleaded, was a complete reorganization of the school system. "It is true that the good education of youth and well-ordered schools are the foundation on which the welfare of society must be built."[21]

Despite the poor results of the Great Elector's efforts at the elementary level, there were two new developments during his reign which resulted directly from princely action. Garrison schools and orphanages were designed to provide elementary education for special groups of children and were the product of electoral initiative. Garrisons which were barracked in fortress cities created special problems that strained the resources of those cities. Military church congregations under the supervision of military chaplains developed in fortress cities. Some had their own garrison churches. Frederick William took the first step to provide garrison schools. At Potsdam, in 1662, he founded a court and garrison school for the children of his soldiers and for the court servants of the Reformed faith.[22] The children of the Berlin and Pillau garrisons were instructed by the *Küster* of the garrison parish. Separate schools did not always exist, but catechism instruction was to be given by garrison chap-

---

21. Quoted by Wöhe, *Geschichte der Leitung,* p. 26, from J. B. Schupp, *Ambassadeur Zipphusius* in *Zugab zu Doct. J. B. Schupp Schriften* (1667), p. 144.
    22. *C. C. March.,* vol. 3, pt. 1, 59 ff.

lains or the *Küster* of the garrison churches. In 1692 a separate Berlin garrison school was established to serve fifty children of the poorest soldiers. A teacher and an army barracks were furnished by Elector Frederick III. A second teacher to serve fifty additional children was added in 1693. The curriculum basically consisted of reading, writing, arithmetic, and religious instruction. Students with aptitude were taught Latin. Teachers were paid six *thaler* monthly out of the garrison marriage fund to which each newly married soldier contributed. At the end of ten years, by 1703, the Berlin garrison school had a school building of its own with three hundred students. The curriculum was expanded to include Greek and Hebrew, and the school was transformed into a Latin school. In 1707 a military orphanage was established in Berlin by Frederick I. The boys of the orphanage received elementary and religious instruction at the garrison school.

Frederick William I expanded this basic concept by adding schools for the children of a regiment wherever it was located.[23] On 21 October 1721 Frederick William established a garrison school at Potsdam for Lutheran children to complement the Calvinist garrison school established in 1662. In the same year he established a Berlin regimental school. Many officers set up legacies for the support of these military schools— to pay teachers' salaries and to buy books. Such schools were necessary because of the large number of army children and because the children were not always welcome in town or city schools. When separate regimental schools were not available, military children often received instruction in the charity schools (*Armenschulen*) of the locality.

The military schools were under the supervision of the garrison commandant or regimental commander. They were Lutheran schools, but provision was made for Calvinist and Catholic children to receive religious instruction from their own garrison or field clergymen. Nonreligious subjects, taught five hours daily, were the responsibility of regimental *Küster*. Frederick William's goal was to make of soldiers' children pious Christians, obedient subjects, brave and loyal soldiers, and good citizens. After 1716, royal military schools and the *Volksschule* for civilian children operated on the same principles at the elementary level. This was one illustration of what might be done to advance elementary education when the prince took the initiative and was not hindered by local traditions or vested interests.[24]

As the reign of the Great Elector had witnessed the solicitude of the prince for the education of military children and the beginning of garrison schools, so this reign also pioneered, in anticipation of the Pietists, in using the institution of an orphanage as an elementary school. Electress

23. Ibid., vol. 3, pt. 1, no. 160, cols. 403-404, "Circular Order of 22 Jan. 1720."

24. For a general and more complete discussion of the garrison school see F. Wienecke, *Beiträge zur Geschichte der Erziehung und des Unterrichts in Preussen—Das preussische Garnisonschulwesen.*

Louise Henrietta, of the House of Orange, took the initiative to found an orphanage in 1665 at her model village of Oranienburg north of Berlin, on the Havel River.[25] This concern for orphans extended beyond mere shelter and care. The Oranienburg Orphanage began with twenty-four children, twelve boys and twelve girls between the ages of eight and ten. Electress Louise granted an annual support of 1,200 *Reichsthaler* plus income in kind. The children were to receive not only catechism instruction and elementary reading and writing, but vocational training as well. As soon as a boy was strong enough, he was to be sent out daily to a nearby master to learn a trade, while still living at the orphanage. Half of his earnings went to the orphanage, and the remaining half was saved for him. The ordinance further provided that if among the boys there appeared a real intellect who could profit from further study, he was to be given the first free vacancy at the Joachimsthal *Gymnasium* at Berlin. At age seventeen or eighteen the girls were put out into good homes to learn domestic skills. If they got married they were given a dowry of 20 *Reichsthaler*.

The orphanage school founded by Electress Louise became a glorious memorial to her. However, its interest to us lies in its foreshadowing of the more significant and more famous orphanage and school for the poor founded at Halle, under Pietist influence, by August Hermann Francke. The combination of elementary and vocational education found at Oranienburg was also a conspicuous feature at Halle.

Only the beginning of a system of elementary schools was made by the Great Elector. City Latin and German schools did recover from the ravages of the Thirty Years' War, satisfied the needs of an urban population, and prepared some young men for the territorial, princely *Gymnasien* and the old and new universities. Requirements to establish *Küsterschulen* in the villages and to compel attendance of village children did not lead to the development of a universal *Volksschule*. Garrison schools and the Oranienburg orphan school were isolated and limited demonstrations of what might be accomplished when the full support of the elector was applied to establishing elementary schools. Rural education in principle and in practice by 1690 had not progressed much beyond the designs of the school ordinance of 1573.

Frederick III (1688-1713)

The real development of a system of elementary schools occurred under the first two Prussian kings and was a direct result of an "alliance" between the Hohenzollern rulers and Pietism. This was a mutually favorable alliance forged during 1691 and 1692. Frederick III offered asylum to the Pietists who were being expelled from the traditional Lutheran territories. In return, Pietist leaders eventually transformed the city of Halle

25. Vormbaum, *Schulordnungen,* vol. 2, no. 33, pp. 636-642, "Foundation and Ordinance of the Orphanage at Oranienburg, 1665."

into the greatest educational center in Germany. Two Pietist personalities played a major part in this alliance: Philipp Jacob Spener and August Hermann Francke. Spener's Pietistic Lutheranism had made him unacceptable to orthodox Lutheranism in Dresden, and in 1691 he accepted the invitation of Frederick III to come to Berlin as provost of St. Nicholas Church, where he remained until 1705. Elector/King Frederick was himself no Pietist, Quietist, or enthusiast in religion, but he had little sympathy for the rigid orthodoxy of the Lutheran and Calvinist establishments, and was drawn to the Pietist concern for the individual conscience and religious toleration. Spener's influence over Frederick in Berlin resulted in protection for Francke and his great social and educational reforms at Halle.

Francke was brought to Halle in 1692 to serve as Professor of Oriental Languages at the projected new university, established in 1694. He also filled a pastorate at Glaucha, a suburb of Halle. Both Francke and Spener were fundamentally interested in religious rebirth, in a full achievement of Luther's doctrine of the priesthood of all believers. This meant discovery by all men of the glory and purpose of God. Education was regarded by the Pietist leaders as the principal instrument to fill man with a proper religious spirit. Religious education was to be achieved by the use of Luther's catechism. Pietism was, however, to transcend the traditional catechism school of the seventeenth century, characteristic of Protestant Germany. Pietist education was not designed merely to lead men or youth to know God through the Scriptures in a dogmatic sense. Pietism differed from dogmatic Lutheranism in that it preached a living, practicing Christianity, and thus it emphasized the development of moral education as a means of improving public life. Education should prepare a youngster to live in this world, and so religious education was accompanied by technical or vocational training. Community welfare, individual moral fulfillment, and the glory of God were all goals of Pietist education. Education should be opened to all men, and the Pietists thus emphasized popular education. There was as much social welfare as catechism in the educational program of Francke.

The city of Halle was fertile territory for Francke's work. Plague (1681), two serious fires (1683, 1684), decimated population (from 13,000 to 7,000) had created a social and moral atmosphere devoid of religious piety if not of religious formality. Halle was famous for its many *Freudenhäuser* (brothels), there was much dancing, drinking, and frivolity on Sundays, people slept through sermons regularly, no one seemed concerned with the education of the youth of Halle, and the children of the poor grew up without any education at all.

Francke at first concerned himself with establishing church discipline and combating religious ignorance by organizing prayer meetings and Bible readings, by intensifying catechism instruction and giving poor children school money out of the church collections so that poverty would not cause neglect of religious education.[26]

Having restored a more intensive religious life to Glaucha and Halle, against the opposition and accusations of the orthodox Lutheran clergy and with the support of Veit von Seckendorff, of the Brandenburg privy council, and of the elector himself, Francke in 1693 turned to the great mission of his life—social reform plans which had nothing less for their aim than the total reconstruction of society. To Francke, the root of all social evil was poverty and poor education. So he set out to eradicate poverty and to educate the youth. Education was the basic solution.

Beginning in 1695 Francke set out on a course of building educational institutions which would include an orphanage, a school for the poor, a German school, a Latin school, a *Gymnasium,* and a teacher-training institute. Basic to the system of schools that he would build were the *Waisenhaus* and *Armenschule.* The fame of these schools designed for the poor attracted so much attention and demand from the more affluent members of Halle that he was forced to establish schools for the other classes. Since his ultimate goal of reconstructing society through education depended upon teachers of the right kind, he was forced to undertake a reform of pedagogy, and to this end he established a *Seminarium praeceptorum* for the training of teachers.

The step-by-step expansion of Francke's institutions is a magnificent story. Concerned with the poor of Glaucha, he took their children into his home to give them religious instruction. Then in 1695 he decided to build a school for the poor, but this resulted in the *Waisenhaus,* an orphanage and a school for orphans which also provided a school for the city poor, as day students, an *Armenschule.* The latter won instant fame, and wealthy burghers and aristocrats sent or sought to send their children to Francke's school. From this urgent pressure evolved several schools to serve the needs of the several social classes.

The *Armenschule* was a German school and was so officially called after 1710 (*Deutsche Schule*). This was a *Volksschule* to serve the children of peasants and craftsmen. Its curriculum consisted of catechism and Bible lessons, reading, writing, arithmetic, music, and other practical things. The number of children in the German schools rose to over 2,000 by 1727.[27]

He also established Latin schools which prepared the children of the wealthy for the university. The *Bürgerschule* (city school) prepared future theologians, jurists, physicians, and merchants. The *Paedagogium Regium* (1702) educated the children of army officers, nobles, and bureaucrats for service to the state.

But Francke believed, as Luther did, in education according to the mer-

---

26. Deppermann, *Der Hallesche Pietismus,* pp. 71-76.
27. Gloria, *Pietismus als Förderer der Volksbildung,* p. 27.

its of the individual. There was abundant crossing of social lines, and children of the lower classes who were qualified were sent to the Latin schools for university preparation.

The increasing number of schools and the rapidly growing student enrollment reemphasized a problem which had plagued seventeenth-century German and Prussian efforts to improve and expand elementary schools, namely, the lack of qualified teachers. Francke found a ready source of teachers among the students of the new University of Halle. For two hours of teaching daily, they were given a free meal at the orphanage. A supply was available, and as many as 134 student teachers were reported before 1700 as having a regular table at the orphanage. From this practice there emerged in 1707 a formal *Seminarium praeceptorum,* a teacher-training institute. Selected students were given two years' free subsistence and training in pedagogy. Such students agreed to serve the Francke schools for three years after that.

It is not our purpose to study in detail the Pietist schools but rather to observe the impact they had on the Hohenzollern kings and thus upon Prussian education. Monarchs and Pietist leaders were of one mind in their concern for the common welfare, for the moral and religious welfare of the individual. Education was to be the means by which the welfare of society and of the individual were to be advanced.

The real significance of the educational contributions and social work against poverty of August Hermann Francke derived from the tolerant and enlightened attitude and benevolent protection extended to Francke and his work by Elector Frederick III and the support and adoption of the whole Franckian establishment by King Frederick William I.

In 1698 Frederick III granted a privilege to Francke which made the *Waisenhaus* an institution of public law and permitted Francke to establish a printing press, bindery, bookstore, a public apothecary, and various income-producing economic ventures. The educational foundations of Francke became in effect state institutions, tax-exempt, self-supporting, licensed by royal privilege.

All of Francke's schools became model schools: the Halle *Waisenhaus* became a model for other orphanages throughout the Prussian territories. The German school set a pattern for the Prussian, elementary *Volksschule*. The *Seminarium praeceptorum* provided a model for other teacher-training institutes. Education for all children, compulsory education even for the poor, became a reality. A curriculum based on the catechism but offering vocational training as well to prepare the Prussian youth to meet the realities of life became a standard curriculum. The use of the German language, even in the Latin schools, as the basic language of instruction was a major innovation. The expansion of the curriculum in the secondary schools to emphasize modern foreign languages and the new sciences with the use of laboratory equipment was a radical step. But the real impact of Pietism was felt at the elementary level. Pietist theologians and teachers, products of the University of Halle and the teacher seminary of Francke spread the idea of the *Volksschule* by establishing schools all over Prussia.

Although Pietism was a religious movement and made religious instruction fundamental in its whole pattern of education, it contributed to the secularization of Prussian schools and the development of a public school system in the eighteenth century. It inspired the legislative efforts of Frederick William I to promote elementary education.

In 1710 Crown Prince Frederick William swore that he would abolish the Pietist establishment when he became king. In August 1711, while Frederick William was passing through Halle, curiosity about Francke's *Waisenhaus* led him to drive around the five-story building of the orphanage and its related buildings, which harbored a dozen schools, a publishing house, an apothecary, and other enterprises. The crown prince admired the buildings, sent an observer inside who gave him a favorable report on the activities of the Franckian establishment, learned from the Halle postmaster that money poured in daily from philanthropic friends and that the Pietist establishment had earned large sums of money from its book business and sales of medical remedies.

A few weeks later, on 23 August 1711, Francke prepared a paper for Frederick William detailing the benefits his establishment had produced since 1695. Astutely or accidentally, he argued not in religious but in mercantilist terms which would appeal to the economy-minded prince. The paper revealed that large sums of money poured into Halle annually from other territories as gifts and from sales. The Franckian institutions aided the economy by spending 30,000 *thaler* annually on clothes and food, and had given much work to craftsmen in building some seventy houses. From these economic activities the excise and sales tax profited considerably, and the post office netted about 500 *thaler* annually. The remedies manufactured and sold by the *Waisenhaus,* such as Hoffman's drops, relieved many sick people. The free meal table for students who taught at the orphanage schools made it possible to give instruction and practice in teaching methods to hundreds of future teachers. The educational institution at Halle served as model schools for the whole state. And the German schools for boys and girls, by emphasizing a practical as well as a Christian education, produced God-fearing, obedient, and hard-working subjects.

Frederick William was impressed after studying this paper and adopted a friendlier attitude towards the Pietists. On 12 April 1713, shortly after becoming King, Frederick William made a surprise inspection of the *Waisenhaus* to assure himself about it. This time he entered the building, spent two hours inspecting and talking, and came away satisfied. He promised to support Francke against any obstacles or opposition. Happily the alliance between the Hohenzollern and Pietism was renewed. On 10 May 1713 Frederick William confirmed the Privilege of the *Waisenhaus* of 1702 in all particulars.[28]

Frederick William I (1713-1740)

The second king of Prussia has been called the father of the Prussian *Volksschule*. If this description is not justified historically, it is no exaggeration to give Frederick William I credit for laying the foundation of the modern Prussian elementary school system. Prior to 1713, and after the Reformation, some progress was made in Brandenburg-Prussia in establishing universities, *Gymnasien*, and city Latin and German schools. It was the Pietists who made the first significant contribution to elementary education and to teacher training. Frederick William I extended the example of the Halle schools to all his territories and had a greater measure of success in rural elementary education than had been achieved prior to his reign.

One of the earliest concerns of the new king was for the German Reformed children of his territories. On 10 July 1713, Frederick William I had established the Reformed Church Directory as the supreme bureaucratic office for the German Reformed churches of all his territories with the exception of Cleves, Mark, and Ravensberg.[29] Not only church but school matters were placed under the directory. The new director issued a school ordinance on 24 October 1713 for inspection of the German Reformed schools. Inspectors and clerics were to see that all parents sent their children to the Reformed schools as soon as they reached the proper age and that the youngsters were not removed from school until the local minister had satisfied himself that the child could read and write adequately and had learned the fundamentals of the Christian religion. In both the Latin and German elementary schools the first consideration was to instill fear and love of God and to instruct in the Christian faith according to the Heidelberg Catechism. Non-Calvinist students were to be allowed to attend but were to be excused from religious instruction in the Heidelberg Catechism. The ordinance further required that in all Latin schools uniform textbooks were to be used so that students could change schools without loss of progress. Perhaps the most suggestive article in the ordinance was the requirement that where there were no schools, but there were children of school age, the inspectors were to assure that wherever there was a Reformed congregation there would also be a Reformed elementary school.[30]

This ordinance foreshadowed the basic trend of Frederick William's legislation concerning elementary education. His acts would apply, gen-

---

28. See Deppermann, *Der Hallesche Pietismus,* pp. 165-171.
29. See Dorwart, *Administrative Reforms,* pp. 102-103.
30. *C. C. March.,* vol. 1, pt. 1, no. 83, cols. 459-461; also in Vormbaum, *Schulordnungen,* vol. 3, no. 6, pp. 210-213.

erally, to all his territories under the new centralist tendency. He would invoke and attempt to enforce compulsory school attendance (*Schulzwang,* which as a principle was as old as the Protestant Reformation and had gained new significance under Francke), and, finally, the king would be concerned with increasing the number of available schools. Unfortunately, this last provision was still left to local parish initiative and support and did not gain any immediate financial support from the royal treasury. However, on 18 March 1715 the king did establish a Reformed school for the Calvinist poor children in Berlin, at the Dom or cathedral.

Frederick William, exercising the rights of patron in villages of the royal domain, gave material assistance to the building of rural schools. He renewed provisions of the edicts of his father of 11 January and 7 February 1711 that rural parishes too poor to erect church and school buildings should get materials free from the royal forests. By an act of 15 February 1714, he guaranteed either the necessary building timber, or the money to buy it, for the erection of village churches and schools on his domain lands. Shortly after, Marquard Ludwig von Printz, who had become the administrative head of several consistories and of public instruction, issued a declaration extending the act of 15 February 1714. His declaration directed noble patrons to provide in their villages, schools, and houses for the teachers.[31] This declaration by no means led to an immediate increase of rural schools on estates of the nobility.

The school ordinance of 24 October 1713, which had been issued for the German Reformed schools, received a counterpart for the Lutheran schools of the electorate in an instruction of 5 March 1715.[32] The provisions on teaching methods with emphasis on religious education, reading, and writing were applied to the Lutheran schools.

This instruction of 5 March 1715, however, took on major significance for another reason. It was an instruction to the church superintendents and inspectors of the electorate to inspect the qualifications and personal conduct of teachers in Brandenburg schools and to determine the income of teachers. It was based on the assumption that in accord with previous legislation the children of Brandenburg attended school in winter and summer. A report was finally made in 1717 after three years' inspection. It was not a favorable report, and among other things it revealed the sad state of the rural school system. The report impelled the Reformed Church Directory and the Lutheran consistory to press the king for compulsory education. In a request of 31 July 1717, the Reformed Church Directory urged the king to issue an ordinance requiring parents to make their children attend school. Frederick William not only approved the request but issued a general ordinance for all his territories affecting all elementary schools. The ordinance of 28 September 1717 is a historic document both

31. See Vollmer, *Friedrich Wilhelm I,* pp. 27-28.
32. *C. C. March.,* vol. 1, pt. 1, no. 90, col. 515.

for what it said or directed and for what historians have said about it.[33]
Friedrich Paulsen, on the basis of this act, hailed Frederick William I
as "the real founder of the Volksschule in Prussia [der eigentliche
Begründer der Volksschule in Preussen]."[34] Heinrich Lewin viewed the
ordinance of 28 September 1717 as having great significance because it
introduced universal compulsory attendance in the Prussian school system.[35] However, F. Vollmer[36] and Max Lehmann[37] put this ordinance in
proper historical perspective, demonstrating that it neither established
the Prussian *Volksschule* nor introduced the principle of compulsion
(*Schulpflicht*).

The ordinance of 1717 was a brief, simple directive requiring that
"hinkünftig an denen Orten wo Schulen seyn die Eltern bey nachdruck-
licher Straffegehalten seyn sollen Ihre Kinder . . . in die Schuel zu-
schicken," that is, it instructed the church directories to see that "in future
in those places where schools exist, parents, under threat of fine, be compelled to send their children to school"—in the winter daily and in the
summer once or twice weekly, so that the children would not forget
what they had learned in the winter and yet could help their parents in
the fields. But, this compulsory attendance was required "an denen Orten
wo Schulen seyn"—only "in those places where schools already existed."
Each child was to pay weekly two *dreier* (sixpence); in the case of impoverished parents this school money was to be paid out of the parish
almsbox.

While it is true, as Lehmann pointed out fifty years ago, that this ordinance did not introduce the principle of compulsory school attendance,
it is, nevertheless, a significant document. First, one should recognize
that the idea of compulsory school attendance was as old as Martin
Luther's preaching. It was Francke at Halle who really made a serious
effort to enforce the principle, particularly by making it possible for the
children of the poor to attend school by paying their school money out
of the local poor fund. The edicts of 24 October 1713 and 5 March 1715
issued by Frederick William I had stressed this principle with respect to
city schools. The ordinance of 28 September 1717, in contrast, was a general edict for all Hohenzollern territories and was particularly concerned
with rural elementary schools. While it did not establish universal compulsory attendance, it asserted the principle as one to be applied universally in the lands of Frederick William I, in town and village. Re-
grettably, it did not gain universal acceptance or success, even where
schools did exist. An edict of 19 December 1736 stated that school visitations by inspectors revealed that the edict of 1717 was not fully imple-

33. Ibid., no. 97, cols. 527-530.
34. Paulsen, *Gelehrten Unterrichts,* 1:577.
35. Lewin, *Preussischen Volksschule,* pp. 42-43.
36. Vollmer, *Friedrich Wilhelm I,* pp. 31-34..
37. Lehmann, "Aus der Geschichte der preussischen Volksschule," in *Preussische Jahr-bücher,* 140 (1910): 209-231.

mented, particularly in rural areas, and that many children were growing up without the rudiments of the three R's and the religious instruction useful for salvation.[38] Thus, twenty years later, the king found it necessary to reissue the edict of 1717 verbatim.

Vollmer concluded that the edict of 1717 had meaning for only one-third of the villages in Brandenburg, where schools existed. There was no requirement that schools should be built where they did not exist, and the royal treasury was not to be used at this time to fill the void. However, Frederick William did require, in 1717, that catechism classes be held each Sunday afternoon by the village preacher for the whole congregation. In Frederick William's eyes, the primary goal of elementary education, after all, was to make pious, devout Christians and obedient subjects. Catechism lessons, prayer, Bible reading, hymn-singing, sermons were all a form of education which could be provided by the village preacher in the course of a Sunday.

Before a well-established system of elementary education, a universal Prussian *Volksschule,* could be established, more would be required than a legislated *Schulpflicht.* Schools would be needed, particularly in the villages, and qualified teachers would have to be supplied. As late as 10 November 1722 a patent was issued permitting the recruiting of *Küster* and schoolmasters in the rural areas from the ranks of craftsmen.[39] However, only tailors, linenweavers, smiths, carpenters, and wheelwrights could be used. The practitioners of these crafts presumably had some skill in writing and figuring, and were useful in the rural economy without competing with the urban craftsmen. This latter protection was evident even earlier when the tax commissaries of Brandenburg in 1718, as agents of the central government at Berlin, were instructed to permit village sacristans and schoolmasters, because of poor pay, to carry on a trade but no other handcraft than one of the five mentioned in the patent of 1722.[40]

The school situation in the Hohenzollern lands was by no means uniform. Brandenburg and Magdeburg, as well as the Rhine territories of Cleves and Mark, were more fortunate than those territories east of the Oder River. The Neumark, East Pomerania, and East Prussia were so poor in schools that the edict of September 1717 had no meaning at all for a large part of the rural population. East Prussia had suffered from the Great Northern War as Brandenburg had from the Thirty Years' War. Village life had been disrupted; churches and schools simply did not exist in many rural areas.

Frederick William took a special interest in the reconstruction of East Prussia.[41] After 1718, his attention, with increasing intensity over the

38. *C. C. March.,* vol. 1, pt. 2, no. 139, cols. 267-268.
39. Ibid., vol. 1, pt. 1, no. 112, cols. 547-550.
40. Ibid., vol. 5, pt. 2, chap. 10, no. 38, col. 672.
41. See Fritz Terveen, *Gesamtstaat und Retablissement: Der Wiederaufbau des nörd-lichen Ostpreussen unter Friedrich Wilhelm I 1714-1740,* chap. 3, "Das Kirchen- und

years, was devoted to improving the school system in both German and Lithuanian Prussia. It may well be that the edict of September 1717 kindled his interest in elementary education, and it was transferred to the educational rehabilitation of Prussia. During an inspection trip through East Prussia in 1718, the king discovered that his subjects in the eastern provinces were not well versed in the Christian faith, and concluded that this was due principally to the dearth of qualified teachers. He wisely associated this condition with the meager salaries and low subsistence level of rural school teachers. It took twenty years before Frederick William made any significant progress, but during those two decades there were at least five serious efforts at school reform.

The king was determined not only to improve teaching in the church schools but to establish a school in each of the larger villages and to raise the subsistence level of schoolteachers. His primary goals were to eliminate ignorance (*grosse Unwissenheit*) and to bring his people to a knowledge of God. He ordered the provincial government, the church consistories, and the domain chambers (*Amtskammer*) to combine their efforts to see that parishes built churches and schools and staffed them with preachers and teachers.

To oversee the projected school reform of 1718 in Lithuanian Prussia, Frederick William appointed as Inspector of Churches and Schools a Heinrich Lysius, a noted Pietist educator and director of the Collegium Fridericianum at Königsberg. Lysius was instructed to collaborate with Francke at Halle on proposals to reform the school situation and to provide adequate and qualified preachers and teachers. For three years Lysius worked at reform, only to be relieved of his position in 1721 with little accomplished. The basic problems of building schools, of expanding the supply of qualified teachers with increased income, of instituting regular full-time instruction in elementary reading and writing were not solved.

Lysius failed not only because he was a Pietist resented by the orthodox Lutheran clergy, but primarily because he was an outsider, a non-Prussian, who was met by resistance from indigenous clergy and noble patrons alike. And yet the overwhelming fact, only slowly recognized, was that no real progress in improving the school or teacher situation in Lithuanian Prussia was possible, because of local poverty, unless the king himself undertook to finance the building of schools.

Frederick William persisted. His genuine paternalistic interest in the welfare and salvation of his people was poignantly expressed in a letter of 8 Feburary 1722 to the Königsberg Government: "wenn ich baue und verbessere das Land und ich mache keine Christen, so hilfet mir alles nit [if I build and improve the land and I make no Christians, then all is

---

Schulretablissement"; also Wolfgang Roehder, *Das Staatserziehungswerk Friedrich Wilhelms I von Preussen* (Altenburg, 1937).

in vain]." Between 1722 and 1732 the king made two more efforts to improve the church and school situations. A plan for reform was drafted in 1728 providing for school construction, teacher supply, compulsory school attendance, and teacher income. But again, as Terveen reported, "Nothing came of this plan."[42] Local resistance and claims of financial hardship caused failure.

After a disappointing inspection journey through Lithuanian Prussia in 1731, revealing that provincial and local authorities had done virtually nothing to add to the number of schools and teachers during the previous decade, Frederick William determined to appoint a special commission to reform the school system of Prussia. A Royal Church and School Commission was appointed in December 1732.

The most difficult problem which the commission inherited was that of providing a subsistence income for the teachers. The commission was to inquire how many schools were still lacking, how many ministers and teachers were needed, and what the financial situation of the parishes was. The king promised to provide construction timber and fuel.

In June 1733, under the supervision of the commission, a questionnaire was distributed in the Lithuanian district of East Prussia among pastors and church supervisors. This questionnaire was designed to provide a detailed report on the existing situation in each parish with suggestions for improvement. The returned reports revealed a distressing financial picture: impoverishment, only a small cash income in each parish. The results of the inquiry of 1733 made it abundantly clear that all the efforts of Frederick William I to reform and improve the school situation in the war- and plague-ravished eastern districts of East Prussia had failed because the king expected the parish to build and maintain schools and to pay the salaries of teachers out of local funds. This was patently not possible—even if traditional and customary.

In November 1733 the Royal Commission selected a model or prototype district in East Prussia to attempt to work out basic principles of school reform. The commission proposed that in each village church a school fund should be established to which the members of the parish would contribute proportionately to their economic capabilities. From this fund school-building costs and teacher salaries were to be paid. The affluent parishes were to advance the necessary money and then be reimbursed from the school fund. Further, the commission proposed that formal school instruction should be conducted during the summer.

A clash between the royal commission and the provincial domain chamber (*Amtskammer*) over the economic feasibility of the plan nullified this effort. By 1735 the commission abandoned the project of a model school district.

The attention of the commission was now directed once again to the

42. Terveen, *Gesamtstaat*, p. 98.

Lithuanian province of East Prussia, where the Salzburg Protestant refugees had been settled after 1731. The king, as early as 16 August 1734, had expressed concern over the need of a school system in this area so that the children of the Salzburg colonists would be assured of receiving instruction in the Christian faith. The Pietist Schultz, accompanied by von Bülow, the king's personal representative, traveled to Gumbinnen and worked out a new program for school reform with the local Lithuanian deputies. This program was forwarded to Berlin on 24 October 1735. Principal innovations suggested by this new project included an emphasis on having a school available for each village at a distance no greater than half a mile, and the provision that where local parish money did not suffice to pay teacher salaries, the royal treasury should lend assistance. The commission concluded that 280 schools were needed for the Lithuanian districts, that the king would have to furnish 7,000 *thaler* for the building program, and that the royal treasury would have to furnish 3,360 *thaler* annually for teacher salaries. The question was raised about the source of the royal contributions, since the regular budget made no provision for them. To this the king replied that a sum of 40,000 *thaler* was to be taken from the domain budget if local church finances were inadequate.

In July 1736 Frederick William traveled to Prussia to take personal charge of the final solution of the problem of school reform in East Prussia, the problem at which he had conscientiously labored since 1718. At a conference on 30 July the king's minister, von Görne, in company with the Royal or Perpetual Commission, drew up "principia regulativa" according to which the Prussian school system should be established. This was a fundamental school ordinance for the whole province of East Prussia issued by royal edict on 1 August 1736 as "Principia regulativa oder General-Schulen-Plan nach welchem das Landschulwesen im Königreiche Preussen eingerichtet werden soll [regulative principles or general school plan according to which the school system of Prussia should be organized]."[43]

Since the *Principia Regulativa* became the basic law for the rural school system of Prussia, its provisions require detailed analysis. School buildings, like the homes of parish priest and sacristan, were to be built and maintained by the individual parishes. The king would furnish building timber; but doors, windows, and Dutch-tile stoves were to be paid for out of the collection moneys. The king would furnish free firewood, but the parishes had to haul it. In town and village each parish was to pay 4 *thaler* annually for the teacher's salary (the teacher was expected to perform certain menial custodial services as well). If a parish was too poor to pay the 4 *thaler,* then the local patron was to pay it.

For subsistence the schoolmaster was to receive in addition certain

43. Vormbaum, *Schulordnungen,* vol. 3, no. 14, pp. 356-358.

items in kind: free use of the village common pasture for some live-stock, a morgen of land (2/3 acre) for garden use, contributions of rye and barley from the collective peasantry of a school district. Each child of school age (5 to 12 years) whether or not he attended school was to pay an annual fee of 15 Prussian *Groschen*. If the schoolmaster was a crafts-man, he was allowed to practice his craft for further support. If not, he was to be permitted to work in the fields at harvest time for six weeks.

The nobility as patrons of the churches in their villages were directed to act in accordance with this school ordinance and to assist their par-ishes in establishing and maintaining schools.

The school law of 1736 furnished the basic principles and pattern for all later school laws. It provided the solution for the two basic problems that had hindered Frederick William's efforts to establish an elementary school system for East Prussia: the financing of school construction and the means for providing teacher income. Not until Frederick William made the decision to subsidize the financing of school construction and teacher salaries out of the Prussian state treasury was a fundamental re-organization of the elementary school system of his eastern province pos-sible. The poverty of the village churches had simply made all previous reform efforts abortive. The king had already spent huge sums in the economic rehabilitation of the war- and plague-ravaged province, includ-ing the cost of settlement of some 20,000 Salzburg refugees. By 1736 East Prussia needed less economic relief.

Frederick William had promised, in 1736, to set aside a sum of 40,000 *thaler* to assist in school rehabilitation. On 29 July 1736 the king added 10,000 *thaler* to this. The money was to be set up as a founda-tion, the capital invested with Prussian merchants at 4-percent interest, and the expected 2,000 *thaler* annual income used to help pay the salaries of teachers in the Lithuanian and Polish districts of East Prussia. On 21 February 1737 the king established a foundation, called the Mons Pietatis, with a capital of 50,000 *Reichsthaler,* under the direction of the Prussian provincial government. The income from this foundation was to be used to assist where normal financing was inadequate in the build-ing of schools and in supporting teachers. It did not intend to establish a public, state responsibility for building schools or paying teacher and minister salaries. In the next four years, after 1736, over 1,100 schools were constructed in East Prussia. Unfortunately, Frederick William's ef-forts to build schools with royal financial assistance were not extended to his other provinces. The completion of this project for the whole king-dom remained a challenge for Frederick II. By cabinet orders of 24 June 1735 and of 26 December 1736, Frederick William did extend the prin-ciple of *Schulpflicht* to Pomerania and to the Neumark, although he did not make the same effort to build schools as he had in East Prussia.

As it turned out, in East Prussia at least, the building of schools was easier than finding a supply of sufficient, qualified teachers to staff them.

Not only in the reign of the second king but for most of the eighteenth century the majority of teachers were craftsmen-teachers, inadequately prepared for their tasks, elementary as they were. Writing and basic arithmetic were often of necessity subordinated to reading, religious education, and hymn-singing. In many areas elementary education by 1740 remained at the seventeenth-century level of catechism schools of *Küsterschule*. Max Lehmann has argued that the *Gymnasien* of Germany, including Prussia, were quite capable of turning out a sufficient number of trained teachers for elementary schools but that no provision was made for this under Frederick William I.[44] This judgment may be a little harsh. It was not so much the failure to train teachers or to expand the teacher-training seminaries as it was the inability of parishes, on whom the burden fell, or the failure of the king to make money available for teachers' salaries that were adequate to attract teachers. The Mons Pietatis of 1737 was helpful to East Prussia but it came late in the reign and was only for the eastern province.

The Pietist interest in teacher training which had led to the establishment of the first teacher-training seminary of Francke at Halle and the practice of providing free meals for future teachers was extended to East Prussia. A teacher seminary was attached to the Königsberg *Waisenhaus* in 1701; and the Pietist Lysius in 1718 established a seminary for the Prussian-Lithuanian province. Free tables were provided at the Königsberg university for theology students who were fluent in Lithuanian and who would serve as teachers and preachers in that area. And during the last five years of his reign, Frederick William I sought to expand the number of teacher-training seminaries in his central and eastern provinces.[45] Over 2,000 elementary schools were founded in the quarter-century of Frederick William's reign, and the task of supplying adequately prepared teachers for them was formidable. Craftsmen and disabled veterans (rescript of 1729) filled the gap as *Küster*.

Frederick William's interest in supplying teachers was expressed as early as 1715 in his instruction to the superintendents of the Lutheran church, who were urged to undertake the training of teachers and to dismiss unqualified teachers.[46] Unfortunately "unqualified" referred to their religious orthodoxy, and the state did not make money available for a systematic teacher-training program. Throughout his reign the king showed more concern for the personal conduct of schoolteachers, requiring inspectors to report any who led an improper life, than he did for increasing the number of trained teachers through state aid.[47]

Although Frederick William devoted his major effort at the elementary level to the rural areas of his kingdom, he did not neglect the military

44. Lehmann, *Preussische Jahrbücher*, 140 (1910): 222.
45. Gloria, *Pietismus als Förderer der Volksbildung*, pp. 60-66.
46. *C. C. March.*, vol. 1, pt. 1, no. 90, col. 515, instruction of 5 March 1715.
47. See, e.g., ibid., no. 137, cols. 567-570.

children, the poor, and the orphaned. He brought the private schools under state regulation. By piecemeal legislation affecting towns and villages in the separate provinces, by making provision for various social or occupational groups, and by regulating private schools, elementary education, by 1740, was being brought closer to centralized supervision, universal standards, and state (i.e., secular) control. The increasing number of regimental schools were directly under royal direction. The most significant expansion of royal activity was in increasing the number of orphanages and *Armenschulen*. The Francke *Waisenhaus* and *Armenschule* at Halle served as models for the king and to inspire the private initiative of Pietist leaders.

In 1724 Frederick William opened his famous military orphanage for boys at Potsdam. The very next year he added a *Mädchenwaisenhaus* (Orphanage for Girls) so that the sons and daughters of the military forces garrisoned at Potsdam could be given catechism and elementary education. In a regulation of 1 November 1724, the king revealed the purpose or motivation for establishing military orphanages at Potsdam and demonstrated how much the Pietist influence had affected him. He proclaimed: "The main purpose of the institution is that the youth may be brought up for the service of God and neighbor."[48] The service of God and one's neighbor—this was to be the goal of elementary education. The military orphanage at Potsdam may well have been the first educational institution in Germany at the elementary level which adopted the principle of confessional parity. All confessions were represented, and there was no confessional requirement for admission. This in time led to a natural separation of catechism instruction from basic elementary instruction in reading, writing, and the crafts. The principle of confessional parity would ultimately receive direct legal recognition in *Das Allgemeine Landrecht* of 1794, Prussia's first common law code, which declared that "No one shall be denied admission to public schools because of differences in confessions of faith."[49]

Frederick William was following his father's example in establishing a *Waisenhaus* at Potsdam. Such an institution, the Friedrichs-Waisenhaus, had already been established at Berlin in 1697 for the children of Prussia's soldiers. Similar institutions were erected in the major cities providing elementary education for hundreds of military orphans resulting from the two great wars between 1688 and 1713. By 1740 the Potsdam orphanage for boys had 1,400 students.[50]

Regimental and garrison schools, as well as military orphanages (which were schools, of course), were necessary because ordinarily no provision was made for these unfortunate children in the regular city schools.

48. Keller, *Volksschulwesens,* p. 66.
49. Walter Landé, ed., *Preussisches Schulrecht,* vol. 6, pt. 1, "Das Allgemeine Landrecht von 1794," pt. 2, chap. 12, par. 10, p. 38.
50. Heubaum, *Deutschen Bildungswesen,* 1:147-148.

Francke, at Halle, had discovered that the children of the urban poor were similarly neglected. His answer was the *Armenschule* (school for the poor). A private institution, it was supported by gifts of the pious and school fees paid out of the parish almsbox. Again, this institution, like his orphanage at Halle, served as a model for an increasing number of *Armenschulen* throughout Hohenzollern territories. These schools, as elementary German schools, both private and public in origin, became an important factor in the development of the Prussian *Volksschule* as a public school system, as the state increasingly took over responsibility for the care and education of the poor.

As early as 1 February 1699, under Pietist influence, a private school was opened at Königsberg for the children of the poor.[51] This school grew out of the activities of Theodor Gehr, who was won over to Pietism in the late seventeenth century. Excited by the example of Francke's school at Halle and fortified by conversations with Francke, Gehr wanted to do something similar at Königsberg. The three cities which made up Königsberg at this time had three Latin schools, a number of parish schools, and about 200 private schools (*Winckelschulen*) at this time. Despite these many elementary schools, there were many children who grew up without education, the children of the poor. It was the problem of the poor which made Gehr want to start a new school. On 11 August 1698, Gehr had begun private instruction in his house for six students. This was a Latin school and Gehr's answer to the poor quality of schooling in the existing Latin schools, which were too humanistic in his judgment. But on 1 February 1699 he opened an *Armenschule* which essentially was a German school for the poor. Both schools met with immediate resistance from zealous Lutherans who brought charges against this Pietist enterprise before the Prussian Lutheran consistory. An investigating committee reported on the high quality of instruction at both the Latin school and the *Armenschule*, but recommended that Gehr's private school be made a public school under regular inspection. During his coronation as king in Prussia at Königsberg, Frederick I issued an edict (21 March 1701) making the private school a "Royal Privileged School." A further royal rescript of 10 May 1703 changed the name of the school to the Collegium Fridericianum. This really consisted of three schools: the Latin school, a German school, and the *Armenschule*. The latter two were basically similar with almost identical curricula of catechism, reading, writing, arithmetic, some elementary history, geography, and nature study. By 1732 the *Armenschule* had to be separated and expanded. It grew into a whole system of public schools for all the city children of Königsberg during the reign of Frederick William I.[52]

51. Ibid., pp. 153-158.
52. G. Zippel, *Geschichte des Königlichen Friedrichs-Kollegiums zu Königsberg Pr. 1698-1898,* pp. 5-49; also Emil Hollack and Friedrich Tromnau, *Geschichte des Schulwesens der Königlichen Haupt- und Residenzstadt Königsberg i. Pr. mit besonderer Berücksichtigung der niederen Schulen,* chaps. 6-7.

At Berlin, on 18 March 1715, Frederick William established at the Calvinist Dom an *Armenschule* for indigent Calvinist children.[53]

Near the end of his reign, in 1738, prompted by the city council of Berlin, Frederick William reached out in still another direction to improve the quality of urban elementary education. At least as early as the sixteenth century, a type of private school had emerged to satisfy the needs of an urban, commercial society wherever existing schools were lacking or church schools were inadequate. Public attitude toward these schools was reflected in their designation as *Winkelschulen*. These were German schools of varying quality usually operated by some unqualified teacher. Despite efforts to suppress them, they flourished into the early eighteenth century presumably because the need for basic education in reading, writing, arithmetic, and "illiberal" subjects was not satisfied by existing or nonexistent public schools. They were frequently hole-in-the-wall schools run by mercenary, unqualified (i.e., uncertified) teachers. For whatever reason, at the request of the city council of Berlin, the king of 16 October 1738 published an "Ordinance Concerning Private Schools in the Cities and Suburbs of Berlin."[54] Fundamentally, the purpose of this regulative ordinance was to assure both certification of the qualifications of the private teachers and the fulfillment of requirements of school attendance as established for the public elementary schools since 1713. No one was to set up a private school unless he was first examined by the superintendent and preacher of the affected locale, had received a written testimonial of his qualifications, and was confirmed by the church directory. Those who were already teaching had to be examined immediately in order to qualify or forfeit the right to hold private classes. The location of the private schools was also subject to the approval of the parish priest so as to provide, by proper distribution in the city, access to as many students as possible.

The qualifications of the elementary teacher, in addition to proper Christian piety, included skill in spelling, reading, writing, and arithmetic, the use of a good method of teaching, and talent to teach the singing of psalms and other songs.

As was generally true in village and town public schools, the parents were expected to send their children to school at the required minimum age, assure regular attendance, and not remove their children from these private schools until they could read, had a mimimum skill in writing, and could pass catechism examination.

Private schools were thus placed under state supervision and were expected to meet the standards established for the *Armenschulen* and rural *Volksschulen*. This general principle would be incorporated in *Das Allgemeine Landrecht* of 1794.[55]

---

53. Vollmer, *Friedrich Wilhelm I*, p. 27.
54. Vormbaum, *Schulordnungen*, vol. 3, no. 17, pp. 440-445.
55. Landé, ed., *Preussisches Schulrecht*, pt. 2, chap. 12, pars. 3, 4, 6, p. 38.

Thus, by 1740, a firm foundation had been prepared for a variety of elementary schools which could and would in the next reign develop into a universal, state-directed primary school system.[56] The paternalistic concern of the first two Hohenzollern kings for the spiritual welfare of their subjects had transformed and broadened the sporadic and ineffectual catechism schools of the seventeenth century both institutionally and substantively. Military schools, orphanage schools, subsidized rural schools in East Prussia, *Armenschulen,* expanded city German and Latin schools, regulated *Winckelschulen* provided a complex variety of elementary facilities. Greater effort to enforce compulsory attendance roughly between the ages of five and fourteen was partially complemented by an increasing number of schools. The need for teachers was recognized, and efforts were made not only to increase the supply but to provide formal teacher training. The Pietist influence permeating Prussian elementary education introduced increasing emphasis on the use of the German language for instruction, expansion of the curriculum to include more natural history, and vocational training.

Although town governments and rural parishes were still responsible for building and maintaining schools, paying teacher salaries, and providing local supervision through the local church officers, royal legislation was assuming the major role in establishing a uniform system of public education in all the Hohenzollern territories.

56. The first universal school regulation for the whole kingdom of Prussia, effective for 100 years, was the "Royal Prussian General Regulation for Rural Schools of 12 Oct. 1763"; see Vormbaum, *Schulordnungen,* vol. 3, no. 25, pp. 539-554.

14

Gymnasium and University, 1650-1740

Secondary and higher education in Germany generally, and in Brandenburg-Prussia in particular, prospered or suffered in direct proportion to the interest and effort of the German princes. The schools above the elementary level were princely schools, territorial institutions established by the territorial prince and supported by him. Those obstacles which to the end of the seventeenth century made it difficult to reform, expand, or establish a universal, elementary public school system had virtually no effect at the intermediate or university level. The needs of the state for educated leaders, theologians, teachers, professional men, and state servants was a compulsive factor in establishing schools at this level. The university, of course, had a medieval origin. The intermediate level of the *Fürstenschulen,* subsequently called *Gymnasien,* owed its origin to a large extent to the influence of the Lutheran Reformation upon the princes and imperial cities of the Holy Roman Empire. The *Gymnasium* offered a higher level of terminal education for many, but fundamentally it became a preparatory school for university admission. It continued and expanded the work of the elementary Latin schools. Instruction at least to the end of the seventeenth century was conducted in Latin.

By the end of the Thirty Years' War, in the several territories which had passed into Hohenzollern hands since the early seventeenth century, educational institutions had suffered serious physical, financial, and personnel damage or loss. Spaniard, Imperialist, Catholic League, Protestant Union, Saxon, Swede—from the Rhine to the Memel—all had ravaged the lands, despoiled the churches, ruined the schools, dispersed the teachers and the students. The Mark Brandenburg had had only two *Fürstenschulen.* In 1648 both existed in little more than name. The Berlin (Lutheran) *Gymnasium* of the Gray Cloister had closed for a year during the Swedish total occupation of the electorate after 1635. In a capital city whose population had shrunk from 24,000 to 8,000 during the lifetime of this intermediate school (i.e., since 1574), the *Gymnasium* of the Gray Cloister in 1650 existed only precariously. The Joachimsthal *Gymnasium* (Calvinist since 1616) had been plundered by imperial troops in 1627, by Swedish troops in 1631, and was completely destroyed, its buildings burned, presumably by Saxon troops, on 5 and 6 January 1636. Students and teachers had to flee, some making their way to Berlin to find asylum at the Berlin *Gymnasium.* But as an operating institution it had ceased to exist.

In East Prussia, on 24 October 1541, Lutheran Duke Albert established a *Pädagogium* (intermediate level) at Königsberg, followed by the founding of a university three years later (17 August 1544).[1] Neither of these schools flourished in the sixteenth century, and both experienced decline as the result of Swedish invasion during the Thirty Years' War. The university did flourish briefly after 1578 under Duke George Frederick.

The Hohenzollern princes inherited, in 1614, in their new territories of Cleves, Mark, and Ravensberg several grammar schools at Duisburg, Wesel, and Bielefeld, and in 1648 and 1680 in Minden and Magdeburg, respectively. All of these beginnings of an intermediate school system experienced hardships and decline as a result of the great war and were in urgent need of reform and resuscitation after 1648.

There was little that the new young elector, Frederick William, could do after his accession in 1640 until peace came to his territories in 1648, and the occupation troops were removed. The need for educated leaders and public servants in all phases of public life was so great that not only Frederick William but the various diets of his territories and city councils made serious efforts after 1648 to restore the old grammar schools to effective status or to establish new intermediate schools. Frederick William and his successors took a keen interest and active part in building *Gymnasium*-level schools and were more successful in this area than they were at the elementary level prior to 1717.

The attitude and policy of Frederick William was best expressed for him by the Estates of his Duchy of East Prussia in the first *Landtag* meeting in 1640. The Estates declared that they had faith "dass Eure Churfürstliche Durchlaucht als dero salus populi suprema lex ist [that the elector's supreme law was the welfare of the people]."[2] They petitioned for the restoration of schools.

A year later the young prince himself asked the advice of the Estates of Brandenburg, in the *Landtag* of 1641, "on means for reestablishment of the University of Frankfurt and the Joachimsthal *Fürstenschule*."[3] The endowment for the latter, which had been granted by the founder in 1607, had been destroyed, and funds were lacking to restore the school or to pay student stipends. Both the diet and the elector expressed concern for the restoration of this school because of the need for trained personnel. But nothing could be done for a decade; other problems were more pressing.[4]

Two other problems had to be resolved before the Joachimsthal *Gymnasium* could be reestablished: location and the confessional status.

---

1. See Hans Langel, *Die Entwicklung des Schulwesens in Preussen unter Franz Albrecht Schultz (1733-1763)*.
2. *UA*, 15:257.
3. *UA*, 10:99-100.
4. See Erich Wetzel, *Festschrift zum Dreihundertjährigen Jubiläum des Königlichen Joachimsthalschen Gymnasiums am 24. VIII 1907*. Pt. 1, *Die Geschichte des Königlichen Joachimsthalschen Gymnasiums 1607-1907*, chaps. 1-2.

Founded in 1607 as a Lutheran school, it had been changed to a Calvinist school in 1616 by the newly converted John Sigismund. The diet of Brandenburg was staunchly Lutheran and in 1641 and 1652 petitioned the elector to appoint only Lutheran teachers.[5] Lutherans preferred to see the school reestablished at either its original location or at Dambeck.[6] There was a Calvinist community in Berlin/Cölln, however, which urged the restoration of the Joachimsthal school at Cölln, in order to make available a center for the teaching of the Calvinist form of Christianity for the benefit of the growing Calvinist community, many of whom were public servants.

In October 1649 the elector purchased a house in Cölln to give the refugee teachers and students a home of their own. This soon proved inadequate, and the prince made several rooms in the electoral palace available for instruction. Intentionally or otherwise, the Joachimsthal *Gymnasium* thus was restored in the city of Cölln and as a Calvinist school. It remained in the palace until 1668, when it was moved to larger quarters at the crossing of the St. George and Holy Ghost streets. By 1688 the school had expanded into more permanent and spacious quarters on Burgstrasse, occupying a substantial three-story building. This would be its home for two hundred years. On the occasion of its first centenary celebration in 1707, King Frederick I reestablished free meals for students.

For the first one hundred years the course of instruction of the Joachimsthal *Gymnasium* was essentially humanistic and theological, with all instruction exclusively in the Latin language. After 1707 the curriculum was expanded to include history and geography, geometry and physics, and in 1725 study of the French language. German, however, did not become the language of instruction until shortly after 1740.

Frederick William I, in a cabinet order of 24 November 1730, decided to establish "within the Evangelical-Reformed Church a seminary or nursery of pious and Christian preachers and teachers for churches and schools."[7] Once again we find expressed the two-century-old Hohenzollern leitmotiv as the king wrote that he was acting out of "untiring paternal concern for the general good."[8] As a result of the cabinet order,[9] an ordinance of 25 July 1731 added a theological seminary to the Joachimsthal *Gymnasium*. It was to consist of twelve students of the Reformed faith who desired to study theology. They were to be given preference as royal candidates for appointments to posts as preachers and teachers.[10] The seminary was not a successful venture and ceased to exist

5. *UA*, 10:233.
6. *UA*, 10:271.
7. Quoted in "Inaugural Address of Prussian Court Preacher Johann Noltenius," published in the separate reprint of the *Ordinance of 25 July 1731—Adding the Theological Seminary to the Joachimsthal Gymnasium*, par. 2. A copy of this may be found in Widener Library, Harvard University.
8. Ibid.
9. Referred to in ibid., par. 14.
10. Ibid., p. 10.

by 1800. The *Gymnasium* itself, however, prospered and remained a Calvinist intermediate school until the nineteenth century and was one of Berlin's distinguished schools to the twentieth century.

The Berlin *Gymnasium* (that of the Gray Cloister) had closed its doors in 1637 for some months because of pestilence. Sheltered within the city and serving as an elementary school as well as intermediate, it continued to serve the Lutheran population of Berlin. It even offered a haven to the fleeing survivors of the Joachimsthal *Gymnasium*. Supported by the city government, the Berlin *Gymnasium* recovered, expanded, and flourished as did the city of Berlin itself after 1650. By the end of the century the school once again had a large enrollment which unfortunately was served by an inadequate faculty of nine grossly underpaid instructors. After 1680 the curriculum was modified in response to the changing needs of the state. By 1713 the upper two classes, in addition to catechism, Latin, and the classics, were offered Greek, Hebrew, history, geography, arithmetic, geometry, and physics.[11]

The Lutheran Berlin *Gymnasium* and the Calvinist Joachimsthal *Gymnasium* of Cölln in the immediate decades after the war satisfied the need for intermediate schools in the capital cities.[12] As the population of Berlin/Cölln grew, however, in part as the result of the settlement of a substantial French colony of Huguenots, two new schools were added in the seventeenth century. In 1681 a *Gymnasium* was established in the suburb of Friedrichswerder; and in 1689 a French *Gymnasium,* planned by the Great Elector, was established by Frederick III to serve the Huguenot refugees.[13] Throughout its history, from its founding date of 1 December 1689 to the twentieth century, French was the language of instruction in this French College, as it was called. Established for the benefit of the French colony, deprived as they were by exile of the splendid schools which the Huguenots had had in France, there was still a more fundamental purpose expressed in the founding edict: "so that the Huguenots in

11. Anton F. Büsching, *Geschichte des Berlinschen Gymnasii im grauen Kloster,* pp. 15-18.

12. There was another city school, rather elusive in definition, which has been given the status of a higher school. This was the Cölln *Gymnasium* which grew out of the *Petrischule,* the parish school of St. Peter's Church in Cölln. Almost a century and a half ago, K. F. Klöden and B. H. Schmidt (*Die ältere Geschichte des Köllnischen Gymnasiums bis zu seiner Vereinigung mit dem Berlinischen Gymnasium*) asserted that the Cölln *Gymnasium* (Petrinische Gymnasium) was the oldest in Berlin, identifying its origin with the official adoption of Lutheranism in Brandenburg in 1539 (p. 8). This position is completely rejected by later investigations. It is not clear when the Latin parish school at St. Peter's expanded its curriculum to achieve status as a *Gymnasium.* Fundamentally it appears to have been an elementary parish school with only a few students above the elementary level. In 1767, the Cölln *Gymnasium* was merged with the larger and flourishing Berlin *Gymnasium,* although the three lower classes continued to meet at St. Peter's Church (see Büsching, *Berlinschen Gymnasii,* pp. 26-29).

13. *Festschrift zur Feier des 200 Jährigen Bestehens des Königlichen Französischen Gymnasium,* introduction by G. Schulze, "Report on the Royal French *Gymnasium* in the Years 1689-1889," pp. 11-28; *Festschrift zur Feier des 260 Jährigen Bestehens des Französischen Gymnasiums Collège Français, Fondé en 1689,* pt. 1, Kurt Levinstein, "Das Collège von der Gründung bis zum Ausgang des Zweiten Weltkrieges (1689-1945)," pp. 2-29.

future can make useful contributions to the general welfare."[14] It was expected that the French refugees would contribute to the common welfare and the cultural life of Berlin. They did in fact provide men for the professions, officers for the army, and capable servants in the Prussian bureaucracy.

A school ordinance of 1695 for the French College prescribed a six-year program of study leading to the university. It was a humanistic program with emphasis on Latin and Greek language and literature, with philosophy and mathematics included. A new plan of study adopted by the Academic Council of the college on 13 September 1703 retained the emphasis on languages and humanistic literature, with some simple mathematics, music, and of course Calvinist religious instruction. In 1720 geography was added, but, surprisingly, history was rejected. This is surprising only in that history, particularly biblical history, was becoming a standard part of the curriculum in the German *Gymnasien.*

Frederick III had endowed the French College in 1689 with an annual income of 540 *Reichsthaler* for salaries and payment of the rent of a house, and they were given free fuel. Its first students were French, but an increasing number of German students, sons of nobles and burghers, entered the college. Nevertheless, the new school almost closed in 1701 because of a decline in enrollment and internal bickering among instructors. The college was saved and given new life by the direct interest and intervention of the king, who helped the French community buy a new house for the school. Direction and responsibility for the college was placed in the hands of a corporation of inspectors who were responsible to the king. This body of seven was soon called the Academic Council.

The French College did not prosper during the first half of the eighteenth century, never having more than an average of thirty-five students before 1740. Academically it did not come up to the standards of the other three *Gymnasien* in Berlin, despite a royal decree of August 1717 which ordered the standardization of textbooks used in all four schools. The problem was mostly a financial one: it was difficult to pay attractive salaries. After 1740 enrollment increased steadily, and in the nineteenth century the French College really began to flourish.

During the century from 1640 to 1740, three Hohenzollern rulers actively demonstrated their concern for education above the elementary level in all their territories. In some instances they responded to the petitions of their subjects to restore territorial *Fürstenschulen,* which had suffered from the Thirty Years' War, or to establish new schools to meet territorial or confessional requirements. In other instances, as, for instance, the French College in Berlin, they acted entirely out of concern for the educational and public welfare of their widespread lands. The growth of inter-

---

14. *Festschrift 200 Jährigen Bestehens,* p. 6, quoted from the edict of establishment of 1 Dec. 1689.

mediate schools—as well as of universities—reflected various pressing factors. Renaissance influence continued to provoke a demand for humanistic education as preparation for the university. The Protestant churches required theological training for Lutheran and Calvinist preachers and teachers. Confessional pressure groups, "national" pride, and the increasing needs of a mercantilist state could be satisfied only by means of expansion of *Fürstenschulen* and universities in all the Hohenzollern territories spread across Northern Europe from the Rhine to the Memel. The response by the princes to these varying forces was reflected not only in more schools but in a changing curriculum. A humanistic-theological curriculum was no longer sufficient. The statist requirements demanded men trained in modern languages, history, geography, and jurisprudence for diplomacy; in cameralist doctrines for public service. The new science demanded expansion of curricula in the new mathematics and the physical and life sciences, with improved laboratory facilities and techniques. Perhaps most significant of all was the realization of the need to teach the German language and grammar and to make German the basic language of instruction at every level from the parish school to the university. It was the good fortune of the Brandenburg-Prussian state to have three rulers between 1640 and 1740 who defined their functions of ruler in terms of service to the state and to their subjects, who understood that the supreme law of the prince was the welfare of the people. All three recognized that salvation of souls, financial solvency, economic development, military success, the glory of the state, and the fulfillment of the individual were ultimately the direct product of and were proportional to the expansion of educational facilities and institutions physically and intrinsically. Latin schools, *Gymnasien, Ritterakademien,* teacher seminaries, and universities all received support, legislative and financial, from the Hohenzollern princes.

In the western territories the County of Mark, acquired in 1614, had no respectable intermediate school. There was a Latin school at Hamm which had had a precarious existence since the thirteenth century. Ruined by the earlier period of the great war, an unsuccessful effort was made by the city magistracy through a school ordinance of 1640 to give new life to the Latin school, which was the only Reformed educational institution in Hamm.[15] As early as 1642 the city fathers of Hamm petitioned Frederick William for the establishment of a *Gymnasium.* In 1650 the Statthalter (regent) of Cleves, John Maurice of Nassau, was ordered by Frederick William to investigate the extent of church resources and other income at Hamm to be used to establish a good school there. These revenues, supplemented by the Elector/Count, made it possible to open a *Gymnasium illustre* in Hamm on 28 May 1657.[16] It was closely associated with the existent Latin school (with which it was united in 1779). The *Gymnasium*

---

15. Vormbaum, *Schulordnungen,* vol. 2, no. 15, pp. 284-287.
16. Ibid., pp. 288-294.

of Hamm was not a flourishing success in the first hundred years, but it did provide for the County of Mark an intermediate-level school of Calvinist orientation.

The city of Halle (not acquired until 1680) had enjoyed a Lutheran *Gymnasium* since August 1565 when the school was founded by the city council with the aid of a gift of a Franciscan monastery and three parish churches offered by the Archbishop of Magdeburg. The city council continued to supervise the school through a Board of Scholars and reorganized and revitalized the *Gymnasium* in an ordinance of 1661.[17] The *Gymnasium* was organized into ten classes, of which the first six were an elementary Latin school and the last four prepared for university admission. As the Calvinist population grew in this center of Lutheran Pietism, King Frederick I found it necessary to found in 1711 a Calvinist *Gymnasium illustre* of Halle. Electoral permission had been given to the Reformed congregation at Halle, on 2 December 1700, to establish a Latin school for instruction in the Calvinist faith. The rapid increase in the numbers of Calvinists led the sympathetic king to grant the building of the Paulist cloister for the school, in 1703. By 1709 the congregation had erected a new and imposing schoolhouse. The healthy and prosperous growth of both the community and the Reformed Latin school led the Reformed presbytery to request the king to elevate the Latin school to a *Gymnasium illustre et regium,* which he did by an edict of 29 August 1709. The presbytery then drafted and published an ordinance for the Reformed *Gymnasium illustre* on 7 January 1711.[18] The new *Gymnasium* began to function on 20 June. There were five classes. Instruction was offered in church history, catechism, Hebrew, French, and Italian in addition to the standard subjects of the *Gymnasium.* Lutherans were permitted to attend, with catechism instruction to be given by their own theologians. Provision was also made for children of needy parents to get free or reduced-cost lodging and meals.

The city council of the city of Minden (the former bishopric was acquired in 1648) took the initiative in 1656 to restore the Minden *Gymnasium* (established in 1530) from the effects of Catholic occupation during the Thirty Years' War. (Between 1622 and 1630 the forces of the Catholic League had waged victorious warfare in northwest Germany against the remnants of the Protestant Union and later against the Danes.) A school ordinance, drafted in 1656 by the burgomaster and city council, was not published until 1697, with electoral approval.[19]

Three years earlier Frederick III had established a Calvinist *Gymnasium,* the *Friedrichschule,* at Frankfurt. This was a logical step, since the

17. Ibid., no. 27, pp. 522-583.
18. Vormbaum, *Schulordnungen,* vol. 3, no. 4, pp. 176-187.
19. Vormbaum, *Schulordnungen,* vol. 2, no. 46, p. 743.

Frankfurt university had been Calvinist since the early seventeenth century.

The other territories, that is, those east of the Oder River, were by no means neglected, but they were continually exposed to the consequences of the series of Northern Wars beginning in 1655. A Latin school in the city of Königsberg in the Neumark, originating in the thirteenth century, was well on the way to expanding to a Lutheran *Gymnasium* by the end of the sixteenth century. It was disastrously affected by the great war and did not regain significance until after 1670. It remained essentially an elementary Latin school until after 1740, becoming the Friedrich-Wilhelms Lyceum in 1790 and a *Gymnasium* in 1817. Given space, in 1698, in the old Augustinian cloister, its student population dwindled to a mere twenty-one by 1725.[20] The schools at Frankfurt served the Neumark.

In East Prussia, the diet of 1661 complained to Frederick William that the three *Fürstenschulen* established in 1586 (at Tilsit, Lyck, Saalfeld) were almost completely defunct and that the young people had no place to go for their education.[21] The Duke was petitioned to appoint able teachers for the *Fürstenschulen*, who could speak Polish and Lithuanian, to make funds available for unpaid salaries as well as stipends for poor students. Little progress was made in East Prussia until the eighteenth century.

Of all the developments aimed at improving, reforming, or restoring intermediate-level schools between 1650 and 1740, none would have as far-reaching impact or significance as the establishment of the *Paedagogium* at Halle in 1695. This was not the result of electoral initiative or action. The *Paedagogium* was one of the several Pietist institutions founded by Francke. The Hohenzollern contribution was in the protection and support extended to Francke and the Pietist enterprises.

Francke opened the *Paedagogium* as a boarding school for the children of more affluent social circles. It was fundamentally a Latin school, but its advanced classes gave it the status of an intermediate-level school for university preparation. By 1700 it was the most advanced school in Germany in methods of instruction and in curriculum. Having no previous tradition and being directly responsive to the educational philosophy of Francke, it was free to introduce innovations, free to adopt the new ideas emerging in the writings of seventeenth-century educational philosophers. The new school retained an emphasis on Latin with all major instruction and lectures conducted in Latin. Greek and Hebrew were available but not required except for theology students. Instruction in the

20. Carl Thiel, *Kurze Darstellung der Geschichte des Gymnasiums zu Königsberg*, pp. 3-16.
21. *UA*, 15:523-524.

French language and in German grammar and writing were major new developments. Improved methods of language instruction were adopted.[22]

While the classical foundation was retained (the major portion of class time was used in language instruction), new subject matter was introduced. Geography and history were added. "No one is to be admitted to history who has not completed the geography course: since without the latter one cannot be learned in history." Biblical history, universal and German history were studied. To the previous elementary arithmetic were added the new geometry, trigonometry, and algebra. A broad exposure to the natural sciences was made part of the curriculum, including botany, zoology, mineralogy, astronomy, physics, anatomy. Laboratory demonstrations and mockups and botanical gardens were supplemented by visits to breweries, forges, and craftsmen shops. Art (drawing) and music were an integral part of the course of study.

The last few years emphasized preparation for university admission with lectures on law, medicine, philosophy, and theology and continued emphasis on Latin. Advanced students, particularly those in theology training, were used as teachers at the Orphanage and the Latin school and received free meals. The purpose was to create an interest in teaching and to inculcate some concepts of teaching methods. From this experience there emerged the formal *Seminarium Selectum Praeceptorum* by 1707. Those selected for this teacher training seminary not only received free meals, but an intensive program in methods of teaching for two years. They were then obliged to teach at the Orphanage for three years.

By 1702 the private *Paedagogium* was given public status by Frederick I and was named the *Paedagogium regium*. The graduates of the Halle *Paedagogium* were in great demand, and became teachers and rectors of the principal *Gymnasien* in the kingdom as well as founders of new schools and teacher seminaries. The influence of the school thus became the most pervasive force in Prussian education in the eighteenth century. Many of the *Paedagogium* graduates continued their studies at the University of Halle, likewise staffed with Pietist sympathizers.

The revolutionary significance of Francke's *Paedagogium* at Halle is found positively in its modernization of the *Gymnasium*-level course of study and negatively in demonstrating the inadequacy of the Renaissance-inspired classical education. The inadequacy was relevant to the needs of the burgeoning modern state, where modern rather than ancient languages were useful in the new diplomacy, where a knowledge of history, law, economics, military science was more practical than skill in rhetoric or

22. See "Ordinance and Method of Instruction to Be Used at the Paedagogium at Glaucha in Halle" (1702), Vormbaum, *Schulordnungen,* vol. 3, no. 1, pp. 53-116; also "Ordinance for the Paedagogium at Halle" (1721), ibid., no. 7, pp. 214-277.

eloquence in poetry. The inadequacy was likewise underscored by the traditional emphasis on humanistic literature and the failure to introduce "the new science." At midcentury the German *Gymnasien,* particularly in North Germany, were not only inadequate in curriculum but were barely surviving as educational institutions. This resulted in the emergence of a special kind of intermediate school, the *Ritterakademie,* an academy for young noblemen.[23] In the European tradition, the nobility and the gentry were born to govern and to command. The education and training which they received was designed to that end. During the sixteenth century sons of nobles had attended Latin schools and *Gymnasien.* After the Thirty Years' War, greater consciousness of social distinction and the impracticality of a burgher education in the classical schools made it seem desirable, even necessary, to have schools exclusively for young noblemen. These men were to be trained for military and civil service in the new absolutist state. French influence was dramatic in making the German princes and nobility aware of their boorish court manners. Gallantry, proper court behavior and social graces, ability to speak the new universal language of French and to converse about the new mathematics, philosophy, and science required a complete reform of the existing curriculum if sons of nobles were to play their proper role in the *Dreiständestaat.*

Several beginnings of specialized schools for sons of nobility had already been made in the late sixteenth century, particularly at Kassel. By 1650 it was necessary to begin again. In Brandenburg-Prussia Frederick William virtually pioneered anew in 1653 in establishing a *Ritterakademie* at Kolberg on the coast of Pomerania. It was designed for twenty-four young noblemen entering at age fifteen to sixteen. Its curriculum and education were aimed at preparing for a military career but included were courtly manners and gentlemanly accomplishments which remained a part of military officer training to the twentieth century: dancing, fencing, riding, and horsejumping. The school's curriculum was one of the earliest methodical efforts to educate the young noble cadets theoretically and to train them practically for their military mission. Although this first academy did not flourish and was dissolved in 1701 by Frederick I, it served as a model for later cadet academies.

Three years later, in 1704, the same Frederick established a *Ritterakademie* in the city of Brandenburg on the Havel, and in 1705 another at Berlin. The first was abolished in 1713 by the new king, Frederick William I. The second was essentially reestablished as a *Kadettenanstalt* in 1717, more distinctly an officer training school for young noblemen.

The ordinance establishing the Royal Cadet Academy at Berlin in 1705 sheds considerable light on the purpose of these schools as well as on

---

23. See Paulsen, *Gelehrten Unterrichts,* pp. 514-524, for a brief, general description; also Heubaum, *Deutschen Bildungswesen,* 1:65, 137, 149.

the educational program.[24] Frederick decided to establish a *Fürstenschule* or *Ritterakademie* at Berlin, he said, because sons of nobles often traveled outside Hohenzollern territories without a proper educational background. This leaves no doubt that the academy was meant to be at the *Gymnasium* level for an exclusive social group. Eligible to attend were the sons of princes, counts, and lords, native and foreign. There was no confessional restriction, only a social one. The minimum age of admission was sixteen. In addition to the aristocratic skills of dancing, fencing, riding, the curriculum was to include Latin (still necessary for an educated man), foreign languages (particularly French, which replaced Greek and Hebrew), ethics, politics, law, history, heraldry, philosophy, physics, mathematics in all forms, drafting, and music. Mathematics and physics were ancillary to instruction in military fortification and engineering. Instruction in military weapons and tactics was also a basic element.

Although this academy was established as a *Fürstenschule,* each student paid a matriculation fee as well as annual tuition, board, and room. Princes paid 750 *thaler,* counts 600, and lesser noblemen 350. The king provided a library of selected books, particularly history and mathematics. The students were also granted the privilege of using the Royal Library, even of borrowing books. After 1717 the academy became more military in purpose and curriculum and was intended to be a source of officers for the Prussian army. By 1722 it had an enrollment of 300 cadets.

Deplorable and ruinous as the situation was in 1648 at the intermediate level, the universities in Hohenzollern territories had reached the very nadir of their academic activity. There were only two universities, that of Frankfurt on the Oder, a Calvinist university, and that of Königsberg in Prussia, a Lutheran institution.

When Elector Frederick William asked the advice of the Brandenburg Estates at the *Landtag* of 1641 "on means for the reestablishment of the University of Frankfurt," the Estates admitted that restoration of the "Akademie zu Frankfurt" was desirable, but they had no means to offer for that purpose. But they did request urgently that Lutheran professors should be appointed in the faculty of theology.[25] These events of 1641 reveal that the university had declined during the war and needed to be restored, that there were a number of vacancies of professorships, and that the university barely existed financially. It would be little exaggeration to say that the Frankfurt university was hardly distinguishable from a good *Gymnasium.* After the war at the *Landtag* of 1652 the Estates again showed their Lutheran colors by requesting the elector to fill the university vacancies with professors only of the Lutheran faith.[26] In the years after 1652, Frederick William helped to restore the university

24. *C. C. March.,* vol. 1, pt. 2, no. 82, cols. 155-164.
25. *UA,* 10:99-100.
26. Ibid., p. 233.

to a more flourishing state with financial subsidies. In return he assumed the right of professorial appointments, which he essentially reserved for Calvinists. In his second testament of 1655, Frederick William expressed particular concern for preserving the University of Frankfurt as a Calvinist university in the event of his succession by a non-Calvinist ruler.[27]

The same sad situation prevailed at Königsberg. In October 1657, the rector and the university senate complained to the Prussian diet about the poor state of the university. Five professorships had become vacant and had not been filled, to the great harm of the students. The Estates were asked to plead with the Duke to fill the vacancies and to obtain increased salaries for the professors.[28] The Estates did present the problem to Frederick William with a most vivid description of how bad things were: "The Academy, the greatest jewel of our fatherland, in contrast to earlier times, is now greatly devastated and has come to be held in disrepute by foreign universities."[29] Not only was the university devastated and held in disrepute by foreign universities, but its small, underpaid, and inadequate faculty limited the number of graduates, who filled the churches of East Prussia with unqualified persons. Again during the sessions of the Great Diet of 1661-1663 the Estates complained that the university was still in bad shape from the recent war (the Northern War, 1655-1660).[30] Faculty vacancies remained unfilled, salaries were poor or not paid, stipends for poor students were lacking, the buildings were in poor condition, and it was impossible for the university to supply the needed pastors and teachers for churches and schools.

Frederick William did help to rehabilitate the University of Königsberg with financial subsidies. However, neither of the two old universities achieved any stature before the eighteenth century. The professional faculties of theology, law, and medicine were considerably below the academic standards of universities in the other German territories. The University of Wittenberg was the chief source of Lutheran theologians and preachers.

The western or Rhine territories of the Hohenzollern in 1650 were completely lacking in university facilities. Frederick William remedied this in 1655 by founding a Calvinist university at Duisburg in the Duchy of Cleves.[31] The Duisburg university was surrounded by more famous institutions, including Calvinist universities in the Netherlands. It never really seemed to fill an urgent local need. In 1652, even before formal inauguration, the philosophy faculty had twenty-five students. A century later there were only thirty-one. Finally in 1818 the university was closed.[32]

27. von Caemmerer, *Testamente,* no. 15, pp. 185-186.
28. *UA,* 15:428-432.
29. *UA,* 15:399.
30. *UA,* 15:523, 657, and vol. 16, pt. 1, p. 29.
31. Werner Hesse, *Beiträge zur Geschichte der früheren Universität in Duisburg.*
32. Wilhelm Rotscheidt, ed., *Die Matrikel der Universität Duisburg 1652-1818.* This work lists the names, origins, and ages of all enrollees between 1652 and 1818, showing the average age at the time of enrollment falling between 16 and 21.

The Great Elector followed in the footsteps of his Hohenzollern ancestors in the measures he took to restore, improve, and expand the number of *Gymnasien* and universities in his territories. He had to overcome the devastating impact of the Thirty Years' War with only the resources of impoverished territories to fall back on, and at the same time he was attempting to play an ambitious role in the grand politics of international affairs. It is not surprising then that his efforts by 1688 had not created any outstanding educational institutions worthy of recognition by foreign intellectual circles. Until 1688 the Hohenzollern princes had not been unique in their concern for the public welfare, nor were they singularly innovating in their educational efforts. They had been creatures of their time, borrowing ideas and institutions from the leading thinkers and the most advanced ruling princes of the time. Some, like the Great Elector, were assiduous in their efforts to improve and reform, to reconstruct and to be constructive in all phases of public life. Education, religious refugees, Jews, commerce, agriculture, manufacturing, the public service, all profited from the positive and enlightened legislation of Frederick William.

It was after 1688, in part because of the transformation of Brandenburg-Prussia under the Great Elector, that the Hohenzollern territories became the political and cultural leader of Protestant Germany. Intellectual, cultural, academic influences radiated out from Brandenburg. This was due to a number of interrelated factors. One word could supply the answer to why Brandenburg suddenly took on great stature in things intellectual— Halle. This city on the Saale River had come into Hohenzollern possession as recently as 1680. In the course of the next two decades, it became the most active center of German Pietism, the home of the complex Franckian educational institutions, and the location of a new university which Paulsen described as "the first real modern university," and it attracted many of the greatest personalities in German intellectual life. The graduates of the *Paedagogium regium,* the *Seminarium Selectum Praeceptorum,* and of the University of Halle, as well as the textbooks, journals, and learned writings published by the *Waisenhaus* printing press, disseminated the ideas and influence of Halle all through North Germany. It was in large measure the devotion and protection of Elector Frederick III and his Hanoverian wife, Sophie Charlotte, particularly protection against the strangulating opposition of the Lutheran orthodoxy and establishment, which permitted these various factors to make Brandenburg the cultural leader of North Germany. Berlin would share some glory with Halle after 1700 when it became the home of the first German Academy of Sciences.

The formal inauguration of a new university at Halle in 1694 was preceded or conditioned by a fortuitous conjunction of forces and events. First Brandenburg had long needed a Lutheran university, since Frankfurt and Duisburg were Calvinist; and Königsberg was both inadequate and too peripheral to the life of Brandenburg. Likewise there was urgent need to provide a friendly home for the new philosophy, the spirit of rationalism, religious toleration, the new concept of public law derived from natural law, a home free of the traditional intellectual framework of scholasticism, Aristotelianism, Latinity, and religious orthodoxy. Brandenburg was fortunate in having a ruler in Frederick III who was receptive to the new intellectual forces in Germany represented by Leibniz, Pufendorf, Seckendorff, Thomasius, Spener, and Francke. The new university was a creation of Elector Frederick, who published his intention to found a university at Halle on 24 June 1691 by appointing a *Cura Academiae* (Board of Curators) charged with this responsibility.[33]

Credit for the real initiative in the idea of establishing a university is generally given to Christian Thomasius, who had been expelled from the University of Leipzig because of his defense of religious tolerance towards the Reformed church, his philosophical rationalism, and the revolutionary innovation of lecturing in German. This new spirit was welcomed in Berlin by the court of Frederick III, who appointed Thomasius Professor of Law at a *Ritterakademie* existing at Halle since 1680. Thomasius began holding lectures, in German, in April of 1690. His lectures on logic and law attracted many of the young noblemen of the *Ritterakademie,* and soon he was compelled to use the great hall of the municipal *Wagehaus* (weighing house) near the town hall.[34] The success of Thomasius, the attraction of his lectures on law for the sons of princes and nobles, and the already existent *Ritterakademie* apparently stimulated the idea of establishing a university at Halle to satisfy the urgent need for training native-born Lutheran preachers and teachers, and to develop a whole cadre of juristically trained servants of the state. Perhaps instigated by Thomasius, these several conditions persuaded Frederick to make his appointment of an academic curia on 24 June 1691. That Halle should be the chosen site was quite natural since as early as 1531 Albert of Hohenzollern, Archbishop of Magdeburg and of Mainz, had obtained from the Papal Legate Campeggio a privilege for the establishment of a university at Halle.[35] Although Albert abandoned his plan because the Lutheran tide was running against him, a twist of fate saw a later Hohenzollern fulfilling that purpose of 1531. The papal privilege was meaningless in the Lutheran territory, but it was used to influence the emperor to issue an imperial privilege for the University of Halle on 19 October 1693.[36]

The imperial privilege or charter was not a necessity, but was a desirable legal advantage if the new university was to enjoy full privileges as a German university. As early as August 1691, Frederick decreed the first orga-

33. Wilhelm Schrader, *Geschichte der Friedrichs-Universität zu Halle,* vol. 2, app. 4, pp. 356-357.
34. For the early history of the university, see J. Christian Förster. *Uebersicht der Geschichte der Universität zu Halle in ihrem ersten Jahrhunderte.* The basic study is Schrader, *Friedrichs-Universität.* Also useful are Hanns Freydank, *Die Universität Halle,* and Leo Stern, ed., *450 Jahre Martin-Luther-Universität Halle-Wittenberg.*
35. Schrader, *Friedrichs-Universität,* vol. 2, app. 1, pp. 351-353.
36. Ibid., app. 8, pp. 361-368.

nizational status of the university.[37] With the *Ritterakademie* and its students and the lectures of Thomasius, there existed a nucleus of an academy of higher learning. The elector authorized the appointment of a faculty mostly from local officials and professional men, provided 3,600 *thaler* for salaries, 500 *thaler* as stipends for indigent students, and assigned classroom space at the weighing house. Fortunately, most of the new appointees declined, thus saving the university from a rather mediocre faculty of parochial fame. Pufendorf, court historian at Berlin, also declined appointment, having no taste for an academic position. However, recruiting in 1692 and 1693 did win significant names to the new faculty. Most fateful was that of August Hermann Francke, who was invited to the pastorate of a parish church at Glaucha (suburb of Halle) and was at the same time (7 January 1692) appointed Professor of Hebrew and Greek at the future university. Another significant name was that of Samuel Stryck, who was appointed Professor of Roman Law and first director of the university. The major plum, however, was the success leading to the appointment, on 13 October 1692, of Veit Ludwig von Seckendorff as the first chancellor of the university. Seckendorff, a distinguished political and cameral philosopher, was one of the most eminent men among the German intellectual titans at the end of the century. His death two months after appointment could not dim the prestige his name as chancellor had given to the planned institution.

The professional staff was to include Thomasius as Professor of Law, J. Breithaupt as the first Professor of Theology, Christoph Cellarius as Professor of History and Philology, and Johann Franz Buddeus as Professor of Philosophy. In the natural sciences, two distinguished names were added to the medical faculty. Friedrich Hoffmann arrived in 1693 and for forty-nine years lectured on physics, chemistry, anatomy, surgery, and practical medicine. Georg E. Stahl, famous for his phlogiston theory, lectured on theoretical medicine and chemistry, complementing Hoffmann. By 1695 fifteen distinguished names had been gathered at Halle to be the first professors of the four faculties. As they arrived between 1692 and 1694 they immediately offered lectures in their specialties, even before the university was officially opened. At the time of the official inauguration of the university on 1-3 July 1694, some 765 matriculated students participated in the ceremony. Between 1694 and 1728, 18,208 students matriculated, the great majority divided almost equally between law and theology.

Thomasius (d. 1728) and Francke (d. 1727) were the guiding lights of the new university. They were strange bedfellows, bound together for a time by their common struggle against Lutheran orthodoxy, whose persecutions they had both suffered at the University of Leipzig. The latter was a Pietist with religious overtones, the former was a torchbearer of

37. Ibid., app. 5, pp. 357-360.

German rationalism. Fundamentally and essentially they were opposites in their intellectual orientation, and Pietism and rationalism would in the early eighteenth century become bitter rivals for control of the university. But their early alliance and the protection of the elector were necessary for survival against the attacks of the Lutheran Estates of the Duchy of Magdeburg and of the Lutheran clergy of Halle. Orthodox Lutherans did not share the spirit of religious tolerance that dictated Hohenzollern policy between 1640 and 1786, was basic to the teachings of the Pietists, and was a natural product of Thomasian rationalism. The Lutheran establishment was more concerned with combating dogmatic heresies (*Irrlehren*) than with education of the poor, was more disturbed by the religious enthusiasm of the Pietists than with its own neglect of religious instruction.

The role of the electoral house in the early history and success of the University of Halle was the dominant factor. Despite local opposition, the university was founded by the state because the welfare and needs of the state required a new university. The elector forbade attacks on the Pietists from Lutheran pulpits and granted permission to Thomasius to lecture on natural law, religious tolerance, and the new rationalism. The Hohenzollern policy of religious tolerance not only encouraged immigration of religious refugees into their lands, but brought to Halle many great minds of different religious convictions. The theological faculty was composed almost exclusively of Pietist Lutherans, but the other faculties were not so limited.

The two forces of Pietism and rationalism at Halle combined to introduce a whole new spirit into Brandenburg and German education. They emphasized, at different levels, a practical education for living in the "modern world." The goal of the new university was to achieve a reformation of the whole life of the state, public and private, through the new sciences and through a practical Christianity. The Pietists introduced a new social doctrine of concern for the poor, widows, and orphans, for elementary education for all, for training teachers in the new methods of pedagogy, and awakened in the Lutheran population a social consciousness of responsibility for others. Carl Hinrichs attributed to the German Pietist concern for social reform the beginning of a road leading to socialism, as others would see English Puritanism leading to the growth of capitalism.[38]

The nontheological faculty, led by Thomasius, introduced the new secular science and rationalism and pointed the way to theoretical absolutism and the German Enlightenment. The new curriculum deemphasized ancient languages while recognizing their importance for the theologian. Emphasis was placed upon the contemporary languages, German and French, the new jurisprudence developed by Samuel Pufendorf, upon

38. *Friedrich Wilhelm I.,* p. 561.

history, the new sciences of the seventeenth century, and the new Cartesian philosophy. The practicality of the new curriculum, as distinguished from the traditional humanistic curriculum which had previously prevailed, achieved its purpose of producing university graduates who not only filled Lutheran pulpits and staffed the new schools, but who also filled the increasing need for public service at town, territorial, and central governmental levels.

During the reign of Frederick William I, a major formal addition was made to the curricular offerings at Halle when the king, in 1727, decided that what he called "Cameralia, Oeconomica und Polizeisachen" were to be taught at the university in the same manner and on the same level as other subjects and sciences. To that end he ordered his minister, University Curator von Knyphausen, to establish a professorial chair for cameralia so that students, before they were employed in public service, would acquire a good, theoretical foundation in these disciplines.[39] When Peter Simon Gasser was appointed to fill the professorship of cameral sciences it was the first such professorship in Germany. In the same year the historian J. Christian Dithmar was appointed to a similar position at the University of Frankfurt. Nowhere in Germany at this time was there a systematic study of theoretical economics, of public finance, or of the management of a national economy. Frederick William was convinced that a strictly juristic or legal training was inadequate for a public administrator who would be concerned with improving a state's economic condition or of increasing the wealth of a nation. So, moved by practical considerations of obtaining for his administrative bureaus men trained in finance and economics, Frederick William I took the first step to establish economics or political economy as a science at a German university.[40]

Until 1727 economics and public finance had always been treated within the framework of some other discipline: theology, moral philosophy, public law, ethics, history. There were, of course, in this age of mercantilism many individuals who wrote about economic affairs, particularly their relationship to the politico-military strength of a state. Since the late seventeenth century various writers, including prominent members of the Halle faculty, had argued that the economic sciences ought to be given separate recognition as a discipline of learning at the universities. The most important work, and the basic text for the first course of Professor Gasser, was the *Teutscher Fürstenstaat* published by Seckendorff in 1656. Pufendorf, Buddeus, Thomasius, and the historian Ludewig wrote and lectured on economic principles and practices. Thomasius re-

39. Acta Borussica: *Die Behördenorganisation und die allgemeine Staatsverwaltung Preussens im 18. Jahrhundert,* vol. 4, pt. 2, no. 140, pp. 216-220, "Cabinet Order to Cnyphausen, 23 July 1727."

40. An excellent and detailed study on the introduction of economics at the University of Halle is that of Bruno Feist, *Die Geschichte der Nationalökonomie an der Friedrichs-Universität zu Halle im 18. Jahrhundert.*

jected the "just price" concept of the theologians and argued the importance of "supply" (scarcity) and actual value in determining price. Ludewig, who became Ordinary Professor of Law at Halle in 1705, argued that there should be a separate and distinct professorship for economics for purposes of training future public officials in public finance and tax administration.[41]

The cabinet order establishing the new professorship in "Cameralia, Oeconomica und Polizeisachen" defined these terms as did Professor Gasser when he published his own textbook, in 1729: *Einleitung zu den ökonomischen politischen und Kameralwissenschaften. Ökonomie*, for which Ludewig was already using the word *Wirtschaft*, referred primarily to agriculture and associated industries useful for the profitable administration of large estates. Grain export, furnishing raw materials for domestic industry, care of the fields, animal husbandry, brewing of beer, management of mills and forests, proper use of services of serfs, all came under economics. *Cameralia* were related to the counting house, including financial administration, budgeting, accounting, taxes. Because the acquisition of bullion in this mercantilist age, a full treasury, a favorable balance in the flow of money in external trade were the dominant concerns, it was not unnatural that the term "cameralism" became synonymous with economics in the German literature of the eighteenth century. *Polizeisachen* referred to the regulation of industry, commerce, urban life, public buildings, bridges, dikes, roads, and guilds. This was an area supervised by the General War Commissariat through its local commissaries.

There is no evidence of great immediate success from this innovation in producing "prudent economists" in large numbers for public service. But it is a strong indication of the "alliance of the Prussian state with the powers of intellectual progress," as Paulsen evaluated the foundation and expansion of the University of Halle.[42]

The university was a state creation, and its statutes, organization, facilities, and privileges were determined by electoral/royal legislative edicts. The elector allocated the money for salaries from several provincial treasuries of the Duchy of Magdeburg. Nevertheless, the academic community participated in drawing up statements concerning the privileges of professors, the status of students, and the privileges of the corporate university. The two basic documents affecting the fledgling university were the "Statutes of the Friedrichs-Universität at Halle and Its Faculties of 1 July 1694,"[43] and the "Electoral Privilege of the Friedrichs-

---

41. Ludewig published an important work on "money" in his *Einleitung zu dem deutschen Münzwesen mittlerer zeiten* (Halle, 1709), in which he discussed the changing value of money in terms of purchasing power and its effect on prices of goods, taxes, rents, interest, etc.

42. Paulsen, *German Education, Past and Present*, p. 120.

43. Schrader, *Friedrichs-Universität*, vol. 2, app. 9, pp. 381-438.

Universität at Halle" of 4 September 1697.[44] The first of these edicts determined the "corpus academicum" as consisting of the traditional four faculties of theology, law, medicine, and philosophy, each headed by an elected dean who served six months. The highest administrative official of the university was the prorector, elected annually by seniority and rotated among the faculties. The office of chancellor had been abandoned after the death of Seckendorff, and that of rector, until abolished by Frederick William I, was reserved for a member of the ruling family. The prorector was aided and advised, particularly in judicial affairs, by a dean's council and an academic senate. The latter was composed of all Ordinary Professors of the four faculties.

Although the university was completely autonomous in its academic and administrative life, it did benefit from the existence of the board of curators appointed in 1691. The *Oberkuratoren* represented the highest administrative body for all universities in Brandenburg-Prussia. Its members were drawn from the ranks of the Real Privy Councillors and were politically responsible for the university at the governmental level.

Without question the most treasured as well as the most controversial privilege of the European university was that of juridical autonomy, which in the case of German universities goes back to the *Authentica Habita* of Emperor Frederick I of 1158.[45] The electoral privilege of 1697 gave to the university complete exemption from all courts (judicial, ecclesiastical, territorial, municipal) and made the university a court of first instance for all members of the academic community: professors, students, officials, and servants. The prorector, assisted when necessary for serious cases by the academic senate, had judicial jurisdiction over all civil and criminal cases involving university members. Civil authorities as well as the military commandant could make arrests and hold criminous students and others in prison overnight, but were required to turn such persons over to the rector for trial and punishment. In capital offenses, before execution, the case was to be referred to the *Justizrat* for confirmation. The *Geheimer Justizrat* (Privy Judicial Council) was the highest court of appeal below the king. The university was privileged to appear directly before this body in Berlin.

The university court had a good measure of business from high-spirited students who frequently brawled with the soldiers of the local regiment or with the townspeople or violated various police regulations. Ill-will on the part of the military resulted from the exemption of students from involuntary military recruiting. Förster, writing in 1799, made it clear that many young citizens registered at the university to acquire student status without serious study in order to "evade the draft."[46] The

44. Ibid., app. 13, pp. 443-451; also in *C. C. Magdeb.*, pt. 1, no. 12, pp. 98-105.
45. See "Privilegium scholasticum" in *Monumenta Germaniae Historica, Legum Sectio IV., Constitutiones et Acta Publica Imperatorum et Regum*, vol. 1, ed. Ludwig Weiland, no. 178, p. 249.
46. *Universität zu Halle*, p. 75.

weighing house, with its halls and rooms, was assigned to the university for lectures, offices, and a university library. The town retained the right to use the great hall for wedding parties and for performances of traveling theater companies. Students were often uninvited guests at the wedding parties and caused disturbances. And then there were the grievances against university students which every town and generation seem to have. These were described in a police regulation of 28 March 1695.[47] It was charged that not only during the day hours but all night as well students in the taverns drank wine, coffee, tea, played cards, rolled dice, consumed sweets and confections, and in general idled their time away. The regulation to curb these "evil" practices was aimed at the local tavernkeepers who were forbidden to serve drinks after 9:00 or 10:00 o'clock in the evening. All games of chance were forbidden, except for chess and ordinary card-playing. Brandy, wine, and liqueurs were not to be sold in the coffee, tea, or chocolate houses. Tavernkeepers were not to make loans of more than 3 *thaler* to students without university permission. This kind of legislation may explain why the students brawled in the streets of Halle with the soldiers and townspeople. The Halle regiment not infrequently was called upon to preserve the peace against riotous students.

With all of its growing pains, normal for the times and for a university town, led by its brilliant array of academic stars, which included Christian Wolff after 1706, the University of Halle rose to phenomenal preeminence among German universities, overshadowing its near neighbors of Leipzig and Wittenberg in the eighteenth century.[48]

---

47. *C. C. Magdeb.*, pt. 1, no. 11, "Regulation Concerning Conduct of Students at Halle in Wine, Tea and Coffee Houses."

48. In a classic case of the violation of university freedom and administrative autonomy, in 1723 Frederick William I dismissed Wolff from his teaching position because of false charges of atheism brought against him by the Halle Pietists. The temporary alliance between Pietism and rationalism had dissolved.

15

The Advancement of Learning

The Hohenzollern interest in advancing the spiritual, educational, intellectual, and cultural welfare of their lands and subjects went beyond building churches, founding schools, and establishing universities. During the century following the Thirty Years' War, several magnificent institutions in the history of Prussian and German learning, scholarship, and culture were founded. These institutions not only were to be significant in their own existence but were to prepare Prussia for the era of enlightenment and to make Berlin a center of monumental beauty, of historical and archaeological scholarship, and of scientific pioneering.

The origins of the great State Library, the Academy of Arts, the Academy of Science, the basic collections for state and Hohenzollern museums, the publishing industry, the magnificent public buildings, the famous Lustgarten and avenue of Unter den Linden which helped make Berlin a major city and beautiful capital are all to be found in this period before 1740. The momentum generated in this century carried through the reign of Frederick the Great to the era of the Humboldt brothers and the founding of the University of Berlin in 1810.

The motives of the three Hohenzollern princes of this century were a mixture of enlightenment, pride, and grandeur, as well as strict utilitarianism. During this period Brandenburg-Prussia was fast becoming the political and military power of North Germany and the leader of German Protestantism. Developments at Berlin and Halle were also to make her the cultural leader of at least North Germany. As Frederick the Great would write in 1748, "Sous Frédéric I. Berlin était l'Athènes du Nord."[1]

The Electoral/Royal Library

The revival of classical learning, the inspiration of literary, political, and theological writings, and the development of the Gutenberg printing press in the age of the Renaissance, all combined to encourage the founding of libraries as depositories for new books and old manuscripts and as centers of scholarly activity. Vatican and Medicean libraries in sixteenth-century Italy exemplified the appearance of private, princely libraries to supple-

1. Adolf Harnack, *Geschichte der Königlich Preussischen Akademie der Wissenschaften zu Berlin,* vol. 2, no. 142, p. 244. For an analysis of the intellectual climate in Brandenburg-Prussia at the beginning of the eighteenth century, and descriptive portraits of influential personalities, see Adolf Harnack, "Das geistige und wissenschaftliche Leben in Brandenburg-Preussen um das Jahr 1700," in *Hohenzollern-Jahrbuch,* ed. Paul Seidel, 4 (1900): 170-191.

ment those of monasteries and universities. The first public libraries in Europe probably were the Mazarin Library in France and the Bodleian Library at Oxford, England. Two minor public libraries were found in Germany before 1661, at Wolfenbüttel and at Gotha. University libraries in Germany were generally not very impressive.

In the Brandenburg Mark at the beginning of the sixteenth century there was no significant collection of books anywhere, either private or princely. The founding of the University of Frankfurt in 1506 stimulated the acquisition of books. Between 1516 and 1540 a university library developed here as the only public library in Brandenburg for over a century.[2] The acquisition of books and the building of libraries was to a large extent dependent upon the existence of domestic printing presses. The first book publisher, a Christoph Weiss, came to Berlin in 1539. More important was the printing house established in 1572 by Leonhard Thurneisser, an enterprising Swiss scientist and dispenser of medical remedies.[3] In a portion of the secularized, Franciscan monastery (the Gray Cloister) he set up a drug factory and a printing press to publish his own writings, including his famous calendar-almanacs which advertised his remedies. So backward was Brandenburg at this time that Thurneisser had to establish a type-making plant and import paper, artists, engravers, and typesetters. His press had its own Latin, Greek, Hebrew, Arabic, Turkish, and Persian type, which along with its excellent engravers contributed to making this a famous printing house. The press survived in Berlin after Thurneisser returned to Basle in 1584. But as was true for so many other educational and cultural innovations of the sixteenth century, the publishing enterprise was almost dormant at the end of the Thirty Years' War.

Elector Frederick William was to be the founder of the first public library in Brandenburg history, the later royal *Staatsbibliothek,* or State Library, in Berlin. The origin of this library was to be found in a *Haus-und Hofbibliothek* or a palace library. There existed in 1650 a court collection of books and early manuscripts acquired by preceding electors, most of which were stored in the palace attic and lacked organization. On 6 July 1650 the elector appointed Joachim Hübner as court historian and court librarian.[4] For eight years Hübner labored as director of all libraries belonging to the dynasty, as reference librarian for public servants, and he was charged with maintaining the best editions and the leading authors and with increasing the number of books. Hübner was expected to catalog and organize the library, but little progress had been made in this direction when Johann Raue was appointed Director of the Palace Library as well as

2. Friedrich Wilken, *Geschichte der Königlichen Bibliothek zu Berlin,* pp. 6-7.
3. Julius Heidemann, *Geschichte des Grauen Klosters zu Berlin,* pp. 62-64.
4. Kurt Tautz, *Die Bibliothekare der Churfürstlichen Bibliothek zu Cölln an der Spree: Ein Beitrag zur Geschichte der Preussischen Staatsbibliothek im siebzehnten Jahrhundert,* pp. 231-233.

of all territorial libraries on 20 July 1658.[5] Raue received this appointment after failing to achieve a uniform, central administration of schools as General Inspector of Schools in the Mark. Between 1658 and 1661 the Palace Library was relocated on the first floor of the apothecary wing of the electoral palace, and Raue began the task of preparing a universal, alphabetic catalogue as well as a catalogue by specialties.

In 1661 Frederick William made the *Hofbibliothek* a public library, a state library, and thus Raue became the first librarian of the Electoral Library of Brandenburg. The apothecary wing of the palace was remodeled by the Dutch architect, Johann Memhardt, so that Raue had three rooms for working space. One room contained the book collection along with paintings, statues, a reading desk, and a world globe. A second room held manuscripts and rare books, an herbarium, a model of Otto von Guericke's Magdeburg hemispheres, and a collection of minerals and stuffed animals. Already in these two rooms there were the beginnings of the Hohenzollern art museum and natural history collection. The third room was a reading room, heated in the winter, for the convenience of the public using the book collection. The latter was small in size in 1661. But beginning with an annual income of 2,500 marks, available for new acquisitions and binding, the library grew steadily by purchase, by gifts, and by adding many items from secularized monasteries and churches. Shortly after "going public" the library was able to purchase from Luther's grandsons, for 1,200 *thaler,* some items from Luther's own writings and library. Libraries of deceased scholars were bought up or donated. Purchases and acquisitions were made all over Germany. In 1677 an important collection of Oriental manuscripts was acquired, and by 1700 Brandenburg was the home of important sinologists. Book-publishing houses established in Berlin aided in making acquisitions. Raue established a library printing press which survived until 1721 and contributed additions. Manuscripts from the newly acquired territories were transferred and preserved in the Electoral Library.

The growing collection of books and other items was first cataloged between 1665 and 1683 by the brothers Christoph and Peter Hendreich. They prepared an alphabetic author and subject catalog which first appeared in 1683 and eventually grew to forty-two volumes. (Christoph Hendreich became library director in 1680 and also served as court historian.) The new library and its cataloged collection of manuscripts made it possible or at least more convenient to begin writing about the history of Brandenburg. The genesis of the great Prussian historiographic tradition, of collecting and publishing the documentary sources of Brandenburg-Prussian and German history, was not unrelated to the organization of materials in the new public state library.

---

5. Ibid., pp. 234-236. The letter patent was drawn up and dated 20 July 1658, but the appointment was not actually delivered until 20 April 1659.

It was the intention of the Great Elector to open the Electoral Library to the public, which was free to make use of the books in the public reading room. The reading room was open, after 1666, every afternoon. Leading public officials could withdraw books upon signing a chit, but only with the express approval of the elector or president of the privy council.

From a relatively insignificant *Hofbibliothek,* the new *Kurfürstliche-bibliothek* or Electoral Library established in 1661 grew so rapidly that by 1687 plans were made for a new and separate library building to be constructed in the Lustgarten adjacent to the electoral palace. Construction of this two-story building with a planned capacity of 40,000 volumes was suspended in 1688. At this time, the Electoral Library consisted of 20,600 printed and bound books and 1,618 manuscripts.[6] It had been necessary for the electoral librarian, in January 1688, to set up four book-binders in his own home to keep up with the binding requirements of the expanding library.[7]

Under Frederick III (I) there was no unusual development, except that the name was changed in 1701 to the Royal Library. It retained this name to the twentieth century.[8] An idea borrowed from French practice sought to increase the library's collection by requiring all Prussian book publishers to deliver two copies of all books published by them to the Royal Library. Not only was this an important decision for the growth of the future State Library of Berlin, but made of the library a historical depository of all books published domestically, thus preserving them for scholarly purposes. Unfortunately during the next reign book publishers frequently failed to deposit the required copies.

A major acquisition was the purchase in 1701 of the private library of Ezechiel von Spanheim, Prussian minister and ambassador to London. Some 9,000 volumes and 100 manuscripts, excelling in history and ancient literature, thus became public property.

Under Frederick William I the arts, sciences, cultural institutions in general had a precarious existence and usually prospered only in proportion to their practical or utilitarian value. The income of the Royal Library was reduced and new acquisitions declined because of the lack of money. No books were purchased between 1722 and 1740. Despite this factor the library grew surprisingly in size. The total number of bound volumes grew from a reported 50,000 in 1715 to 72,000 by 1740, as the result of gifts and other acquisitions. The Royal Library of Berlin in 1740

---

6. There were many duplicates in the collection, which in part explains the exaggerated estimate of some historians that there were 80,000 volumes in 1688 (e.g., Ferdinand Schevill, *The Great Elector* [Chicago: The University of Chicago Press, 1947], p. 381).

7. Tautz, *Bibliothekare,* p. 258.

8. After World War II the former Royal Library became a victim of physical, geographical, and ideological division. The portion in East Berlin is designated as the *Deutsche Staatsbibliothek* to distinguish it from the *Staatsbibliothek* of Berlin.

was exceeded in size by only a few European libraries at Paris, Rome, Vienna, and Helmstedt.[9] Oelrichs, the Library's first historian, writing in 1752, described it as "one of the largest and finest in Europe."

Project for a World University, 1667

Shortly after he had transformed the court library into a public library in 1661, Frederick William became seriously intrigued with a project submitted to him by a Swede, Benedict Skytte, in 1667. The suggestion was for nothing less than a world university, which as a *universitas gentium* would be a worthy United Nations creation in the twentieth century.[10] It would be a "university for the nations, sciences, and arts." What Frederick William had in mind was an asylum for all persecuted intellectuals of Europe, a center for pure and applied sciences. There would be no restrictions on the teaching of every free art or science. Here would gather learned men of all nations and religions, pursuing truth and protected by international treaty from the dangers of war. Whether or not inspired by Bacon's *New Atlantis,* this dream would have been the realization in fact of Solomon's House. In this sense the project was perhaps closer to being an academy of sciences[11] than a universal university.[12] In 1700 Jablonski noted that the 1667 project was much like the proposal of 1700 for a Society of Sciences. Although Frederick William offered to support the grand design with an initial 15,000 *thaler* and other revenues, nothing came of the plan. Had there been a Seckendorff or Leibniz to collaborate with this enlightened prince, the project might have been more than stillborn. Failure of fulfillment, however, was not the immediate issue. The very fact that Frederick William was capable of seriously considering a creation of this kind was reflective of the Hohenzollern concern for the advancement of learning, for the promotion of

9. The most valuable and reliable narrative of the history of the Prussian State Library is that of Eugen Paunel, *Die Staatsbibliothek zu Berlin, Ihre Geschichte und Organisation während der ersten zwei Jahrhunderte seit ihrer Eröffnung, 1661-1871,* pp. 1-44. Another recent and useful source is *Deutsche Staatsbibliothek 1661-1961,* vol. 1, *Geschichte und Gegenwart,* and vol. 2, *Bibliographie* (very complete compilation). Friedrich Wilken, *Geschichte der Königlichen Bibliothek zu Berlin,* is the basic book from which the later modern histories have borrowed heavily. The first history of the Royal Library was that of Johann C. C. Oelrichs, *Entwurf einter Geschichte der Königlichen Bibliothek zu Berlin.* It offers much information on the early history and acquisitions as preserved in the short history prepared by the second director of the Library (Christoph Hendreich, *De Scribenda historia bibliothecae regiae Berolenensis* [Berlin, 1725]). Kurt Tautz (*Bibliothekare*) contributes portrait studies of the various librarians of the Electoral Library and their services in the seventeenth century.

10. Since the grand plan was never more than that, it was filed away in the archives and forgotten until it was discovered by D. E. Jablonski in 1700 ("Notice Concerning the Plan of the Great Elector to Establish a European University [1667]" [by Jablonski], in Harnack, *Preussischen Akademie,* vol. 2, no. 1, pp. 3-4).

11. Heubaum, *Deutschen Bildungswesen,* 1:64.

12. Harnack, *Preussischen Akademie,* vol. 1, pt. 1, p. 3.

the intellectual and cultural welfare of his territories within a framework of religious toleration to be found only in the United Netherlands at this time. It was an amazing and ambitious project for a small German territory, without the financial resources of the western states, to undertake. The idea emerged again at the turn of the century and resulted in an academy of sciences.

The Royal Society of Sciences in Berlin

The efforts of the Great Elector to build institutions of learning and scholarship were gloriously carried on and magnified by his successor, Frederick III, who founded the University of Halle (1694), an Academy of Arts (1696), and a Society of Sciences in 1700. The name of Leibniz, librarian and historian at the court of the elector of Hanover, was to be intimately connected with the founding of the Society of Sciences. In a letter of 31 December 1700 Leibniz (1646-1716) admitted he had talked with Skytte in 1667 about the abortive plan for a universal academy (after Skytte had departed from Berlin for Frankfurt am Main where Leibniz was then resident).[13] Although he never gave credit to the Swede for planting the idea in his consciousness, it was from this time (1667-1668) that Leibniz made the one great goal of his life the establishment of an academy somewhere in Germany comparable to the Royal Society in London and the Royal Academy in Paris. The incitement may have come from these foreign examples. As a philosopher of optimistic rationalism, Leibniz asserted the principle that the purpose of all activity was the advancement of the "general welfare." In his commentary of 1669-1670, "on establishment of a society in Germany,"[14] he spoke of "der gemeine Nuz," and in other writings[15] he mentioned "le bien public" and "das gemeine Beste" as the goals to be achieved through a society of scholars working in the arts and sciences. Leibniz expressed the view that Germans had done much to pioneer new discoveries in the sciences— physical, mechanical, natural—but had in the seventeenth century failed to develop or expand upon these discoveries. Germany he proclaimed as the mother of chemistry; the leader in mining techniques; the school of all mechanics in making clocks, water-power devices, fire-fighting machines, air pumps, and hydraulic machines; the birthplace of modern astronomy, of copper engraving; and foremost in the world of medicine, medical remedies, and the life sciences.[16] But now, after the war, he found that schools, academies, education, crafts, arts, and sciences were in a state of ruin and disorder. To restore the arts and sciences to a

13. Ibid., 2:4.
14. Ibid., 2:9.
15. Ibid., 1:16-17.
16. Ibid., vol. 2, no. 4, pp. 19-26, Leibniz's second draft of 1669-1670 for a society in Germany to advance the arts and sciences.

flourishing state, Germany needed to follow the example of England and to establish an academy of sciences. And the princes of Germany were capable of this, he asserted. He appealed over two decades to the electors of Mainz and Hanover as well as to the emperor in an effort to establish somewhere in Germany a society or academy of learned men who would bring the arts and sciences once again to a prosperous condition. Only in Brandenburg at the court of the Hohenzollern prince did he receive a favorable answer.

Leibniz became aware of Brandenburg and Berlin because of his employment by the House of Hanover and his close relationship with Sophie Charlotte, who married Elector Frederick III on 28 September 1684. Sophie Charlotte brought to Berlin a love of the arts and sciences. A pupil of Leibniz, a friend of learning and of learned men, an admirer of French culture, she became the link between Leibniz and the elector and helped bring to fruition the idea of an academy of science. Some would call her the real founder of the Berlin Society. To further his goal, Leibniz attempted to win appointment as court historiographer in 1694 in Berlin on the death of Pufendorf, but failed because of court politics.[17]

The series of events which led to the reality rather than the dream of a society of learned men began in 1697, when Sophie Charlotte became interested in building an astronomical observatory as part of the new electoral stables being erected in the new suburb Dorotheenstadt. When informed of this, Leibniz seized upon the project to urge the electress to expand or attach to the observatory an academy of sciences. The Calvinist court preacher, J. T. Jablonski, with access to the elector, endorsed the plan of Leibniz and worked closely with the electress and Leibniz to draw up plans and to convince the elector that the glory of his name and the welfare of his territories would be enhanced by the founding of such an academy.

Another significant development occurred at Regensburg when, on 23 September 1699, the Protestant delegates at the Imperial Diet decided to adopt the Gregorian calendar by dropping the eleven days following 18 February 1700.[18] Leibniz combined this calendar revision with an idea borrowed from Germany's great mathematician, Erhard Weigel of Jena University, namely, a calendar monopoly to be granted to the Berlin Observatory and the associated Society of Sciences. In March and May 1700, Jablonski submitted to the elector a proposal to build an observatory in Berlin and to establish an academy of sciences.[19] Books and instruments, he

17. Eberhard von Danckelmann was the dominant adviser to Frederick III at this time and a court enemy of the Electress Sophie Charlotte. When he fell in 1697, Sophie's influence over the elector grew as did her success in spending Brandenburg money on lavish artistic ventures.

18. Harnack, *Preussischen Akademie,* vol. 2, no. 22, p. 58, "Agreement of the Evangelical Princes at Regensburg."

19. Ibid., vol. 2, nos. 23, 24, pp. 58-68.

said, were already available in the collection of the new Electoral Library. The costs of salaries and other expenses could be met by giving the academy a calendar monopoly. An observatory tower and an academy meeting place could be built on the new stables. At the same time Jablonski recommended Leibniz as the first president of the proposed academy.

As early as 19 March 1700 Frederick declared his intention to establish the proposed Academy of Sciences and an observatory in Berlin.[20] After granting the new academy a calendar monopoly on 10 May,[21] the elector issued a formal letter of foundation for a Society of Sciences on 11 July 1700.[22] The following day a letter appointing Leibniz as president was issued.[23] Leibniz continued to hold his position at Hanover as court librarian, but was allowed to visit Berlin periodically to assist in launching the new project, to select members, and to edit its first publication.

Many individuals were responsible for the founding of the first academy of sciences in Germany, the Royal Society of Sciences of Berlin. Besides Leibniz and Sophie Charlotte, there were learned Prussians in Berlin, kindred spirits of men like Leibniz, Spener, Thomasius, Francke, and intimates of the spirited electress. Men like Jablonski and like Ezechiel von Spanheim, in whose home in Berlin learned men had for many years held regular, informal meetings, were the ones who carried the Leibniz plan to fruition. But all of these efforts would have been in vain except for the support of the Elector Frederick. On the eastern frontier of Germany he did what emperor and electors had refused to do in Vienna, Mainz, Dresden, and Hanover. He established a center for the advancement of scientific learning, a focal point for the gathering of learned minds. Frederick again demonstrated the Hohenzollern sympathy for improved educational institutions, the recognition of the basic relationship between the material and spiritual welfare of their lands and people, and the advancement of learning. Frederick, like his father, within the limitations of a poor land, was prepared to support institutions of education, culture, and science.

Leibniz and Jablonski had primarily concerned themselves with the sciences (physics, chemistry, astronomy, geography, mechanics, optics, algebra, and geometry). To this Frederick, as a royal contribution, added a requirement that the new society should cultivate and foster a knowledge and use of the German language, German history, and law. Thus Harnack gives Frederick credit for being the real spiritual founder of the philological-historical section of the later Prussian Academy of Sciences.[24]

20. Ibid., vol. 2, no. 25, p. 68.
21. Ibid., vol. 2, no. 37, pp. 87-89.
22. Ibid., vol. 1, pp. 93-94.
23. Ibid., vol 2, no. 54, pp. 115-116.
24. The magisterial work of Adolf Harnack on the history of the Royal Prussian Academy of Sciences in Berlin is the most thorough study of this institution and the principal source used. Vol. 1 is a narrative based on vol. 2, which is a complete collection of the sources dealing with the history of the Academy.

In March 1700, Frederick gave instructions that the electoral *Baumeister* Grünberg should begin construction of an observatory tower as part of the royal stables. And on 18 May 1700 Gottfried Kirch was appointed the first astronomer of the society with the duty of preparing an annual calendar the sale of which was an exclusive monopoly of the society.[25]

In a general instruction for the Society of Sciences, issued on founding day, Frederick also declared that he would make available to the members of the society the Electoral Library, his clock and instrument collection, as well as any rare, foreign animals, plants, and minerals that came into his possession.[26] Tools, implements, water mills, arsenals, forges, smelters, and works of art in the Thiergarten (zoological garden) and Lustgarten were all placed at the disposal of the society members. The purposes of the society were fundamentally to promote the sciences through experiment, study, foreign correspondence, observations, development of new inventions and technology, and improvements in agriculture so that science could serve the general welfare. It was to promote the purity of the German language and attempt to increase the fame and welfare of the German nation. Frederick urged that the society, through friendship with Czar Peter of Russia, seek to establish scientific observations in Russian Asia of astronomical and geographical nature (Alexander von Humboldt would do this a century later). He hoped to extend evangelical missionary work to China via the backdoor of Siberia. The Prussian African Company was to assist in the research of the Society.[27]

The general instruction of 1700 served as the constitutional charter for ten years, using the Royal English Society as a model. The king assumed the role of protector. The society would consist of a president, a governing council, and elected members.

For ten years the Berlin society existed on paper. A formal inauguration and dedication of observatory and meeting place was postponed until the tower was built. This unfortunately required ten years, years of war and wasteful court extravagance which frequently bordered on the scandalous, making the necessary money scarce. However, the society did begin to function, the calendar was published according to Kirch's calculation, and 55 sessions were held before 1711. Most of the scientific work accomplished during this decade was due to Kirch (1639-1710) and Johann Leonhard Frisch (1666-1743). Kirch was a pupil of Weigel and was regarded as the foremost astronomer of Germany. In 1680[28] Kirch made the first telescopic

25. Harnack, *Preussischen Akademie,* vol. 2, no. 38, p. 90.

26. Ibid., no. 50, pp. 103-109.

27. Founded in 1682.

28. I am indebted to my colleague, Edgar Everhardt, himself a discoverer of two comets, for the reference on Kirch's comet (Sergei Konstantinovich Vsekhsvyatskii, *Physical Characteristics of Comets* [Moscow, 1958], pp. 120-123; trans. and ed. by staff of Israel Program for Scientific Translations [Jerusalem: S. Monson, 1964]; published for the National Aeronautics and Space Administration and the National Science Foundation, Washington). In 1702 Kirch's wife discovered a second Kirch comet.

discovery of a comet, later observed by Newton, who made reference to it in his *Principia Mathematica.*[29] At Berlin Kirch continued his observations of comets and variable stars. His accurate calendars earned the society's only income during this time. Frisch helped to develop the silk industry of Prussia, improved the famous Berlin (Prussian) blue dye, made significant contributions to German language studies, and authored the publication of a Latin-German dictionary. As a natural scientist he was distinguished for his writings on the insects and birds of Germany.

These ten years were difficult ones. The society had no meeting place, no observatory, no instruments, no library, no money for publications, particularly of the results of Kirch's observations. The society was close to dissolution by 1706. Leibniz came to Berlin and worked hard to revive it and stimulate its scientific work. His efforts were successful. The completed observatory tower was turned over to the society in August 1709; and in May 1710 the society's first volume was published: *Miscellanea Berolinensia.* It contained sixty articles in three different areas: literature, physical-medical, mathematical-mechanical. By this publication the society earned its way into the scientific world. However, as Harnack wisely observed, "The volume is evidence that the new science of the second half of the seventeenth century had found a place in Berlin. The special spirit of the Eighteenth Century is not yet revealed in it."[30] The spirit of the Enlightenment was not to be found in this volume, although the new science of the seventeenth century was thereby made at home in Berlin.

The Royal Society of Sciences was granted a new constitution on 3 June 1710.[31] It was now legally endowed with the middle tower of the new royal stables as an observatory with rooms for a meeting chamber. The society was divided into four departments: (1) physics, medicine, chemistry; (2) mathematics, astronomy, mechanics; (3) German linguistics and history; (4) literature, particularly ancient Hebrew, Greek, and Latin, as well as propagating the faith among pagans and infidels. Each department elected a director for life by majority vote. The four directors rotated the office of vice-president annually and through the governing council actually ran the affairs of the society, because Leibniz, president until 1716, spent most of his time in Hanover. Each department was required to meet once monthly, thus in effect providing for a weekly meeting of the Society when a paper was to be presented.

The formal, festive inauguration of the Royal Society occurred on 19 January 1711 in the new meeting chamber of the observatory tower.[32]

29. Sir Isaac Newton's *Mathematical Principles of Natural Philosophy and His System of the World,* trans. Andrew Motte in 1729, vol. 2, *The System of the World* (Berkeley: University of California Press, 1962), bk. 3, proposition XLI, problem XXI, example, pp. 507-508. In Newton's first edition of 1686 see p. 490.

30. Harnack, *Preussischen Akademie,* 1:165.

31. Ibid., vol. 2, no. 99, pp. 192-196.

32. A description of the actual inauguration ceremony can be found in ibid., vol. 2, nos. 107, 109, pp. 204-210.

Leibniz left Berlin in 1711 never to return. Frederick I died in 1713. With the departure of the inspirer and the founder, the Royal Society declined in activity and became almost ineffective in the following years. The new king was no friend of learning and culture in general and despised the society. He thought seriously of abolishing it, but was dissuaded from this so long as the society could support itself and be of practical value.

By 1715 the society had lost its most active members, with the exception of Jablonski and those connected with the Anatomical Theatre. Frederick William I was not really hostile to learning, only to vain and idle learning. His support of the fields of medicine, chemistry, the cameralist sciences reveals that it was the usefully productive sciences which interested him. The learned men of the society after 1713 were an unproductive body, publishing only five more meagre volumes of the *Miscellanea* by 1740.

It has been argued that Frederick William's disdain for the society was best expressed by his appointment in 1718 of Jacob Paul Gundling as the second president of the society.[33] There are those historians who have found the key to this king's personality in his love for tall soldiers and his appointment of an alcoholic historian as president of the Royal Society of Sciences. Gundling had been appointed Professor of Civil Law, History, and Literature at the new *Ritterakademie* in Berlin in 1705. With the abolition of the academy in 1713 by Frederick William, Gundling was unemployed and gradually became an alcoholic. In the same year, however, the king appointed Gundling newspaper reader and analyst, and he became an influential advisor on political and economic matters. But his weakness for drink gradually turned him into a learned buffoon at the meetings of the *Tabakskollegium,* the King's informal kitchen or cellar cabinet. Harnack, however, maintains that Gundling had not yet become a comical figure in 1718 when he was appointed to the office vacant since the death of Leibniz. Actually he published a number of books on history, statistics, and geography, as well as a *Codex diplomaticus Brandenburgicus.* The Codex was a compilation of several thousand documents important in promoting archival studies. In 1724 he obtained for the society a royal order that its library receive a copy of all books published in Prussia. He also won for the society a monopoly for publication of all geographic maps and the right to publish collections of law. When, in January 1735, Frederick William transferred some 3,000 books on mathematics and medicine from the Royal Library to the society, the academy library was launched on a solid foundation.[34] Judged by his scholarly production, Gundling was qualified to be a member of the society's historical section. But his own personal deterioration was a reflection of the decline of the society's effectiveness, influence, and

33. Ibid., no. 131, p. 232.
34. Ibid., no. 139, pp. 240-241.

respect. Not until after 1733, when the old court preacher Jablonski, who had been a member since 1700, was appointed president, did the society regain vitality and productivity. It was under the next ruler, Frederick the Great, that the Society of Sciences came into its own. Reorganized, with royal support, it became between 1740 and 1746 the Royal Academy of Science and Belles-Letters, and between 1746 and 1756 was under the presidency of the great French mathematician, Maupertuis.

During the first four decades of the eighteenth century, the Royal Society of Sciences of Berlin was not a great success. It did not, as Harnack said, "call forth a new cultural epoch," for Berlin or Prussia. As Minister von Viereck reported to Frederick II on 9 June 1740, the society achieved European recognition and high respect while Leibniz was president.[35] But after 1716, as Frederick the Great described in his own historical sketch of the society, the society fell "dans une decadence entière" and "en léthargie."[36] Only chemistry, medicine, and anatomy functioned actively and made those practical, useful contributions which Frederick William I admired. Yet the fact remains that Berlin was the first home of a princely established center of scientific research and publication in Germany, and it inspired the founding of those of Vienna, Dresden, and St. Petersburg. From this beginning emerged the great Academy of Science still functioning today in Berlin.

The Academy of the Arts

The expanding power of the Hohenzollern territories after 1650 was manifested and reflected in a variety of ways. Brandenburg-Prussia not only became the most powerful Protestant state in the Holy Roman Empire as manifested by its growing political, military, and territorial strength, but it was to emerge in the eighteenth century as an intellectual and cultural leader as well. Halle with its university would dominate the intellectual development of northern Germany. Berlin with its Royal Library and Royal Society of Sciences would become a center for historical and scientific research. Berlin, however, was the capital of widely scattered territories, and the Hohenzollern rulers intended to transform the small, insignificant town of 8,000 inhabitants of 1648 into a city which by its size and beauty would compare favorably with the great capitals of Europe, and by its splendor reflect the might of the state. In this the three rulers between 1650 and 1740 were successful. The modern city of Berlin was laid out during this century. The great baroque buildings, erected before 1740 and added to significantly by Frederick the Great, gave to Berlin the architectural style and magnificence which survived until the destruction of World War II.

35. Ibid., no. 145, pp. 246-247.
36. Ibid., no. 142, pp. 244-245.

A major symbol of this artistic outburst was the Academy of Arts, founded in 1696. It was more a product of and a helpmate for the artistic development of Berlin than a cause of it. But, like the later Society of Sciences, it demonstrated the Hohenzollern urge to promote the cultural welfare of the state. For the first king of Prussia, Frederick, it may well have been a simple urge for ostentatious splendor, comparable to the attainment of the royal crown in 1701. But, beyond this goal of pomp, it meant introducing a great variety of fine and practical arts among the skills of Berlin artists and craftsmen. Not only did architecture, painting, and sculpture profit from Hohenzollern support, but glass and ceramic industries were developed. Tapestries, gold, silver, and coppersmiths, foundries for casting bronzes, botanical gardens, baroque furniture all contributed to the beauty of the city and to the pleasure of the residents.

The first Hohenzollern interest in the arts expressed itself under Joachim II in the second half of the sixteenth century. The design of a Renaissance electoral palace by Kaspar Theiss, the paintings of Lucas Cranach, and the work of various Saxon artists were a good beginning. Berlin could already boast of several distinguished church edifices. However, the Thirty Years' War was a cultural and artistic setback for Berlin, for Brandenburg, as it was for most of Germany. By 1650 it was necessary to begin again. The young Frederick William, who laid the foundation for the great Prussian State Library, also revealed an interest in art collection and city building that laid the foundations for great museums and outlined the design for a beautiful capital. His exile to the Netherlands between 1635 and 1638 and his first marriage to Louise Henrietta of Orange resulted in an influx of Dutch architects, engineers, and artists. Italy contributed many reproductions, and French influence became dominant at the end of the century. These foreign artistic influences, however, encouraged the growth of a covey of Prussian artists and artistic craftsmen of all kinds.

No sooner was the great religious war ended by the Peace of Westphalia than Frederick William began to make Berlin into a modern city. This was to be a city filled with works of art. He imported a whole colony of Dutch artists, chief among whom was the engineer Memhardt who was the great city architect, designing the new fortress city and outlining plans for expansion. Equally important was the initiative taken by Frederick William in developing an appreciation of the muses and graces in his principality, to develop appreciation of the arts, to attract learned men and artists to Berlin, to emancipate the Brandenburg cultural spirit.[37] Frederick William also began collecting works of art and natural

37. Valuable references on the cultural and artistic development of Brandenburg-Prussia between 1650 and 1740 include: W. von Oettingen, "Die bildenden Künste unter König Friedrich I," *Hohenzollern-Jahrbuch,* ed. Paul Seidel, 4 (1900): 231-246; G. Thouret, "Einzug der Musen und Grazien in die Mark," ibid., pp. 192-230; P. Seidel, "Die bildenden

history, collections which became the foundations of the later state and Hohenzollern museums in Berlin. He gave instructions for the purchase of paintings and sculpture from foreign countries, including copies of Italian masterpieces. Portraits of the Hohenzollern electoral dynasty were created to become part of the Hohenzollern museum. Copper engravings, scientific books and journals, Japanese lacquer and porcelain, Dutch Delftware, French tapestries became a part of the Berlin art world. In addition, perhaps stimulated by gifts of a Dutch uncle, Maurice of Nassau, through the Dutch East India Company, the Great Elector bought many artifacts of natives of newly discovered lands. Unusual specimens of nature started another kind of collection. In 1686 Frederick William inherited a valuable coin and medal collection from Elector Karl Ludwig of the Palatinate which was added to a sizable coin collection begun by Joachim II. In true mercantilistic fashion, to prevent a *thaler*-drainage in payment for these items of luxury, Frederick William established a faience factory in Berlin (1697) to produce Delftware and a glass factory to make crystal and ruby glass, and he planned the beginning of a tapestry-weaving industry with the aid of French Huguenot refugees after 1685. The leading tapestry weaver was Pierre Mercier the Younger, out of Aubusson, who was appointed court tapestry weaver by the Great Elector in 1686.

Only the beginnings were made by Frederick William. After 1688 his son expanded his collection almost passionately. Five rooms of the Berlin palace were used to store the growing collection of antiquities, art works, and natural history specimens. Stuffed animals, minerals, fossils, amber pieces, seashells, antique furniture, painted miniatures, carved stones, sculpture in wood, marble, plaster, alabaster, and bronze, silver and gold pieces, wax figures, glass in all forms, brass candelabra, paintings, mirrors, tabourets, items of chinoiserie, the famous coin collection, copper engravings, huge Gobelin-style tapestries (in 1699 there were over 800 tapestries covering the walls of the palaces of Berlin and Potsdam), faience works (anticipating the later magnificent porcelain industry of Berlin) filled the palace and established a solid basis for several later museums. Shortly after 1700 King Frederick I acquired many priceless pieces of art from his Orange heritage—oil paintings and silver and gold pieces in particular.

When Frederick William acquired the Palatinate coin collection in 1686, it was accompanied by one Lorenz Beger who in 1693 became supervisor of the State Library, the coin collection, the art collection, and the

Künste unter König Friedrich I," ibid., pp. 247-268; Richard Borrmann, ed., *Die Bau- und Kunstdenkmäler von Berlin;* Friedrich Nicolai, *Beschreibung der Königlichen Residenzstädte Berlin und Potsdam,* 3d ed., 3 vols.; Lorenz Beger, *Thesaurus Brandenburgicus,* 3 vols. (1696-1704); Max Arendt, Eberhard Faden, and Otto-Friedrich Gandert, *Geschichte der Stadt Berlin, Festschrift zur 700-Jahr-Feier der Reichshauptstadt;* Ernst Consentius, *Alt-Berlin Anno 1740,* 2d ed.; Willi Drost, "Schlüter und das Berliner Barock," in *Berlin in Vergangenheit und Gegenwart: Tübinger Vorträge,* ed. Hans Rothfels.

natural history collection. Beger perhaps deserves credit for arousing the Prussian and German interest in archaeology and antiquities by purchasing the antiquities collection of Belloir (some 40 marble pieces, 80 bronzes, and many artifacts) which became the foundation of the Antiquarium of the later Royal Museum of Berlin. Between 1696 and 1704 Beger published three folio volumes (*Thesaurus Brandenburgicus*) depicting in copper etchings the antiquarial collection as well as the royal palaces and their interiors. It served as an invaluable source book for subsequent histories of Prussian art and architecture.

By 1690 there were many artists of all kinds in Berlin—Dutch artists, a growing number of French Huguenots, and some Italian. An increasing number of German artists and artisans joined this foreign colony. At this time the Berlin colony of artists began having thoughts of establishing a private art academy. A suggestion made to Elector Frederick, in 1694, by Augustin Terwesten that an academy of arts, modeled on that of Paris, be established was readily adopted by Frederick, and an electoral Academy of Arts was formally established in 1696. Although almost the whole of Frederick's reign was taken up by two great European wars (1688-1697, 1702-1713) involving Brandenburg-Prussia, he himself was possessed by a profound love for the arts of peace. Spending money like a Maecenas on artists, on beautifying Berlin with new buildings, he lavishly pursued glory, pomp, and etiquette and held great festivities, all in imitation of the extravagant French court of Louis XIV. It mattered not that he bankrupted his territories.

As soon as the elector approved of the suggestion of an academy for artists to foster creative work and artistic theory, he directed Johann Arnold Nering, the electoral *Baumeister,* to prepare the second floor of the front facade of the new royal stables as a home for the proposed academy. Since 1687, in the new city of Dorotheenstadt, Nering had been building the *Marstall* at the head of Unter den Linden. The huge stables would later also be the location of the Royal Observatory and the Society of Sciences. Six rooms were made available, and the academy was opened on 1 July 1696.

The fundamental statute for the governance of the academy was not published until 20 March 1699. It proclaimed that the academy was established "to encourage the arts of painting, sculpture, and architecture." But it involved much more than these fine arts. Essentially the academy was composed of two elements: a school of instruction and an association of academic artists. Although it was meant to be an advanced school, one room was reserved for elementary instruction. In another, modeling in plaster was taught. And in other rooms instruction was given in city architecture and military fortification, anatomy and drapery arrangement for painters, and drawing from live models supplemented by a large number of plaster models of ancient statues supplied by the elector from Italy.

In 1694 Andreas Schlüter, the most significant German sculptor of the time, was brought to Berlin as court sculptor. He was made a member of the academy and a sometime instructor in sculpting. In 1696 he replaced Nering (d. 1695) as court architect. For ten years Schlüter and his workshop dominated artistic and architectural production in Berlin. His workshop was filled with artists of all kinds to produce wood carvings, sculptures, stucco work, paintings, bronze works, and all sorts of decorative items for the palace and other buildings. He redesigned, modified, and enlarged the palace in Cölln. His most famous creation was the huge bronze equestrian figure of the Great Elector, which for two centuries gave lustre to Die Lange Brücke, the bridge designed by Nering to span the Spree River between Berlin and Cölln north of the Palace Square. Schlüter for a decade was to play the role of a Prussian Le Brun, designing art works to be completed by others. His workshop and the Academy of Arts did much to promote the decorative arts up to 1713. The smith's crafts, brazier skills, casting of bronze statues, the striking of commemorative medals, church bells, artistic cannon kept Berlin's foundries busy. The Gobelin tapestry industry required designers and weavers. The nature of artistic production expanded so that in 1706 the academy's name was altered to that of Royal Academy of Arts and Mechanical Sciences. Its members included silk-embroiderers, artistic weavers, goldsmiths, clockmakers, opticians, and mechanics. The academy prospered to 1713, training many apprentices who became producers of the objects of art which would decorate the palace, the Berlin arsenal, and many other public buildings.

Under the austerity regime of Frederick William I, the decorative arts ceased to flourish as they had under his father. Many artists, among them leading royal architects, left Berlin for other states, including Saxony and Russia. Berlin had to yield to Dresden as the art center of northern Germany. After 1713 the academy declined to little more than a drawing school where surveyors and artistic craftsmen were apprenticed. Portrait painters, necessary for dynastic purposes, were retained. Among them Antoine Pesne was the most important. Frederick William himself joined the ranks of productive painters.[38] The second king ordered many silver pieces for the palace, as well as mirror frames, console tables, and candelabra. He did not completely neglect the decorative arts, but no longer did the academy or the arts enjoy the lavish support of the previous reign. On the other hand, the building program in Berlin received wholehearted support from Frederick William.

Monumental Berlin

The true significance of the promotion of the decorative arts by the Hohenzollern rulers after 1650 cannot be fully appreciated if it is thought

38. See Jochen Klepper, *In tormentis pinxit*, 2d ed. (Stuttgart, 1959).

of only in terms of art collections and museums. To some extent, of course, there was a concomitant releasing or development of the creative spirit that flowed over into other arts in the eighteenth century, such as music, literature, the theatre.

The purpose of the Brandenburg princes, however, was to use the arts to beautify, to ornament the capital city of Berlin and particularly the many new public buildings which were part of this artistic explosion. Thus the building program, the architectural monuments and style, the city planning and expansion of Berlin to provide for the private and public needs of a population which grew from 6,000 to 90,000 in a century were an integral part of making *Alt-Berlin* a beautiful city.

In 1650 the capital of Brandenburg consisted of the twin cities of Berlin and Cölln, divided by the Spree River, which branched out trident-fashion so that a northern arm encircled Berlin and a southern branch Cölln. The two cities were in effect islands. The main stream of the Spree flowed northwest with Berlin slightly to the northeast opposite Cölln. In Berlin the only buildings of value were the Cloister Church of the Franciscans, St. Nicholas and St. Mary churches, and the buildings of the Gray Cloister occupied by the Berlin *Gymnasium*. In Cölln were found St. Peter's Church, the Dominican Dom, and the delapidated palace. This was the unpromising heritage of Frederick William. In the course of the next forty years the capital area expanded. Three new cities were added. Friedrichswerder was developed first, receiving a city charter in 1662. It lay across the Spree west of Cölln, and was planned by Memhard after 1655 as a residential area for court servants and public officials.

Directly west of Friedrichswerder and Cölln, facing the Spree River, a new city called Dorotheenstadt was laid out by the second wife of the Great Elector. This was begun in 1674. It was a suburb lying outside the city walls. Its principal topographical feature was the broad avenue known as Unter den Linden, extending from Friedrichswerder to the location of the later Brandenburg Gate on the edge of the Tiergarten, the Elector's hunting preserve.

In 1688 Frederick III laid out a fifth city, again west of Friedrichswerder and south of Dorotheenstadt, and called, not surprisingly, Friedrichsstadt. Dorotheenstadt and Friedrichsstadt were princely cities located outside the city walls and were governed by electoral officials. The three cities within the walls each had individual city halls, city magistracies, and burgomasters. However in 1709 the five cities and several unchartered suburbs were all incorporated into the one city of Berlin with a single city administration.

The oldest ground plan of the cities of Berlin and Cölln, drawn by Johann Gregor Memhard about 1650, graphically shows the topographical features and the early important buildings. At the point where the Spree River began to flow between Berlin and Cölln, a dam, known as the Mühlendamm, was thrown across the river perhaps as early as the thirteenth century. The flooded waters were used to drive various mills located along the shores. This dam furnished a causeway or crossing between Berlin and Cölln, and the earliest settlements were made here. On the north side in Berlin the oldest marketplace, later called the Molkenmarkt (dairy market), and the oldest church, St. Nicholas, were located only a short distance from the Mühlendamm. Southward on the Cölln side a fisherman's wharf was the basis for a fish market. Here too was located the parish church of Cölln, St. Peter's.

In the thirteenth century a second market called the *Neuer Markt* (Newmarket) was established some distance from the river opposite St. Mary's Church. It made available garden produce, fish, and meat. In the upper reaches on the northeast side of Berlin were located the Franciscan complex of buildings, the Gray Cloister, and the *Klosterkirche.* The Holy Ghost Church and the Berlin city hall were the only other significant edifices in 1650. The city hall was located on the main throughway of Georgenstrasse (later Königsstrasse) leading from the Palace Square in Cölln across Die Lange Brücke north to the St. George Gate where St. George Hospital and cemetery were located.

The chief significance of Cölln was that here was located the electoral palace built in the sixteenth century. The map of Memhard shows the early palace, the attached apothecary wing to the north, and the Dominican cathedral adjacent to the south. Between 1618 and 1632 a lofty water tower was built on the southwest corner. Drawing water from the Spree River by hydraulic water ram, it then by gravity supplied water to all compartments of the palace.

North of the palace lay a swampy area, in part used for a kitchen garden to serve the electoral table. Memhard converted this area after 1659 into beautiful gardens. Here facing the apothecary wing was the famous Lustgarten, a formal garden with flowers and trees of all kinds and increasingly filled with the growing collection of statuary. Beyond the Lustgarten were the fountains of the Wassergarten with water furnished from the nearby water tower. A summer pavilion, an aviary, a kitchen garden added to the beauties of this development. At the same time Memhard began a necessary renovation of the palace itself.

West of the Lustgarten was a bridge across the Spree, the Hundebrücke (later Schlossbrücke). It was across this bridge in the marshy meadows that Memhard laid out Friedrichswerder, the new residential city for officials and bureaucrats. The street leading from the bridge was planted with linden and chestnut trees. Not this street but its extension to the west in the new city of Dorotheenstadt would become Unter den Linden.

Frederick William faced a herculean task in 1648. He could hardly be expected to undertake a vast new construction program for a population which did not exceed 20,000 in 1685. His first concern was to transform Berlin, Cölln, and Friedrichswerder into a fortress city; Memhard achieved this between 1658 and 1683. Six-foot walls, pierced by six major city gates, gave the city the appearance depicted in the map of Berlin of 1688 drawn by J. B. Schultz. Surrounded by moats and canals, with new bridges joining the separate cities, Frederick William's major intracity contributions were paved streets, security, sanitation. The city of the next two centuries, however, was outlined by Memhard's city plans. The useless city walls and moats would be torn down in 1736 and filled in by Frederick William I to provide new building sites. But the palace area with its Lustgarten, the main streets of the inner city, the projected Linden Promenade, and the future growth of the city to the west were to be a permanent heritage. The only significant monumental contributions of this reign were the rebuilding of the palace and the construction in 1687 of the Spinnhaus on an island just above the Mühlendamm. It was the first workhouse in Berlin for beggars, the poor, the idle, where spinning wool yarn and other crafts were taught. It was a large square building, useful but of no great architectural significance.

It was during the reign of Frederick III (I) that Berlin profited from this prince's love for magnificence, lavishness, and the shine of external appearances. The population of Berlin boomed to 55,000 by 1710. New public buildings to meet a variety of public needs were constructed. The new royal dignity required a proper setting, and as Arendt described Frederick, "His mind was more oriented towards the appearance of might." Since a beautiful Berlin best exemplified the "appearance of might," it was the first king who actually began the conversion of Berlin into a modern, European capital city. A series of distinguished architects serving as electoral/royal *Baumeister* designed a multitude of buildings, parks, churches, summer houses, church and gate towers, private homes. The French baroque influence was dominant, but by the turn of the century a Prussian architectural style was emerging which might with some liberty be described as Prussian Palladian.

After Memhard the important city architects were Nering (1688-1695), Schlüter (1696-1706), Eosander von Göthe (1706-1713), Philip Gerlach under Frederick William I. These men were joined by various other architects such as Martin Grünberg, Michael Smids, and Jean de Bodt.

Nering designed and began the construction of two buildings which became famous in Berlin history, the Berlin arsenal (Zeughaus) and the royal stables (Marstall). He also designed Die Lange Brücke. The arsenal was begun in 1695 and was erected in Friedrichswerder opposite the Lustgarten between the Schlossbrücke and the Neue Thor. In effect it was at the head of Unter den Linden. Years later Friedrich Nicolai wrote "the arsenal is one of the most beautiful buildings in Europe."[39] It was a huge building 280 feet square, two stories high. Its beauty came not just from its baroque structure and portals but from the dozens of statues, some in clusters, of mythological or allegorical military significance, designed by Andreas Schlüter. Most of these statues, some forty-

39. Nicolai, *Königlichen Residenzstädte,* 1:163.

15. City Plan of Berlin by J. B. Schultz of 1688

eight, rested on a balustrade which ran completely around the roof. This building was first suggested by the Great Elector as a central gun factory, and it did in fact serve the Prussian army as an arsenal until 1877. The lower floor was a workshop, the upper floor was used as a museum. A foundry *(Gieshaus)* for casting the cannon and other pieces designed at the arsenal was located to the rear.

The building of the royal stables was started as early as 1687. It was located in Dorotheenstadt at the beginning of Unter den Linden, or Dorotheenstrasse. Two stories high, it covered two city blocks enclosing two huge courts. Designed as a necessary facility for housing the royal horses as well as the mounts of the electoral royal house guard, it soon acquired a loftier purpose. In 1695 a portion of the second floor became the home of the Academy of Arts. By 1710 an observatory tower had been erected, and the tower became the location of the Society of Sciences. For two hundred years or more this was known as the Academy Building. Under Frederick the Great the Royal Stable/Academy Building would be joined by the Berlin Opera House, the new State Library Building, and the Prince Henry Palace (which became the home of the University of Berlin in 1810).

After 1688 Nering laid out the new city of Friedrichsstadt with its perpendicular streets and established for it a style of architecture to which all new construction had to conform. He expanded the Berlin city hall and designed the Parochialkirche and many imposing city houses.

Nering's successor was Andreas Schlüter, who came to Berlin as court sculptor. Architecturally his major contribution was in connection with the remodeling of the royal palace. Where the Great Elector had for thirty years engaged in what Nicolai called *Flickwerk* or patchwork to restore the delapidated, leaking palace, after 1688 Frederick decided on a complete remodeling, to vastly expand the palace and to bring all previous construction together externally into a harmonious and symmetrical whole. Schlüter was selected as architect, and in 1697-1698 he prepared plans for a whole new baroque facade and a complete interior transformation. Two major inner courts were planned, as well as a rebuilding of the old water tower to make a huge bell tower. The new Academy of Arts and the workshop of Schlüter designed and contributed interior decoration including murals, stuccowork, mirrors, tapestries, furniture, ceiling decorations, carved figures, grand stairways, candelabras in a completely baroque magnificence.

Reconstruction and building began in 1699 and were not completed until 1716. Schlüter did not complete the work. In 1706 he was relieved of his position as palace architect by his jealous rival Eosander von Göthe. His downfall was occasioned by the collapse of the *Münzturm* (mint tower), as the old water tower was called after the electoral mint was relocated in the tower during the previous reign. Frederick had determined to convert the *Münzturm* into a lofty bell tower. Schlüter designed a tower 280 feet high, but his construction was faulty. He did not provide an adequate foundation around the old tower to support the weight of the added construction, and the tower began to sink. Because of the danger of total collapse, the tower had to be taken down and Schlüter was discredited. He continued as sculptor, however, and designed the magnificent bronze sarcophagi of Queen Sophie Charlotte (1706) and of King Frederick I (1713).

Many other buildings, both public and private, were designed by various architects during the reign of Frederick, adding to the beauty of the city. Grünberg designed the Grosse Friedrichshospital (1697-1716), an orphanage and elderly persons' home, located near the Spree River on the Berlin side above the Mühlendamm. Eosander after 1710 designed a summer palace for Crown Princess Sophie Dorothea, called Monbijou, on the north side of the Spree opposite Dorotheenstadt. It was a beautiful palace with galleries full of the new porcelain, German as well as Oriental. A Jewish synagogue was erected in Berlin near the *Neuer Markt* between 1700 and 1714. The Garrison Church near the Spandau Gate on the north side of Berlin was begun in 1701 but was completely rebuilt by Philip Gerlach in 1722 with a seating capacity of 4,000. Many churches with lofty spires were erected between 1700 and 1740 to serve the growing population: Parochialkirche, Bohemian Church, French Churches for the Huguenots, Deutsche Kirche (completely classical in style with dome and Corinthian columns), and many others.

The business and commercial needs of the growing city also led to new construction. The Mühlendamm, with marketplaces on both sides of the river, attracted many merchants. Because of the fire hazard, a shopping arcade of a number of stone buildings was constructed on the crossing, providing space for retail shops. Berlin's first stock exchange was located here between 1693 and 1738, when Frederick William I moved the Berlin Börse to the former *Lusthaus* (pavilion) of the Lustgarten. A home designed by Schlüter for the favorite Colbe von Wartenberg in 1702 became the central post office, at the foot of Königsstrasse just off Die Lange Brücke.

Many of the buildings begun in the reign of Frederick I were completed by Frederick William I. Many churches were built by the latter, and goaded by a jibe of his Hanoverian cousin, George I of England, Frederick William was responsible for beautiful spires which graced the Berlin skyline from afar. Philip Gerlach completed the building program in Friedrichsstadt and left his mark with such buildings as the *Kollegienhaus,* where the many judicial colleges of Berlin met.

By 1740 Berlin had grown into a city of 90,000 people. It had become a city filled with beautiful buildings, gardens, parks, the linden promenade. Architects, sculptors, artists of all kinds, supported and directed by the personal interest of the Hohenzollern rulers, had indeed transformed the insignificant town of 1648 into one of the most beautiful capitals of Europe.

16. Royal Palace and Great Elector Statue

17. Throne Room in the Berlin Palace

Part V

Public Health and Medical Sciences

V

Public Health and Medical Sciences

It was in the spirit of a regulative state that the domain of public health was subjected to princely legislation. Concern for the physical welfare of their subjects as well as the material benefits of a healthy and productive population induced European statesmen like Colbert and others, in the second half of the seventeenth century, to adopt measures designed to safeguard the health of both human and animal populations. These measures were manifold. The very concept of an administrative control and regulation of medical practice, by various genuine and pseudomedical practitioners, became incorporated in the emerging bureaucratic states. Requirements of licenses to practice, setting professional standards, delineation of functional jurisdiction, fee and price fixing, elimination of quacks and quack remedies became a matter of state regulation. Improvement of medical education and state support of facilities and institutions which would advance medical knowledge were complementary to public support of universities, general education, and national culture. Public sanitation was enforced by the state as naturally as city planning, building codes, and fire protection. The prevention of human and animal epidemics by state regulation for the first time since the fourteenth century became a possibility.

After the middle of the seventeenth century, various states of Europe developed a tendency to intervene in the whole area of public health for purposes of administrative regulation. In Germany, the Hohenzollern princes of Brandenburg were among the first to subject medicine and public health to state regulation and supervision under the police power of the state. Such state intervention, designed to promote individual and general welfare, was a normal expansion of the functions of the welfare state at the end of the seventeenth century.

16

The State Board of Medicine and Public Health

In the year 1685, Elector Frederick William took the first statutory step to place the whole realm of public health and all those professionally concerned with it under the administrative supervision of the state. This was done through promulgation of a medical ordinance, the first such comprehensive ordinance for medicine in Brandenburg history. Its primary provision was the establishment of a *Collegium Medicum,* a state board of medicine.[1]

The decision and action of the elector in 1685 were neither sudden nor unprecedented. Other German territories as well as non-German states had already established such medical boards for the purpose of regulating the practice of medicine in all its forms.[2] Walter Artelt and Manfred Stürzbecher have recently pointed out that the incentive for the establishment of a Brandenburg *Collegium Medicum* went back to 1661, when a number of court physicians in Berlin submitted a petition and a draft to the elector proposing such an institution.[3] The proposal of the several court physicians was submitted to the privy council for discussion. From these discussions emerged a revised draft or concept of a medical ordinance in 1662. This draft, however, did not reach fruition as an electoral edict. It was not until 12 November 1685 that Frederick William promulgated a medical ordinance establishing an administrative, bureaucratic, state board of medicine.[4] The final edict of 1685 revealed the elector's intention to place public health, and those involved in protecting it, under state control and supervision. It did not seek primarily to protect the corporate interests of physicians, as did the petition of 1661.

The justification for state intervention was based on reports coming to the Great Elector about abuses in the practice of medicine, in the preparation and distribution of medical remedies, and in the cure of sickness. These reports alarmed the prince, not only because "the science given by God to man for his welfare" was abused, but because on account of

1. See Reinhold A. Dorwart, "The Royal College of Medicine and Public Health in Brandenburg-Prussia, 1685-1740," *Medical History,* vol. 2, no. 1 (Jan. 1958), pp. 13-23.
2. Alfons Fischer saw the idea of a medical board to supervise public health developing in the sixteenth century *(Geschichte des Deutschen Gesundheitswesen,* 1:183-188).
3. Walter Artelt, *Medizinische Wissenschaft und Ärtzliche Praxis im Alten Berlin,* pp. 22 ff.; Manfred Stürzbecher, *Beiträge Zur Berliner Medizingeschichte,* pp. 6-27. Stürzbecher's comments on the prehistory of the medical ordinance of 1685 represent the most thorough and competent analysis of the developments between 1661 and 1685 presently available.
4. "Edict Concerning the Newly Established *Collegium Medicum* and the Conduct of Physicians, Surgeons, and Apothecaries," *C. C. March.,* vol. 5, pt. 4, sec. 1, no. 16, cols. 11-24. The text of the medical ordinance is also published in Stürzbecher, *Beiträge,* pp. 27-34.

those abuses, the health and lives of his people were endangered. Therefore, as evidence of his fatherly concern for the welfare of his people, he
decided to establish in 1685 a college or board of medicine in Berlin and
to place in its charge the medical profession and all the people associated
with it: physicians, apothecaries, barbers, surgeons, midwives, oculists,
herniotomists, lithotomists, and bathkeepers.[5]

The Board of Medicine was to consist of both laymen and professionals.
Real Privy Councillors, one of whom would serve as president, would
represent the civil element and give greater authority and dignity to the
board. The president would report its decisions directly to the elector.
The professional element would include the elector's personal and court
physicians, and the two physicians-in-ordinary of the medical faculty of
the University of Frankfurt. Other territorial physicians might be added
as associate members if their capacity, erudition, and experience war-
ranted. The physician members of the board were to elect a dean who
would ordinarily preside over discussions, would convoke the board, pro-
pose agenda for discussion, and would conserve the documents, records,
and seal of the board.

The very first function of the board was that of certification. All
physicians present or future who practiced or wished to practice in the
electorate of Brandenburg were to report to the board in person or in
writing, make known their methods of treating diseases, and produce
the public testimonials which had admitted them to practice. The board
would then pass on their qualifications and admission to practice. New-
comers were to refrain from the practice of medicine without approval
of the Board of Medicine. In the Neumark and other areas bordering the
Oder River, the board was to confer with the medical faculty of the university in matters concerning certification.

If the city magistrates or nobles in the counties wished to take on
a physician, the candidate had to be submitted to the board for approval.
Those who had studied at the University of Frankfurt and who graduated
from its medical faculty were to receive first consideration, in accord with
previously extended privileges.

This in effect instituted for the first time a state licensing system for
physicians. The requirement of submitting credentials of qualifications
and of receiving approval and license from the board to practice was also
extended to include apothecaries, barbers, surgeons, oculists, herniotomists, tooth-extractors, and midwives. All these were required to announce themselves to the *Collegium Medicum,* submit their qualifications to practice, be examined by the board or by approved physicians

5. The term "Collegium" or "college" does not refer to an academic institution. It was a
governmental bureau, a state board or commission, an administrative organ of the state
authorized to supervise the entire field of medicine and public health, and at times to serve
as an administrative court. To avoid confusion, *Collegium Medicum* will be translated as
"Board of Medicine."

in local areas, and then practice only if they had gained approval of the board. Journeymen and apprentices of licensed apothecaries, barbers, and surgeons were to be presented to the board or an approved physician before being dismissed from service and given proper testimonials of their qualifications and good conduct.

A second major assignment in the elector's effort to raise standards in the medical profession was for the board to instruct all those subordinated to it in a proper code of conduct, which the board would also enforce.

Physicians, for example, were directed to associate with each other in friendly fashion. They were forbidden to entice patients away from each other, or to criticize their colleagues. It would be proper for a physician to call in other physicians as consultants in diagnosis or prescription. No physician was to refuse such a call, since this affected a patient's welfare. Physicians were to inform themselves in exact detail of the condition of their patients and to reveal to no one what they learned. They should not demand exorbitant fees, particularly of the poor, but should serve poor and rich equally well. Jurisdiction over medical fees and accepted remedies was likewise assigned to the Board of Medicine.

When surgeons received cases of dangerous wounds or bad accidents, they were to call in approved physicians in ample time, were to heed their advice, and refrain from prescribing internal medicaments. Grocers, spice-merchants, alchemists, distillers, confectioners, perfumers were likewise forbidden to meddle with medical affairs, treatment, or remedies. Bathkeepers were not to prescribe internal medicine or encroach upon the professional areas of physicians, apothecaries, or barber-surgeons. In similar fashion, midwives were to prescribe no internal medicine on their own, and were to consult physicians in serious cases.

Oculists, herniotomists, and tooth-extractors who were approved were to be permitted to practice only at the public fairs and only for a period of four days. Charlatans, quacksalvers, and all deceivers who did not belong to the medical profession were not to be tolerated at all, much less old women, spell-makers, and others who used unseemly, magic, superstitious, and mysterious means.

In order to promote professional skill the physicians of the board were instructed, as often as it was possible to obtain cadavers, to perform dissections in a place to be assigned by the elector so that young medical students, surgeons, midwives, and others might acquire practical knowledge of human anatomy.

The newly established Board of Medicine was to be supported by fees charged for the examinations and testimonials. The costs of inspection of apothecary shops were to be borne by the towns and the apothecaries.

Manfred Stürzbecher's discovery of an unpublished item from the German Central Archives at Merseburg has provided new information on the medical ordinance of 1685.[6] This item, dated 30 November 1685, provided the information that the ordinance was published and forwarded to all city magistracies and district commissaries. The issue of the effectiveness of the ordinance of 1685 is still open to question. A Board of Medicine apparently did come into being in Berlin. But the other provisions of the ordinance were not carried out: licensing of all medical practitioners, regulation of fees, prices, and professional conduct, and inspection of apothecary shops. A price list for guidance of apothecaries in selling their medical remedies apparently was not drawn up by the medical board and approved by the elector until 22 June 1692.

The new price list was published in connection with a new and revised medical ordinance of 30 August 1693.[7] The new medical ordinance was drafted by the Board of Medicine on orders of the elector, presumably because of the inadequacy, ineffectiveness, or neglect of the ordinance of 1685. The ordinance of 1693 confirmed that of 1685, and, then, in separate but inclusive ordinances for physicians, apothecaries, barber-surgeons, and midwives, with far more explicit detail and strictness, it once again attempted to place the whole domain of medicine under state administration and supervision. Published and distributed like that of 1685, the ordinance of 1693 apparently suffered the same ineffectiveness. Less than a year after publication, on 1 May 1694, Frederick III was forced to issue a "Circular Order" to the magistrates of the Brandenburg cities telling them to publish the several ordinances of 1693, so that ignorance of them could no longer be pleaded as defense by medical practitioners.[8] The elector stated in his Circular Order that although the ordinance had been promulgated to the magistrates of the Mark, "there has been no result from this publication." There still were difficulties in getting effective medical policing, but the ordinance of 1693 appears to have had greater impact on effective regulation of medical practitioners and enforcement of canons of professional conduct than did the medical ordinance of 1685. The significance of the 1685 ordinance derived from its statutory originality and from its establishment of the State Board of Medicine, which could be used by the elector to enforce medical regulation.

Physicians and others were again required to register with the board and submit their qualifications for practice. They were forbidden to prepare medicaments except for secret preparations unavailable in an apothecary shop. Referrals to specific apothecaries by physicians for

6. Stürzbecher, *Beiträge,* p. 41, n. 59. In 1958 (see n. 1 above) I had expressed the judgment that the medical ordinance of 1685 had had little immediate effect, and that the edict itself had not been published. Stürzbecher has corrected this in part.

7. *C. C. March.,* vol. 5, pt. 4, sec. 1, no. 16, cols. 23-60.

8. Ibid., col. 59, "Circular Order Concerning Publication of the Medical Ordinance," of 1 May 1694.

mutual gain were forbidden. Members of the medical profession were forbidden to leave towns or places where they had earned a living if such places became infected with plague. For their protection, however, physicians need not enter infected houses, but were permitted to advise and to prescribe treatments from outside on the basis of information provided by hardier persons who had access to the patient.

The perpetual problem of fees and payment of fees was recognized by the ordinance. Experience indicated, it said, that patients were not particularly grateful, and physicians were forced to haggle like charlatans and shopkeepers with their patients and often demanded fees out of proportion to their services. The elector therefore established a fee schedule for medical calls and services. The fees varied from three *Groschen* to four *Reichsthaler* for a prescription obtained at the physician's home, for first and for successive calls, and whether for ordinary or contagious sickness, for night calls, for country calls involving travel, for autopsies, and for embalming. For curing venereal disease the physician could make his own terms. A conscientious physician was expected, out of Christian love, to help those who were too poor to pay.

Surgeons were to be sober people and ready and capable night and day to offer their skill to their neighbors. Master surgeons who were called to treat serious injuries or wounds inflicted by a second party were to make a temporary quick bandage and then reveal to local police officials the gravity of the wound so that the evildoer might be apprehended and properly punished.

Surgeons were definitely inferior professionally and subordinate to physicians in the hierarchy of medical practitioners. When both a surgeon and a physician were on a case together, the surgeon was to defer to the physician. Surgeons were to refrain from all internal cures, and in the treatment of syphilis by mercury and salivation, surgeons were to act only with the assistance of a physician. Barbers apparently were prone to overcharging their patients—asking a higher fee on grounds of a difficult operation or threatening not to treat a serious wound unless they were paid more. So again a fee schedule was prepared establishing proper fees for protection of both the surgeon and the patient. The fees ran from twelve *Groschen* to twenty *Reichsthaler*. For these fees surgeons dressed ordinary wounds, bone-penetrating wounds, wounds caused by sticking or stabbing, head wounds (ordinary or with injuries to the cranium or pericranium, or those in which the cranium was depressed with a fissure); treated injuries requiring trepanning; set leg fractures, longitudinal fractures of limbs, and dislocations; treated contusions, abscesses, tumors of all kinds, sore throats, inflammations; performed amputations and bloodletting. And again the poor who could not pay were to be treated out of Christian love and conscience. The surgeon's domain was external treatment by and large, and that of the physician was internal.

Midwives were an essential part of the public health services at this time. All obstetrical functions were performed by them. They too were required to register and submit their qualifications to the Board of Medicine if in the Berlin area or to the town physician approved by the board away from the capital. Like surgeons, midwives were required to live honorable, pious, and sober lives because their services might be required day or night. They were to treat women in labor with gentleness and discretion, were not to encourage labor without proper indications, nor without necessity place a woman on the delivery chair nor hold her there unduly long. Midwives should be prepared in emergencies to summon another experienced midwife for advice, or even a physician, particularly in cases where either the mother or the unborn child was dead while the other still lived. Physicians must be called in when any part of the afterbirth was not completely removed.

Midwives were forbidden to administer to any person, married or not, any medical remedy, potion, or powder whereby the fetus might be injured, killed, or expelled from the womb dead or alive or to give advice on such. They were forbidden to give forcing remedies to facilitate or advance menstrual flow. Apothecaries were forbidden to prepare for or to sell to midwives any such remedies. This was in the domain of the physician. Prescribing of any and all forms of internal remedies was forbidden to midwives. And, finally, if they were approached by a suspicious person requesting advice for illicit purposes, the midwives were to report this at once to the local magistrates or to the board so that possible harm might be prevented.

The functions of the apothecary were most intimately linked with the practice of internal medicine and with the functions of the physician. In this period of the late seventeenth century, when the first efforts were made at establishing professional standards of conduct and qualifications for practice, it is obvious that the professional fields of service of physician and apothecary needed to be sharply delineated. Apothecaries were forbidden to visit or prescribe for patients or give them any medicaments without a physician's approval. Physicians in turn could bypass the apothecary and prepare their own remedies only to a limited extent.

The work of the apothecary was in large measure carried out under strict supervision of approved physicians. This particularly applied to the preparation of chemical remedies. Until 1698, when a Brandenburg pharmacopoeia was published describing methods of preparation, apothecaries were required to consult with a physician on the method of preparing chemical compounds.[9]

The Board of Medicine by the terms of its establishment was more

9. All medical compounds kept in apothecaries for ordinary usage were to be prepared according to the Pharmacopoeia of Augsburg and other approved books, until such time as the Berlin *Collegium Medicum* should prepare its own pharmacopoeia. This was achieved in 1698.

than a certifying board. It was a part of the machinery of public administration which was taking shape in the late seventeenth and early
eighteenth centuries. It not only served as a professional body, but had
a court authority to pronounce sentence and decree punishment against
violators of the medical ordinance. But much of its effort in medical administration was futile in the early years after 1685, because it lacked
means of enforcement. By a patent of 25 June 1701 the king ordered
the police *(Landreuter)* to enforce the board's decisions.[10] But such orders
were to be signed by the president of the board, a member of the Real
Privy Council.

Early in his reign Frederick William I attempted to make state intervention and regulation of medical practice more effective than it had
been since 1685. In a letter patent of October 1713, he took note of
grievances which still persisted in medical matters and remarked that
many of his subjects had suffered in health, even in life, because of the
incompetence of those who undertook to be physicians.[11] He reemphasized the requirements of examination and certification, particularly forbidding unlicensed transient physicians and medical students to practice
medicine in his kingdom. Codes of professional conduct and limitations
of professional activity were reasserted. Apothecaries were not to fill
prescriptions unless written or approved by a physician. Grocers were
not to sell medical remedies. Surgeons were to refrain from internal treatment. Retired soldiers, old women, midwives, and chemists were forbidden to engage in any medical treatment.

To protect the gullible from medical mischief, the king insisted that
dentists, lithotomists, herniotomists, as well as charlatans and quacks,
be allowed to practice their business at the annual fairs only for the
number of days permitted in the medical ordinance of 1693. And, *horribile
dictu,* it was necessary to order the public executioners and skinners to
refrain from all medical treatments, internal and external. Thus perhaps did the legends arise in folklore about the quackery of horse doctors!

The insistence of the second king on stricter compliance with medical ordinances makes it clear that the first quarter-century of medical
police administration was not filled with success. However, the basic
problems were recognized, and procedures were elaborated for raising
standards of medical practice and for safeguarding the public health.
Most important of all was the affirmation of the principle that it was
a proper and necessary function of the state to regulate and supervise
those persons active in the medical arts.

The Royal Board of Medicine had administrative jurisdiction in all

10. *C. C. March.,* vol. 5, pt. 4, sec. 1, no. 16, col. 69, "Patent Concerning Execution of the
Published Sentences of the *Collegium Medicum.*"
11. Ibid., no. 16, cols. 71-75, "Patent Concerning Elimination of Certain Grievances
in Medical Administration," of 9 Oct. 1713.

of Brandenburg, including the Neumark east of the Oder River. In effect it could function adequately only in the capital city of Berlin. In order to extend its jurisdiction effectively into other Brandenburg towns and to enforce the provisions of the various medical ordinances, an office entitled Adjunct Physician was created in 1714.[12] A local physician was appointed to serve as adjunct to the royal board. He was directed to submit to the board lists of physicians, apothecaries, surgeons, midwives, and bathkeepers of the local area to determine if they had been examined and licensed. If not, the adjunct was to administer the necessary examination of qualifications and the royal board would grant approval to practice on the basis of the adjunct's report. He was to forward to Berlin all complaints and grievances and violations of standards of medical practice for investigation and administrative action.

The basic issue and problem remained that of licensing qualified physicians. In 1718 a royal declaration ordered strict enforcement of the 1685 requirement that no one was to practice medicine without approval of the Board of Medicine.[13] Such approval was to be given only after a qualifying examination during which the candidate would be given a *casuum practicorum* to solve from his own knowledge and experience.

In 1685 the Board of Medicine had been set up to supervise medical affairs only in the territory of the electorate of Brandenburg. Under Frederick William I the general tendency in the Hohenzollern possessions was in the direction of extension of centralized control from Berlin over all territorial administrative organs. For most aspects of state life, the principal instrument of this control was the General Directory established in 1723.[14] On 4 December 1724 the king personally ordered the General Directory to establish provincial *Collegia Medica* in each of his territories to administer all medical affairs in the provinces in accordance with the basic medical ordinance of 1685.[15] All provincial boards were administratively subordinated to the Berlin board which, on 17 December 1725, was elevated to the superior dignity of an *Oberkollegium Medicum* (Supreme Medical Board), thus centralizing medical administration for the whole kingdom in Berlin.[16]

The membership of the provincial boards was selected by the Berlin board and consisted of two physicians, two surgeons, and two apothecaries, with an administrative director from the Provincial War and Domain Chamber. They were empowered to examine and qualify physi-

12. Ibid., no. 16, col. 75, "Ordinance Concerning the Office of Adjunct to the Board of Medicine," of 18 April 1714.

13. Ibid., no. 20, cols. 203-206, "Declaration That No Physician Shall Practice Until He Has Presented Himself before the *Collegium Medicum*," of 3 Jan. 1718.

14. See Reinhold A. Dorwart, *The Administrative Reforms of Frederick William I of Prussia*, pp. 161-180.

15. *C. C. March.*, vol. 5, pt. 4, sec. 1, no. 29, cols. 235-236, "A Royal Order That a *Collegium Medicum* Shall Be Established in Each Province," of 4 Dec. 1724.

16. Ibid., no. 32, cols. 252-253.

cians, surgeons, and apothecaries for practice, to inspect apothecary shops, and were to report on medical and surgical affairs to the board in Berlin.

The efforts begun in 1685 to establish high standards of practice and professional conduct, to eliminate quacks, and to restrict internal and external medical treatment and preparation of drugs and remedies to those who were properly qualified by no means met with unqualified success. Tradition, superstition and gullibility, the boldness of quacks, the relatively limited knowledge in the field of medicine, and above all the inadequate means of enforcement of the rulings of the royal board still permitted the existence of abuses and threats to the medical welfare of the people. This was the view expressed by Frederick William I on 27 September 1725 as he issued a new "General and Stricter Medical Ordinance."[17] The king bluntly stated that he intended to end these abuses and malpractices "once and for all." However, rule by edict, even in a paternalistic welfare state, did not always accomplish the desired and desirable end.

The new ordinance of 1725 in general followed the pattern of the one of 1693. It confirmed the jurisdiction of the Board of Medicine and placed it under the direction of the Court Marshall, Ludwig von Printz, for greater authority and prestige. The board was to include available privy councillors, court physicians, the physician ordinary, and the oldest practitioner in Berlin. The king's personal surgeon, the court apothecary, two of the cleverest surgeons in Berlin, and two experienced apothecaries were to be added as consultants whenever surgical and pharmaceutical affairs came up for discussion. Representatives of the medical faculty of Frankfurt university, on the board since 1685, were now left off.

The ordinance of 1725 reaffirmed the edict of December 1724 in the matter of establishment of provincial boards of medicine. But a new element was introduced. To assure proper professional standards in qualifying candidates for medical practice, the board members themselves had to meet new standards. Physicians, surgeons, and apothecaries appointed to the provincial *Collegia Medica* must have completed the appropriate "postgraduate" training course offered at the Anatomical Theater in Berlin (e.g. anatomy, surgical operations, or pharmaceutical chemistry).[18]

A constant source of grievance and complaint by laymen had to do with medical fees and prices of medical remedies. To prevent collusion among physicians, surgeons, and apothecaries the *Oberkollegium* at Berlin was given authority to fix these fees and prices throughout the kingdom.

In order to assure that the provisions of the various medical ordinances

17. Ibid., no. 32, cols. 219-236.
18. The following chapter will discuss medical education and the significance of the Anatomical Theater.

were observed and violations punished, it was necessary to have means of enforcement. As early as 1693 a *Hoffiscal* (court fiscal) had been assigned to the *Collegium Medicum* of Berlin.[19] This official was a treasury-police agent who was to be alert at all times for violations of the ruler's edicts so that the royal fisc would receive its share of fines. The one assigned to the medical board was to act against violations of the medical ordinances. In 1716, General *Fiscal* Duhram was directed to alert all his agents to violations of the medical edicts and to report them to the medical board for investigation and judgment. The *Oberkollegium,* after 1725, served as a court with exclusive jurisdiction in medical affairs. A law expert was assigned to the board to prepare correct citations and sentences in connection with complaints and violations.[20]

In 1701 the *Landreuter* were required to enforce the board's decisions and sentences, and in 1719 the *Steuerräte* (central tax agents) were directed to enforce observance of all edicts emanating from the Berlin Board of Medicine.[21] Frederick William was making use of the new bureaucratic machinery of the central government to attempt stricter observance of the medical ordinances.

The so-called "stricter" medical ordinance of 1725 renewed and expanded the original (1685) code of professional conduct affecting physicians, surgeons, bathkeepers, midwives, and apothecaries. Increasing emphasis was placed on qualifications and training. Physicians, applying for the privilege to practice medicine, were required to diagnose an assigned test medical case on which they would be examined, and if the Board of Medicine so requested, would complete the course in anatomy offered at the Royal Anatomical Theater in six lecture periods before their requests for a license to practice would be approved.[22] Internal treatment was reserved exclusively as a professional function of approved physicians. But, in turn, the latter were to refrain from all external, surgical treatments and from dispensing pharmaceutical remedies. However, if a physician should possess a specific remedy which for certain sicknesses was considered superior and more effective than usual remedies, he was to be permitted to sell one or two samples at a fair price to an apothecary and then to prescribe it for his patient—but only after this remedy had been tested by other reliable physicians and examined and approved by the Board of Medicine.

Testing and giving board approval to unusual remedies were necessary in order to curb the practice of some greedy physicians of preparing

19. See Dorwart, *Administrative Reforms,* pp. 190-192 for the office of *fiscal.*

20. On this see *C. C. March.,* vol. 5, pt. 2, sec. 1, no. 77, "Royal Rescript to the Supreme Board of Medicine on Proper Procedure to Be Followed in Fiscal Cases," 18 Jan. 1736.

21. *C. C. March.,* vol. 5, pt. 4, sec. 1, no. 24, cols. 209-212, of 11 July 1719.

22. The Board of Medicine had never fulfilled the assigned mission of 1685 to instruct surgeons, midwives, and medical students in human anatomy by performing dissections with the assistance of its member-physicians.

certain remedies under new names and concealing in them harmful narcotic ingredients, which were then sold at a high price to apothecary and patient alike. Such unscrupulous physicians were accustomed to praise those apothecaries who connived with them in this deceit as the best in all Berlin.

When a resident physician was lacking in small towns and villages, capable surgeons or apothecaries were given permission to practice medicine and to dispense remedies without prescription. The latter were urged to avoid drugs for catharsis, vomiting, forcing menstruation, as well as opiates, narcotics, and coarse sialagogues.

Physicians were forbidden to recommend a surgeon or an apothecary to a patient; the patient was free to make his own choice.

To protect the financial interests of approved physicians, surgeons, and apothecaries, they were granted in 1725 a priority over all creditors in the event of liquidation of assets, of deaths, and of bankruptcies of their patients. These medical practitioners were to use the published price and fee list as a guide.

With surgeons, too, greater emphasis was placed on training and qualifications. In order to be admitted to practice in Berlin and in the provinces, surgeons had to give evidence of completion of an apprenticeship and of seven years of service (as journeymen), part of which had to be as a regimental surgeon. They likewise had to furnish a certificate of completing the course in surgical operations at the Royal Anatomical Theater. Only those who had completed the course and had been examined by the Board of Medicine and the guild of surgeons were to be permitted to call themselves surgeons and operators. No one was to be allowed to practice external surgery except those surgeons approved by the royal board.[23] In severe and dangerous cases surgeons were to call in physicians who would take charge. In particular, in the treatment of venereal diseases, or other diseases where treatment involved sialogogues, no surgeon was to undertake treatment without assistance of a physician. Nor were surgeons to let blood when a patient had a high fever without consulting a physician. Physicians were emerging as the truly professional medical people while the surgeon was still looked upon as a craftsman of the surgeons' guild.

The pattern of upgrading professional training for members of the health sciences was not neglected in the case of apothecaries and midwives. Before being approved by the Board of Medicine, midwives were now (1725) required to attend the Anatomical Theater and to be instructed by the Professor of Anatomy in the composition and

23. On 5 April 1725 the king ordered that there be no more than 26 surgeons—20 German and 6 French—in his capital cities (*C. C. March.,* vol. 5, pt. 4, sec. 1, no. 32, app. 10, cols. 238-239). In 1736, because of the growth of population in the capital, he increased the total membership of the surgeons' guild to 32 (24 German and 8 French), but required that all five parts of the city have their resident surgeons and that none should have their operating quarters too close to one another (ibid., no. 39, cols. 263-264).

anatomy of the genital parts. They were not to induce labor before the proper time, and were to consult other midwives as well as physicians and surgeons when abnormal situations arose.

Apothecaries, like the surgeons, in applying to the Board of Medicine for a license, had to furnish evidence of satisfactory apprenticeship and a period of at least seven years' service. Those in the Berlin area were required to take the course in pharmaceutical chemistry taught by Caspar Neumann, Professor of Practical Chemistry. In metropolitan Berlin, since 1720, only twelve apothecary shops were allowed, nine German and three French. Administrative regulations of standards of preparation, storing, labeling, pricing, cleanliness, requirement of prescriptions from licensed physicians, protection of apothecaries from illegal competition from dry grocers, all sought to place the apothecary on an ethical basis which would protect the health of the king's subjects.

Much can be learned on the status of the health professions in the early eighteenth century from certain negative provisions of the ordinance of 1725. Hernial surgeons, dentists, and spice merchants who appeared at the annual fairs were forbidden to practice in Prussian cities unless they were granted a special privilege. All internal and external medical treatment was denied to medical students, preachers, chemists, distillers, Jews, shepherds, quacks, old wives, and soothsayers. The implication is obvious. There were imposters and charlatans preying upon the gullibility and superstition of the people, exploiting the limited knowledge and skill in medical treatment and medical remedies (the "miracle" drugs and spices of the eighteenth century), and abusing the lack of professional standards which characterized the first half of the eighteenth century. Therefore, the greatest effort of the king in the regulation and administration of public health was to grant exclusive rights to practice to those who were trained, examined, and licensed and who took an oath to observe the required code of professional ethics.[24]

In 1727 Frederick William I observed that "the goal [of his 1725 ordinance] has not been fulfilled."[25] The major complaint seemed to be the failure of the several professional services to refrain from infringing upon the assigned functional jurisdiction of the others. He modified his previous orders to allow physicians traveling in rural areas where no apothecaries were available to prepare and dispense selected remedies to patients. In cities, physicians were permitted to give remedies to patients who were too poor to pay both a physician and an apothecary.

24. For examples of the oaths required of practicing physicians, surgeons, apothecaries, dispensers, dry grocers, bathkeepers, and midwives, see ibid., no. 32, apps. 21-29, cols. 244-248.
25. "Declaration of the General Medical Ordinance of 27 Sept. 1727," ibid., no. 36, cols. 257-260.

They were also allowed to prepare and sell necessary pharmaceuticals in small towns where there were no apothecaries.

Surgeons were allowed to prepare certain external medicaments not generally available in apothecary shops, but not the usual things for external care such as plasters and unguents.

More important, perhaps, because of the expense involved in taking the prescribed courses in operating for surgeons, and in pharmacy for apothecaries, such courses in the future were to be required only of those who wished to practice in the larger cities.

After 1727 the medical ordinance seemed to meet with considerable success in improving standards of professional qualifications and conduct, in keeping unauthorized persons from engaging in medical and surgical treatment, and in regulating the sale of medical remedies.

In 1736 the king turned his attention once more to the guild of surgeons in issuing a "General Privilege and Guild Charter for Barber-Surgeons."[26] It was now required that each new surgeon who was accepted in a guild would contribute twenty *Reichsthaler* to the guild treasury for the purchase of surgical instruments so that the most modern instruments could be kept available. Surgeons then borrowed these instruments from the guild for their operations.

A distinction was made at this time between surgeons who could operate and work on external cures and barber-surgeons, who were permitted to treat flesh wounds, engage in shaving, cupping, clysterizing, and bloodletting by venesection, but were not allowed to undertake serious surgical treatment or operations.

Regimental and garrison surgeons were exempted from the usual limitations placed on surgeons with respect to internal treatment, but were required to follow instructions of the king's Chief Field Physician and Surgeon-General. Surgeons were again forbidden to undertake, without participation of a physician who would be in charge, the cure of syphilis and other venereal diseases because of serious mistakes which had occurred as a result of salivation caused by internal mercurial medicines or by application of a mercury unguent. A number of deaths were reported from improper treatment. Surgeons were permitted to prepare and administer certain *decocta lignorum* (vegetable decoctions) in the case of certain external surgical diseases, such as buboes, chancres, and *testiculis venereis.*

A growing emphasis on professional training, on professional qualifications, and on certifying and licensing to separate the qualified from the quacks marked the successive, regulative efforts of the Board of Medicine in the domain of public health. To assure attainment of the higher professional training, incorporating the latest scientific developments, physicians, surgeons, apothecaries, and midwives were required to complete appropriate training courses: a course in human anatomy for physi-

26. Ibid., no. 39, cols. 259-276.

cians, a course in surgical operations for surgeons, a course in pharmaceutical chemistry for apothecaries, a specialized course in genital anatomy for midwives. In order to make this training available in a manner more satisfying and more complete than that offered by the anatomical exercises at the Anatomical Theater, Frederick William I by an Edict of 14 December 1723[27] established a Royal College of Medicine and Surgery to serve as a medical faculty which would teach these courses at the Anatomical Theater located in the observatory tower at the royal stables. This academic College of Medicine and Surgery in Berlin served as a medical school while the Supreme Board of Medicine continued to supervise the whole realm of public health and all of its servants in the whole kingdom through its several provincial *Collegia Medica*. Some members of the administrative board also served as professors at the new College of Medicine and Surgery.

In order to defray the administrative expenses of the new *Oberkollegium* of 1725, the king granted a Privilege[28] to this board to publish and sell the medical ordinance of 1725, the new Brandenburg pharmacopoeia, and the price list for remedies. All persons engaged in the various medical arts and crafts were required to buy a copy of the ordinance. Only physicians and apothecaries were required to purchase price list and pharmacopoeia. Along with fees paid at the time of qualifying examinations, the boards of medicine were to a large extent self-supporting.

Sanitation

Safeguarding public health involved more than administrative regulation of those who practiced medicine in some form or who engaged in preparation and retail sale of medical remedies. This was recognized by the Hohenzollern princes in their efforts to promote sanitation in public life, and to prevent pollution of air and water resources. The problems of urban sanitation were exemplified in the efforts after 1648 to make Berlin a clean city. Wells were frequently polluted with debris and dead animals. Rivers and canals were used to dispose of rubbish and filth. The streams, canals, and sluices often became clogged, stagnant, odoriferous, and were sources of danger to public health.

The first measures of public sanitation came under supervision of urban administration for streets, wells, and buildings. The increasing threat of plague and cattle disease, as the result in part of the many wars and

27. See Artelt, *Medizinische Wissenschaft*, pp. 62-63, and Herbert Lehmann, *Das Collegium medico-chirurgicum in Berlin als Lehrstatte der Botanik und der Pharmazie*. See also the following chapter on medical education.

28. *C. C. March.*, vol. 5, pt. 4, sec. 1, no. 32, app., cols. 254-256, "A Concession to the *Oberkollegium Medicum* of a Monopoly on Publication and Sale of the Medical Ordinance, the Dispensatory, and the Price List of Medicines," of 17 Dec. 1725.

movement of thousands of persons, induced the first Prussian King, Frederick I, to establish a *Collegium Sanitatis* or Board of Sanitation, probably in 1709.[29] It was, in fact, originally called a *Pest-Kollegium* or Plague Office, thus emphasizing its origin as an administrative response to the growing threat to public health from the spreading plague. At first its assigned mission was to establish and enforce administrative regulations to protect the royal lands from contagious, epidemic diseases among humans and from the spread of cattle disease. In response to a royal request the Board of Sanitation drafted a Pest Regulation and Medical Plan for Berlin and Brandenburg, both of which were published in November 1709.[30] The former established an organization for fighting the plague prescribing the functions of all medical personnel in case of emergency. The second was a medical plan for treating and curing infected persons, listing recommended medicaments.

After 1720, the Board of Sanitation expanded its public health activity. It became concerned with everything in public life or practice that could be injurious or harmful to public or personal health: adulteration of wine, beer, and vinegar, unbaked bread and food spoilage, burial of the dead in cities, pollution of the Spree River from cesspools and sewers, and so forth.

---

29. A Patent of 3 Oct. 1709 directed the *Collegium Sanitatis* to punish public servants who overcharged for the issuance of passes for travel from plague-infested areas. This was the first mention I found of the *Collegium Sanitatis*. See ibid., vol. 5, pt. 4, sec. 2, no. 14, cols. 293-296. An edict of 12 Dec. 1708 ordered provincial governments to appoint plague physicians and plague surgeons to make preparations for a probable plague attack (ibid., no. 10, cols. 287-292). Presumably, some time after this, the Board of Sanitation came into existence as an administrative bureau concerned with defensive measures against the spread of the plague.

30. Ibid., no. 16, cols. 295-340, "A Regulation of 14 Nov. 1709."

17

Medical Education

In the half century after 1685 the *Collegium Medicum* of Berlin succeeded in bringing all branches of the public health services under state regulation, supervision, and inspection. Licensing and certification, following submission of credentials and examination of applicants, implied establishing minimum standards of professional qualification. The establishment of the Berlin Board of Medicine and of the later provincial boards, however, made no direct institutional contribution toward advancing medical education or training in associated medical sciences. The directive of 1685 requiring the Berlin board to perform dissections for the benefit of medical students, midwives, and surgeons was never carried out.

Nevertheless, the first quarter of the eighteenth century witnessed the establishment of the medical sciences in the kingdom of Prussia on a truly scientific, systematic, and professional basis.[1] By 1725 medical education had acquired a modern format, making available the most recent achievements in the pure sciences in the first formal, prescribed curriculum. Modern medicine and modern concepts of medical education could hardly have been introduced sooner, for they were a product of the scientific revolution of the seventeenth century. Under the influence of Robert Boyle, Georg Stahl, and Herman Boerhaave, chemistry was slowly emancipating itself from alchemy. Despite the significant work of Vesalius, the study of human anatomy was just arriving at the point of systematic, scientific understanding and teaching at the beginning of the eighteenth century. This was soon followed by developments in knowledge of morbid anatomy. The work of Jung, Tournefort, and Leeuwenhoek made significant contributions to the understanding of living organisms. Medical education naturally profited from the new sciences of chemistry, botany, and anatomy.

In addition to the academic and professional application of advances in the medical sciences, a number of formal institutions, new or modifications of existing facilities, made important contributions to educational purposes. Hospitals were expanded to offer facilities for clinical training. The royal botanical garden, herbarium, and the Court Apothecary Shop became available for teaching purposes. The new Society of Sciences with its section on physical and medical sciences published results of its research. An anatomical theater and an academic College of Medicine and Surgery offered the practical instruction necessary in order to achieve

---

1. See Reinhold A. Dorwart, "Medical Education in Prussia under the Early Hohenzollern, 1685-1725," *Bulletin of the History of Medicine,* vol. 32, no. 4 (July-Aug., 1958), pp. 335-347.

higher standards of professional training for all persons involved in the practice of medicine or cure of disease. All of these facilities were concentrated in Berlin, which became the medical center of Prussia. The medical facilities of the universities of Frankfurt and Halle were eclipsed by the progress made in Berlin.

The Society of Sciences, founded in 1700, provided personnel, financial support, and space for medical teaching and research. Of the four sections into which the society was divided by royal statute, only the one devoted to physics, chemistry, and medicine became involved with the advancement of medical education in Prussia. At the very first meeting of this section in 1711, Friedrich Hoffmann, Professor of Medicine at Halle and a leading court physician in Berlin, proposed that the society establish an anatomical theater within the observatory tower. He argued that the primary purpose of the society was not to write books but to engage in research.[2] This was a thrust at the literary, classical sections. He further offered to lecture on anatomy with the aid of cadavers for demonstration purposes—if the theater and the necessary instruments were provided.[3] At the same meeting, Hoffmann urged that a chemical laboratory be established by the society.

Although the Society of Sciences, in 1711, approved the idea of establishing an anatomical theater under its sponsorship and control, nothing came of it. Personal and professional jealousy was the cause. Dr. Andreas Gundelsheim, the most influential court physician of the time and a jealous rival of Hoffmann, opposed it successfully. He had refused appointment to the Society of Sciences, which he despised. He used his influence with the crown prince and second king, Frederick William I, to discredit the society and eventually to drive Hoffmann out of Berlin and back to Halle. The society was denied financial support for its proposed anatomical theater. Access to the space in the observatory tower, which it had allocated for the theater, was not granted.

The need for an anatomical theater was too great for such a project to be defeated because of personal jealousy or jurisdictional conflict with the administrative *Collegium Medicum*. By 1713 the institution of an anatomical theater by the society was moving along, and it was hoped that the favor of the new king could be won, since he was interested in anatomy and botany as they related practically to medicine. But Gundelsheim moved

2. See Adolf Harnack, *Geschichte der Königlich Preussischen Akademie der Wissenschaften zu Berlin*, 1:176. While Hoffmann gets credit for the original proposal for an anatomical theater, the minutes of the governing directory of the society state that Krug von Nidda, director of the section on medicine, physics, and chemistry, proposed to the society that an anatomical theater be installed in the upper floors of the observatory tower and it was approved. Presumably, von Nidda brought this proposal up to the directory from his section, where Hoffmann had first introduced it. See ibid., 2:227.

3. The first anatomical theater in the Hohenzollern territories had been established at the medical school of the University of Frankfurt in 1684. It made little contribution to practical anatomy. Not even a dozen cadavers were sectioned here during the seventeenth century (see Artelt, *Medizinsiche Wissenschaft*, p. 24).

in and claimed anatomy and botany for himself. He succeeded, in 1713, in obtaining from the king an order establishing an anatomical theater in Berlin. It was this royal action, and not the initiative of the society, that established the theater, which was not under control of the society.

Meanwhile, the society had completed preparation of space for an anatomical theater in the tower, and had provided the necessary instruments for dissection as well. Gundelsheim had satisfied his own self-importance by preventing the union of society and theater. Since he was not qualified to perform sections, he was content to have the society furnish the space, the instruments, and a member of the society to do the actual teaching. Dr. Christian Spener was appointed Professor of Anatomy by the king, and on 2 December 1713 he performed his first lecture-section. By the time of his early death, 5 May 1714, he had performed ten sections.[4]

Although the society had no control over the theater and received no credit for its contributions, in 1714 the king ordered it to pay 1,000 *Reichsthaler* out of its treasury for the support of the theater. The society, interested in the advancement of science and eager to maintain association with the theater, was happy to support the latter with money, space, and instruments, as well as a Professor of Anatomy from its membership.

After Gundelsheim's death in May 1715, Frederick William turned the direction of the theater over to the Society of Sciences completely. He ordered the society to "put the theater in good order and to see that dissections were performed regularly throughout the year at regular and convenient times."[5] Dr. Heinrich Henricius became Professor of Anatomy, succeeding Spener. The society, after 1717, became completely responsible for the financial support, direction, and supply of cadavers to the theater, although it continued as an independent institution. As late as 1730, Dr. Augustinus Buddeus described the Anatomical Theater as "a separate institution, with which the society was not to interfere."[6]

Whatever the circumstances and impediments, the important thing was that between 1711 and 1714, Berlin had acquired an anatomical theater, with royal favor. The first major step had been taken to upgrade medical education, particularly for surgeons (both civilian and military) and midwives. The issue of the credit for sponsoring it was unimportant, and the Society of Sciences recognized this in supporting the theater wholeheartedly with space facilities, personnel, funds, professors, and a new chemistry laboratory.

Along with anatomy, the greatest emphasis in the early eighteenth-cen-

---

4. See Manfred Stürzbecher, "Beitrag zur Geschichte der Berliner Anatomie," *Berliner Medizin* 9 (1958): 236-239. See also Manfred Stürzbecher, "Zur Geschichte des Anatomischen Theaters in Berlin im 18. Jahrhundert," *Medizinische Mitteilungen* 20 (1959): 102-106.

5. See Harnack, *Preussischen Akademie,* 1:228, 2:228. Royal Order of 15 May 1717, ibid., vol. 2, no. 133, p. 235.

6. Ibid., 2:227.

tury interest in medicine was placed on chemistry and botany. The study and application of chemistry had been promoted by the Court Apothecary Shop, established since 1585. Pharmaceutical chemistry in Berlin emerged from the drug chambers and laboratory of the court apothecary located in the electoral palace.

The study of botany, distinguished in Germany through the work of Valerius Cordus, Conrad Gesner, and Joachim Jung, was advanced after 1700 through the efforts of Gundelsheim. On Gundelsheim's proposal, Frederick William in 1713 had ordered the conversion of the Royal Hop Garden (an herb and kitchen garden, lying outside the Potsdam Gate) into a botanical garden or *hortus.* The garden belonged to the court apothecary but was placed under the direction of Gundelsheim.[7] After his death, by royal order of 2 April 1718, the Society of Sciences assumed direction and financial support of the apothecary garden, in return for which the botanical garden was made available for practical study in medical botany.[8]

To supplement the living specimens of the *hortus,* Berlin was also favored with Gundelsheim's founding of an herbarium. He started the Berlin herbarium with a vast personal collection of plants gathered during a two-year journey in the Orient in the company of J. P. de Tournefort, Professor at the Paris Jardin des Plantes. In 1715 Gundelsheim's collection was donated to the Society of Sciences, which maintained it and made it available for instruction in botany and pharmacognosy.[9] In 1719 the king directed the society to assume financial responsibility for and care of all foreign plants in the greenhouses at Oranienburg.[10]

Another institutional development of the late seventeenth and early eighteenth centuries contributing to the advancement of medical training and practice was in the expansion of hospital facilities.[11] The oldest hospitals in Berlin dated back to the thirteenth century and were church-inspired. The Holy Ghost, St. George, and St. Gertrude hospitals did not have a large capacity, and served essentially as poor houses, caring for the aged and infirm. To these older facilities there were added in the second half of the seventeenth century hospitals for the French Huguenot

7. The minutes of the governing directory of the Society of Sciences recorded, on 2 Jan. 1715, a proposal of Dr. Gundelsheim that the Anatomical Theater and the botanical garden be joined to the society. Nothing came of this, even after the death of Gundelsheim in May. See Harnack, ibid. 2:228.

8. Harnack, ibid., vol. 2, no. 136, p. 236.

9. See Lehmann, *Collegium medico-chirurgicum,* pp. 50-52, on the early history of the Berlin *hortus* and herbarium.

10. Harnack, *Preussischen Akademie,* vol. 2, no. 137, pp. 237-239. The society complained on 23 Dec. 1719 that its funds would not permit it to add this burden. Already, it argued, the society had to support a library, an anatomical theater, a chemical laboratory, an observatory, a botanical garden and herbarium, a collection of natural history specimens (Spener's *Naturalia* had been purchased in 1714), minerals, and a variety of optical, dissecting, and chemical instruments.

11. See Artelt, *Medizinische Wissenschaft,* pp. 64-65.

community in Berlin, separate hospitals for lepers and for plague victims, and military hospitals. The Dorotheen Hospital was built in 1674
by the Great Elector to care for impoverished foreigners who, for lack of
medical care, were just left to die. In 1711 it was converted to a home
for the insane, until 1727 when the *Irrenhaus* (insane asylum) was built.

Two of the more significant hospitals were the Grossen-Friedrich Hospital, begun in 1697 as the first large hospital for both the sick and the
mentally ill, and the Royal House of Charité. The Friedrich Hospital
was designed as a general poorhouse for orphaned children and for
insane, sick, or aged adults. It became strictly an orphanage after 1725.
The Charité originated in 1710 as a *Pesthaus* or isolation hospital to
care for the poor of Berlin if the threatening plague should strike the
city. The plague failed to reach the city, and Frederick William used it
between 1713 and 1726 as an infirmary for the Berlin garrison. Persuaded
by a surgeon for the poor, Christian Habermaass, to make this hospital
a training school for physicians and surgeons, on 18 November 1726
Frederick William ordered the military infirmary to become a general
hospital for Berlin, dedicated to the care of the poor. In 1727 it received
the name of the "Charité."[12]

The Charité became the center of practical medicine, where surgical
operations were observed by trainees. It served for training interning
medical students, for training midwives, and next to Würzburg it was the
home of the first clinic in Germany.[13] The Charité served a variety of
needs. It was a hospital; it was a nursing home for the infirm and destitute senior citizens; it offered maternity facilities for married and unmarried women; and it had a special pavilion for venereal and contagious
diseases. The Charité was one of the earliest centers for the study of skin
disease as well as venereal disease. The beginnings of clinical dermatol-
ogy are found here in the early eighteenth century.[14]

In the same year that the Charité was converted to general hospital
service, 1726, the king established an insane asylum where the mad, insane, and melancholy could receive proper care. The poor received free
care.

Other felicitous developments contributing to the advancement of
medical knowledge and practice, as well as reflecting on that advancement, were the publication of Brandenburg's first pharmacopoeia, the
Dispensatorium Brandenburgicum of 1698, and the first Berlin medical
journal, the *Acta Medicorum Berolinensium,* which between 1717 and
1730 reported the results of autopsies designed to discover the cause of

12. See Friedrich Nicolai, *Beschreibung der Königilichen Residenz-Städte Berlin und
Potsdam,* 2:626-633, for a discussion of the hospitals and poorhouses of Berlin.
13. The first experimental and successful inoculation against smallpox in Prussia was
begun in 1769 at the Charité. See Artelt, *Medizinische Wissenschaft,* p. 147.
14. Manfred Stürzbecher, "Zur Geschichte der Dermatologie in der Berliner Charité im
18. Jahrhundert," *Zeitschrift für Haut- und Geschlechtskrankheiten* 26 (1959): 319-324.

death. The pathological reports built up medical statistics on the causes of death and provided a case history to further diagnosis and prognosis.

The threat of the spread of bubonic plague to Brandenburg in 1709 and the actual outbreak of an epidemic of rinderpest-like cattle disease in 1711 led to systematic efforts on the part of the medical profession not only to understand the symptoms of plague and epizooty, but to make suggestions for prevention and cure on the basis of systematic investigation of both epidemics.

The climax of a quarter-century of institutional expansion of facilities for the advancement of medical knowledge and medical education in the kingdom of Prussia came in 1723 with the new Royal College of Medicine and Surgery, established by a royal edict of 14 December 1723.[15] Aside from the administrative efforts to raise standards of conduct and qualification after 1685, the first impulse for the advancement of medical science came from the Society of Sciences. This impulse was quickened by the establishment of the Anatomical Theater in 1713, and the latter in turn became the origin of the later *Collegium Medico-chirurgicum*. Associated with these institutions which emphasized the theoretical side of medicine, surgery, chemistry, and botany were the Court Apothecary Shop, the botanical garden, and the new hospitals which offered opportunities for practical experience.

During the reign of Frederick William I there existed a curious relationship among these several bodies, separate at all times and yet closely associated with and dependent upon each other. No inclusive and comprehensive university school of medicine emerged, of the type found at the medical faculties of Halle and Frankfurt. Financially and in terms of personnel, the Society of Sciences was the key institution. In terms of space facilities and instruments, the Anatomical Theater was the base of all instruction. The Society of Sciences furnished from its membership the several professors who taught at the Anatomical Theater (1713-1724) or who composed the faculty of the College of Medicine and Surgery after 1724. The society paid the salaries of most professors and their assistants, subsidized the Anatomical Theater, the botanical garden and herbarium of Berlin, and contributed to the purchase of anatomical and surgical instruments for use at the theater. After 1735, the society also maintained a medical library begun by a donation of the king from the Royal Library.

The Society of Sciences was housed on the second floor of the royal stables. The Anatomical Theater was on the same floor, and its facilities

15. It is no longer possible to ascertain the facts surrounding the actual founding of the Royal College of Medicine and Surgery. The documentary evidence for the founding of the college on 14 Dec. 1723 has been lost and is known by reference from instructions of 1724 directed to the new college. See Lehmann, *Collegium medico-chirurgicum*, pp. 12-13; and Artelt, *Medizinische Wissenschaft*, pp. 62-63.

consisted of the demonstration auditorium, instrument room, skeleton room, cadaver-preparation room, and offices. These facilities were important because they were the scene of the earliest formal academic medical teaching in Berlin. In effect, the Anatomical Theater was Berlin's first medical school.

The Anatomical Theater

The original suggestion of 1711 that the Society of Sciences establish an anatomical theater in Berlin came to naught. Frederick William I, however, was won over to the project in 1713 by the suggestion of Holtzendorff, the king's personal physician and surgeon-general of the Prussian army, that such a theater would train native regimental surgeons for the expanding Prussian army. The curious mixture of personal traits in this soldier-king, his intense interest in the Prussian army as well as his paternalistic concern for the welfare of his subjects, combined in the decade between 1713 and 1725 to advance the cause of medicine and medical education enormously. The first step (1713) of offering scientific training in anatomy by dissection on a more systematic basis reached a climax, for this period, in the establishment (1723) of a professional College of Medicine and Surgery offering the first comprehensive curriculum of medical education, and incorporating the newest developments in related sciences.

The Anatomical Theater was established "for the training and improvement of surgeons for the benefit of the general welfare." Surgery in the early eighteenth century was still more of a barber's craft than a learned profession. The first major step in promoting the surgeon's craft to a scientific basis was taken by providing facilities for anatomical dissections, and by ordering the Society of Sciences to furnish the lecturer whenever a cadaver became available. Demonstrations were held on no regular plan, apparently, but only when cadavers of malefactors became available. The first Professor of Anatomy was Dr. Christian Spener, who was to lecture three times weekly on anatomy and perform sections as often as possible. Between December 1713 and May 1714 he completed ten section-demonstrations. A cabinet order of 15 May 1717 expanded the source and supply of available cadavers by requiring that suicides as well as bodies of deceased in the poorhouses and workhouses be turned over to the theater.

Until 1719 anatomical demonstrations occurred on an occasional schedule without planning. This would not attain the desired goal, and accordingly, by a regulation of 5 March 1719, the king declared that "anatomical exercises should be practiced all through the year at convenient hours and at fixed times."[16] Since the Anatomical Theater in

---

16. *C. C. March.,* vol. 5, pt. 4, sec. 1, no. 23, cols. 207-210, "Establishment of the Anatomical Theater, 5 Mar. 1719."

itself was an empty vessel, its potential could be filled only by utilizing the personnel, financial, and directive capacities of the Society of Sciences. The society was instructed to schedule anatomical exercises, to prepare a curriculum, provide professors, and furnish cadavers, all at its own expense. Arguing that "it is most important for a good surgeon that he understand anatomy well and that he be instructed in the fundamentals of surgery helpful in his practice," the king decreed in 1719 that anatomical demonstrations were to be held publicly during the winter session from Michaelmas to Easter. The demonstrations were to be held on human cadavers, sections of animals, or taught by means of anatomical preparations, three times weekly, for the benefit of surgeons and of medical students. With some awareness of pedagogical technique, the king instructed that "because in teaching anatomy it is important to observe the whole business of dissection," the anatomical explanation and dissection of whole cadavers should be undertaken by the current Professor of Anatomy. All this was to be done according to a scheduled plan of lectures for the session, to be announced by printed notice.

The Society of Sciences was ordered to prepare the schedule of anatomical exercises, demonstrations, and lectures for the entire year. The curriculum was to include, in addition to the sections of the winter schedule, lectures on all types of cases occurring in surgical practice, on all types of wounds, and on external diseases of the limbs. During the summer semester there were to be scheduled weekly public lectures on techniques of surgical operation and on bandaging, such as a good regimental surgeon needed to know.

Unscheduled opportunities for instruction were also recognized as possibly arising in the Friedrich Hospital or in the Berlin workhouse. If surgeons wished to section a body on these premises, proper facilities were to be provided for them. If unusual operations were to be performed at the hospitals, the Professor of Anatomy and interested surgeons were to be called. Likewise, whenever autopsies were to be performed at the theater on bodies of persons who had died of unknown or incurable diseases or who had been murdered, the Professor of Anatomy was to be summoned so that he might notify candidate surgeons who could thus participate in the examination of the fatal wounds, or if necessary be of assistance in the autopsy.

The Regulation of 1719 also provided that there be a permanent prosector on hand, selected by the director of the theater and the Professor of Anatomy. This man was to assist the professor in anatomical sections and make ready the cadavers and anatomical preparations.

Once it was well established as a center of instruction for anatomy, the Anatomical Theater became a base upon which to build and expand medical education and training. In 1722 a royal ordinance extended instruction in anatomy to midwives. Subjects of dissection were to be the bodies of female persons who died in poorhouses, as well as unmarried women who died while pregnant, or during and after birth.[17] The Criminal Court of Berlin was ordered to prevent concealment of any such deaths, and to see that the bodies were delivered to the theater "for the good of the public and the instruction of midwives."

The Royal College of Medicine and Surgery

The College of Medicine and Surgery was established in December 1723. Its purpose was to expand the original anatomical and surgical instruction at the Anatomical Theater to include lectures and demonstrations in medicine, botany, chemistry, and pharmacy. Its creation further confused the institutional organization in Berlin for the advancement of the medical sciences. The College of Medicine and Surgery appears to have been no more than a faculty appointed by the king, seven in number originally. Without a budget, without a "campus," the new college was dependent upon the Society of Sciences for its professors' salaries, upon the Anatomical Theater for classrooms, laboratories, and anatomical sections, upon the Court Apothecary Shop for its chemistry laboratory, and again upon the Society of Sciences for use of the botanical garden and herbarium.[18]

One significant administrative change occurred with the establishment of the new college. To it, its two directors and dean, was transferred from the Society of Sciences the responsibility of announcing and supervising its lecture courses. The Society of Sciences and the Anatomical Theater henceforth, apparently, would furnish staff and facilities. Curriculum, standards, methods would be within the administrative jurisdiction of the Royal College. In the well-regulated Prussian state of Frederick William I, however, it was a royal regulation of 1724, addressed to the college, which took the initiative in detailing the names of the first professors, the subjects, order, and methods of instruction.[19] The regulation was both climactic and revolutionary in the history of medical education in Prussia. Its curriculum was the climax of some twenty-five critical years of effort to place the medical and public health professions on a sound scientific basis. It was revolutionary in its comprehensive inclusion of the developments in related sciences. Moreover, the encouragement given to the work of the new faculty of outstanding scholars not only carried on the tradition of Glauber and Jung, but established new traditions of achievement in chemistry, pharmacy, and botany.

17. Ordinance of 28 Aug. 1722, ibid., no. 25, cols. 211-212.
18. With so many scientific and educational institutions developing at Berlin in the first quarter of the eighteenth century, the failure of Prussia to establish a university of Berlin before 1810 is almost astonishing. Even more so was the failure to establish a fully integrated medical school.
19. "Regulation Concerning the Lectures to Be Held at the Anatomical Theater in Connection with the Newly Established Royal College of Medicine and Surgery, 1724," *C. C. March.,* vol. 5, pt. 4, sec. 1, no. 26, cols. 211-216.

The royally instituted curriculum of 1724 takes on a considerable measure of importance as a reflection of the progress made in the medical sciences, in the late seventeenth and early eighteenth centuries, from Galenic traditions to awareness of new developments. A description and analysis of the curriculum will reveal the content and status of medical education at Berlin in that year. In the plan of lecture courses ordered by the regulation, Dr. Heinrich "Henrici," as Professor of Therapeutics, was to lecture four hours weekly on medical and surgical pathology, to explain such with practical illustrations and observations, to suggest methods of cure, and finally to note the common errors in medical practice and discuss how to correct them.

The most important personality in 1724 was Dr. Augustinus Buddeus, Professor of Anatomy and Physics. He was to lecture on anatomy and perform dissections in the winter months, as that was the most agreeable time for anatomical demonstrations. The order of instruction required first that he explain the outer layers and the divisions of the human body. After this introduction he was to explain the structure of the ordinary parts of the anatomy under the principal topics of myology (muscles), angiology (blood vessels), neurology, and splanchnology (the internal organs). Following this exposition of the anatomical parts, Dr. Buddeus was to begin an explanation of surgical operations. First he was to discuss the true characteristics of all wounds and how to heal them. Next, in describing the execution of the most important surgical operations, he was to explain the anatomical structure of the area where the skilled hand of the surgeon would operate, the reasons why the particular operation was unavoidable and how this could be recognized, how the operation could be performed under all circumstances, and, finally, what good or bad effects could be hoped for or should be feared in the postoperative period. With dissection and anatomy completed in the winter session, during the summer semester Dr. Buddeus was to begin demonstration of surgical bandages and their applications. This was described as one of the most useful aspects of surgery, and both practicing and candidate-surgeons could expect to profit from the demonstrations. This was a type of instruction deemed particularly useful to regimental surgeons. For the demonstrations, new, specially constructed models were to be used.

Dr. Buddeus was also to lecture in the summer months on osteogenesis, since osteology or explanation of human bone structure was fundamental to anatomy. For this he would use appropriate laboratory preparations. Likewise, since dislocations and fractures of the bones constituted a considerable portion of surgery, the Professor of Anatomy would also give the history of surgical instruments useful for such treatments, and demonstrate practical application of the most important ones.[20] The

20. Surgical instruments, particularly new ones, were customarily owned not by the individual surgeon but by the surgeons' guild in each town. They were purchased from a

summer-session instruction in operating closed with an explanation of the lethality of wounds and the preparation of an intelligent report of an autopsy on a murdered body, that is, a report anatomically correct for police purposes.[21] The busy Professor of Anatomy and Physics was to accomplish all this in two half-yearly sessions, teaching at the Anatomical Theater eight hours weekly.

A third course of instruction prescribed in 1724 was *materia medica* (including both pharmacognosy and pharmacology) and pure botany. This was the task of Dr. Michael Matthias Ludolff, director of the botanical garden and Professor of Botany. The *materia medica* was to be taught in the winter months, while the summer months would permit demonstration of the plants found in the botanical garden. So that students would be familiar with each genus even when no live species were available in the garden, a dried specimen from the herbarium was to be used. This was necessary so that the Tournefort method of classification might be demonstrated.[22]

Two hours weekly of *materia medica* and of botany were to be supplemented by two hours of *chymia rationalis pharmaceutica* taught by Dr. Johann Heinrich Pott, Professor of Chemistry and founder of ceramic pyrochemistry. This material was to be taught in a prescribed order: (1) description of and working of chemico-pharmaceutical medicaments, (2) the handling of these and the precautions necessary thereto, (3) the chemical-physical reasons and principles of their working, and (4) the application of their products to medicine and surgery. The theoretical lectures of Pott had to correlate with the practical laboratory work of Neumann.

Caspar Neumann, court apothecary, toxicologist, and Professor of Practical Chemistry, was to abstract from chemical physics the necessary and useful chemical pharmaceuticals and then pursue the procedures and experiments useful and necessary to medicine and surgery. He was to prepare the experiments and demonstrations, using appropriate chemicals or chemical products, and acquaint the students with the necessary furnaces, earthen, glass, and metal vessels, and instruments. This training was necessary for physicians particularly, because apothecaries were not always qualified to make chemical preparations. Apothecaries,

---

guild fund derived from entrance fees paid by new members. The instruments were loaned out as needed. See, e.g., ibid., no. 39, col. 263, Guild Charter of 15 March 1736.

21. Legal medicine was taught for the first time in Germany at the new Royal College of Medicine and Surgery in 1724. It became a regular part of the medical curriculum when the college was incorporated into the medical faculty of the new Friedrich-Wilhelm University of Berlin in 1810. See Manfred Stürzbecher, "Zur Geschichte des Gerichtsmedizinischen Unterrichts in Berlin," *Medizinische Mitteilungen* 20 (1959): 137-141.

22. J. P. de Tournefort (1656-1708) in his *Elements of Botany* (1694) established principles of plant classification according to the structure of flowers, and set up a system of twenty-two classes of plants. In Berlin and elsewhere the Tournefort method dominated the eighteenth century until replaced by the Linnaean method of classification under Ludolff's great successors, Gleditsch and Willdenow.

however, would overcome this deficiency by taking this very course. Instruction was to be conducted two hours weekly in the Court Apothecary Shop, a well-equipped chemical laboratory.

Four hours of mathematics were to be taught throughout the year by Johann Georg Schutz, Professor of Mathematics. In the first half year instruction included decimal arithmetic, theoretical and practical geometry, trigonometry, and the art of gauging. This mathematical preparation led naturally, if surprisingly, into a half year's instruction in defensive and offensive fortification.

The seventh and final course of instruction prescribed in the curriculum of 1724 was conducted in the winter months by Gabriel Senff, Demonstrator of Surgical Operations. For benefit of surgeons he was to show the procedure of operations, particularly how, where, and why to perform operations on human bodies. Then he was to demonstrate the appropriate instruments and which were the most suitable to the various operations, and what form of dressing was the most convenient to apply after completion of surgery.

The opportunity offered to surgeons and physicians or to medical students by the establishment of such a complete, integrated, and advanced course of instruction in anatomy, operations, and related subjects was by no means regarded as an unmixed blessing by medical persons, particularly surgeon-candidates. It was another hurdle designed to eliminate the quack or unqualified barber. It was an effort to place surgery on a loftier scientific and professional basis. But it was a hurdle; it took time, required aptitude, and cost money. In his efforts to raise the standards of all practitioners in the general area of public health, Frederick William, by an ordinance of 29 March 1724, required that surgeon-candidates take the course in anatomy under Dr. Buddeus and the course in operating procedure under Field Surgeon Senff at the College of Medicine and Surgery, before taking qualifying examinations and being granted the privilege of practicing by the administrative Board of Medicine.[23] Successful candidates were required to serve for a time as regimental field surgeons among the troops.

The surgeon in the reign of Frederick William I had not yet been freed from the status of a craftsman. He was inferior in status to the physician and subordinate to him in medical authority when they worked together, precisely because of the difference between the learned professional and the craftsman. The physician was a graduate of a medical faculty. The surgeon was a member of the guild of barber-surgeons and received his training in the traditional manner of the guilds. Boys who were proficient in reading and writing and the necessary Latin were apprenticed for a period of four years to a master surgeon for training in

23. "Ordinance That Surgeons before Their Examinations Will Complete a Course in Anatomy, 29 March 1724," *C. C. March.*, vol. 5, pt. 4, sec. 1, no. 27, col. 239.

the craft. After seven years' service as a journeyman surgeon, part of it as a regimental surgeon, this guildsman could apply for examination and qualification as a master surgeon.[24] Since 1724, however, surgeons who wished to practice their craft in the larger cities were required to complete the course in anatomy and in operations. Those who had completed the required course and passed the qualifying examination were the only ones of the guild who were permitted to call themselves surgeons and operators as opposed to their lesser colleagues, the barbers and bleeders.

The same requirement of the course in anatomy was imposed upon all physicians in town and country who wished to practice medicine in Brandenburg.[25] Certification requirements for midwives and pharmacists likewise required taking courses in genital anatomy and pharmaceutical chemistry respectively at the new college.[26] The offerings of the College of Medicine and Surgery thus were special courses of a wide range designed to lift the professional skill of those who practiced the healing arts through exposure to the latest developments and techniques.

Thus, for almost a century, until the establishment of the University of Berlin in 1810, the Anatomical Theater and the Royal College of Medicine and Surgery served as a center of scientific research and teaching, making its own contributions to science, introducing into the scientific life of Prussia the new discoveries and theories developed in foreign countries, and producing a galaxy of scientific personalities.

24. "General Medical Edict and Ordinance" of 27 Sept. 1725, ibid., no. 32, cols. 226-227; and "General Privilege and Guild Charter for Barber-Surgeons in the Mark Brandenburg" of 15 March 1736, ibid., no. 39, cols. 262, 272.
25. Ordinance of 24 Aug. 1724, ibid., no. 28, col. 236.
26. Medical edict of 27 Sept. 1725, ibid., no. 32, cols. 233, 221.

18

The Apothecary and Public Health

The promotion and security of public health are the result of a combination of several complementary factors. As we have learned in the two previous chapters, administrative regulation by the state and advancement of medical education did contribute considerably to this end. Certification and licensing of medical practitioners, establishing of codes of professional behavior, protection of the several medical arts from unfair competition or encroachment by related practitioners, legislation against charlatans and quacks, fixing of fees and prices, elevation of professional standards and qualifications, and state-aided improvement of medical education and training were all the result of a new era in the history of Brandenburg public health which began with the electoral edict of 12 November 1685.

The most significant development in the medical arts, after 1685, resulted from the application to the art of healing of the new knowledge being discovered in the pure sciences. The knowledge and skills of the medical practitioners were so enormously increased in the early eighteenth century that one can begin to recognize them as emergent professional men of science.

At the beginning of the seventeenth century, the public health services of medicine, surgery, pharmacy, midwifery, and related arts had made little progress towards the attainment of professional, scientific standing. Only the physician could be described as a learned, professional man, because he had completed an academic course. Surgeons, barbers, bathkeepers, and apothecaries were craftsmen who acquired their skills in the traditional guild system of training apprentices. Stürzbecher makes the point that the distinction between a learned profession and a craftsman was revealed in the Berlin *Bürgerbuch* (Register of Citizens) in that a craftsman had to acquire *Bürgerrecht,* municipal citizenship, before he was allowed to practice his craft.[1] Apothecaries came under this legal status and requirement.

The apothecary developed from a merchant-retailer of spices, herbs, and remedies to a man with a distinctive professional status based on scientific training. In the period between 1685 and 1740 the apothecary began to make the important transition from a merchandising tradesman, struggling to maintain a retail monopoly against competing grocers, to that of a profession based on the progress made in botany and the new

---

1. See Manfred Stürzbecher, "Die Heilberufe im Berliner Bürgerbuch," *Berliner Gesundheitsblatt* 5 (1954): 142-143; also Alfons Fischer, *Deutschen Gesundheitswesen,* 1:322-323.

science of pharmaceutical chemistry. Fischer has written that "the success of physicians depends on the status of medical science and in turn the latter depends on the evolution of the natural sciences."[2] This is equally true for those who prepare the medical remedies, the apothecaries. Their importance to public and to personal health increased to the degree in which their knowledge and skill reflected "the evolution of the natural sciences" in the eighteenth century. The development of scientific pharmacy in Berlin began under Casper Neumann in the Court Apothecary Shop and was furthered by the course in pharmaceutical chemistry taught at the College of Medicine and Surgery.

Early History

As concerns the apothecary in Germany from the later Middle Ages to the reign of Frederick III, two aspects are noteworthy. First, the origin of the apothecary is to be found in the spice trade. He began as an importer and retailer, a dealer in spices, herbs, drugs, sugar, and various exotic or luxury items. In the sixteenth century, particularly, apothecaries were wealthy merchants. There was a gradual shifting of occupational activity from purveying spices and drugs to preparation of medical remedies. This was a slow development, gaining considerable momentum from the scientific progress of the eighteenth century.

Second, the apothecary in Germany was not organized in guilds. This was in stark contrast to the apothecary in England, France, Italy, and elsewhere in Europe.[3] Apothecaries in Germany not only did not have their own guild, but seldom were members of any other guild. The most likely, for instance, would have been that of the dry grocers, the *Materialisten* or *Krämer*.

These two aspects, the shopkeeper origin and the lack of an apothecary guild, directly affected the status and development of the apothecary in a variety of ways. His position and status were determined by the granting of a princely privilege granting him a monopoly on drug sales. This brought him into economic competition and conflict with the grocer, and, in turn, because of the monopoly, led princes to attempts at price-fixing. "It is highly characteristic of Germany, unlike such countries as Italy and France, that the pharmaceutical profession always was regulated by governmental regulations rather than being self-governing."[4]

2. Fischer, *Deutschen Gesundheitswesen*, 1:119.
3. Lester S. King, *The Medical World of the Eighteenth Century*, p. 4. More particularly see Manfred Stürzbecher, "Zur Biographie Alt-Berliner Apotheker," *Beiträge zur Geschichte der Pharmazie und Ihrer Nachbargebiete*, 2 (1956): 49-75; also Stürzbecher, "Zur Geschichte der französischen Apotheken in Berlin," *Pharmazeutische Zeitung*, vol. 103, no. 9 (27 Feb. 1958), p. 210.
4. Edward Kremers and George Urdang, *History of Pharmacy*, p. 114.

The first known apothecary privilege granted in Berlin was that given in 1481 to Johann Tempelhoff.[5] This privilege was granted by the city council of Berlin and was confirmed by the elector in 1482. It gave to Tempelhoff a monopoly in Berlin and Cölln for the sale of spices, herbs, drugs, confections, brandy, wax, and distilled water. At the same time, grocers were forbidden to sell these items. Prior to this, Stürzbecher sees no direct connection between the Berlin apothecary and the field of medicine. He was a *Gewürzkrämer,* a spice merchant. After the end of the fifteenth century, the apothecary becomes associated with Berlin's public health administration. This was concretely expressed by an electoral order of 1499 which required the elector's court physician to inspect the privileged Berlin apothecary shop. This is, perhaps, the earliest example of medical policing in Brandenburg history. After the late seventeenth century, supervision and inspection of apothecary shops in the electorate passed to city physicians and the Berlin Board of Medicine.

In 1520 an apothecary oath was required of Peter Hohenzweig on the occasion of his appointment as Berlin's privileged apothecary.[6] In a formula which would be often repeated in the next two centuries, he swore to look after the best interests of Berlin's inhabitants, to prepare all prescriptions exactly as written by the physicians, and not to alter or modify such prescriptions. He further swore not to keep prepared remedies beyond the period prescribed, and not to sell to unauthorized persons, without prescription, laxatives, poisons, and abortive drugs.

The acts of 1499 and 1520 confirm the fact that the apothecary was becoming identified with the preparation or compounding of medical remedies, in accordance with physicians' prescriptions, thus distinguishing him from the normal grocer. He continued to be a spice-merchant, importing and selling foreign spices, herbs, sugar, brandy, and other privileged items. But now he came under public supervision because his activities had a bearing upon the health of the community. The lack of a guild organization made public policing necessary.

The medical remedies which the apothecaries prepared in the fifteenth and early sixteenth centuries from their supplies of herbs and drugs were prepared by methods directed by the prescribing physicians. The earliest pharmacopoeias in Germany appeared in Nuremberg (1542), Augsburg (1564), and Cologne (1565).[7] Following the publication, apothecaries were directed to use the methods of preparation described in these pharma-

5.   Manfred Stürzbecher, "Zur Wirtschaftsgeschichte des älteren Berliner Apothekenwesens," *Deutsche Apotheker Zeitung* (1957), p. 1038, first delivered as a paper at the meeting of the International Society for the History of Pharmacy, at Heidelberg, Oct. 1957: see also Stürzbecher, "Beitrag zur Entwicklungsgeschichte des Berliner Apothekenwesens," *Beiträge zur Geschichte der Pharmazie,* no. 3 (1959), pp. 29, 47-48.
6.   For a copy of this oath of 4 July 1520, see Stürzbecher, "Beitrag zur Entwicklungsgeschichte," pp. 49-50.
7.   Fischer, *Deutschen Gesundheitswesen,* p. 83.

copoeias. That of Augsburg gained the dominant influence. The Pharmacopoeia Augustana of 1564 contained reference to some 1100 medicaments, probably all "Galenicals."[8] While botany and vegetable drugs predominated, men like Leonhard Thurneysser and his pupil, the apothecary Michael Aschenbrenner, in Berlin applied the beginnings of Paracelsian chemistry to medical remedies.[9]

As the apothecary after 1500 became a preparer of remedies, a dual jurisdictional conflict developed. Physicians frequently encroached on the work and livelihood of the apothecary, and the apothecary frequently practiced medicine. And similarly, a conflict developed between apothecaries and grocers which was not completely resolved even in the eighteenth century. Grocers or spice merchants could sell herbs and spices in bulk, but frequently used journeymen-apothecaries to prepare remedies. These would be problems inherited by the *Collegium Medicum* in its administration of the public health practitioners.

One other significant development in the period before 1685 was that of price regulation. Price regulation of many consumer items by government and guild probably began as early as the Carolingian era. It was a necessary result of the growth of towns and the beginning of a money economy after the year 1000. This regulation of prices affected the necessities of life—food and raw materials. It was in accord with church doctrine and the "divine" sanction of public promotion of the general welfare.

The regulation of prices for remedies sold by apothecaries had a slightly different rationale. Although such a regulation was as old as the medical edict of 1240 of Emperor Frederick II (Hohenstauffen), it did not have effect in Germany until the sixteenth century. Price-fixing of medical remedies was a necessary adjunct to the lack of competition inherent in the monopoly granted by apothecary privileges and in the restriction of the number of apothecary shops permitted in cities.[10] There were only three privileged apothecaries in Berlin and Cölln until the end of the seventeenth century.[11]

Price control in seventeenth-century Brandenburg was not limited to medical remedies. Wages of craftsmen and prices of a multitude of items, primarily necessities of life, were regulated by public authority, usually the elector. This was a necessary response to the inflation and scarcity of goods and money resulting from the Thirty Years' War. This

8. Kremers and Urdang, *History of Pharmacy*, p. 66.

9. Stürzbecher, "Leonhard Thurneysser," *Berliner Medizin* 9 (1958): 42-43; Stürzbecher, "Michael Aschenbrenner, Apotheken und Münzmeister," *Medizinische Monatsschrift* 8 (Aug. 1957): 539-541. Aschenbrenner was granted an apothecary privilege for Berlin and Cölln in 1588, although he probably served as court apothecary as early as 1571.

10. See Kremers and Urdang, *History of Pharmacy*, pp. 117-119; Fischer, *Deutschen Gesundheitswesen*, pp. 161-164; Stürzbecher, "Beiträg zur Entwicklungsgeschichte, pp. 34-37.

11. Eberhard Faden, *Berlin im Dreissigjährigen Kriege*, p. 53.

18. The Apothecary Arrives with His Clyster

19. Tobacco Smoking in 1630

was an era of the *Wipper* and *Kipper,* money clippers and counterfeiters. In 1623 a price list was published fixing the value of the Brandenburg *thaler* and fixing the prices of hundreds of commodities and services.[12] Apothecaries and grocers were placed in the same category, indicating that they had not yet been completely divorced. The price list of 1623, no matter how ineffective, set the standards of prices until the new price list of 1693.

The Brandenburg Apothecary after 1685

A new chapter in Brandenburg public health began in 1685. This new phase was the result of a vigorous, persistent, and continuous state intervention in the entire domain of medicine and public health. One direct result in the eighteenth century was an improvement in the professional status of the apothecary. This intervention, while traditional in the German territories, was also a manifestation of the theory of government of the Hohenzollern princes, whose guiding principle was a paternalistic concern for the welfare of their subjects. This principle was expressed by Frederick William in the apothecary privilege granted to Christoff Pentzer on 5 August 1667.[13] He stated that it was "ein hoch nötiges Ding [a most necessary thing]" that well-appointed apothecary shops should exist wherever there were large communities (as in Berlin and Cölln) for the protection of public health. This could not be effective, he argued, unless special privileges were granted to apothecaries. It was necessary for the common good.

In many aspects, state regulation of apothecaries after 1685 followed historical precedent and tradition. Licensing through electoral privileges, monopoly, public inspection, apothecary oaths, price fixing were already determined by state legislation. Until 1700, conservatively, the apothecary was fundamentally a shopkeeper with little professional standing and little scientific training.

The publication of the medical ordinance of 1685 which established the Board of Medicine as a bureaucratic body to supervise medical practitioners has been generally regarded as a milestone in the history of Brandenburg public health. Whatever the economic or professional motivation that prompted electoral publication of the ordinance of 1685, it had far-reaching results. One of the basic functions of the Board of Medicine was to establish standards of professional conduct for apothecaries. This in turn led to upgrading apothecary training under the impact of the new sciences. The result was a professional man of science.

12. *C. C. March.,* vol. 5, pt. 2, sec. 10, no. 5, cols. 587-622, "A Price Ordinance Prepared by the burgomasters and city councils of Berlin and Cölln and Published by Elector George William, 17 March 1623."
13. Published in Stürzbecher, "Beitrag zur Entwicklungsgeschichte," pp. 50-54.

The dominant role of the physician in public health administration is readily observed in the omission of apothecaries from membership on the Board of Medicine created in 1685. The increased stature and professional standing of the apothecary, in turn, was recognized in 1725 when two pharmaceutical assessors were added to the Supreme Board of Medicine in Berlin.

A major function of the Board of Medicine was to serve as a certifying board. Before new apothecaries were to be allowed to practice, they were first required to present themselves to the Board for examination. Licensed apothecaries were to present their dispensers (journeymen and apprentices), when taken on or dismissed, to the board in Berlin or its member representatives at the Frankfurt university medical faculty. In other electoral towns the board-approved physician-in-ordinary performed this function. The purpose was to approve the new employees and to assure that testimonials of good conduct and proficiency were granted to the dismissed. Ethical conduct meant that all apothecaries and their clerks, in accord with their civic oaths, would abide by the apothecary price list, would not alter by name, weight, or measure any prescribed remedy, would show proper respect to physicians, would refrain from any secret understandings with physicians for personal gain or to the harm or disadvantage of patients. They were to fill faithfully all prescriptions written by approved physicians, refrain from doctoring or visiting the sick, and especially were not to sell, without approval or foreknowledge of a physician, any purgatives, emetics, diuretics, opiates, or poisons.

The edict of 1685 also sought to protect the apothecary against the retail competition of grocers, spice merchants, alchemists, distillers, confectioners, and perfumers who were forbidden to dispense medical remedies. Grocers since 1650 had been subject to inspection to assure that they did not stock such prepared remedies.[14]

To protect the health of citizens, the Board of Medicine was to authorize and supervise regular inspections of all licensed apothecary shops except the Court Apothecary. Annually or oftener, with the aid of city or town magistrates and physicians throughout Brandenburg, the board was to inspect the stocks of drugs and prepared remedies, condemning the old and defective items. The inspectors were to instruct the apothecaries, their journeymen-dispensers, and the apprentices in their duties. And, finally, the inspectors were to make certain that drugs and remedies were sold at a proper price. To determine this, the medical board was instructed to prepare a price list for electoral approval. This was not accomplished until 1693.

14. Visitations of grocers were provided for by ordinances of 20 Sept. and 24 Nov. 1650, 20 Oct. 1698, 4 Sept. 1709 and 30 Sept. 1710, indicating that grocers persisted in selling medical remedies.

The medical edict of 1685 was published, but its various regulative provisions were either unenforced or ineffective.[15] A second and more successful effort occurred in 1693 with the publication of a revised medical ordinance and an attached price list.[15] The elector directed the board in more detail to establish standards of professional conduct for all medical practitioners. Physicians were forbidden to prepare medicaments for sale in competition with the apothecaries. A separate, inclusive ordinance for apothecaries detailed a code of conduct, procedures, and methods of preparation for the apothecary.

Apothecaries were forbidden to treat the sick or to prescribe or sell remedies without a physician's approval. Licensed physicians were to attend the unpacking, weighing, and pricing of exotic or foreign items. Similarly, in compounding remedies, apothecaries were to use only ingredients which were first examined by physicians for weight and quality. Chemical remedies were not to be prepared by apothecaries, much less by itinerant alchemists, on their own. Until such time as a territorial pharmacopoeia was published and a standard method of preparation described, apothecaries were directed to consult with physicians on the method of compounding chemical remedies. Other medical compounds, the ordinary Galenicals, were to be prepared according to the methods prescribed in the Augsburg *Pharmacopoeia* and other approved books. After preparation, all compounds were to be stored in containers with the year and date of preparation inscribed. Unlabeled containers found during annual inspections were to be rejected.

Venoms and poisons were to be kept well secured and isolated from other remedies. Separate scales, mortars, pestles, sieves, mullers, and tammies were to be used for measuring and weighing poisons to avoid contamination of instruments used in regular compounding. Apothecaries were to be discreet in the sale of poisons and to sell to no one, particularly unknown or suspect persons, without a physician's written prescription. Responsible persons who needed poisons in their work were permitted to buy such upon showing their certificates.

Opiates and purgatives were to be prepared with great care and accurate measurement. No apprentice of less than four years' experience was to sell or prepare them except in the presence of the apothecary or an experienced journeyman. If a journeyman-dispenser began to fill a prescription, he was not to turn to other business or allow another to complete the preparation in order to avoid dangerous error.

Rigid control over prescriptions was demanded for the protection of the individual. Apothecaries were forbidden to criticize prescriptions, to deprecate them secretly, or to dissuade patients from using them. Instead they were to fill prescriptions exactly as written without changes, omis-

15. *C. C. March.,* vol. 5, pt. 4, sec. 1, no. 16, cols. 11-24 (edict of 1685); and cols. 23-60 (edict of 1693).

sions, or false weight or measure. If prescriptions were illegible or contained errors, the apothecary was to consult with the prescribing physician and make no unauthorized correction. Journeymen were to be closely supervised in their preparation of remedies. They were to be instructed to keep their utensils clean and to use no copper or brass mortars if internal remedies required the addition of acids. Prescriptions from unlicensed physicians, barber-surgeons, and bathkeepers, particularly for purgatives, emetics, and emmenagogues, were not to be accepted or filled. The ingredients for forbidden drugs were not to be sold.

All compounded prescriptions were to have inscribed on them the day, month, and year of preparation and the price for later inspection purposes. The prepared medicines were to be placed in thoroughly clean containers and marked with the signature on the prescription. Medicines of a strong nature, which might be dangerous to the individual, were not to be refilled without the express approval of a physician. The regulations and efforts to safeguard preparation of remedies have obviously changed little in over two centuries.

To assure that the licensed apothecary shops were well managed and conformed to the published regulations, annual unannounced inspections were to be conducted by city physicians and town officials. They were to demand to see all medical ingredients, check their quality, inspect dates on prepared remedies, and the local physicians could ask to see their own prescriptions for inspection purposes.

Administrative supervision and regulation of Brandenburg apothecaries in the two ordinances of 1685 and 1693 went far beyond the measures of the preceding two centuries. However, they failed to meet with unqualified success, enforcement, or approval. The apothecaries complained about the severity of restrictions on their activities, as well as about continued violations of their privileges by unauthorized retailers or quacks. They themselves were often guilty of violating measures designed to protect the public welfare.

In 1696, in response to complaints of apothecaries, Frederick III eased restrictions on retail sales in Brandenburg apothecary shops.[16] Unrestricted sales of some simple medicaments, without a physician's prescription, were permitted. Such items included antispasmodic powders, sedatives, mild laxatives and lenitives (demulcents) such as manna, cassia, tamarindus, senna, rhubarb, prunes, raisins, mithridates, and theriac (poison antidotes) so long as these were not sold in excess quantity. Prescriptions were still required for strong purgatives such as turpeth, agaric, jalap, scammony, diagrydiate, catapuce, antimony, mercury, and their preparations. The same applied to opiates and vomitoria.

---

16. Ibid., cols 59-65, "Declaration on the Medical Ordinance [of 1693] on Several Points Concerning the Apothecaries," 30 May 1696.

The declaration of 1696 also reasserted the exclusive privilege or monopoly of the apothecaries against infringement by physicians who dispensed certain medicinal herbs or grocers, spice merchants, or distillers. Internal remedies not only were to be prescribed by competent persons but were to be prepared only by those who were competent.

There were complaints about the table of prices attached to the medical ordinance of 1693. The elector, however, declared in 1696 that since the apothecaries had assisted in drawing up the price list, it should remain unchanged. It was recognized, nevertheless, that because of war conditions and their effect on European commerce, there was considerable price fluctuation on imported drugs and spices. Therefore, the elector urged the Board of Medicine to enforce the price list with discretion, so that neither dispenser nor consumer would suffer. In 1715, after two major European wars, a revised price list of all medicines found in apothecaries was published.[17] Medicines and drugs were listed alphabetically by Latin, German, and French names, with the established price for each. The list reveals the medicines and drugs used by Brandenburg apothecaries at this time. Almost 400 different main categories with many subtypes included oils, spirits, essences, syrups, waters, tinctures, and unguents. The items included such things as ordinary sugar candy, opium, laudanum, laxatives, purgatives, amulets, extracts of roots, flowers, herbs, and parts of animals (e.g., musk of deer).

Responsibility for fixing the prices of medical remedies was assigned to the Berlin Board of Medicine by a rescript of 30 July 1700. After 1725 this was extended to the Prussian provinces through the newly-created provincial medical boards. For the first time, in 1724-1725, apothecaries were assigned as regular members of the administrative boards.[18] Two apothecaries joined the provincial boards. The court apothecary had been a regular member of the central board in Berlin since 13 June 1724. And it was further provided in 1725 that two experienced Berlin apothecaries were to be added as consultants or assessors in Berlin, whenever pharmaceutical affairs were under discussion at the central board. The presence of apothecaries as members of the boards of medicine reflected their increased professional prestige and assured greater protection of their special interests. Apothecaries appointed to the medical boards were required to have completed appropriate training courses at the new College of Medicine and Surgery in Berlin.[19]

Since 1520 apothecaries had been required to take an oath regarding their function. The ordinances of 1685 and 1693 continued this requirement. A patent of 1700 expressly required such an oath of all apothecaries and dispensing clerks in the whole electorate of Brandenburg.[20]

17. Ibid., cols. 77-184.
18. *C. C. March.,* vol. 5, pt. 4, sec. 1, no. 32, cols. 220-221, par. 4.
19. Ibid., pars. 3, 4.
20. "Patent Concerning Swearing in of Apothecaries," 17 Jan. 1700, *C. C. March.,*

In Berlin this was to be done before the Board of Medicine, in the provincial towns before a resident physician. If the apothecary was owned by a physician, he was required to employ a pharmaceutical dispenser who had to be properly sworn in. In addition to the regular oath, apothecaries in towns lacking a resident physician took an additional oath that, since the care of the sick would devolve upon them, they would advise the sick according to their knowledge and conscience and would prepare medical remedies for them. In serious cases, exceeding their knowledge and ability, they would refer the sick to the nearest doctor.

In 1713 the new king, Frederick William I, attempted to eliminate certain continuing grievances.[21] Apothecaries again were warned not to fill any prescriptions not written or at least approved by a physician, on pain of a heavy fine. Grocers, and particularly journeymen-apothecaries employed by them, were ordered to cease selling medical remedies on pain of forfeiting their grocers' trade.

The issue of monopoly and privilege was not easily solved by edict. Evasion of restrictions was frequent, and in 1725 the king addressed an ordinance to the Royal Board of Medicine specifying that grocers were not to stock or sell medicines and medicinal spices, but only edible food items.[22] In turn, apothecaries were not to stock or sell edible foods, only medical remedies. A conflict arose at this time over the right to sell coffee and tobacco. On the basis of a declaration of 22 April 1727, the apothecaries claimed these items, since grocers were allowed only victuals.[23] This issue was not finally settled until the end of the century.

State regulation of individual activity for the protection of the common good is not a function readily and happily accepted by the regulated individual. Particularly in areas of consumer protection, those engaged in purveying, vending, or offering services for fees are as likely to be moved by greed, avarice, or personal profit as by a sense of public service. Sanitation, adulteration of products, short weight or measurement, overpricing, quackery, and humbug, even by supposedly learned or professional men, illicit competition by unqualified or uncertified personnel are all phases of economic life which in all centuries have invited state intervention by regulation to protect the private citizen and the public

---

vol. 5, pt. 4, sec. 1, no. 16, cols. 65-69. Oath of an apothecary: "I swear that I will carefully do my duty and operate my shop with propriety and that I will conform to the Price List and Apothecary Ordinance [of 1693] in that I will not alter the prescribed remedies in name, weight, or measure, will not substitute one substance for another, will have all prescriptions properly filled, and will refrain from ordinary treatment and visiting of patients, and particularly will not sell without a physician's approval any strong purgatives, vomitoria, drugs, opiates, or poisons."

21. "Patent Concerning Elimination of Certain Grievances in Medical Administration," 9 Oct. 1713, ibid., no. 16, cols. 71-75.

22. "Ordinance On What Goods Apothecaries and Grocers Should Stock," 12 May 1725, ibid., no. 30, col. 241.

23. See Manfred Stürzbecher, "Zur Frage des Kaffee- und Tabakhandels in Apotheken," *Geschichtsbeilage der Deutschen Apotheker-Zeitung* 6 (1955): 405-407.

welfare. Obviously, there would be no need for such public regulation if those persons who served the public were moved by noble principles. And, conversely, it is natural that such persons would seek to avoid restrictions imposed on them by regulation and by standards of certification and professional qualification.

The medical ordinances of 1685 and 1693 made a significant *legislative* beginning in the administrative regulation of all phases of public health—although some of the medical policing was not new. There was resistance and evasion, partly because of poor enforcement provisions. In 1725 the first major effort was made by Frederick William I to review and revise the principles and standards of regulation of the various branches of public health service, to reaffirm or redefine the privileges of each, and to establish canons of professional conduct, qualifications, and improvement.[24] After describing the conditions endangering the health and welfare of his subjects, Frederick William declared his intention to abolish the abuses and malpractices which had crept into the practice of medicine. Here we are concerned only with apothecaries.

Recognizing the close relationship between the health of his land and subjects and the effort, knowledge, and faithfulness of apothecaries, the king instituted a qualifying procedure for the latter on the basis of professional examinations. All apothecaries wishing to settle in Berlin or in provincial towns or cities to open a shop were required first to register with the Supreme Board of Medicine, present their certificates of apprenticeship and evidence that they had served at least seven years as journeymen-dispensers. Then they had to attend the required course in pharmaceutical chemistry taught by Caspar Neumann. Upon completion of the course, the applicants were to be examined by the medical board (which included the court apothecary and two pharmacy associates). If approved by the board, the applicants then took the apothecary oath (see note 20). The provincial boards were to follow the same procedures for applicants outside Brandenburg and were to forward the results of examinations to Berlin for final approval or rejection.

The year 1725 is a turning point in the advancement of pharmacy to a high professional status. No longer was a good character, knowledge of Latin, and apprentice-journeyman training sufficient. Apothecaries had to satisfy certification boards by demonstrating attainment of certain minimum qualifications before receiving licenses to practice. Formal, academic instruction in pertinent courses of theoretical and practical chemistry was required. Apothecaries were required to attend the lecture course in chemical-pharmaceutical remedies taught by Dr. Johann Pott. This was followed by the course of Caspar Neumann. By experiments and demonstrations, using appropriate pharmaceutical chemicals and

24. "The General Medical Edict and Ordinance of 27 Sept. 1725," *C. C. March.,* vol. 5, pt. 4, sec. 1, no. 32, cols. 219-236; for sections on apothecaries see cols. 228-233.

chemical products, Neumann was to instruct his students in the proper use of furnaces, earthen, glass, and metal vases and instruments necessary in the compounding of chemical preparations. With this type of formal training, qualified apothecaries would be able to replace physicians in the preparation of chemico-medical remedies.

As a result of the new requirement representing an upgrading of professional training and qualification, the king ordered that "in future no one other than proper apothecaries who had really learned the profession shall be allowed to manage or to buy an apothecary shop."[25] This directive was aimed at the grocers and physicians who persisted in using journeymen-apothecaries to prepare medicines for sale, in illicit competition with licensed apothecaries. To make the public aware of the distinction, the king, still in 1725, further required that the certified apothecaries place a sign over their shops saying "Privileged Apothecary," while the competing grocers were to display a "Grocery Shop" or "Spice Shop" sign.

At this time, the edict of 1725 suggests that there were in metropolitan Berlin only twelve authorized apothecary shops, nine German and three French, serving perhaps 75,000 persons.[26] In addition there was the Court Apothecary Shop located in a wing of the royal palace. Since 1719 this shop and chemical laboratory had been under the supervision of Caspar Neumann.

The Court Apothecary Shop furnished medicines to the royal family, members of the court, and personnel employed in the General Directory in Berlin and at the gun factory at Potsdam. It also issued medicines for the five garrison regiments, to invalided and pensioned war veterans, to hospitals, poorhouses, orphanages, church and school employees, pregnant women, and to colonists migrating to East Prussia. Many received medicines free of cost. Most higher officials received only a 50-percent discount. Because of abuses of various kinds by those who had access to the Court Apothecary Shop, Frederick William on 7 June 1725 issued a regulation to curb these abuses.[27]

No prescriptions were to be accepted from or filled for persons entitled to free medicines unless they had been written and signed by the king's personal physician, a court physician, or by garrison physicians. Certain exceptions were authorized for the personal surgeon of the king and for regimental field surgeons. The king warned that the practice of having two or three physicians send in prescriptions at the same time for one patient suggested conspiracy and deceit. The court apothecary was to

25. Ibid., col. 232, par. 14.

26. Ibid., col. 229, par. 2, refers to a royal ordinance of 27 Dec. 1720 in which the king directed the Berlin magistracy to limit the number of licensed apothecaries to twelve. The practice of granting privileges to apothecaries was terminated in the revised apothecary ordinance of 1801 (Stürzbecher, "Zur Wirtschaftsgestchichte Berliner Apothekenwesens").

27. *C. C. March.*, vol. 5, pt. 4, sec. 1, no. 31, cols. 215-220.

report such connivance so that the offending person could be deprived of his privilege. The same penalty was to be imposed on those who obtained free medicines and then sold them or gave them to others. Many members of the court were less interested in *materia medica* than in other items available at the Court Apothecary Shop, "which really do not serve for the restoration of lost health but serve to arouse lust and wantonness, for sprucing up and for gallant wooing." Since this was "contrary to the purpose of the court apothecary," the king forbade the free dispensing of even the least portion of pomade, sugar, sugar candy, virgin wax, almond, oil, balsam, snuff, perfume, and so forth to anyone except the royal family. Others were required to pay or were to be referred to the commercial shops. Physicians were forbidden to prescribe simple drugs, expensive oils, and other uncompounded elements. These items could be dispensed only as part of preparations or remedies. While the king attempted to place strict control over dispensing free medicines to eligible persons, he was generous in providing medicines for the poor, who could not pay the regular retail prices.

The Court Apothecary Shop in 1725 was much more than a convenient stockroom or prescription room for members of the court. It had a long and distinguished history both as a dispensary and as a chemical laboratory. After the installation of Caspar Neumann as court apothecary in 1719, it was completely modernized and became one of the most famous European apothecary shops.[28] Neumann had traveled extensively and studied chemistry in various European centers, gaining recognition as a distinguished chemist in London. He made Berlin a center of chemical studies (along with Dr. Pott and E. G. Stahl) through his practical research and his teaching at the College of Medicine and Surgery. The chemical laboratory of the Court Apothecary Shop was for a long time the best equipped in Berlin and was used for pharmaceutical instruction. The Court Apothecary Shop, its associated botanical and herb garden, and the contributions of Neumann were primarily responsible for the significant advancement of pharmacy to a scientific profession after 1725.

The ordinance of 1725 repeated and revised previous regulations concerning the daily practice and professional conduct of apothecaries, establishing standards designed to protect public health. Apothecaries were required to prepare all compounds, medical remedies, or chemicals according to the *Brandenburg Dispensatory,* and on pain of a fine of 25 *Reichsthaler* were to charge neither more nor less than the listed prices for prescriptions, and were not to alter or substitute ingredients. Poisons and other dangerous materia were to be well safeguarded as described above. No poisons were to be sold to anyone without a prescription. No internal medicines were to be sold except as prescribed by an approved physician. No apothecary was to recommend to residents one physician as

28. Manfred Stürzbecher, "Caspar Neumann," *Berliner Medizin* 8 (1957): 156-158.

against another. Nor were they to dispense medical compounds and nostra not approved by the medical board but prescribed by greedy physicians, on pain of a fine of 100 *Reichsthaler* for the first offense and loss of their privilege for a second.

Ordinary internal and external treatments as well as dispensing of medical compounds without prescription were completely forbidden to apothecaries and their dispensers, except that simple remedies such as mild laxatives, demulcents, and soothing powders could be sold in moderate doses. No exception was made for emetics, purgatives, emmenagogues, mercury and antimony preparations, opiates, antidotes, and sudorifics. Triennial inspections were to be made to assure that regulations were being observed and standards met.

In order to protect the apothecaries who must meet the required standards and ethics and must keep on hand a fresh supply of herbs, roots, flowers, conserves, various waters, and other preparations, grocers were forbidden to deal in any medical remedies. To clarify the situation, Frederick William permitted grocers to handle items which did not concern the field of medicine, such as all kinds of foreign foods and spices, comfits, pastries, confectionaries, also Dutch gin, French, Rhenish, and simply distilled brandies. The forbidden list included distilled spirits or waters, unguents, plasters, essences, tinctures, elixirs, pills, powders, or electuaries, that is, medicines, simple or compounded, for internal or external use. Also excluded were items going under the general name of *Olitäten* (medicines or perfumes containing oil) except for olive oil, linseed oil, oil of mace, cloves, cinnamon, pepper, cubeb, and rosewood.

All grocers, chemists, distillers, and their clerks were required to take an oath that they would not sell the forbidden medicines.

Grocery shops and distilleries were to be visited semiannually with the assistance of a number of apothecaries, and any prohibited goods were to be confiscated.

Grocers were forbidden to employ journeymen-apothecaries on pain of a fine of 100 *Reichsthaler* for grocers and permanent exclusion from the apothecary profession for guilty journeymen. Physicians likewise were forbidden to employ such journeymen as laboratory assistants and then use them to prepare medicines for sale.

The goal of assuring monopoly of preparation and sale of medical remedies to the apothecaries was not easily achieved. To the privileged apothecary it was primarily an economic issue. He was expected to maintain a complete inventory of all ingredients necessary for the protection of health. He had lost his monopoly on confections, brandies, and other items after the Thirty Years' War. To survive economically, then, his monopoly on sale of medicinal preparations was a necessity. On the other hand, the lure of profit was too much to resist for physicians, surgeons, midwives, bathkeepers, grocers, and spice merchants. A glance at the

20. *Toothextracting at the Fair*   21. *An Apothecary Shop*

shelves of twentieth-century retail establishments reveals that the issue is a persistent one.

Between 1690 and 1725 there were at least eight occasions when the Prussian king had to order grocers to cease abusing their retail guild privileges at the expense of the apothecaries.[29] An edict of 1726 extended this prohibition to traveling hawkers who offered medical remedies and quack nostra at a discount.[30] To Frederick William I, however, the issue was more than a matter of protecting a privilege. His genuine paternal concern for the welfare of his people caused him to strike out against greed, fraud, and quackery that in any way might cause harm to the health of his subjects. And only those persons who had been examined and certified by the Royal Board of Medicine were to be permitted to practice medicine or prepare and dispense medical remedies.[31]

29. *C. C. March.*, vol. 5, pt. 4, sec. 1, no. 32, apps. 14-20, cols. 241-244.

30. "Edict That the General Medical Ordinance of 1725 Shall Be Strictly Observed, 1 Feb. 1726," ibid., no. 34, cols. 255-258.

31. Dr. Manfred Stürzbecher, of Berlin, Germany, was kind enough to forward to me reprints of many of his articles published in learned periodicals in Germany, articles which otherwise would have escaped my notice. I take this opportunity to express my appreciation of this courtesy. A complete bibliography of his many articles may be found in his *Beiträge zur Berliner Medizingeschichte.*

19

Epidemics and Practical Medicine

Administration, education, and regulation represented one side of the broad spectrum of public health. They represented an institutional element, the visible agents, the external evidence that there was a body of medical knowledge and a variety of medical practitioners available to protect the public health. Hospitals, medical training centers, health practitioners, administrative boards of medicine, as well as expansion in the body of medical and scientific knowledge, however, are or should be means to achieve a public good. They are empty vessels which take on meaning only when they are applied to the prevention and cure of disease, illness, and injury, and thereby serve mankind generally and individually. This is the other side of public health—the people who benefit from the available external agencies. Only when the latter are applied in practice is there indication of the level of advancement in knowledge, of the status of the medical sciences, and of the degree of political awareness and social responsibility applied to reducing human suffering from disease.

In the period between 1685 and 1725 three Hohenzollern rulers demonstrated their interest in promoting health facilities. In the first decades of the eighteenth century, two crises provided an opportunity to demonstrate practically the Hohenzollern concern for the health of both the human and animal population of Brandenburg-Prussia. The state was forced to respond to the twin dangers of plague and epizooty. This response not only reveals a paternalistic concern for the welfare of subjects and territories, but offers a clear insight into the level of medical knowledge, the methods of treatment, and the concept of disease existent in the early eighteenth century. Human and animal pathology had progressed to a point of awareness of contagion and the related importance of sanitation, of recognition of symptoms and the course of a disease, which permitted preventive measures but provided practically no cures.

The last major outbreaks of the bubonic plague in Central and Western Europe occurred between 1664 and 1721. In the area of northeastern Germany and Northern Europe, this period was punctuated by the last great epidemic of 1709-1711.

At almost the same time a serious epizootic outbreak, affecting most of Europe, threatened to destroy the cattle herds of Brandenburg. In the decade after 1709 the cattle herds of Europe were reduced by several million. The danger stemmed from an epidemic of a rinderpest-like cattle disease.

The great crisis and threat of epidemic of 1709 originated in the east, in the war between the Swedes and the Russians. The war ran over into neutral East Prussia and Poland and served to spread both the bubonic plague and cattle disease in epidemic proportions. The problem for the rulers of Prussia was first to prevent the spread of disease across the Oder River, and, if that failed, to combat the disease with all available means.

Plague

Prior to 1709 Brandenburg had already been forced to take preventive measures against the danger of plague. There were several outbreaks in Europe after 1664. The danger had been avoided by a policy of closing the borders and isolating local outbreaks.[1] Quarantine, isolation, restriction on travel were the principal agencies to prevent spread of contagion.

The major eruption of plague in 1708-1709, however, produced a more systematic study of the plague and of means of prevention and cure. Berlin and Brandenburg were never directly affected by the contagion, both because of the preventive measures taken by the state and because of the elaborate organization of a civil defense machinery to guard Berlin. Brandenburg was cut off from Eastern Europe. Until late 1709 the major effort was directed towards keeping the plague out of Brandenburg by various police measures of sealing the borders and reducing travel, by quarantine methods, by banning commercial intercourse with infected areas or cities, and by plans to isolate any locally infected villages.[2]

By the end of 1709 the danger to Berlin and Brandenburg reached its peak, as the plague assumed serious epidemic proportions in neighboring lands. Frederick I, on 14 November 1709, issued "A Regulation and a Medical Plan on What to Do in Connection with the Current Dangerous Occurrences of the Plague in Towns, Villages, and Hamlets."[3] The regulation was no more than an intensification of the general program of prevention. It did offer one of the earliest examples of planning a civilian defense organization against major catastrophe. It outlined an organization of personnel to be appointed beforehand with detailed, assigned functions to perform in the event the plague actually broke out. Under the broad supervision of public health directors in each city, there were to be wardens, street inspectors, designated plague physicians, apothecaries, nurses, midwives, pastors, coffin-carriers, gravediggers, and decontaminators of infected houses. Pesthouses and hospitals were to be set up for quarantine purposes. The plague personnel would live in isolation from the healthy population in event of plague. Their functions would be to detect individual outbreaks of disease, provide services to in-

---

1. See patents of 31 July 1664, 30 Oct. 1680, 13 July 1681, and 19 July 1682, in *C. C. March.*, vol. 5, pt. 4, sec. 2, nos. 1, 3, 4, 8, cols. 279-286.

2. Edicts of 19 May 1708, 12 Dec. 1708, 5 Aug. 1709, and 17 Sept. 1709, ibid., nos. 9, 10, 11, 13, cols. 285-294.

3. Ibid., no. 16, cols. 295-340.

fected persons, enforce various sanitation requirements, prevent public gatherings of people, protect property, make burial arrangements, and finally decontaminate and fumigate infected houses and materials. Food, medicine, salaries, housing for the dislocated, care of the poor were to be provided out of public funds.

Associated with the regulation was a medical plan proposed by the new Board of Sanitation. A description of the symptoms of the plague as well as suggestions for precautions and cures reflected a more systematic approach to the problem of the plague in the medical profession. It revealed the best medical opinion of the time as to the nature of the disease, how to identify it, and how to combat contagion. The best medical opinion, unfortunately, was not very good medical science. The fundamental concept of disease had been altered little since the days of Hippocrates, Celsus, Al-Razes, Avicenna, and the physicians of the Renaissance era. Medicine, the concept of disease, the art of healing were still based essentially on principles of humoral pathology. Clean air, a good diet, hygiene and sanitation, isolation for contagious disease were supplemented by certain vegetable drugs to restore the humoral balance. Bleeding was still regarded as a useful treatment in the early eighteenth century.

The medical plan described the recognizable symptoms of the plague. These signals included sudden tremors over the whole body followed by a high continuous fever, severe headache and vertigo, much uneasiness of the heart, nausea and inclination to vomit, stitches in the side, backache, listlessness and heaviness of all limbs, great inclination to sleep, shortness of breath, a dry and bitter mouth, sunken and weepy eyes. And, finally, boils and plague swellings would appear in glandular areas as behind the ears and under the shoulder blades. On some there would appear black and brown spots, carbuncles, pustules, and swollen glands on the belly, legs, and arms.

After the symptoms were observed, treatment was to begin by inducing sweating to drive out the disease, using remedies containing theriac and bezoar. If an infected person could not be brought to a sweat, the use of sudorifics was prescribed by applying alexipharmics. It was believed that the internal poison could be drawn out through sweat pores by diaphoresis. Since heavy sweating weakened the body, various heart stimulants were recommended. Placing a piece of sugar-covered lemon in the mouth would quicken the heart and repel disease, it was believed at the time.

If buboes occurred under the shoulder blades, in the groin, or elsewhere, bloodletting cups of plasters of magnetic arsenic were to be applied. An onion heated in hot coals and stuffed with theriac and bound to the buboes might draw out the infection. The boil had to be opened and suppuration encouraged so that the infection would not work back to the heart. If buboes would not respond to suppuratives, then they were to be relieved by diaphoresis. If a scirrhus hardness was left, the buboes were to be excoriated with plasters (melitot, diachylon, or of tacamabacca).

The medical plan of 1709 indicated, apparently without endorsing it, that some people sought to keep the infection from spreading to the heart by drawing a circle around the bubo with an Oriental sapphire. Others used a butter of antimony to paint a circle around the carbuncle to keep the infection from spreading. In fact, some maintained that with this treatment the carbuncle fell off.

There was a great fear of the plague entering Berlin in late 1709 and again in late 1710. Severe restrictions on travel and on transit trade were imposed.[4] By the end of 1711 the king felt that those territories of his which had been beset by the plague were freed of it.[5] They were now granted their former freedom of trade and foreign intercourse, although various restrictive precautions remained in effect for a number of years and were enforced again in 1713 against Hamburg and some Hapsburg territories, and against France in 1721.[6]

Epizooty[7]

To a large extent the threat to the cattle herds of Brandenburg from a rinderpest-like epidemic was warded off by the first efforts at a scientific approach to the problem of cattle disease between 1711 and 1732. The measures taken to prevent disease, to isolate it once it had broken out in local areas, the efforts to identify the symptoms and to discover effective remedies for the disease again offer interesting historical insight to the status of veterinary knowledge and practice in the first decades of the eighteenth century. The parallels with contemporary efforts to combat plague are quickly observed in several aspects. The systematic efforts exerted towards the prevention and cure of the rinderpest-like cattle disease were the results of direct governmental legislation and directive. The progress made in combating the disease, as well as the development of veterinary science, was dependent upon the concern and support of the paternalistic rulers. The efforts at cure were burdened with the same traditional concept of disease which circumscribed the efforts made to cure the plague. And this most of all was due to the fact that in 1700 there really was no veterinary science. Animal disease of necessity fell into the province of those who normally were concerned with human sickness. Since the same body of knowledge was applied to both plague

4. Edicts of 24 Nov. 1709, 12 July 1710, 1 Aug. 1710, 30 Oct. 1710, 24 Nov. 1710, ibid., nos., 17, 20, 21, 27, 28, cols. 339-360, passim.
5. Ibid., no. 35, cols. 383-388, 2 Nov. 1711.
6. Ibid., nos. 38, 39, cols. 389-396; nos. 50, 51, cols. 417-420.
7. For a fuller discussion see Reinhold A. Dorwart, "Cattle Disease (Rinderpest?)—Prevention and Cure, 1665-1732," *Agricultural History*, vol. 33, no. 2 (1959), pp. 78-85.

and epizooty by the same group of practitioners, methods of treatment, prevention, cure followed an almost identical pattern.

Prior to the threat of 1711 there had been some indication of the awareness of the spread of disease by infection from dead cattle, as may be judged from seventeenth-century regulations governing the disposal of dead animals. However, there is no evidence that there was any scientific discrimination between the dangers of putrescence and those of contagious infection. The danger from dead animals which were diseased resulted from the methods of disposal. Meat was used for baiting wolf traps; hides were used for making leather buckets. Carcasses were disposed of by local burying, by throwing them into rivers and streams, or by permitting dogs to eat the carcasses. It was the law of the land that dead cattle were to be surrendered to the public executioners and skinners for disposal. Between 1655 and 1684 several edicts were issued by the elector ordering noble and peasant alike to report all dead cattle.[8] That the basic purpose of disposal by public executioner was to prevent the spread of disease was stressed in a patent of July 1684.[9] Until 1711 these precautions were normal and routine prevention measures against the spread of disease due to the putrescence of dead cattle. But in this year the Hohenzollern lands between the Elbe and Oder rivers were faced with the spectre of a genuine epidemic of cattle disease.

The rinderpest-like epizooty erupting in southern Russia in 1709 spread to East Prussia, Poland, and Silesia. By 1711 the disease had gotten out of control and was spreading westward into Pomerania and Brandenburg. The threat of general epidemic to the cattle herds of Brandenburg resulted in the ordering of stringent protective measures by Frederick I on 7 December 1711.[10]

A quarantine of eight days on the borders and import restrictions were basic precautionary measures, in order "to prevent the ruin of the lands."[11] Whenever an authentic report was received of disease in neighboring territories, importation of cattle was forbidden without quarantine. The disease was considered under control in East Prussia by 1717 but import restrictions were imposed as late as 1729.[12]

If, despite quarantine and controlled import, the disease occurred within the frontiers, the next step was to isolate it to prevent development

8. *C. C. March.,* vol. 5, pt. 4, sec. 3, no. 1, cols. 423-424, patent of 14 Sept. 1665. Ibid., no. 2, cols. 424-425, patent of 1667 and no. 3, cols. 425-428, patent of 1682. These patents reveal as much concern over the violation of the privileges of the executioners and skinners to dispose of carcasses as for the prevention of disease.

9. Ibid., no. 4, cols. 427-428. The official concern for proper disposal of dead cattle was extended from Brandenburg to the duchies of Magdeburg and Pomerania and to the principality of Halberstadt by electoral edict on 22 April 1689 (ibid., no. 5, cols. 427-430). The edict of 1684 was reissued in 1704 and in 1707, indicating general evasion of the requirement to bury dead animals.

10. Ibid., no. 8, cols. 433-434.

11. Ibid., no. 11, cols. 437-438, 14 Feb. 1714, and no. 13, cols. 439-442, 20 Oct. 1716.

12. Ibid., no. 17, cols. 443-444, 11 Sept. 1717; no. 27, cols. 459-476.

of an epidemic. The danger of contagion was to be forestalled by segregation of infected cattle, decontamination of pastures, barns, and feeding equipment, and burial of complete carcasses with quicklime treatment. Infected villages were isolated with the use of armed guards to prevent movement of persons and all animals.

A major problem in preventing the spread of cattle disease to epidemic proportions was recognition of the disease when it occurred. The danger of infection by contagion had long been recognized. To prevent this it would be necessary to identify the symptoms. The first genuinely systematic efforts at scientific investigation of cattle disease in Brandenburg began in 1711, by order of the basic edict of 1711. It required the circulation of printed questionnaires in the areas where cattle disease existed among the farmers who lost cattle and among the skinners who disposed of the carcasses. It was hoped that the answers to the fifteen questions would yield information on the nature and symptoms of the disease. On the basis of this information, a publication suggesting remedies would be prepared.

From accumulated experiences with the epidemic between 1711 and 1716, and on the basis of the answers to the questionnaires required since 1711, Frederick William I in 1716 issued a bulletin, "A Basic Instruction on How to Recognize the Cattle Disease, How to Protect the Healthy Cattle from It, and How to Cure the Sick."[13]

The disease was described as producing a noticeable, intense shuddering over the whole body and skin of the animal. The infected animal suffered from loss of appetite, hung its head almost to the ground, and appeared listless. Breath was hot and foul, eyes were inflamed. The mouth and tongue were dry and hot and often black, while boils and blisters appeared in the throat. With some there was both stoppage of urine and constipation; others suffered from diarrhea and much belching. In most cases all teeth became loose.

In 1723 dissections of cattle carcasses by the territorial and city physicians of Halberstadt added more information on the nature of the disease.[14] Study of the viscera of several dead animals revealed nothing abnormal about the heart, lungs, liver, and spleen. However, the gallbladder was extraordinarily enlarged; the intestines were inflamed and full of foul matter. The inadequacy of veterinary knowledge in 1723 relative to this cattle disease was underscored by the physicians' confession that "whatever became infected died and infected others."

The final step in this first scientific investigation of epizooty was a search for preventive remedies and cures. The effort produced a curious mixture of traditional remedies and products of the new chemistry. The

13. Ibid., nos. 14, 27, app. 1, cols. 467-471. First issued in 1716, it was reissued on 24 Dec. 1729.

14. Ibid., no. 27, app. 2, cols. 471-476, "Physical and Medicinal Research in Cattle Disease and Recommended Remedies, of 6 Dec. 1723."

greatest weakness was the lack of controlled experiments. A great variety of powders and drugs of plant origin were recommended, along with chemical preparations. But the edict of 1729 finally admitted that all conceivable medical remedies had been applied with no apparent favorable efforts. No remedies were discovered by which cattle unable to resist the disease by their own mettle could be saved. Although veterinary medicine in the first half of the eighteenth century failed to discover either preventive remedies for contagion or cures for infection, the methodological approach, and the systematic observation and study of cattle disease in Brandenburg at this time, pointed in the direction of a veterinary science.[15]

15. For an interesting comparative essay on this subject see Shelby T. McCloy, "Relief for Epizootics," in *Government Assistance in Eighteenth-Century France.*

Part VI
Public Security

20

Fire Protection

Fire, like contagious disease, can be a calamity endangering the lives, welfare, and property of a community. Uncontrolled among the combustible materials of the villages and towns of this era, fire could be catastrophic in its effects upon the lives of peasants and burghers, as well as upon the economic resources of a community. The threat to public security from fire evoked among city and territorial governments a variety of measures to minimize the danger or effects. This threat can be compared to the dangers of contagious disease with considerable historical and methodological justification. The defense against fire, as against disease, in the three hundred years after 1500, developed through three phases. The primary and basic phase was fire prevention and elimination of fire hazards. When this failed and fire occurred, fire-fighting techniques had to be developed and applied. In the sixteenth century, equipment, appliances, and techniques were almost completely identical to those used in the cities of the Roman Empire. By the eighteenth century, the advancements in technology resulted in improved fire-fighting appliances. However, when all efforts at fire prevention and fire-fighting failed to avert material disaster, a third development offered some relief. In the early eighteenth century, the state took the initiative of launching the first fire insurance companies as a means of alleviating at least the financial loss of real and personal property.

The German territories, after the seventeenth century, were more advanced than most European countries in developing fire-fighting techniques and fire-fighting appliances, and in organizing fire-protection administration. Because of the inadequacy of fire-fighting technology in the sixteenth and seventeenth centuries, the major legislative emphasis was on fire prevention. Although cities like Hamburg, Nuremberg, and Amsterdam made major contributions during the seventeenth century in invention of fire-fighting appliances, such as the fire pump and leather delivery hose, the electorate of Brandenburg proved to be the most progressive of the German territorial states in developing means of combating the hazards and ravages of fire.

Fire Prevention[1]

As early as 1515, a police ordinance for the cities of Brandenburg or-

1. See Reinhold A. Dorwart, "German Fire Protection 300 Years Ago," *Quarterly of*

dered certain fire precautions to be taken by town residents.[2] These precautions were repeated in greater detail in 1540 by Margrave John for his territory of the Neumark.[3] The emphasis was on fire prevention. As late as 1650 most houses were covered with straw or wood shingles and equipped with wood or clay chimneys. Town councils were made responsible for quarterly inspections of houses and shops, checking the safety conditions of fireplaces, chimneys, firewalls, and hearths. Council approval was needed for ovens in breweries, bakeries, and kitchens. The use of covered lanterns, rather than torches, was required for night entry into stables of public inns. No new house construction or reroofing was to be permitted unless tile roofs were installed.

The danger of fire caused by careless individuals or by criminal arsonists in village, field, and forest was to be guarded against by forbidding peasants, shepherds, and herders to carry fire for their convenience into pasture or forest.[4] A series of edicts against arsonists between 1570 and 1616 made it clear that those who lived by violence and extortion at the expense of helpless peasants and unprotected tavernkeepers did not hesitate to use arson as blackmail.[5] Wandering rogues, gypsies, escaped serfs often maliciously started fires in villages.

After the devastation of the Thirty Years' War, Frederick William, who was intent upon rebuilding and restoring his lands, turned to developing improved fire protection. He repeated the earlier warnings against careless handling of fires in homes, barns, inns, and forests in a fire edict of 1660.[6] In 1661 he ordered the removal of all straw and hay roofs within his towns and their replacement by tile.[7]

By 1672 a more determined and more comprehensive effort to advance fire protection through electoral decree was made for Berlin and Cölln. A fire ordinance of 15 July 1672 set the pattern for the next sixty years of legislative effort to protect Berlin and Brandenburg from the danger of fire.[8] The first part of this ordinance dealt with the "Removal of That Which Represents a Fire Hazard and Causes Damaging Fires." The removal of fire hazards to some extent involved improved building codes as well as a certain amount of city planning. Constant threat of punishment or fine for nonobservance revealed a passive resistance among the elector's subjects because of the expense involved in taking the necessary

the National Fire Protection Association, vol. 51, no. 3 (Jan. 1958), pp. 195-205. Illustrated with examples of early fire-fighting equipment.

2. *C. C. March.,* vol. 6, pt. 2, app. 1, col. 6.

3. Ibid., vol. 5, pt. 1, sec. 1, no. 1, cols. 9-11.

4. Ibid., no. 2, col. 24, police ordinance of 1550.

5. Ibid., vol. 5, pt. 5, sec. 1, no. 9, cols. 19-22, mandate against arsonists of 1570.

6. Ibid., vol. 5, pt. 1, sec. 2, no. 1, cols. 139-142, fire edict of 23 May 1660.

7. "Patent That Fire Appliances Be Available and That Straw and Hay Roofs Be Eliminated," ibid., no. 2, cols. 141-144.

8. "A Fire Ordinance Approved by the Great Elector for Berlin and Cölln," ibid., no. 3, cols. 143-156.

corrective action. Fireplaces, ovens, and chimneys were to be built of stone or tile, with masonry firewalls separating them from wood structure. Quarterly sweeping of chimneys was required. All storage sheds used to hold unthreshed grain or surplus hay were to be removed from within the city walls. Protective measures were aimed at certain craftsmen who by the nature of their work or materials presented a potential fire hazard. Hoopers, cabinetmakers, latheturners, wheelwrights, and others who produced wood shavings and chips were ordered to remove and safely dispose of such chips daily. Shoemakers were instructed to remove their tanning vats outside the city along the river. Ropemakers, torchmakers, butchers, and soapboilers were subjected to similar preventive measures.

A ban was placed on tobacco smoking and the use of open torches of pitch in city stables or haylofts, as well as on the open streets at night. Covered lanterns were to replace the torches.

After 1660, the rural areas of Brandenburg did not get serious attention until a fire ordinance of 1701.[9] Referring to the fact that frequently whole villages were reduced to ashes, and sometimes were not rebuilt for years, the ordinance sought to eliminate fire hazards in villages. Cottages were required to have chimneys, usually omitted in rural construction. Bakeovens were to be built outside the cottages and not used for drying flax. Ovens for drying flax, the village forge, and drying kilns for hops were to be located a safe distance from village houses.

The first major revision of the ordinance of 1672 was issued in 1707.[10] Chimneys, ovens, kilns were to be built of brick, two bricks deep and wide enough for quarterly sweeping. Wood raingutters were to be replaced by tin or by stone drains. Safe storage of combustible materials (wood chips, grease, gunpowder, empty barrels) was required. A clue to public response to the preventive measures is found in an order that the Berlin military commandant was to assign necessary noncommissioned officers to protect the fire inspectors.[11] As late as 1723 Frederick William I exasperatedly complained that there had been no lack of fire-prevention regulations but too much failure to observe them, so that serious fires still occurred.[12]

9. "Fire Ordinance for the Rural Areas in the Mark Brandenburg, 26 Jan. 1701," ibid., no. 7, cols. 169-172.

10. "A Revised Fire Ordinance for the Royal Capital Cities and Suburbs, 3 May 1707," ibid., no. 13, cols. 191-214.

11. Inspection and enforcement of the fire ordinances were the keys to the success of fire protection but both were frequently lacking. In 1686 Frederick William complained that the regular inspection of all places where fires were used in Berlin was not occurring and ordered the city council to resume such inspections ("Circular Rescript to the Magistrates Concerning Inspections of City Fire Installations, 3 Nov. 1686," ibid., no. 5, cols. 167-168). In an ordinance of 7 April 1691 the burgomasters and city councillors of the capital cities were given four weeks to get rid of straw and shingle roofs in the city and to see that they were replaced by tile (ibid., no. 6, cols. 167-170).

12. "Edict of Failure to Observe Adequately All Previous Fire-Prevention Ordinances in Town and Country, 12 June 1723," ibid., no. 38, cols. 263-266.

In the thirty years after 1707 no further significant progress was made in fire protection. Perhaps little more could be done at the time other than strict enforcement of existing regulations, particularly those in building codes which might affect new construction in the expanding cities. In 1708 and in 1709 Frederick I made an effort to reduce the danger of general conflagration by ordering the building of firewalls at frequent intervals between city residences.[13] Firewalls were to pass completely through a city block from street to street, two feet above the height of roofs. Because the cost of such building modification was to be borne by affected householders, civic resistance to this progressive safety requirement led to its suspension in 1710.[14] A general fire ordinance of 1718 extended to all the cities of Brandenburg the general fire-prevention provisions ordered for Berlin in 1707.[15] A fire ordinance for Greater Berlin of 31 March 1727 could do no better than concern itself with the elimination of some forty different types of fire hazards, all familiar from previous legislation.[16]

Fire Fighting

If, despite all precautions, fire were to break out in a town, the next phase obviously was that of extinction or fire-fighting. Between 1515 and 1740 there was a tremendous improvement in the appliances and techniques of fighting fires and in the administrative machinery to organize public capacity to fight fire.

The police ordinances of the sixteenth century make it clear that fire-fighting appliances were rather primitive. The arsenal consisted of fire hooks, ladders, and leather buckets. A brass squirtgun to apply water directly to the fire was a "major" weapon.[17] Water barrels on sled runners

13. "Edict That Firewalls Should Be Raised at Fixed Distances, 3 Sept. 1708," ibid., no. 18, cols. 225-228; "Patent on Rearing of Firewalls, 20 Aug. 1709," ibid., no. 21, cols. 229-230.

14. "Notification That the Requirement to Build Firewalls Be Suspended, 26 June 1710," ibid., no. 24, cols. 235-236.

15. Ibid., no. 28, cols. 241-246. The new king's first edict concerning fire prevention had appeared 14 Jan. 1716 (ibid., no. 27, cols. 237-240). It listed the familiar fire hazards, ordered inspection of all chimneys, required having on hand proper fire-fighting equipment and digging an ample number of wells.

16. Ibid., no. 42, cols. 267-310. This ordinance was drafted by the Electoral War and Domain Chamber and approved by the king on 2 April 1727.

17. The most common water-throwing device in the seventeenth century was the syringe or handsquirt (*Handspritze*). A brass tube usually, though sometimes made of wood, one and one-half inches in diameter, about two and one-half feet long, it held from two to four quarts of water which was expelled by a plunger through a nozzle of one-half inch bore. It was filled from tubs of water placed near the scene of the fire (see Thomas Ewbank, *A Descriptive and Historical Account of Hydraulic and Other Machines for Raising Water*, p. 315). See Ewbank for reproduction of a squirtgun taken from Georg Agricola, *De Re Metallica* (Basel, 1556), p. 308, or the translation by Herbert C. Hoover and Lou H. Hoover (New York, 1950), p. 377. The closest modern analogy to the syringe is the stirrup pump made famous during World War II.

drawn to the scene of a fire were used to fill buckets and fire squirts. All householders and business establishments were expected to possess ladders, hooks, buckets, and squirts, while the city council maintained the water vats.

However limited the technology of fire fighting was in the sixteenth century, the destruction of the Thirty Years' War reduced available equipment to spades, axes, and some surviving squirts.[18] Linking the severe losses from fire during the war years (1655-1660) to the lack of fire-fighting equipment, Frederick William in 1660 ordered city authorities in Brandenburg to acquire useful appliances, which meant those used in the sixteenth century.

However, in 1672 the basic fire ordinance of that year took the first progressive steps in improving fire-fighting technology and in organizing a community for fighting fires.[19] Prior to the time when professional fire-fighting brigades stood ready with their equipment to respond to fire alarms, it was necessary to make use of personnel in a community who ordinarily had other occupations. Under the Great Elector the whole community of a city could be mobilized with specifically assigned functions. In cities favored with garrisons, the soldiers played a major role in fighting fires, protecting property, and policing the streets.

Fire watch and alarm were the first prescription. Civilian night watches and military patrols were used in Berlin and Cölln to watch for fires. The musicians' guilds were required to furnish fire lookouts in the city towers day and night. Horns and drums were used to raise a fire alarm if fire or smoke were detected.

Available fire-fighting equipment was stored in ladderhouses of the city guard corps and in the two city halls of Berlin and Cölln. Parallel legislation to keep the streets clear of debris and to increase the number of public wells made it possible to move water barrels on sleds from the wells to the scene of the fire. Every city guild was required to furnish ten leather buckets with "bucketeers." The city authorities and the neighboring householders were to supply the handsquirts.

The occupational structure of Berlin society was exploited by assigning certain functions to pertinent guilds. Coopers and tubmakers maintained the water tubs for use with the fire squirts. Carters and teamsters hauled the city-owned ladder wagons and water pumps, while other citizens who owned horses reported to the public wells to drag the water sleds to the fire.[20] The large, horse-drawn water pumps were operated by the braziers,

18. *C. C. March.,* vol. 5, pt. 1, sec. 2, no. 1, cols. 139-142, fire edict of 23 May 1660.

19. "A Fire Ordinance Approved by the Great Elector for Berlin and Cölln," ibid., no. 3, cols. 143-156.

20. Just when the earliest pump engine for fire-fighting was used is difficult to say, but probably in the early seventeenth century. Suction and piston pumps were used in the sixteenth century for lifting water and the principle was applied in the seventeenth century to fire extinction. See Abraham Wolf, *A History of Science, Technology, and Philosophy in the 16th and 17th Centuries,* 2d ed. (London, 1950), pp. 512-521, 524-536, 541-542. One

who could service the brass parts if necessary. Carpenters and masons reported with fire axes and hooks prepared to rip down houses to stop the spread of fire. Brewers were to come, each with a fire squirt. All other guilds were to send apprentices with the required leather buckets to keep the fire pumps filled with water from the barrels.

The actual fighting of the fire resulted from directing a flow of water on the fire from the many small hand squirtguns, the manually operated fire pumps, and bucket brigades. Water barrels had to be kept filled to furnish water for the squirts and pumps. Ladders and fire hooks were used to scale houses, get up on roofs, or tear down walls.

This orderly mobilization of a whole community with the fullest exploitation of the best equipment of the age probably equalled the best fire-fighting technique in any European city of the time. Six years earlier London had nothing comparable with which to fight the Great Fire of 1666. In England fire-fighting brigades came into being after the establishment of private fire insurance companies who wished to reduce their financial risks. In Brandenburg private and public professional fire-fighters came much later. Fire-fighting was accomplished by volunteer personnel, manning equipment publicly or privately owned, mobilized and directed by public officials.

The Berlin fire ordinance of 1707 made the first major revision of the ordinance of 1672.[21] It placed particular emphasis on possession or availability of equipment. Each householder was to have on hand at least two leather buckets, a squirtgun, and a ladder. Thirty-seven guilds were made responsible for stocking an assigned number of leather buckets at the guild halls of the five cities.[22] The two city halls were to maintain hook and ladder wagons, carrying an additional supply of handsquirts.

At the beginning of the eighteenth century, the major weapon on which the success of fire extinction depended (and for which the elaborate preparation of buckets and of bucket brigade was designed) was the large metal fire pump, manned by pumping teams from the braziers guild. Each city and suburb had a number of these pumps available: four in Berlin, three in Cölln, two in Friedrichswerder, and one in Dorotheenstadt. Ten

---

of the earliest pump engines of modern times was described in Germany at Nuremberg in 1656 as forcing a stream of water one inch in diameter eighty feet high. Forty feet was perhaps the average height reached in the seventeenth century. At first one lever and one piston were used, then followed the use of two pumps, alternating pistons, two levers manually operated with a resultant constant stream of water. The two pumps were placed in a cistern or tank which was moved on sleds or wheels. Piping at first was made of rigid copper which was replaced successively by flexible leather, then canvas hose. The water tank was kept filled by the bucket lines. While there were technical improvements, particularly in the first decades of the eighteenth century, this manually operated water pump remained standard for over a century until the steam engine was added. See Ewbank, *Hydraulic and Other Machines*, pp. 315-338, passim.

21. "A Revised Fire Ordinance for the Royal Capital Cities and Suburbs, 3 May 1707," *C. C. March.*, vol. 5, pt. 1, sec. 2, no. 13, cols. 191-214.

22. Berlin, Cölln, Friedrichswerder, Dorotheenstadt, and Friedrichsstadt.

22. *Fire-fighting in the Seventeenth Century*

23. *Night Watch*

large fire pumps for a population of approximately 60,000 in 1707 was a remarkable achievement.[23] Nicolai reported that the first fire station in Berlin *(Spritzenhaus)* to hold these fire pumps was built in 1706.

Even more remarkable was the addition of fireboats in this year, on the canals and river running through Berlin.[24] Since many buildings along the canals and sluices were not easily accessible for fire fighting, the *Hausvogt* (commandant of the Berlin prison) was made responsible for keeping ready two flat-bottomed boats equipped with large fire pumps. This was a singular innovation and addition to the fire-fighting capabilities of Greater Berlin.

The civilian governor of Berlin, supported by the military commandant, was made responsible for the public fire-fighting equipment, for service and inspection of all facilities including wells.

After 1707 fire-fighting equipment and techniques made no further progress in the next quarter of a century. In 1727 the metropolitan city of Berlin was divided into nineteen precincts.[25] Each precinct had two fire wardens to take charge of all fire-fighting, salvage, and rescue work. This marked the beginning of a professional, expert force. Fire and water commissioners, under the fire warden, supervised fire-fighting on the scene and assured a steady flow of water from the wells, canals, and river to the fire pumps. The captains of pumping crews attached to each pump or fireboat were called fire chiefs. In the first half of the eighteenth century, organization and technology had made considerable progress in effective fire-fighting. Fire pumps could pour a stream of water at an approximate rate of 50 to 100 gallons per minute. Supplemented by squirtguns, bucket brigades, hook and ladder units, these pumps probably gave Berlin one of the most efficient fire-fighting organizations among European cities of the eighteenth century.

Fire Insurance[26]

If the two defensive weapons of fire prevention and fire-fighting failed, the damage and fire loss could be disastrous, as the Great Fire of London had demonstrated. Accordingly, throughout Europe and in Brandenburg

---

23. London in 1667 (after the Great Fire) with a population of about 400,000 was required to have twelve engines, and in 1863 with more than 1,000,000 residents, it had only forty hand-engines (Frederick H. Haines, *Chapters of Insurance History* [London, 1926], pp. 44, 162).

24. The first floating fire engine in London appeared probably about 1760, the second in 1767 (Francis B. Relton, *An Account of the Fire Insurance Companies, Associations, Institutions, Projects, Established and Projected in Great Britain and Ireland During the 17th and 18th Centuries* [London, 1893], p. 437).

25. *C. C. March.*, vol. 5, pt. 1, sec. 2, no. 42, cols. 267-310.

26. See Reinhold A. Dorwart, "The Earliest Fire Insurance Company in Berlin and Brandenburg, 1705-1711," *The Business History Review*, vol. 32, no. 2 (1958), pp. 192-203.

as well, a third defensive weapon was introduced, the concept of risk coverage.

The idea of property insurance against loss to protect the large investments in the expanding cities of the second half of the seventeenth century was borrowed from marine experience. A rather complete form of marine insurance had evolved after the fifteenth century from the practices known as bottomry and respondentia.[27] From this precedent apparently there emerged, in the course of the seventeenth century, the idea of insurance against the risks of fire.

The earliest emergence of the idea of fire insurance companies occurred in England and in the German territories.[28] The neighboring, maritime countries of France, the Austrian and United Netherlands, and the Scandinavian states followed slowly only after the middle of the eighteenth century. Probably the oldest fire insurance company in the world is the Hamburger Feuerkasse incorporated in 1676 in the Imperial City of Hamburg.[29]

The only Northern European state which made contemporaneous progress in the early development of fire insurance companies was the electorate of Brandenburg. In 1705 Frederick I set up a fire insurance project sponsored by and managed by the state.[30] A regulation of 15 October 1705 established a Fire Insurance Office in Berlin, for the purpose of handling fire insurance funds.[31] This was an administrative bureau of the

27. For a discussion of the origins of marine insurance, see Florence de Roover, "Early Examples of Marine Insurance," *Journal of Economic History* 5 (1945): 172-200. Bottomry refers to a loan against the ship as pledge, respondentia a loan against the goods shipped.

28. Fire insurance probably existed in Germany before it did in England. *Feuerkassen* (fire indemnity funds) and *Brandgilden* (fire guilds) were known in individual German towns in the early seventeenth century. See Relton, *Account of Fire Insurance Companies,* p. 7. For a brief summary of the origin of fire insurance concerns in Great Britain, see Alwin E. Bulau, *Footprints of Assurance,* pp. 125-145. Presumably, a proper claim to the distinction of being the first fire insurance company in England might be made by Barbon's Fire Office formed in 1680 and incorporated in 1688. See also D. E. W. Gibb, *Lloyds of London: A Study in Individualism* (New York, 1957).

29. Bulau, *Footprints,* p. 245. The first fire insurance company in France was chartered in 1754, although a Bureau des Incendies was established in 1717 to aid fire victims with funds contributed by public charity. "All in all, fire insurance in eighteenth-century France was in an embryonic state"; see Shelby T. McCloy, "Fire Relief and Prevention," in *Government Assistance in Eighteenth-Century France.* On France see also Bulau, *Footprints,* pp. 235-236.

30. Certain marked distinctions between the early development of fire insurance companies in England and Brandenburg may be noted. Basic was the distinction between the private undertaking and enterprise that marked the English concerns and the form of state socialism found in the first Brandenburg companies. One advantage accruing to the peoples of Brandenburg from this distinction was that fire-fighting was not left to individual enterprise and competition as advertising build-up. The state likewise sponsored and regulated the acquisition of the latest and best fire-fighting machines, their proper maintenance and manning in case of fire, and offered the advantage of this protective apparatus to all citizens equally. It will also be noted that subscription to the English concerns was voluntary and that membership in the Brandenburg company became compulsory for all houseowners, a factor, it will be discovered, in its undoing.

31. *C. C. March.,* vol. 5, pt. 1, sec. 2, no. 9, cols. 173-176.

state which was in the insurance business and had a state monopoly on that business. It was neither a chartered, private fire insurance company nor a regulative office of insurance companies. The Fire Office of 1705 is interesting historically because it emerged immediately with many features regarded as standard in modern insurance practice.

Brandenburg householders, in town and country, were to register the declared value of their houses and other buildings with the Fire Office. Buildings were to be appraised before registration, unless cost value was established by documents. Insurance rates were set on a sliding scale, decreasing after the first year. To assure greater care on the part of the owner for fire prevention, a one-third deductible clause was introduced.[32] That is, an owner could assume one-third of the risk himself by declaring only two-thirds of appraised value.

Upon certification by the local magistrate to the Fire Office of loss by fire, the owner was to receive payment within eight weeks of the whole or partial declared value, according to appraised damage. Prior to receiving payment, the injured owner had to give assurance that the insurance money would be used for rebuilding.

A novel feature of the regulation of 1705 provided that a proprietor who insured his house might also insure household furnishings and personal property, including livestock. This proffered protection of personal property was withdrawn in 1711, not to appear again until 1812.

Presumably because of a reluctant response by proprietors, a significant modification of the basic regulation was made on 1 June 1706.[33] Fire insurance for buildings was made compulsory for all proprietors in Brandenburg. A low, standard insurance rate of 3 *Groschen* per 100 *Reichsthaler* or about $1.25 per $1,000.00 of declared value was set. Proprietors were required to declare value at a minimum of one-third of the appraised value. The one-third deductible option was retained.

There was considerable resistance to this compulsory fire insurance, particularly from the rural nobility. Because of this resistance, by a mandate of March 1708 the king granted exemption from premium contributions to the serfs and peasants resident in villages of baronial estates.[34] The nobleman, however, would be required to assume responsibility for replacing peasant losses from fire.

32. It is interesting to note the presence of a two-thirds loss clause and a three-quarters value clause in fire insurance in America today.

33. "General Fire Insurance Regulation," *C. C. March.,* vol. 5, pt. 1, sec. 2, no. 10, cols. 175-182.

34. "Mandate Concerning the Royal Prussian General Rural and Urban Fire Insurance Office, 21 March 1708," ibid., no. 14, cols. 213-216. While the Hohenzollern rulers did feel a deep paternal responsibility for the welfare of their subjects, the principal motive behind the fire insurance project was to assure speedy reconstruction of houses and buildings in cities, towns, and villages throughout Brandenburg. Relief from taxes and grants of aid from the state were insufficient to assure immediate reconstruction. Reconstruction was necessary if Brandenburg-Prussia was to continue her economic growth and expansion. So the

In 1708 two tragic occurrences curtailed the Prussian state's venture into fire insurance. In the summer of 1708 the city of Krossen on the Oder River was almost completely burned out. A royal directive of 2 August 1708 ordered the Fire Office treasury to pay 70,000 *Reichsthaler* to the burned-out residents of the city, thereby theoretically justifying the wisdom of instituting fire insurance.[35]

Unfortunately, the fire indemnity payment was not available. Due to peculation the treasury was empty.[36] This scandalous situation resulted in a loss of confidence in the Fire Office and weakened the effort to provide fire insurance on a practical basis. Because of continued and open resistance, the king finally abolished the Fire Insurance Office on 17 January 1711.[37]

The failure of the first Fire Office in Brandenburg was merely the failure of an institution, not of an idea. This first venture served as a prelude to the permanent development of fire insurance companies under Frederick William I.

Acting in response to numerous requests for a mutual indemnity society, Frederick William in 1718 approved the institution of the Städtische Feuersozietät von Berlin, the City Mutual Fire Society of Berlin, composed of Berlin houseowners.[38] It was not a fire insurance company, but a mutual fire indemnity society requiring no premium payments. A member fire victim would be indemnified by member contributions. The listed appraised valuation of member houses determined the share paid by each. This was again a compulsory venture. But this time it met with success because it applied only to city property owners, who had indeed requested such protection.

In the next five years the example of the City Mutual Fire Society of Berlin was followed by three other similar societies in the province of Brandenburg, in the city of Stettin, and in the province of East Prussia.[39] These public fire insurance societies or companies were successful and per-

---

state went into the fire insurance business to spread the risk and to make reconstruction capital available in the event of catastrophe.

35. *C. C. March.,* vol. 5, pt. 1, sec. 2, no. 16, cols. 217-224.

36. Brandenburg-Prussia in 1708 was in a serious financial predicament because of the mismanagement and embezzlement of various treasury funds by two scheming court favorites who syphoned out of all special treasuries into the household treasury whatever funds were available, without concern for the future. The Fire Insurance treasury was completely devoid of funds in 1708 in spite of the royal promise of 1705 that the insurance premiums would not be used for any other purpose. This embarrassing situation served to discredit the king's effort to establish a fire insurance program for his territory. See Hans Prutz, *Preussische Geschichte* (Stuttgart, 1900), 2:335-336.

37. *C. C. March.,* vol. 5, pt. 1, sec. 2, no. 25, cols. 235-238.

38. "Regulation Concerning the Operation of a General Society in the Capital Cities for Protection Against Fire Damage," ibid., no. 30, cols. 249-254, a regulation of 29 Dec. 1718.

39. *Feuersozietät der Provinz Brandenburg* (1719), *Stettiner Öffentliche Feuerversicherungsanstalt* (1722), and *Feuersozietät für die Provinz Ostpreussen* (1723).

manent and were the forerunners of a continuous development of public, mutual, and joint-stock companies, insuring both real and personal property in the following three centuries.[40]

---

40. See Bulau, *Footprints*, pp. 245-247, for interesting illustrations of the fire marks used by these Brandenburg-Prussian fire offices.

21

Police Protection

The earliest definition of *Polizei* was the maintenance of good order, the preservation of peace and public security. This function, basic to the origin of state and government in whatever form, was primarily concerned with preventing crime. Good order and public security essentially included protection of life and property. Violence in any form and destruction or loss of property were to be prevented, deterred, or punished by the police of the state. Travel and commerce on highways and rivers required protection against robbers and other violent persons. Beggars and thieves, gypsies, vagabonds, and riotous persons made life and property in towns and cities insecure. This police function is so fundamental to the existence of a polity that when it fails, the political community faces dissolution and anarchy.

In the historical period of this study from the later Middle Ages to the eighteenth century, the basic emphasis on this aspect of police power was constantly present in all police ordinances. During this period the police power legally inherent in the governing forces expanded to concern itself with personal morality, economic and social regulation, consumer protection, education, city building, sanitation and public health, care of the poor, and other aspects of personal, community, and public life. By the beginning of the eighteenth century a distinction began to emerge between promotion of individual and general welfare as a function of the state and the strictly police function of protection of life and property. Maintaining peace and order, upholding the law, preventing violence and destruction would become the narrow original police function symbolized by a uniformed police force during the nineteenth century. Promotion of individual and general welfare would become a function of the regulative power of the state inherent in the broadest legal sanction of the police power of the state. The distinction may be expressed in simplified terms as between the criminal jurisdiction of the state and its civil jurisdiction in promoting the good life.

As early as the fifteenth century the new Hohenzollern electors of Brandenburg were concerned with providing highway security and ending lawlessness so that commerce and trade could flourish. The Imperial Diets between 1495 and 1548 sought to establish peace and order in the German territories. The social unrest, peasant uprisings, soldiers free from the wars of the emperor, all combined to create conditions of disorder and lawlessness. The very first imperial police ordinances placed legislative priority on achievement of internal peace, justice, security, and good order. Any effective achievement of public security in Germany would, however, be the work of territorial princes, feudal and manorial landlords, and city governments.

Rural security until the eighteenth century was most ineffective. Peasants were victimized by unemployed mercenary soldiers, threatened by bands of gypsies, and were even helpless before the violence of noble landowners. At the historic Brandenburg *Landtag* of 1549, the town delegates requested the elector to enforce the imperial *Landfriede* (public peace), proclaimed at the Diet of Augsburg of 1548, particularly regarding safety on the highways, by permitting the towns to pursue and arrest disturbers of the peace and highwaymen. Travelers and merchants were not safe on the highways, and the *Landsknechte* annoyed the poor people in the villages.[1] The Elector did order the *Landfriede* of 1548 to be enforced in the Mark and ordered all law enforcement officials to protect the highways so that all persons could pass in safety.[2] Grievances submitted to the elector by the Brandenburg towns in 1555 complained about wandering gypsies who harmed the poor people of the villages.[3]

A major development of some importance was the electoral directive of 1540 that night watches were to be established in all towns.[4] During the first half of the seventeenth century, night watches fell into abeyance and had to be restored by the Great Elector. Night watches were concerned as much with fire precaution as with thievery and mugging, and they were the crude beginnings of regular city police forces. Town councils were made responsible for suppressing, apprehending, and punishing all evildoers within the town, except that an apprehended nobleman guilty of murder was to be remanded to the prince for trial.[5] Edicts of 1565, 1567, 1572, and 1573 made it clear that the police ordinance of 1540 was not effectively enforced and that public security on the highways and in the villages was constantly endangered.[6] Much of this, of course, had to do with vagabonds and footloose wayfarers. Various local officials, nobles, prelates, bailiffs, town magistrates, and village elders were enjoined to preserve the peace, but were either incapable of doing so or not interested. Frequently law enforcement failed because the lawbreakers were harbored by the local people. Peasants were often as not intimidated as well as abused. The greatest menace to peace came from ex-soldiers who had possession of muskets.

During the Thirty Years' War practically all law enforcement failed. Enemy soldiers and "friendly" soldiers lived off the land, and neither life nor property in town or village was secure. After the war Frederick William struck out against marauding soldiers, gypsies, and wandering vaga-

---

1. Friedensburg, *Kurm. Ständ. Joach.,* vol. 1, no. 155, p. 434.
2. Ibid., no. 165, p. 487.
3. Ibid., vol. 2, no. 327, p. 71.
4. *C. C. March.,* vol. 5, pt. 1, sec. 1, no. 1, col. 12.
5. Ibid., col. 16.
6. Ibid., vol. 5, pt. 5, sec. 1, nos. 1, 2, 3, 4, cols. 1-12.

bonds. Mounted gendarmes patrolled the highways, night watches were restored in towns, and some progress was made in maintaining law and order. City militia and the growing standing army quartered in cities offered greater protection than had existed previously.

Two new factors after 1650 created urban police problems. The growing number of apprentices and journeymen responding to the growth of manufacturing and the growing number of students responding to expansion of *Gymnasien* and universities introduced in some towns and cities an element prone to riotous behavior. The tendency to carry dirks and daggers among pages, lackeys, students, apprentices, and journeymen posed an obvious threat to urban peace. An edict of 1704 forbade this practice.[7] In 1708 students at the Berlin *Gymnasien* and city apprentices were ordered to cease wearing dirks.[8] Nevertheless, in June 1709 the king complained that everybody was carrying dirks in spite of previous bans, with the result that many stabbings, murders, and robberies occurred. The governor of Berlin was ordered to punish all violators.[9] In the city of Halle, university students frequently had to be pacified by the soldiers of the local regiments.

During the first four decades of the eighteenth century, considerable progress was made in developing a rural gendarmerie[10] and an urban police force backed by local military forces. Agents of the central government, particularly the rural *Landräte* (district commissaries) and urban tax commissaries representing the General War Commissariat, supervised the police function of local officials. In Berlin, *Gassenmeister* (street police) enforced the law in the streets, market inspectors in the marketplaces. The city was divided into two police districts with a police superintendent in charge of all police activity in each district.[11] The city police force was subordinate to the united city council (after 1709), but here as in other cities of Brandenburg-Prussia the local garrisons were available to assist the city police when necessary.[12] In rural areas, cavalry squadrons assisted the rural gendarmes in ferreting out robber bands or in driving gypsies and foreign beggar rabble out of the country.

Enforcement

Through a myriad of police edicts to achieve the public good, one vex-

7. Ibid., vol. 5, pt. 1, sec. 1, no. 11, cols. 93-94.

8. Ibid., no. 14, cols. 95-96.

9. Ibid., no. 16, cols. 97-98.

10. "General Instruction Concerning Various Police Matters According to Which the Rural Gendarmes (*Ausreuter*) of the General War Commissariat Should Be Guided, 15 Sept. 1713," ibid., no. 17, cols. 97-102; "Instruction for *Ausreuter* in the Neumark and Sternberg, 30 Sept. 1733," ibid., no.·24, cols. 111-120.

11. "Instruction for Superintendents of Police in Berlin, 23 May 1735," ibid., no. 27, cols. 121-130.

12. Patent of 16 July 1735, ibid., no. 29, col. 134.

ing problem persisted in Brandenburg-Prussia for over two centuries. This was the frustrating problem of enforcement. The efforts of paternalistic rulers to promote individual and general welfare by edict did not always meet with success. One reason for failure was ineffective enforcement. For those who find this explanation inadequate—and it is—the author invites reflection upon the failure of law enforcement in the mid-twentieth century. There are enormous analogies between the problems of the welfare state in the early modern period and the problems of our own century and society. Ineffective enforcement is a product of many factors. Inadequate police forces, corruption of police officials, hostile public opinion, greed and profit motives, rejection by individuals of governmental compulsion, reluctance to accept the goals and purposes to be achieved in the name of welfare, all these are factors. In some areas, of course, there is the psychological problem of the criminal instinct. This, perhaps, is less germane to the general nature of the welfare state. Why do people evade or violate police regulations intended to promote the general good? Sumptuary legislation invades private life most intimately. Restraint of natural human instincts, on moral or public grounds, is not readily accepted by the individual. Consumer protection in the marketplace, protection against quack or untested medical remedies must contend with instincts of greed and profit and gullibility. Prevention of air and water pollution, acceptance of sanitation requirements, elimination of fire hazards and littering of streets are dependent upon genuine individual concern for the welfare of others. Respect for minority groups in a society, concern for the poor and the unfortunates of society are a reflection of community and individual values of tolerance, compassion, and perhaps self-negation. All in all it is in the very nature of the legislation of a welfare state to regulate, to compel, to intervene in the private life of the citizen to achieve a greater good. The citizen does not always accept the goal of the greater good if he as an individual must pay the price.

In the lands of the Hohenzollern between 1500 and 1700 the machinery for enforcement, police and bureaucratic, was quite inadequate. The prince issued edicts. Local village, town, and city officials were expected to enforce the edicts. There was no professional police force. Rural officials were subject to influence by local gentry, or they connived for personal profit with lawbreakers. The use of cavalry squadrons in rural areas and of local garrisons in cities to support local police officials reveals the limited capability of the police. There was a great variety of policing required by law: medical, market, and sanitation police, fire wardens, customs inspectors, all had special functions. By the beginning of the eighteenth century, however, a growing bureaucratic machinery, centrally appointed and controlled, began to achieve stricter enforcement. Rural gendarmes subordinated to the *Landräte* and *Steuerräte,* who in turn were agents of the General War Commissariat, were appointed by the king in increasing numbers. Their specific assignments were to enforce the multitude of police edicts. But not even Frederick William I, with his symbolic cudgel, could win complete enforcement. By 1735 the second king of Prussia had made considerable progress in establishing a rural and urban police force and a bureaucratic machinery, which together would be molded into a tradition of Prussian efficiency, obedience, and service to the state. But the basic problem, an old one and a current one, remained: resistance to administrative regulation and compulsion by those who are regulated and compelled.

22

Conclusion

In the previous pages I have described many facets of public life in the Hohenzollern territories of Brandenburg-Prussia. Paramount in the development of these various phases of public life was the role of the Hohenzollern princes. By their regulative legislative acts, these princes intervened in the daily life and in the private and public activities of their subjects. This intervention was determined and made necessary by the exigencies of historical change, by the challenges of the new secularism, and by an embryonic modernism. Guided by the prototype of the later medieval cities, the new, secularized territorial state assumed ever-expanding functions not previously fulfilled by the patrimonial feudal prince.

Although individual regulative acts were an ad hoc response to particular problems, crises, and individual needs in private and public life, the legislation of the Hohenzollern princes was guided by fundamental principles and by a particular concept of the function of state and of prince. Heirs of a Christian-feudal heritage of office, the princes declared that they acted out of "väterliche Sorge" (paternal concern) for the welfare of their subjects. At no time in these two centuries was this expressed better than by the declaration, in 1640, of the Estates of the Duchy of East Prussia that the supreme law of the prince was the "salus populi."

Expressed in various terms, the ideas of the "general welfare" or the welfare of the people are as old as the origin of the first polities sanctioned by law. In the immediate post-medieval period, the term *Polizei* was adopted in the German legal terminology to designate various areas of princely concern which transcended the basic functions of law and order. The police power of the state, expressed tangibly through various legislative forms, increasingly came to be used to promote the general good and individual welfare. Thus was born what would later receive from historians the rubric *Polizeistaat*.

I have defined *Polizeistaat* as "welfare state" because the contemporary regulative legislation and the contemporary political philosophers equated *Polizei* with *Wohlfahrt*. *Wohlfahrt* and *Polizei* before 1800 certainly incorporated, by definition and in practice, more inclusive areas of public life than does the twentieth-century effort to limit "The Welfare State" to a function of social welfare services. Only Pauline Gregg, of recent writers, appears to define the present version of welfare state more inclusively: "The Welfare State I take to be the whole of the present socio-political-economic organization, and not merely the welfare services provided by the State." She also recognized that only the name is twentieth-century and that "the conception of the Welfare State occurred some four hundred years ago with the break-up of the social institutions of the Middle Ages."[1]

I have rejected the scholarly arrogation of the historical template of "Welfare State" exclusively to the twentieth-century social service state. The concept of the welfare state has been an integral and inseparable aspect of the modern state. It has passed through three stages or phases reflecting the changing nature of the evolving western polities. It would be a historical oversimplification to suggest that the political evolution of the western states and the development of the welfare state have moved forward *pari passu*.

Fundamental to the idea of the welfare state has been the principle and exercise of administrative and legislative regulation and intervention by the political arm of the polity. The nineteenth-century *Zeitgeist* of laissez-faire and political liberalism separated the regulative state of an aristocratic-mercantilist world from that of a democratic-industrial society. Nevertheless, the purpose of state intervention in public life and the regulation of the activities and behavior of the individual consistently has been defined as the promotion of the welfare, security, prosperity, and rights of the individual, as well as the advancement of that abstract being, the common good, *das gemeine Wesen*.

What gives distinction to each stage and contributes to the historical evolution of the idea of welfare state is what each stage incorporates under its definition of "welfare" and under its legislative regulation.

Against the definition of the welfare state argued in the Introduction, I have, in the six parts of this study, examined in practice the application of this theory to many phases of public life by the Hohenzollern rulers of Brandenburg-Prussia.

1. Pauline Gregg, *The Welfare State, An Economic and Social History of Great Britain from 1945 to the Present Day* (Amherst: The University of Massachusetts Press, 1969), Preface, p. 4.

Bibliography

Index

Bibliography

Primary Sources

Acta Borussica: Die Behördenorganisation und die allgemeine Staatsverwaltung Preussen im 18. Jahrhundert. 15 vols. in 17. Edited by Gustav F. Schmoller et al. Berlin: Paul Parey Verlag, 1894-1936. *(Denkmäler der Preussischen Staatsverwaltung im 18. Jahrhundert,* pub. by the Royal Academy of Sciences.)

Acta Borussica: Die Handels-, Zoll- und Akzisepolitik Brandenburg-Preussens bis 1713. Vol. 1, edited by Hugo Rachel. Berlin: Paul Parey Verlag, 1911.

Baader, Joseph, ed. *Nürnberger Polizeiordnungen aus dem XIII bis XV Jahrhundert.* Stuttgart, 1861. *(Bibliothek des Litterarischen Vereins in Stuttgart 63.)*

Bahr, Hans, ed. *Quellen zur brandenburgischen-preussischen Geschichte.* 3 vols. Leipzig: R. Voigtländers Verlag, 1914-1919. From the beginnings of Brandenburg history to the reign of the Great Elector.

Book of Vagabonds and Beggars, see *The Book of Vagabonds and Beggars.*

Caemmerer, Herman von, ed. *Die Testamente der Kurfürsten von Brandenburg und der beiden ersten Könige von Preussen.* Munich: Duncker and Humblot, 1915. (Veröffentlichungen des Vereins fur Geschichte der Mark Brandenburg.)

Deutsche Schulgesetzgebung. Introduction by Gerhard Giese. Langensalza: J. Beltz, 1931. *(Kleine pädagogische Texte.* Edited by Elizabeth Blochmann, Herman Nohl, Erich Weniger. Book 19.)

Erneuerte Verordnungen und Gesetze für das Königliche Joachimsthalsche Gymnasium. Berlin, 1767. The ordinances of Frederick II of 1767 for the Joachimsthal *Gymnasium.*

Friedensburg, Walter, ed. *Kurmärkische Ständeakten aus der Regierungszeit Kurfürst Joachims II.* 2 vols. Munich: Duncker and Humblot, 1913-1916. *(Veröffentlichungen des Vereins für Geschichte der Mark Brandenburg.)*

Goldast, Melchior, ed. *Collectio Constitutionum Imperialium.* Frankfurt a/M., 1713.

Harnack, Adolf. *Geschichte der Königlich Preussischen Akademie der Wissenschaften zu Berlin.* 2 vols. Berlin, 1900. Vol. 1, *Von der Gründung bis zum Tode Friedrichs des Grossen;* vol. 2, *Urkunden und Aktenstücke.*

Kuentzel, Georg, ed. *Die Politischen Testamente der Hohenzollern.* Leipzig: B. G. Teubner, 1911. *(Quellen zur deutschen Geschichte.)*

Landé, Walter, ed. *Preussisches Schulrecht.* Vol. 6, pt. 1. Berlin: C. Heymann, 1933. In series: *Verwaltungsgesetze für Preussen,* ed., Max von Brauchitsch; new edition by Bill Drews and Gerhardt Lassar.

Luther, Martin. *Luther's Werke.* Edited by Georg Buchwald et al. 3d ed., 8 vols. Berlin: C. A. Schwetschke and Son, 1905.

Meinardus, Otto, ed. *Protokolle und Relationen des Brandenburgischen Geheimen Rathes aus der Zeit des Kurfürsten Friedrich Wilhelm.* 7 vols. in *Publicationen aus den Preussischen Staatsarchiven.* Leipzig: S. Hirzel, 1889-1919.

Monumenta Germaniae Historica, Legum Sectio IV, Constitutiones et Acta Pub-

lica Imperatorum et Regum. Vol. 1. Edited by Ludwig Weiland. Hanover, 1893.

Mylius, Christian Otto, ed. *Corpus Constitutionum Magdeburgicarum Novissinarum oder Königliche Preussische und Churfürstliche Brandenburgische Landes-Ordnungen, Edicta und Mandata in Herzogthum Magdeburg wie auch in der Graffschaft Mansfeld von anno 1680 biss 1714.* Magdeburg and Halle, 1714.

———. *Corpus Constitutionum Marchicarum.* 8 vols. in folio. Berlin and Halle, 1736-1741.

Raumer, Georg W. von, ed. *Codex diplomaticus brandenburgensis continuatus.* Pts. 1 and 2. Berlin, 1831-1833.

Riedel, Adolf, ed. *Codex Diplomaticus Brandenburgensis. Sammlung der Urkunden, Chroniken und sonstigen Quellenschriften für die Geschichte der Mark Brandenburg und ihrer Regenten.* 41 vols. in 21. Berlin, 1838-1869.

Sämpliche Fürstliche Magdeburgische Ordnungen/ und vornehmsten Mandata, welche der Hochwürdigste, etc. Herr Augustus, Postulirter Administrator dess Primat-und Ertz-Stiffts Magdeburg . . . Leipzig, 1673.

Schulze, Berthold. *Brandenburgische Besitzstandskarte des 16. Jahrhunderts: der ritterschaftliche, geistliche, städtische und landesherrliche Besitz um 1540.* (*Historischer Atlas von Brandenburg.* New series, no. 1.) Berlin: W. de Gruyter, 1962.

Seckendorff, Veit Ludwig von. *Teutscher Fürstenstaat.* 5th ed., expanded. Frankfurt a/M., 1678.

———. *Teutscher Fürsten-Staat.* 9th ed. Edited by Andres Simson von Biechling. Jean, 1754.

The Book of Vagabonds and Beggars: With a Vocabulary of Their Language. Edited by Martin Luther (1528). Translated by John C. Hotten, 1860.

The Book of Vagabonds and Beggars with a Vocabulary of Their Language and a Preface by Martin Luther (1528). Edited and translated by David B. Thomas. London: Penguin Press, 1932.

Urkunden und Actenstücke zur Geschichte des Kurfürsten Friedrich Wilhelm von Brandenburg. Edited by Bernhard Erdmannsdörffer et al. 23 vols. in 26. Berlin, 1864-1929.

Vormbaum, Reinhold, ed. *Die Evangelische Schulordnungen des 16en-18en Jahrhunderts.* 3 vols. Gütersloh, 1860-1864.

Wolff, Christian Freyherr von. *Vernünfftige Gedanken von dem gesellschaftlichen Leben der Menschen und insonderheit dem gemeinen Wesen zu Beförderung der Glückseligkeit des menschlichen Geschlechts.* 6th ed. Frankfurt and Leipzig, 1747. (First published Halle, 1721.)

Secondary Materials

Arendt, Max; Faden, Eberhard; Gandert, Otto-Friedrich. *Geschichte der Stadt Berlin. Festschrift zur 700-Jahr-Feier der Reichshauptstadt.* Berlin: Mittler, 1937.

Artelt, Walter. *Medizinische Wissenschaft und Ärztliche Praxis im alten Berlin. In Selbstzeugnissen.* Pt. 1. Berlin: Urban and Schwarzenberg, 1948.

Babucke, Heinrich. *Zur Erinnerung an die Ubersiedelung des Altstädtischen Gymnasiums zu Königsberg, Pr.* Königsberg, 1889.

Bauch, Gustav. *Die Anfänge der Universität Frankfurt a. Oder.* Berlin, 1900.

Baumgart, Peter. "Absoluter Staat und Judenemanzipation in Brandenburg-Preussen." *Jahrbuch für die Geschichte Mittel- und Ostdeutschland* 13-14 (1965): 60-87.

Benser, H., and Stürzbecher, Manfred. "Die Heilberufe in Angermünde." *Medizinische Monatsschrift* 8 (1957): 137-140.

Blättner, Fritz. *Das Gymnasium; aufgaben der höheren Schule in Geschichte und Gegenwart.* Heidelberg: Quelle and Meyer, 1960.

Boehn, Max von. *Die Mode: menschen und moden im siebzehnten jahrhundert nach bildern und stichen der zeit.* Munich, 1913.

———. *Die Mode: menschen und moden im achtzehnten jahrhundert nach bildern und stichen der zeit.* Munich, 1909.

Bornhak, Conrad. *Geschichte der preussischen Universitätsverwaltung bis 1810.* Berlin, 1900.

Borrmann, Richard, ed. *Die Bau- und Kunstdenkmäler von Berlin.* Berlin, 1893.

Brunn, Friedrich Leopold. *Einige nähere Nachrichten von der Gründung, frühern Einrichtung und den Schicksalen des jetzigen königlichen joachimsthalischen Gymnasiums.* Berlin, 1825. A history of the *Gymnasium* from 1607 to 1640.

Bühler, Johannes. *Deutsche Geschichte.* Vol. 4, *Barock.* Berlin: W. de Gruyter, 1950.

Bulau, Alwin E. *Footprints of Assurance.* New York: Macmillan, 1953.

Büsching, Anton F. *Geschichte des Berlinschen Gymnasii im grauen Kloster.* Berlin, 1774. Büsching was the school director.

Consentius, Ernst. *Alt-Berlin Anno 1740.* 2d ed. Berlin: Gebrüder Paetel, 1911.

Dehio, Georg. *Geschichte der Deutschen Kunst.* Vol. 3. 2d rev. ed. Berlin: W. de Gruyter, 1930. Excellent illustrations.

Deppermann, Klaus. *Der Hallesche Pietismus und der preussische Staat unter Friedrich III. (I.).* Göttingen: Vandenhoeck and Ruprecht, 1961.

Deutsche Staatsbibliothek 1661-1961. 2 vols. Vol. 1, *Geschichte und Gegenwart,* ed. Horst Kunze et al. Vol. 2, *Bibliographie,* compiled by Peter Kittel. Leipzig: Verlag für Buch- und Bibliothekwesen, 1961.

Deutsches Wörterbuch. Edited by Jacob and Wilhelm Grimm. 15 vols. Leipzig: S. Hirzel, 1854-1919.

Dilthey, Wilhelm. *Zur preussischen Geschichte.* Edited by Erich Weniger. 2d ed. Stuttgart: B. G. Teubner, 1960. *(Wilhelm Dilthey's Gesammelte Schriften,* Vol. 12.)

Donner, Andreas Matthias. "Over de Term 'Welvaartsstaat'." In *Mededelingen der Keninklijke Nederlandse Akademie van Wetenschappen.* New series, Vol. 20, no. 15, pp. 551-565. Amsterdam: Noord-Hollandsche Uitg. Mij, 1957.

Dorwart, Reinhold A. *The Administrative Reforms of Frederick William I of Prussia.* Cambridge, Mass.: Harvard University Press, 1953.

Drost, Willi. "Schlüter und das Berliner Barock." In *Berlin in Vergangenheit und Gegenwart: Tübinger Vorträge.* Edited by Hans Rothfels. Tübingen: Mohr, 1961. *(Tübinger Studien zur Geschichte und Politik, no. 14.)*

Duller, Eduard. *Deutschland und das deutsche Volk.* 4 vols. Leipzig, 1845. Vol. 4 consists of 35 color plates of costumes worn in various parts of Germany, chiefly in the eighteenth century.

Eisenbart, Liselotte C. *Kleiderordnungen der deutschen Städte zwischen 1350 und 1700. Ein Beitrag zur Kulturgeschichte des deutschen Bürgertums.* Göttingen: Musterschmidt, 1962. *(Göttinger Bausteine zur Geschichtswissenschaft* 32.)

Ewbank, Thomas. *A Descriptive and Historical Account of Hydraulic and Other Machines for Raising Water.* 15th ed. New York, 1864. A classic work, useful for information on fire-fighting devices and engines.

Faden, Eberhard. *Berlin im Dreissigjährigen Kriege.* Berlin: Deutsche Verlagsgesellschaft für Politik und Geschichte, 1927.

Fay, Sidney B. "Bismarck's Welfare State." *Current History* 18 (Jan., Feb., Mar. 1950): 1-8, 65-70, 129-133.

Feist, Bruno. *Die geschichte der nationalökonomie an der Friedrichs-Universität zu Halle im 18. jahrhundert.* Halle: O. Hendel, 1930.

Festschrift zur Feier des 200 Jährigen Bestehens des Königlichen Französischen Gymnasium. Edited by Georg Schulze, school director. Berlin: A. Haack, 1890.

Festschrift zur Feier des 260 Jährigen Bestehens des Französischen Gymnasiums Collège Français, Fondé en 1689. Edited by Kurt Levinstein, school director. Berlin: W. Büxenstein, 1949.

Fine, Sidney. *Laissez Faire and the General-Welfare State.* Ann Arbor: University of Michigan Press, 1956.

Fischer, Alfons. *Geschichte der deutschen gesundheitswesen.* 2 vols. (1933.) Hildesheim: G. Olms, 1965.

Förster, Johann. *Uebersicht der Geschichte der Universität zu Halle in ihrem ersten Jahrhunderte.* Halle: Waisenhaus Verlag, 1799.

Francke, August Hermann. *Der grosse Aufsatz: Schrift über eine Reform des Erziehungs- und Bildungswesen als Ausgangspunkt einer geistlichen und sozialen Neuordnung der evangelischen Kirche des 18. Jahrhunderts.* Edited and introduced by Otto Pedczeck. Berlin: Akademie-Verlag, 1962.

Freydank, Hanns. *Die Universität Halle.* Foreword by Theodore Ziehen. Düsseldorf: Lindner-Verlag, 1928.

Gasser, Simon Peter. *Einleitung zu den Ökonomischen, politischen und Kameraliswenschaften.* Halle, 1729. Gasser was the first professor of cameralism at the University of Halle, 1727-1745.

Geiger, Ludwig. *Berlin 1688-1840. Geschichte des geistigen Lebens der preussischen Hauptstadt.* Berlin, 1893.

Gilbert, K. R. *Fire Engines and Other Fire-Fighting Appliances.* London: Her Majesty's Stationery Office, 1966. A Science Museum illustrated booklet.

Gloria, Elisabeth. *Der Pietismus als Förderer der Volksbildung und sein Einfluss auf die preussische Volksschule.* Osterwieck: Zickfeldt, 1933.

Greenfield, Kent R. *Sumptuary Law in Nürnberg: A Study in Paternal Government.* Johns Hopkins University Studies in Historical and Political Science, series 36, no. 2. Baltimore: The Johns Hopkins Press, 1918.

Halphen, Louis. "L'idée d'état sous les carolingiens." *Revue Historique* 185 (1939): 59-70.

Handwörterbuch der Staatswissenschaften. Edited by Ludwig Elster, Adolf Weber, Friedrich Wieser. 9 vols. 4th ed. Jena: G. Fischer, 1923-1929.

Harnack, Adolf. "Das geistige und wissenschaftliche Leben in Brandenburg-Preussen um das Jahr 1700." In *Hohenzollern-Jahrbuch,* 4: 170-191. Edited by Paul Seidel. Berlin: Giesecke and Devrient, 1900.

Hartung, Fritz. "Der Aufgeklärte Absolutismus." In *Staatsbildende Kräfte der Neuzeit: gesammelte Aufsätze* pp. 149-177. Berlin: Duncker and Humblot, 1961.

Heidemann, Julius. *Geschichte des Grauen Klosters zu Berlin.* Berlin, 1874.

Heise, Werner. *Die Juden in der Mark Brandenburg bis zum Jahre 1571.* Series: *Historische Studien,* no. 220. Berlin: Ebering, 1932. Includes an excellent bibliography on the history of the Jews in Brandenburg.

Heman, Carl. *Die Bildungsideale der Deutschen im Schulwesen seit der renaissance.* Basel, 1892.

Henne am Rhyn, Otto. *Illustrierte Kultur- und Sittengeschichte des deutschen Sprachgebietes.* Stuttgart: Strecker and Schröder, 1918.

Herz, Rudolph. *Berliner Barock: Bauten und Baumeister aus der ersten Hälfte des 18. Jahrhunderts.* Berlin: Deutsche Verlagsgessellschaft für Politik und Geschichte, 1928.

Hesse, Werner. *Beiträge zur Geschichte der früheren Universität in Duisburg.* Duisburg, 1879.

Heubaum, Alfred. *Geschichte des deutschen Bildungswesen seit der Mitte des 17. Jahrhunderts.* Berlin: Weidmann, 1905.

Hinrichs, Carl. "Der Hallesche Pietismus als politisch-soziale Reformsbewegung des 18. Jahrhunderts. Berlin: Deutsche Verlagsgessellschaft fur Politik und schlands 2 (1953): 177-189.

Hollack, Emil, and Tromnau, Friedrich. *Geschichte des Schulwesens der Königlichen Haupt- und Residenzstadt Königsberg i. Pr. mit besonderer Berücksichtigung der niederen Schulen. Ein Beitrag zur Kulturgeschichte Altpreussens.* Königsberg i. Pr., 1899.

Holtze, Friedrich. *Das Strafverfahren gegen die märkischen Juden im Jahre 1510.* Berlin, 1884. *(Schriften des Vereins für die Geschichte Berlins,* no. 21.)

Jordan, Julius, and Kern, Otto. *Die Universitäten Wittenberg Halle vor und bei ihrer Vereinigung.* Halle: M. Niemeyer, 1917.

Jordan, Wilbur K. *Philanthropy in England 1480-1660.* New York: Russell Sage Foundation, 1959.

————. "The English Background of Modern Philanthropy." *American Historical Review,* vol. 66, no. 2 (Jan. 1961), pp. 401-408.

Just, Leo, ed. *Handbuch der Deutschen Geschichte.* 5 vols. Constance: Akademische Verlagsgesellschaft Athenaion, 1956-1968. Vol. 5, *Athenaion-Bilderatlas zur deutschen Geschichte.* Edited by H. Jankuhn, H. Boockmann, and Wilhelm Treue.

Kaeber, Erich. "Geistige Strömungen in Berlin zur Zeit Friedrichs des Grossen." *Forschungen zur Brandenburgischen-Preussischen Geschichte* 54 (1943): 257-303.

Kaeber, Ernst. *Bürgerrecht, Bevölkerungs-, Herkunfts- und Berufsstatistik Berlins bis zur Mitte des 18. Jahrhunderts.* Berlin: Gsellius Verlag, 1934.

Kaemmel, Heinrich. *Geschichte des deutschen schulwesens im übergange vom mittelalter zur neuzeit.* Leipzig, 1882.

Keller, Friedrich E. *Geschichte des preussischen Volksschulwesens.* Berlin, 1873.

Kern, Fritz. "Vom Herrenstaat zum Wohlfahrtsstaat." *Schmoller's Jahrbuch für Gesetzgebung, Verwaltung und Volkswirtschaft im Deutschen Reiche* 52 (1928): 393-415.

King, Lester S. *The Medical World of the Eighteenth Century.* Chicago: University of Chicago Press, 1958.

————. "Medicine in 1695: Friedrich Hoffmann's *Fundamenta Medicinae.*" *Bulletin of the History of Medicine* 43 (1969): 17-29.

Klöden, K. F., and Schmidt, B. H. *Die ältere Geschichte des Köllnischen Gymnasiums, bis zu seiner Vereinigung mit dem Berlinschen Gymnasium.* Berlin, 1825.

Krause, Günter. *Die aufsicht des staates über die öffentliche volksschule im geltungsgebiet des allgemeinen landrechts.* Schlochau: E. Golz, 1926.

Kremers, Edward, and Urdang, George. *History of Pharmacy.* 2d ed., rev. Philadelphia: J. B. Lippincott, 1951.

Krieger, Leonard. "The Idea of the Welfare State in Europe and the United States." *Journal of the History of Ideas* 24 (1963): 553-568.

Langel, Hans. *Die Entwicklung des Schulwesens in Preussen unter Franz Albrecht Schultz (1733-1763).* In *Abhandlungen zur Philosophie und ihrer Geschichte,* book 32. Edited by Benno Erdmann. Halle: M. Niemeyer, 1909.

Lehmann, Herbert. *Das Collegium medico-chirurgicum in Berlin als Lehrstätte der Botanik und der Pharmazie.* Berlin: Triltsch and Huther, 1936.

Lehmann, Max. "Aus der Geschichte der preussischen Volksschule." *Preussische Jahrbücher* 140 (1910): 209-231.

Lewin, Heinrich. *Geschichte der Entwicklung der Preussischen Volksschule und der Förderung der Volksbildung durch die Hohenzollern.* Leipzig: Dürr'sche Buchhandlung, 1910.

Liebe, Georg H. *Das Judentum in der deutschen vergangenheit. Mit 106 abbildungen und beilagen, grösstentheils aus dem 15. bis 18. Jahrhundert.* Leipzig: E. Diederichs, 1903.

Lowenthal, Marvin. *The Jews of Germany: A story of sixteen centuries.* Philadelphia: The Jewish Publication Society of America, 1936.

Luther, Martin. *First Principles of the Reformation.* Edited and translated by Henry Wace and C. A. Buchheim. London, 1883.

McCloy, Shelby T. *Government Assistance in Eighteenth Century France.* Durham, N.C.: Duke University Press, 1946.

————. *The Humanitarian Movement in Eighteenth Century France.* Lexington, Ky.: University of Kentucky Press, 1957.

McPeek, James A. S. *The Black Book of Knaves and Unthrifts in Shakespeare and Other Renaissance Authors.* University of Connecticut Publications Series. Storrs, Conn., 1969.

Marcus, Jacob. R. *The Jew in the Medieval World: A source book, 315-1791.* Cincinnati: The Union of American Hebrew Congregations, 1938.

Merk, Walther. "Der Gedanke des gemeinen Besten in der deutschen Staats- und Rechtsentwicklung." In *Festschrift Alfred Schultze zum 70. Geburtstag,* ed. Walther Merk, pp. 451-520. Weimar: Bohlau, 1934.

Nabakowsky, Johanna. *Die Pädagogik an der Universität Halle im 18. Jahrhundert.* Osterwieck: A. W. Zickfeldt, 1930.

Nicolai, Friedrich. *Beschreibung der Königlichen Residenz-Städte Berlin und Potsdam.* 3 vols. 3d ed. Berlin, 1786. First published 1769.

Niemeyer, August Hermann. *Geschichte des Königlichen Pädagogiums seit seiner Stiftung bis zum Schluss des ersten Jahrhunderts.* Halle: Waisenhaus Press, 1796. A centennial history by the director of the *Pädagogium,* who was a descendant of its founder.

Niemeyer, H. A. *Vollständiger Bericht über das Königliche Pädagogium zu Halle.* Halle, 1836.

Oelrichs, Johann C. C. *Entwurf einer Geschichte der Königlichen Bibliothek zu Berlin.* Berlin, 1752.

Oettingen, W. von. "Die bildenden Künste unter Friedrich I, Die Königliche Akademie der Künste zu Berlin." In *Hohenzollern-Jahrbuch* 4: 231-246. Edited by Paul Seidel. Berlin: Giesecke and Devrient, 1900.

Owen, David. *English Philanthropy, 1660-1960.* Cambridge, Mass.: Harvard University Press, 1964.

Painter, F. V. N. *Luther on Education.* Philadelphia, 1890.

Paulsen, Friedrich. *Geschichte des Gelehrten Unterrichts auf den deutschen schulen und universitäten vom ausgang des mittelalters bis zur gegenwart.* 2 vols. 3d ed. Leipzig: Veit, 1919-1921.

————. *German Education, Past and Present.* Translated by T. Lorenz. London: T. F. Unwin, 1908. Originally published as *Das Deutsche Bildungswesen in seiner geschichtlichen Entwicklung.* Leipzig, 1906.

Paunel, Eugen. *Die Staatsbibliothek zu Berlin; ihre Geschichte und Organisation während der ersten zwei Jahrhunderte seit ihrer Eröffnung, 1661-1871.* Berlin: W. de Gruyter, 1965.

Petersohn, Jurgen. "Wissenschaftspflege und Gelehrte Bildung im Herzogtum Preussen im letzten Viertel des 16. Jahrhundert." *Jahrbuch für die Geschichte Mittel- und Ostdeutschlands* 11 (1962): 75-110.

Redslob, Edwin. *Barock und Rokoko in den Schlössern von Berlin und Potsdam.* Berlin: Rembrandt-Verlag, 1954. Beautiful color photographs and illustrations of the decorative work of the interiors of Berlin palaces.

————. "Die Städtebauliche Entwicklung Berlins." *Jahrbuch für Geschichte des Deutschen Ostens* 1 (1952): 203-224.

Reimann, Georg J. *Das Berliner Strassenbild des XVIII und XIX Jahrhunderten.* Berlin, 1954.

Relton, Francis B. *An Account of the Fire Insurance Companies Associations Institutions Projects Established and Projected in Great Britain and Ireland During the 17th and 18th Centuries.* London, 1893.

Richter, Albert. *Bilder aus der Deutschen Kulturgeschichte.* Pt. 2. Leipzig, 1882.

Roberts, Daniel. *Victorian Origins of the British Welfare State.* New Haven: Yale University Press, 1960.

Rotscheidt, Wilhelm, ed. *Die Matrikel der Universität Duisburg 1652-1818.* Duisburg: Rhein. National-Dr., 1938.

Sachar, Abram L. *A History of the Jews.* 2d ed., rev. New York: A. A. Knopf, 1940.

Sachar, Howard. *The Course of Modern Jewish History.* Cleveland: World Publishing Co., 1958.

Schottland, Charles I., ed. *The Welfare State: Selected Essays.* New York: Harper and Row, Torchbook Series, 1967.

Schrader, Wilhelm. *Geschichte der Friedrichs-Universität zu Halle.* Pt. 1, 2 vols. Berlin, 1894.

Schultz, Alwin. *Allgemeine Geschichte der Bildenden Künste.* Vol. 3. Berlin, 1896.

————. *Das Häuslichen Leben der Europäischen Kulturvölker vom Mittelalter bis zur zweiten Hälfte des XVIII Jahrhunderts.* Munich: R. Oldenbourg, 1903.

Segall, Joseph. *Geschichte und Strafrecht der Reichspolizeiordnungen von 1530, 1548, 1577.* Breslau: Schlettersche Buchhandlung, 1914.

Seidel, Paul. "Die bildenden Künste unter Friedrich I, Kunst und Künstler am Hofe." In *Hohenzollern-Jahrbuch* 4: 247-268. Edited by Paul Seidel. Berlin: Giesecke and Devrient, 1900.

Selle, Götz von. *Geschichte der Albertus-Universität zu Königsberg in Preussen.* 2d ed., rev. Würzburg: Holzner, 1956.

Sellenthin, Hans-Gerd. *Geschichte der Juden in Berlin.* Berlin: Jüdische Gemeinde, 1959.

Specht, Franz. *Geschichte des unterrichtswesen in Deutschland von den ältesten zeiten bis zur mitte des dreizehnten Jahrhunderts.* Stuttgart, 1885.

Stern, Leo, ed. *450 Jahre Martin-Luther-Universität, Halle-Wittenberg.* 3 vols. Halle-Wittenberg: University Press of Martin-Luther-University, 1945-1952. Vol. 2, *Halle (1694-1817) und Halle-Wittenberg (1817-1945).*

Stern, Selma. *The Court Jew: A Contribution to the History of the Period of Absolutism in Central Europe.* Translated by Ralph Weiman. Philadelphia: Jewish Publication Society of America, 1950.

———. *Der Preussische Staat und die Juden.* 4 vols. Tübingen: Mohr, 1962. Pt. 1: *Die Zeit des Grossen Kurfürst und Friedrich I;* pt. 2: *Die Zeit Friedrich Wilhelms I.* Each part includes a separate volume of documents.

Stiller, Felix. "Das Berliner Armenwesen vor dem Jahre 1820." *Forschungen zur Brandenburgischen und Preussischen Geschichte* 21 (1908): 175-197.

Stürzbecher, Manfred. *Beiträge Zur Berliner Medizingeschichte. Quellen und Studien zur Geschichte des Gesundheitswesen vom 17. bis zum 19. Jahrhundert.* Introduction by Johannes Schultze. Berlin: W. de Gruyter, 1966.

Tautz, Kurt. *Die Bibliothekare der Churfürstlichen Bibliothek zu Cölln an der Spree: Ein Beitrag zur Geschichte der Preussischen Staatsbibliothek im siebzehnten Jahrhundert.* Leipzig: O. Harrassewitz, 1925.

Terveen, Fritz. *Gesamtstaat und Retablissement: Der Wiederaufbau des nördlichen Ostpreussen unter Friedrich Wilhelm I, 1714-1740.* Göttingen: Musterschmidt' Wissenschaftlicher Verlag, 1954. (*Göttingen Bausteine zur Geschichtswissenschaft* 16.)

Thiel, Carl. *Kurze Darstellung der Geschichte des Gymnasiums zu Königsberg.* Schwedt, 1823.

Thiel, Erika. *Geschichte des Kostüms. Europäische Mode.* Berlin: Henschelverlag, 1960.

Thiele, Gunnar. *Geschichte der Preussischen Lehrerseminare.* Berlin: Weidmann, 1938. (*Monumenta Germaniae Paedagogica,* vol. 62, pt. 1).

Thouret, Georg. "Einzug der Musen und Grazien in die Mark." In *Hohenzollern-Jahrbuch* 4: 192-230. Edited by Paul Seidel. Berlin: Giesecke and Devrient, 1900.

Troeltsch, Ernst. *The Social Teaching of the Christian Churches.* Translated by Olive Wyon. 2 vols. New York: The Macmillan Company, 1931.

Ulbricht, Karl. "Geburt, Hochzeit und Tod in Volksbrauch und Volksglauben der Kreise Lebus und Beskow-Storkow." *Zeitschrift fur Volkskunde,* ed. Fritz Boehm. New series, vol. 1, no. 2 (1929), pp. 196-200; vol. 1, no. 3 (1930) 292-298; vol. 2, no. 3 (1931), pp. 282-88.

Vincent, John M. *Costume and Conduct in the Laws of Basel, Bern, and Zurich 1370-1800.* Baltimore: The Johns Hopkins Press, 1935.

————. "European Blue Laws." *Annual Report of the American Historical Association,* 1897, pp. 355-373.

Vollmer, Ferdinand. *Friedrich Wilhelm I und die Volksschule.* Göttingen: Vandenhoeck and Ruprecht, 1909.

Wehrmann, Martin. *Die Begründung des evangelischen Schulwesens in Pommern bis 1563.* Berlin: A. Hofmann, 1905. In *Beiträge zur Geschichte der Erziehung und des Unterrichts in Pommern,* no. 7. (*Mitteilungen der Gesellschaft für deutsche Erziehungs- und Schulgeschichte.*)

Wetzel, Erich. *Festschrift zum Dreihundertjährigen Jubiläum des königlichen Joachimsthalschen Gymnasiums am 24. VIII 1907.* Pt. 1, *Die Geschichte des Königlichen Joachimsthalschen Gymnasiums 1607-1907.* Halle: Waisenhaus Press, 1907.

Wienecke, Friedrich. *Beiträge zur Geschichte der Erziehung und des Unterrichts in Preussen—Das preussische Garnisonschulwesen.* Berlin: Weidmann, 1907.

Wiese, L., ed. *Verordnungen und Gesetze für die höheren Schulen in Preussen.* 2d ed. Berlin, 1875.

Wilken, Friedrich. *Geschichte der Königlichen Bibliothek zu Berlin.* Berlin, 1828. This is the basic work on which all books about the Royal State Library were based for the first 150 years of the library's history.

Wöhe, Kurt. *Die Geschichte der Leitung der preussischen Volksschule von ihren Anfängen bis zur Gegenwart.* Osterwieck: Zickfeldt, 1933.

Woody, Thomas. *Fürstenschulen in Germany after the Reformation.* Menosha, Wis.: George Banta, 1920.

Wyper, James. "Traditions of the Fire Insurance Business." *The Hartford Agent,* vol. 32, no. 5 (Nov., Dec. 1940), pp. 73-76, 108-111. Pub. by the Hartford Fire Insurance Co., Hartford, Conn.

"Ye Old Tyme Fyre-Fightynge." *Industrial Fire Chief,* pt. 1, vol. 7, no. 5 (July-Aug. 1927), pp. 11-13; pt. 2, vol. 7, no. 6 (Sept.-Oct. 1927), pp. 12-13. Part 2 offers illustrations of early equipment. Pub. by Foamite Childs Corp., Utica, N.Y.

Zippel, G. *Geschichte des Königlichen Friedrichs-Kollegiums zu Königsberg, Pr. 1698-1898.* Königsberg Pr., 1898.

Index

Academy of Science, Prussian. *See* Society of Sciences
Academy of the Arts, 226-229
Acta Medicorum Berolinensium (Berlin medical journal), 259
Alenu (Jewish prayer), 128, 135
Allgemeines Preussisches Landrecht (Civil Code), 18, 21, 190, 192
Alt-Berlin, 230-235
Anatomical Theater, 248-250 *passim,* 253, 256-257, 260-263
Anti-Semitism, 114, 115-116, 118-120, 121
Apothecaries, 245, 251, 268-283
Apothecary oath, 277-278
Apothecary Shop, Court, 258, 266, 280-281
Arsenal, Berlin (*Zeughaus*), 232
Ausreuter (rural police), 49, 56, 65, 72, 74, 75, 109, 246, 249

Baptism, 30-33
Becher, Johann Joachim, on education, 162
Beger, Lorenz, *Thesaurus Brandenburgicus,* 227-228
Beggars and vagabonds, 95-111 *passim*
Berlin: after *1648,* 79-81, 85-88; poor relief, 102-103; cultural center, 214, 225; medical center, 256; unified city administration, 230. *See also* Alt-Berlin
Betrothals. *See* Weddings
Blasphemy, 27
Board of Medicine, 107, 240-253, 271, 273-274, 277, 278
Board of Sanitation, 253-254, 286
Bossuet, Bishop Jacques, 5
Botanical garden, Berlin, 258
Brauthahn, 37
Briggs, Asa, 1
Buddeus, Augustine (physician), 257, 264
Bugenhagen, Johann, school reform in Pomerania, 172
Building code, 81-82, 296
Building inspectors, 81-82
Bürgerrecht, 268

Cadet school, Royal, in Berlin (*Kadettenanstalt*), 203
Cameralism, 1, 5; university chair of at Halle, 210-212
Capitulary of *789,* Charlemagne's, 145
Castle, electoral: origin, 80; reconstruction, 234
Cattle disease, 260, 287-290

Cemeteries, 41; Jewish, 115, 134
Charité, general hospital, 259
Charity, 8; and the Christian Church, 95, 102
Charles V., Emperor, introduces *Polizei,* 15
Christian Church, its welfare function, 8, 20
Church buildings in Berlin, 151, 230, 235
Class distinctions, regulation of, 31, 35, 37, 64, 93
Cleves, Duchy of, schools in, 170-171, 195
Clothing regulation, 45-50
College of Medicine and Surgery, Berlin, 253, 260, 263-267
Collegium Fridericianum (Konigsberg grammar school), 191
Collegium Medicum. See Board of Medicine
Comenius, Johann Amos, on education, 161
Compulsory education, idea of, 143, 144-145, 149, 165, 173, 182, 183
Concept of government, medieval, 6-7
Curriculum: school, 147, 149, 150, 152, 157, 175, 179, 196-204 *passim,* 209-210; medical, 264

Diet of Augsburg (*1548*), 96
Diet of Worms: of *1495,* 14; of *1521,* 15
Dilthey, Wilhelm, 13, 18
Dithmar, J. Christian (cameralist), 210
Dom, Berlin, 80, 182
Dorotheenstadt, 80, 230

East Pomerania, elementary schools, 171-172
East Prussia: elementary schools, 171; school reform, 184-189
Education, ideas on, 160-165
Enforcement of regulations, problems of, 26, 49, 66, 69, 71, 73-75, 105-106, 111, 278-279, 295, 307-309

Fairs, annual, 56-59
Fire-fighting technology, 293, 296-300
Fire Insurance Office, 300-304
Fire ordinances: of *1672,* 294, 297; of *1718,* 296
Fiscals, 42-43, 71, 128, 136, 249

Francke, August Hermann, 164, 176-179, 208
Frankel, Charles, 1
Frederick I, Emperor: and Jews, 116; and universities, 212
Frederick II, of Prussia, 18, 214, 225
Frederick III, of Brandenburg, on education, 164, 168, 176, 207, 222
Frederick William, the Great Elector, 77-78, 85, 121, 168, 195, 206, 226; Jewish policy of, 122-125
Frederick William I, of Prussia, 18, 42, 49, 67, 68, 72, 76, 82, 106-109, 164, 180, 224, 261; and the *Volksschule,* 181-193
French College, 197-198
Friedrichsstadt, 80, 83, 230
Friedrichswerder, 80, 230
Friedrich Wilhelm Canal, 57, 58
Frisch, Johann Leonhard (Academy member), 222-223
Funerals, 40-44
Fürstenschule (intermediate school), 147, 148, 150, 154-157, 194-204

Garrison schools, 174-175, 190
Gassenmeister (city police), 105-106, 307
Gasser, Peter Simon (cameralist), 210
Gehr, Theodor (Königsberg educator), 191
General Directory, 247
General War Commissariat, 49, 71, 74, 75, 82, 211, 307, 308
German schools (elementary), 146, 152, 178, 191
Göthe, Eosandervon (court architect), 232, 234
Grammar schools. See *Fürstenschule*
Greenfield, Kent R., 8, 11
Gundelsheim, Andreas (physician), 256, 257, 258
Gundling, Jacob Paul (historian, president of Society of Sciences), 224
Gymnasium, of the Gray Cloister, 154, 194, 197. See *Fürstenschule*
Gypsies, 95, 98, 99, 104, 105, 109

Halle, city of, 177; schools at, 178-180; *Paedagogium,* 201-203; educational center, 206; university, 206-213

Hartung, Fritz, 5
Hawkers and peddlers, 60, 68-74, 76
Hendreich, Christian (state librarian), 216
Henrichius, Heinrich (anatomist), 257, 264
Herbarium, Berlin, 258
Hintze, Otto, 17
Hoffmann, Friedrich (physician), 208, 256
Hofjude, 121, 130
Hook, Sidney, 8, 9, 12, 18
Hospitals, 258
Housing, 78-86
Huguenots in Berlin, 80, 197, 227

Jablonski, J. T. (court preacher, president of Society of Sciences), 220, 225
Jews: Edict on Jews of *1157,* 113; First Crusade, 114; first expulsion, *1446,* 117; second expulsion, *1510,* 119; third expulsion, *1571,* 120; *Bürgerrecht,* 114, 117; numbers, 118, 122; edict of *1671,* 122-124; under Frederick William I, 130-139
Joachim II: and diet of *1536,* 62; and diet of *1549,* 27, 63-64; attitude toward Jews, 119-120; education, 151
Joachimsthal Gymnasium, 154-157, 194-196
Jordan, Wilbur K., 8, 10

Kindelbier, 30, 32
Kirch, Gottfried (astronomer and Academy member), 222-223
Krieger, Leonard, 5, 6, 7, 19
Küsterschule (catechism school), 148, 154, 173

Laissez-faire, 2, 9, 20, 21
Landrat, 73, 75, 307, 309
Landreiter. See *Ausreuter*
Landsknechte (soldiers), 96, 97, 107
Landtag (Diet), Brandenburg: of *1536,* 62; of *1549,* 63, 64, 306
Latin schools, 146, 147, 148, 152, 179
Leibniz, Gottfried Wilhelm, 219-221, 223
Liber Vagatorum (The Book of Vagabonds), 94
Library, State, 215-218
Licensing medical practitioners, 241-242, 247, 267, 274, 279

Index

Lippold (court Jew), 119-120
Ludewig, Johann Peter (Halle Professor of History), 210, 211
Ludolff, Michael Matthias (botanist), 265
Lustgarten, 80, 231, 235
Luther, Martin: on luxury, 46; on beggars, 96; on Jews, 118; on education, 143-145, 150
Lysius, Heinrich (Pietist educator), 185

Magdeburg, Duchy of, 27, 55, 79, 125; schools in, 172-173
Margrave John, of the Neumark, 25, 27, 28, 55, 77, 96
Market inspectors, 59, 68, 75
Markets, weekly, 59-60, 66, 68-69; Berlin, 231
Maurice, Duke of Saxony, and the *Fürstenschule*, 147
Medical education, 255, 263-264
Medical journal, Berlin, 259
Medical ordinances: of *1685*, 240, 273-274; of *1693*, 243; of *1725*, 248, 281
Melanchthon, Philip, 146, 147, 150
Memhard, Johann Georg (city architect), 80, 226, 230, 231
Midwives, 245, 250, 262
Miscellanea Berolinensia (Academy publication), 223, 224
Molckenmarkt (dairy market), 68, 231
Mons Pietatis of 1737 (educational fund), 188
Mühlendamm, 68, 230, 235
Museums, Berlin, origins, 226-228

Nering, Johann Arnold (court architect), 228, 232, 234
Neumann, Caspar (court apothecary and chemist), 251, 265, 269, 279-281
Nuremberg sumptuary legislation, 9

Observatory, Berlin, 220, 228
Oranienburg, 80, 180, 258
Orphanages: Oranienburg, 176; Halle, 178; military, 175, 190

Paulsen, Friedrich, 147, 149, 183, 211
Pharmacopoeia: Brandenburg, 245, 259, 281; Augustana, 270-271, 275
Pietism, 18, 164-166, 176, 209
Plague, bubonic, 260, 284-287

Police ordinances
  Brandenburg; of *1334*, *1540*, 25; of *1580*, 46; of *1549*, 64-65
  imperial, of *1521*, *1530*, *1548*, *1577*, 15
Police power, 2, 4, 11, 19, 21
Political Testaments (Hohenzollern), on education, 167-168
Polizei, 3, 14, 15, 19, 305, 310
Polizeistaat, 3-12; Prussian form, 12-19, 310
Poor relief, 94, 100-105
Population, Brandenburg: in *1564*, 66; in *1648*, 77-78; in *1713*, 80; Berlin, 235
Pott, Johann Heinrich (chemist), 265, 279
Pound Roscoe, 4, 21
Prices and fees, regulation of, 243, 244, 248, 271, 273, 277
Principia Regulativa (basic school law), 187
Printz, Marquard Ludwig von (minister for church and public instruction), 182, 248
Pufendorf, Samuel, 17, 208, 220

Ratichius, Wolfgang, 161
Raue, Johann, general inspector of schools, 169-170, 174; electoral librarian, 215-216
Reformed Church Directory, 181, 182
Regulative function of the state, 10, 12, 15, 246; sanction for, 3, 12, 13, 17, 18, 20, 21
Retail trade, 60-74, 124
Richberg, Donald R., 21
Ritterakademie, 148, 150, 203-204, 212-213

Sabbath observance, 28-29
Sanitation, urban, 85-90, 262-263
Schlüter, Andreas (sculptor and court architect), 80, 229, 232, 234
School ordinances: of *1573*, 152-153, 170; of *1717*, 182-183; of *1736*, 187; Saxon ordinance of *1528*, 149; Magdeburg ordinance of *1658*, 172-173
Schools: *Klosterschule*, 145; elementary, 146, 152-154, 169-193; Latin, 146; *Volksschule*, 148, 153, 175, 178, 182; at Halle, 178-180. *See* Curriculum
Schottland, Charles I., 4
Schupp, J. B., on education, 174

327

Schutzbrief, for Jews, 113; of *1334* and *1344,* 114-116

Schutzgeld, paid by Jews, 113, 123-127 *passim*

Seckendorff, Veit von, 5; definition of Polizeistaat, 16-17; on education, 162-164; at Halle university, 208

Seminary of Preceptors, at Halle, 179, 202

Society of Sciences, 219-225, 256, 257, 258, 260-262

Sophie Charlotte, Queen of Prussia, 220

Spanheim, Ezechiel von, 217, 221

Spener, Christian (anatomist), 257, 261

Spener, Philip J. (Pietist), 101, 176-177

Spinning houses, 99, 102, 113, 232

Staatsbibliothek, 215-218

Stables, Royal (*Marstall*), 222, 223, 228, 232, 234

Stadtbuch, Berlin, 114, 115

Stahl, Georg (physician and Halle professor), 208, 255

Steuerrat (tax commissioner), 73, 81, 102, 249, 307, 309

Stryck, Samuel (professor and university director at Halle), 208

Sumptuary legislation, 3, 11; defined, 25-26

Surgeons, 242, 244, 250, 252-253, 261, 266-267

Tempelhoff, Johann (apothecary), 270

Temple, William, Archbishop of York, 1

Theiss, Caspar (Renaissance architect), 80, 226

Thomasius, Christian, 17, 161, 207-209

Thurneisser, Leonhard, 215, 271

Troeltsch, Ernst, 8, 9

Universities: Frankfurt, 157-158, 204; Königsberg, 205; Duisburg, 205; Halle, 206-213; juridical autonomy, 212

University government, 217-218

Unter den Linden, 80, 230

Urban renewal, 79, 83-85

Vagabonds, sixteenth-century types, 94-96

Vincent, John M., 6, 8, 11

Viner, Jacob, 1

Waisenhaus (Orphanage), at Halle, 178, 179, 180

Wayfarers, criminous, 96, 97, 98, 109-111

Weddings and betrothals, 33-40

Weights and measures, 54-56

Welfare, definition of, 2, 3, 4

Welfare state: definition of, 3, 9, 10, 14, 18, 20; origin of, 5, 7, 8, 20

Winckelmann, Johann Justus, on education, 161

Winckelschulen, 192

Wolff, Christian, definition of welfare state, 17-18, 213

World university, project for, 218-219